CONTENTS

IAN HARRISON

ADVANCED ACCOUNTING

FOR A2

SECOND EDITION

HODDER
EDUCATION
AN HACHETTE UK COMPANY

ACKNOWLEDGEMENTS

Gratitude is due to many people when writing any book; this book is no exception. I thank the team at Hodder Education for their understanding and patience, and Jane Worraker for her careful checking of the manuscript. I must thank my wife Sandie for her proofreading and word-processing and for her comments and guidance which are very much appreciated and most of all for her tolerance and good humour during the preparation of this book.

There may be occasions when a critical reader might feel that I have over-simplified some concepts. However, I make no apologies for this as the main readership will be the average 18-year-old studying at Advanced Level or first-year degree level and my explanations are written with a view to aiding their understanding of what is often seen as a more difficult subject.

Orders: please contact Bookpoint Ltd, 130 Milton Park, Abingdon, Oxon OX14 4SB. Telephone: (44) 01235 827720. Fax: (44) 01235 400454. Lines are open from 9.00 to 5.00, Monday to Saturday, with a 24-hour message answering service. You can also order through our website: www.hoddereducation.co.uk.

If you have any comments to make about this, or any of our other titles, please send them to educationenquiries@hodder.co.uk

British Library Cataloguing in Publication Data
A catalogue record for this title is available from the British Library

ISBN: 978 0 340 97359 2

First edition published 2004
This edition published 2009
Impression number   10 9 8 7 6 5 4 3 2 1
Year   2012 2011 2010 2009

Copyright © 2009 Ian Harrison

Hachette UK's policy is to use papers that are natural, renewable and recyclable products and made from wood grown in sustainable forests. The logging and manufacturing processes are expected to conform to the environmental regulations of the country of origin.

Artwork by David Graham
Cover photo © Peter Dazeley/Stone/Getty Images
Typeset by Fakenham Photosetting Ltd, Fakenham, Norfolk
Printed in Italy for Hodder Education, an Hachette UK Company, 338 Euston Road, London NW1 3BH.

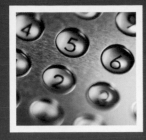

INTRODUCTION

You have just completed an AS course in Accounting. This has been an ideal foundation course for your A2 year. You should have laid a solid foundation necessary to help you build up to the more difficult and complex topics that you will now encounter.

At AS Level much emphasis was placed on knowledge and understanding of the various topics. You learned how to apply that knowledge and understanding to various situations.

The Advanced Level course that you are embarking on requires higher-order skills, especially those involving the ability to analyse and evaluate a topic.

As an A Level student you will be assessed on your ability to:

- demonstrate your knowledge and understanding of accounting information systems
- assemble and classify accounting data, presented to you, in an understandable way
- know and apply accounting concepts in a variety of scenarios
- interpret and analyse accounting information in a way that will enable you to evaluate alternative courses of action and make reasoned judgements
- communicate your results and findings in a variety of ways that will suit the many users of accounting information
- understand and appreciate the value of accounting information as well as its inherent limitations.

Studying and revising for any examinations should not be a last-minute affair. In order to gain the grade that you deserve, you should make detailed notes throughout the duration of the course.

Jot down notes of interesting items from the radio and television, from newspapers and from what friends and relatives tell you about the business world.

Accounting needs much practice. If you have run out of questions on a particular topic, revisit questions or borrow past question papers from your school or college library. Visit the appropriate websites to 'get the feel' of recent examination papers and check your answers against any mark schemes that are available.

Practise the topics with your friends – this will help you, as well as them.

Certain items have to be learned by heart in any subject – there is no substitute for this. Layouts must be learned, as well as certain definitions and formulae. This is vitally important. There can be no excuses. Practise for 5 or 10 minutes per day – you will soon master any topic you wish to remember. This is how you learn the words of pop songs – regular practice.

Why is it that your teachers know so much about their subject areas? Yes, they did study it at a high level at university, but the other reason is that they have probably repeated certain topics to many classes over many years and this practice has meant perfection!

REVISION

Start to revise in plenty of time – please do not leave it to the last minute. The A2 year is not as long as it seems: it is not 12 months – it can be as short as seven or eight months. Deduct holidays from this and an odd few days off with a sports injury or a cold and you could be looking at five and a half months – work it out!

Remember to spread your revision across all your subjects – no employer or university wants a grade A in one subject and two or three fail grades. Be like the juggler and keep all your subjects going at the same time.

Try to find spare times at school or college to revise – this will free up some time at home.

Prepare a revision timetable for each week – and stick to it – it is easier to stick to a regular routine of study than it is to do it in a haphazard way. Regular study works best.

The more you put in, the more you will get out of it!

If you revise while listening to music, remember that this is not possible in a crowded examination hall so you need to have practice sessions in complete silence – sounds awful, doesn't it? But this is necessary because you will have to spend up to two and a half hours in the examination room at one time, sitting and working in silence.

Varying your methods of revision will help you to avoid getting bored – have regular breaks or a change of subjects or topics.

Try:

- reading aloud
- talking yourself through a difficult topic
- giving yourself tests
- working with a friend and testing each other (make sure that when you set a question, you know the answer!). Try to avoid gossip sessions when working with a friend!
- summarising answers to written questions
- using mnemonics
- practising sections of questions before building up to the whole question.

As a guide to how well you know a topic, ask yourself: 'Could I explain this topic to someone who does not know much (if anything) about accounting so that they would understand it?' If you can answer 'Yes', then you probably understand the topic. If you have to answer 'No' – then more revision is necessary.

When you are waiting outside the examination hall, ready to start your examination, I bet that some of your friends will wish you good luck. Luck has nothing to do with the result you obtain – the result will be a reflection of the time spent revising and practising.

Examination results are awards for honest endeavour. Remember this as you go through this book!

CHAPTER
ONE

Loose Ends

The aim of this book is to take you one stage further in the study of accounting. *Introducing Accounting* covered the topics that you needed to cover for tackling your AS examinations; this book covers the topics that you will encounter on your A2 course. It has been written with, I hope, the minimum of jargon, to make it as understandable as possible. Clearly, there are some topics that cannot be completely de-mystified, but an attempt has been made.

As in *Introducing Accounting*, chapter objectives identify the key points to be covered in the chapter you are about to read and there are references to the sections of the specifications covered.

Each time a new term is introduced it will appear in a definition box.

Examination tips are also identified as the chapters progress. Each chapter will explain the topic, then there will follow examples of questions that an examiner may ask. Each worked example is followed by the answer. It is a good idea to cover over the answer with a spare sheet of paper while you attempt it. If you get stuck you can then uncover the answer and hopefully carry on and perhaps finish the example.

Throughout the text there are numerous questions for practice purposes. Questions are graded, starting with simpler ones and building up to more complex questions as you proceed through the chapter.

Odd-numbered questions have the answers at the end of the book. Even-numbered questions do not have the answers.

In the main, even-numbered questions are very similar to the odd-numbered questions so if you get stuck you can use the odd-numbered question to help you out.

Past examination questions have deliberately been omitted as these can be readily obtained from the examination boards. These will then provide a further useful resource for you to use in addition to the questions provided for you in this book.

Details of past papers available can be obtained from the appropriate website.

Do have a look at these sites because they will give you an idea of how questions look in the context of each paper. The mark schemes will give an indication of what the examiner is looking for in your answer. But do remember that the mark schemes have been prepared for use by examiners who have had a full day's training on the papers, followed by several hours of instruction from senior examiners.

Try www.aqa.org.uk and www.ocr.org.uk.

It is so very important that you practise questions from each topic. The old adage 'practice makes perfect' still applies today and the more practice you get, the better your grade will surely be.

The more time you spend on your studies, the greater your reward will be when the results are announced.

Specification coverage:
OCR FO12

By the end of this chapter you should be able to:
- prepare departmental accounts
- prepare a reconciliation statement of control account balances with schedules of debtors and creditors
- prepare and use a suspense account.

DEPARTMENTAL ACCOUNTS

Accounting is an information system. It is used to communicate information to the users of final accounts. It communicates information to managers, to owners, to lenders of finance and to many others. Sometimes the information that is obvious hides other information that is less obvious.

EXAMPLE

Tony owns and runs a newsagent's shop. As well as newspapers, Tony sells magazines, sweets and chocolates, cigarettes and bottles of fizzy drinks. His profits have been fairly static over the past five years or so at around £26,000. 'Quite a nice living', you might say.

However, if we look more closely at Tony's profits and analyse them very carefully, we may discover that all is not quite what it seems:

- profit from the sale of newspapers is £12,000 per annum
- profit from the sale of magazines is £8,500 per annum
- profit from sales of sweets and chocolates is £4,400 per annum
- profit from the sale of cigarettes is £1,870 per annum
- loss on sales of fizzy drinks is £770 per annum.

If Tony ceased to sell fizzy drinks, his profit would rise to £26,770. So perhaps Tony should close down the section of the shop that is devoted to stocking and selling the drinks.

But Tony may be prepared to sell the drinks as a 'loss leader' because he knows that very few of his customers buy only a drink. They usually buy a drink and a magazine or a drink and a chocolate bar etc. So if he stopped selling the drinks, other products might suffer too.

Accounting information might not tell us the whole story. We need as much accounting information as possible to enable us to make informed business decisions.

Departmental accounts provide us with information that will enable us to assess the profitability of separate sections of a business.

WORKED EXAMPLE

Sanjay owns and runs a shop that sells baby linen, prams and cots. He provides the following information relating to the year ended 31 March 20*9:

Departments	Baby linen £	Prams £	Cots £
Stock at 1 April 20*8	1,380	2,350	560
Stock at 31 March 20*9	1,540	1,970	430
Purchases	23,760	35,780	2,350
Sales	45,980	60,460	5,890
Wages	12,560	16,670	2,340

The following expenses cannot be attributed to any particular department:

	£
Rent and rates	4,200
Lighting and heating expenses	6,600
Administration costs	1,200
Other expenses	900

The baby linen section occupies half of the floor space of the shop; prams occupy one-third and cots occupy the remainder.

Sanjay has decided to apportion rent and rates and lighting and heating expenses in proportion to the floor space occupied by each department. Administration and other expenses are to be shared equally.

Required

Prepare a departmental income statement for the year ended 31 March 20*9.

	Baby linen		**Prams**		**Cots**	
	£	£	£	£	£	£
Sales		45,980		60,460		5,890
Less Cost of sales						
Stock at 1 April 20*8	1,380		2,350		560	
Purchases	23,760		35,780		2,350	
	25,140		38,130		2,910	
Stock at 31 March 20*9	1,540		1,970		430	
		23,600		36,160		2,480
Gross profit		22,380		24,300		3,410
Less Expenses						
Wages	12,560		16,670		2,340	
Rent and rates	2,100		1,400		700	
Heat and light	3,300		2,200		1,100	
Administration	400		400		400	
Other expenses	300		300		300	
		18,660		20,970		4,840
Net profit/(loss)		3,720		3,330		(1,430)

Answer

It can clearly be seen from the results that the cots department is unprofitable. If Sanjay closed down the cots department his profit would rise to £7,050.

Or would it?

We have already mentioned the interdependency of one department to another in Tony's business; this may also be true in the case of Sanjay's business.

Let us consider the way in which expenses have been shared between the departments. Apart from the wages, the other expenses have been apportioned on a purely arbitrary basis. Their apportionment may not reflect accurately the amount of the resources actually used by each department. The accurate way to apportion the expenses is to ask how much rent and rates would be saved if the cots department was closed. If we said that £380 would be saved then that must be the amount of rent and rates that should be charged to the cots department. How much would be saved on heating and lighting if the department was closed? If the answer was £620 then that is the correct charge to the cots department. This method, although time consuming, would reveal the true extent of the profitability of each department.

As well as considering the profitability of the department and its impact on other departments, other factors should be considered: the impact on customer confidence and workers' morale, among others.

A better approach is to take the **marginal cost approach**. This is considered in depth in Chapter Fourteen.

QUESTION 1

The following information is given for Jan's electrical store:

Stock	at 1 January 20*8 £	at 31 December 20*8 £
Kitchen goods	6,980	7,450
DIY goods	4,870	5,090
Leisure goods	8,820	7,690

	Kitchen goods £	DIY goods £	Leisure goods £
Sales for the year	97,876	73,752	102,653
Purchases for the year	42,631	30,884	38,005

Required

Prepare an extract from the departmental income statement for the year ended 31 December 20*8.

QUESTION 2

Cedric provides the following information relating to his business:

	Nail bar £	Hairdressing £	Cosmetics £
Stock at 1 March 20*8	230	860	340
Stock at 28 February 20*9	185	1,010	350
Sales	18,357	46,679	28,763
Purchases	4,784	25,879	8,472

Required

Prepare an extract from the departmental income statement for the year ended 28 February 20*9.

QUESTION 3

Maurice Duvall owns and runs a shop specialising in continental cheeses and meats. He provides the following information for the year ended 31 October 20*9.

	£
Stocks of cheeses – 1 November 20*8	2,860
31 October 20*9	1,790
Stocks of meats – 1 November 20*8	1,540
31 October 20*9	1,680
Purchases – cheeses	29,960
meats	43,750
Sales – cheeses	88,630
meats	125,330
Wages of sales assistants – cheeses	12,660
meats	21,110
Administrative salaries	8,560
Insurances	4,800
Repairs to meat fridge	840
Electricity	2,400

	£
Rent and rates	7,200
Lighting and heating expenses	1,680
General expenses	8,550
Motor expenses (including depreciation)	11,500

The cheese department occupies two-thirds of the total floor area; the meat department occupies the remainder.

Overheads are to be apportioned as follows:

■ according to **floor area** – electricity, rent and rates and lighting and heating
■ **equally** between the two departments – administrative salaries, insurances and general expenses
■ **motor expenses** are to be apportioned one-fifth to cheeses and four-fifths to meats.

Required

Prepare a departmental income statement for the year ended 31 October 20*9.

QUESTION 4

The following information is given for Sandra's boutique:

	£
Wages	108,000
Rent and rates	9,400
Insurances	9,500
Depreciation	24,000
General expenses	17,400
Purchases – Department A	72,000
Department B	64,000
Department C	18,000
Sales – Department A	180,000
Department B	120,000
Department C	60,000
Stock at 1 February 20*8 – Department A	5,800
Department B	4,600
Department C	1,800
Stock at 31 January 20*9 – Department A	5,500
Department B	4,900
Department C	1,600

■ Departments A and B each occupy 4,400 m²; Department C occupies 2,200 m².
■ Wages and depreciation are to be apportioned in proportion to sales revenue.
■ Rent and rates are to be apportioned according to floor area occupied.
■ Insurances and general expenses are to be apportioned equally.

Required

Prepare a departmental income statement for the year ended 31 January 20*9.

CONTROL ACCOUNTS – FURTHER CONSIDERATIONS

In *Introducing Accounting* we prepared control accounts and used them to verify the entries in the sales ledgers and purchases ledgers. It is unusual at A2 Level to require candidates to prepare a straightforward control account. (The exception to this is, of course, when it is part of a larger synoptic question.)

Questions at A2 Level generally deal with errors and events that are discovered after the schedule of debtors and the control accounts have been drawn up.

These questions are designed to test candidates' knowledge of:

■ how control accounts are prepared
■ the sources of information used to write up the personal ledger accounts
■ the sources of information used to prepare the control accounts
■ the relationship between the control account and the personal ledger accounts.

It is worth spending a little time revisiting *Introducing Accounting* to remind yourself how the day books are used to write up both the personal ledger accounts and the control accounts.

Remember that some control accounts are kept as part of the double-entry system; they are **integrated** into the double-entry system. Some control accounts are kept purely as memorandum accounts and the personal accounts are kept as part of the double-entry system.

Whether control accounts are part of the double-entry system or whether they are memorandum accounts, they are always prepared in the same way.

A **schedule of debtors** is a list of all debit balances extracted from the sales ledger(s). Also known as a schedule of trade receivables.

A **schedule of creditors** is a list of all credit balances extracted from the purchases ledger(s). Also known as a schedule of trade payables

● EXAMINATION TIP

Remember that any credit balances extracted from the sales ledger must be shown in the trial balance (and later the balance sheet) as trade payables.

Any debit balances extracted from the purchases ledger must be shown as trade receivables.

The most popular type of question to be set at A2 Level requires candidates to reconcile the balance shown in the control account with the total of the balances extracted from the appropriate personal ledger.

This type of question will give a list of errors. Some of the errors will require:

■ an adjustment to a personal account in the sales ledger (or purchases ledger) only – hence this will have an effect on the schedule of debtors (or creditors) extracted from the ledger
■ an adjustment to the appropriate control account only – hence this will have an effect on the balance brought down in the control account
■ an adjustment to both a personal account in the sales ledger (or the purchases ledger) and an adjustment to the control account too.

WORKED EXAMPLE

Amandeep Bola maintains control accounts as part of her general ledger. She has prepared a sales ledger control account for February 20*9 with information derived from her subsidiary books. The debit balances shown in the control account at 28 February 20*9 amounted to £9,040. This failed to agree with the schedule of debtor balances extracted from the sales ledger on that date. This showed total debtors of £9,372.

After preparing the control account and the schedule of debtors, the following errors were discovered:

1. The debit side of John Taylor's account in the sales ledger had been overcast by £100.
2. A credit sale of £340 to Akit Patel had been debited in error to the account of Anjni Patel. Akit's account had been debited to correct the error but no entry had been made in Anjni's account.

WORKED EXAMPLE *continued*

3. A credit sale to Janice Mulch of £108 had been correctly entered in the sales day book but had not been entered in her sales ledger account.

Required

Prepare a statement reconciling the total debtors shown by the schedule of debtors with that shown in the control account at 28 February 20*9.

Answer

	£	
Total debtor balances as per schedule	9,372	All these errors have an effect on one
Less Overcast	(100)	of the accounts in the sales ledger.
Entry in Anjni's account	(340)	None of them has any effect on the
Add Entry to Janice's account	108	sales ledger control account.
Control account balance	9,040	

WORKED EXAMPLE

Leslie Buttersby has prepared a purchases ledger control account as a memorandum account for December 20*8. The creditors shown in the control account at 31 December 20*8 amounted to £6,488; this amount failed to agree with the total of creditors' balances extracted from the purchases ledger at that date. The schedule of creditors totalled £4,316.

The following errors were discovered during January 20*9:

1. A page of the purchases day book was undercast by £1,000 in December.
2. The balance of £7,937 on the purchases ledger control account at the end of November 20*8 had been carried forward into the December control account as £9,737.
3. Credit balances amounting to £1,372 had been transferred to the sales ledger. These 'set-offs' had not been entered in the purchases ledger control account.

Required

Prepare a statement showing the adjustments to the balance shown by the purchases ledger control account.

Answer

	£
Balance as per control account 31 December 20*8	6,488
Add Amount of undercast	1,000
Less Transposition error	(1,800)
Set-offs	(1,372)
Corrected control account credit balance	4,316

WORKED EXAMPLE

Charlie Parlez maintains control accounts as part of his general ledger. He has prepared a sales ledger control account for the month of August 20*9. The debit balance shown in the sales ledger control account at 31 August 20*9 failed to agree with the schedule of debtors extracted from the sales ledger at that date. The total of the balances extracted from the sales ledger at that date was £16,561. The following errors were subsequently discovered:

1. The debit side of Melvyn Chan's account in the sales ledger had been undercast by £10.
2. A credit sale of £427 to David Austen had been debited to the account of Darren Morris in error.
3. A credit sale of £633 to I. Gourd had not been entered in the sales day book.
4. A page in the returns day book had been undercast by £100.
5. The account of Juan Badun shows a debit balance of £137. Although an entry to write this debt off as being bad had been entered in the journal, no entries had been made in any ledgers.
6. The provision for doubtful debts was increased in August from £1,740 to £1,930; no entry had been made in any ledger.

Required

Calculate:

a   the corrected total of sales ledger balances after the errors have been corrected
b   the total of debtor balances at 31 August 20*9 as shown in Melvyn's sales ledger control account **before** the errors had been corrected.

Answer

a

	£
Debtor balances as per uncorrected schedule	16,561
Add Adjustment to Melvyn's account (1)	10
Add Missing entry from account of I. Gourd (3)	633
Less Bad debt (5)	(137)
Corrected debtors' balances	17,067

b

	£
Correct debtors balance as per control account	17,067
Less Sale to I. Gourd (3)	633
Add Sales returns day book undercast (4)	(100)
Add Bad debt written off (5)	(137)
Original debit balance on incorrect control account	16,671

- Correction (2) does not affect the schedule of debtor balances nor does it affect the sales ledger control account – it is a transfer from one debtor to another.
- Correction (6) does not affect the sales ledger – it is a book entry only: debit profit and loss account; credit the provision account.

○ EXAMINATION TIP

Remember that the solution to this type of problem is not dependent on whether the control accounts are integrated or kept as memorandum accounts. The time when there will be a difference in your answers is when you are required to show the double entries.

A credit sale to R. Dickens for £97 had been omitted from the sales day book.

Required

Journal entries to correct the error.

Answer

For an integrated system:	£	£
Dr Sales ledger control account	97	
Cr Sales		97
For control accounts kept as memorandum accounts:		
Dr R. Dickens	97	
Cr Sales		97

QUESTION 5

Alex Brown has prepared a schedule of debtors which has totalled £4,775. He has discovered the following errors which he believes may affect the list of debtors, balances that he has extracted from his sales ledger at 31 May 20*9:

1. A balance on the account of T. Stamp, a credit customer, of £146 has been brought down on 1 June 20*8 as £416.
2. The sales day book has been undercast by £1,000.
3. An entry for C. Oyne of £718 in the sales day book has not been posted to his account in the sales ledger.
4. P. Ence, who owes Alex £316, could not settle his debt and the amount was to have been written off in May – no entries have been made in the books of account to record this.

Required

Calculate the corrected total of debtors at 31 May 20*9.

QUESTION 6

Melody Gnobu has prepared a purchases ledger control account for May 20*9. The balance carried down was £11,319. In June 20*9 she discovered the following errors:

1. The purchases returns day book had been undercast by £100 in May 20*9.
2. A payment to I. Gloope for £612 on 12 May 20*9 had been entered in the cash book but had not been entered in Gloope's account.
3. Transfers of balances (set-offs) amounting to £4,372, in May 20*9, had not been entered in any control account.
4. The total discount allowed account had not been entered in any control account.

Required

Calculate the correct balance to be carried forward into the purchases ledger control account for June 20*9.

QUESTION 7

Julie Blackwell maintains control accounts as an integral part of her double-entry system. She has prepared a sales ledger control account for January 20*9.

She has also extracted a schedule of debtors from her sales ledger at 31 January 20*9. The total of debtors failed to agree with the balance carried forward to the February control account of £4,361.

The following errors have been discovered:

1. A copy of the sales invoice sent to Clax & Co for £301 had been destroyed and no record of the transaction had been made in the books of account.
2. Discounts received of £126 had not been entered in the control account.
3. The balance brought down on 1 January amounting to £2,717 had not been entered in the control account.

4. A credit sale to J. Fitzwilliam of £991 had been entered in the sales day book but had not been posted to the ledger.
5. Cash sales for 4 January 20*9 amounting to £1,488 had not been entered in the books of account.
6. A credit sale of £637 to Betty Cluck had been entered in the sales day book as £376.

Required

a The correct total of debtors shown in the sales ledger control account at 31 January 20*9.
b The total of debtors balances at 31 January 20*9 before the errors were corrected.

QUESTION 8

Rita Blundiski maintains control accounts as memorandum accounts. Her purchases ledger control account prepared for September 2009 does not agree with the £27,520 total of creditors extracted from her purchases ledger. On examination, Rita discovers the following errors:

1. A purchases invoice for £543 for goods purchased on credit from J. Bull had not been received. No entry had been made in the book of prime entry.
2. The total of the discount received column in the cash book had been overcast by £101.
3. One whole page in the payments cash book totalling £4,728 had been posted to the wrong side of the individual creditors' accounts.
4. Bad debts for September amounting to £1,342 have not been written off in the books of account.
5. A purchases invoice received from Pough & Blow Ltd, for £1,467, had been entered in the purchases day book as £7,164.
6. Transfers (set-offs) from the sales ledger, to the purchases ledger, amounting to £1,467, had not been entered in either control account.
7. A balance of £211 in the account of Patsy D. Khan at 31 July 20*9 had been carried down on 1 August as £1,121.

Required

a Calculate the corrected total creditors at 30 September **after** errors 1–7 have been taken into account.
b Calculate the original balance on the purchases ledger control account at 30 September 20*9 **before** errors 1–7 were taken into account.

SUSPENSE ACCOUNTS

Suspense accounts are sometimes examined at A2 Level, especially as part of the synoptic assessment. Remember that if a trial balance does not balance, you cannot reasonably expect your final accounts to balance if you use the figures from the trial balance to prepare financial statements.

To allow a set of draft financial statements to be prepared, a suspense item is included in the trial balance in order to make it balance. If the 'balancing' amount is a debit, the suspense item is included in the balance sheet as a current asset. If the suspense item is a credit, then this will appear in the balance sheet as a current liability.

Here are three examples to remind you of how a suspense account is used.

WORKED EXAMPLE

The sales day book has been overcast by £100.

Required

Prepare journal entries to correct the error.

Answer

The sales day book provides the entry to the double-entry system (remember the ticket booths into the football ground in *Introducing Accounting*).

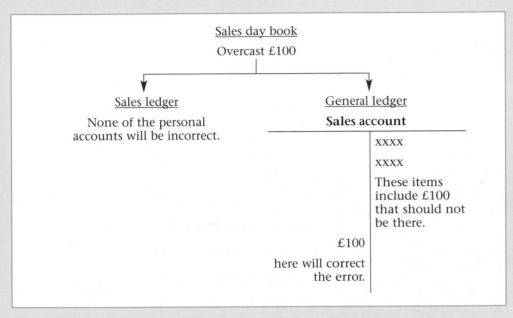

So we have put in £100 on the debit side of the double-entry system. Where can we put a credit entry to maintain our system? In the rent account? In the wages account? Of course not! If you cannot find a corresponding entry easily and comfortably, you will need to use a suspense account.

So:	**Dr**	**Cr**
Sales account	£100	
Suspense account		£100
Correction of error – sales overcast by £100.		

Rent paid of £4,000 has been entered in the rates account in error.

Required

Prepare journal entries to correct the error.

Answer

Rates account		
xxxx	4,000	
xxxx		

We need to credit the rates account to get it right and debit the rent account

Rent account	
xxxx	
xxxx	
4,000	

Do we have a debit entry and a credit entry? Of course – easy – so no need for entries in any other account.

continued ➤

WORKED EXAMPLE *continued*

So:	Dr	Cr
Rent account	£4,000	
Rates account		£4,000

Correction of error of commission £4,000 paid for rent incorrectly entered in rates account.

WORKED EXAMPLE

The discounts received column in the cash book totalling £953 has been posted to the debit of the discounts allowed account as £539.

Required

Prepare journal entries to correct the error.

Answer

Discounts allowed		
xxxx	539	Entry to remove incorrect posting of discount received.

Discounts received		
	xxxx	Entry to post correctly discount received.
	xxxx	
	953	

Do we have a debit entry and a credit entry (of the same amount)? No – we have credit entries totalling £1,492 – we need a debit entry of £1,492. Where can we put the debit entry to maintain the double-entry system? In the rent account? In the wages account? Of course not! Again, we have failed to find an easy, comfortable, corresponding entry, so we will have to rely on our old friend – the suspense account.

So:	Dr	Cr
Suspense account	£1,492	
Discount allowed		£539
Discount received		£953

Correction of error – discount received £953 posted in error to discount allowed account as £539.

Note that in these examples I have not used figures when denoting the original error(s); this helps many students – it avoids triple-entry book-keeping!

QUESTION 9

Patricia Gooi extracted a trial balance from her ledgers at close of business on 31 May 20*9. The trial balance totals failed to agree. (Patricia maintains an integrated set of control accounts in her general ledger.) In June 20*9 Patricia found the following errors:

1. The advertising account had been overcast by £100.
2. A cheque paid to Ralph Simpson for £720 had been posted to the credit of the control account.

3. Goods to the value of £120 withdrawn for Patricia's own use had been recorded only once in the books of account; as sales.
4. Repairs of £1,600 to a machine had been debited to the Machinery account.

When these errors had been corrected, the trial balance totals agreed.

Required

Prepare:

a journal entries to correct the errors that Patricia discovered (narratives are not required).
b a suspense account showing clearly the original trial balance difference.

QUESTION 10

Vincent Schelling extracted a trial balance from his ledgers at close of business on 30 April 20*9. The trial balance totals failed to agree. (Vincent does not maintain integrated control accounts in his general ledger.) In early May Vincent discovered the following errors:

1. Purchases returns of £702 had been incorrectly debited to the purchases account as £207.
2. £450 drawings for April had been posted to the wages account.
3. The sales day book had been overcast by £1,001.
4. A cheque paid to Sammy Lim for £71 had been posted to the credit of his account.

When the trial balance errors had been corrected, the trial balance totals agreed.

Required

Prepare:

a journal entries to correct the errors (narratives are not required)
b a suspense account showing clearly the original trial balance difference.

QUESTION 11

Bert Aked extracted a trial balance from his ledgers at close of business on 31 January 20*9. The trial balance totals failed to agree. (Bert maintains integrated control accounts in his general ledger.) The following errors were discovered in early February 20*9:

1. Bert had injected £5,000 additional capital into his business. This sum had been debited to the bank account and credited to the sales account.
2. Commission payable of £2,100 had been entered in the general ledger as commission receivable £1,200.
3. A credit sale of £650 to Pippa Bramley had been debited to the account of Pippin Cox.
4. £73 discount allowed entered in the cash book to Shirley Knott had been debited to the account of Andy Knott as £37.
5. Purchase returns of £140 sent to D. County had been entered in the account of S. County.

When these errors had been corrected the trial balance totals agreed.

Required

Prepare:

a journal entries to correct the errors (narratives are not required)
b a suspense account showing clearly the original trial balance difference.

QUESTION 12

Joyce McIntyre extracted a trial balance from her ledgers at close of business on 31 December 20*9. The trial balance totals failed to agree. (Joyce does not maintain integrated control accounts in her general ledger.) Joyce found the following errors in early January:

1. Goods returned by Sanaa Malik of £302 had been completely omitted from the books of account.
2. Rent receivable amounting to £650 had been posted to the rent payable account as £560.
3. A debit balance of £240 in the sales ledger account of S. Neal had been transferred to her purchase ledger account as £420.
4. The bank overdraft figure of £1,750 on 1 December had been included in the debit bank column in the cash book.
5. Goods purchased on credit from D. Hickson of £903 had been entered in the account of H. Dickson.

When these errors had been corrected, the trial balance totals agreed.

Required

Prepare:

a journal entries to correct the errors (narratives are not required)
b a suspense account showing clearly the original trial balance difference.

CHAPTER
TWO

Incomplete Records

There are two main types of organisation that may not keep a full set of double-entry records. They are

- small cash-based businesses
- clubs and societies.

In this chapter we shall consider the former.

SMALL CASH-BASED BUSINESSES

Much of the work of any professional accountant is taken up with the preparation of the final accounts of small businesses; because many of these businesses carry on their business on a cash basis, they will not keep a full set of ledgers in which to record their business transactions.

QUESTION

Name three businesses that conduct most of their business on a cash basis.

Answer

Your answer could have included businesses like Roland's Hair salon; Wong's Chinese take-away; Wendy's Mini-market.

Since there will be few (if any) credit customers in my answer it is extremely unlikely that Roland, Wong or Wendy will keep a sales ledger.

Remember that a sales ledger will contain the accounts of all credit customers. Since the vast majority of the customers of those businesses pay cash, there is no need to open an account for them.

Also, many (if not all) of the purchases of goods for resale and the services consumed will be paid for by using cash or by writing cheques. Roland will buy his perms from his local hairdressing cash and carry; Wong will pay by cheque for the gas used to cook the food that he sells; Wendy will pay for her telephone calls by cheque or by using cash. None of these traders will find it necessary to keep a purchases ledger.

The main book for the recording of transactions for these businesses will be a cash book in which all transactions using cash or cheques will be recorded. The information contained in the cash book will be supplemented by bank statements, till rolls, invoices and receipts.

The task that is faced in this situation is to build up a more complete picture of the financial transactions that have taken place during the financial year than the one that is shown by the cash book on its own.

There are two main types of questions set in examinations:

- where candidates are required to calculate the organisation's profit or loss
- where candidates are required to prepare an income statement for the organisation.

It is important that you are able to recognise each type of question.

Specification coverage:
AQA ACCN 3;
OCR F012

By the end of this chapter you should be able to:
- calculate net profit or loss using the net asset method
- prepare final accounts for businesses who do not keep a full set of financial records
- calculate cash and stock losses.

CALCULATION OF THE PROFIT OR LOSS OF A CASH-BASED BUSINESS

The key to recognising this type of question is found in the word used in the question. That word is 'required'. It is quite simple really – if you read the question very carefully.

This type of question will always ask you to calculate the profit or loss.

There are five stages to this procedure. You will recognise them. They have already been used in Chapter 2 of *Introducing Accounting*.

In this type of business there is no ledger, and therefore there are no accounts. There can be no balances, so there can be no sheet for balances (ie a balance sheet).

Can you remember how you calculated the profit or loss for a business using the net asset method?

A **statement of affairs** is exactly the same as a balance sheet.

- **Stage 1: Calculate the opening capital** (net assets) of the business either by listing the assets and then deducting the liabilities or by preparing a statement of affairs.
- **Stage 2: Calculate the closing capital** (net assets).
- **Stage 3: Deduct the opening capital from the closing capital.** This will indicate the profit or loss retained in the business.
- **Stage 4:** Some profits may have been taken out of the business during the year in the form of cash and/or goods (or services) as drawings. These **drawings** (profits) **have to be added to the retained profits**.
- **Stage 5:** Sometimes the proprietor of a business may inject new capital into the business. This extra capital will increase the assets owned by the business at the end of the year; in turn this will increase the figure we have calculated as retained profit (it could reduce the figure calculated as a retained loss).

  Obviously, the amount of capital introduced is not an increase in net assets earned by the business so it must be disregarded in our calculation. So **deduct capital introduced**.

We can summarise these stages:

	Closing capital
Deduct	Opening capital
Retained profit	xxxxxxxxxxxx
Add	Drawings
	xxxxxxxxxxxx
Deduct	Capital introduced
Profit for the year	xxxxxxxxxxxxxx

WORKED EXAMPLE

As at 1 January 20*9 Gemma had the following assets and liabilities: vehicle at valuation £2,400; equipment at valuation £5,400; stock £670; debtors £45; bank balance £1,730; creditors £260.

One year later, at 31 December 20*9, she had the following assets and liabilities: vehicles at valuation £12,400; equipment at valuation £4,860; stock £590; debtors £55; bank balance £2,540; creditors £180.

During the year Gemma withdrew £16,750 cash from the business for her household expenses. She also withdrew goods for her personal use, to the value of £1,230.

Required

Calculate the business profit or loss for the year ended 31 December 20*9.

WORKED EXAMPLE *continued*

Answer

	£	
Closing capital	20,265	(12,400+4,860+590+55+2,540−180)
Less Opening capital	9,985	(2,400+5,400+670+45+1,730−260)
Retained profits	10,280	
Add Drawings	17,980	(16,750+1,230)
Profit for the year ended 31 December 20*9	28,260	

Note the wording of the question: it said 'calculate'.

WORKED EXAMPLE

Dreyfus supplies the following information relating to his business:

	at 1 April 20*8 £	at 31 March 20*9 £
Premises at cost	60,000	60,000
Machinery at valuation	36,000	32,400
Vehicles at valuation	12,600	11,340
Stock	1,650	2,120
Debtors	135	120
Creditors	470	430
Bank balance	1,450	3,560

During the year ended 31 March 20*9 Dreyfus made drawings of £23,700.

In February Dreyfus inherited £7,800 from a distant relative; he paid this sum into the business bank account.

Required

Calculate the business profit or loss for the year ended 31 March 20*9.

Answer

	£	
Closing capital	109,110	(60,000+32,400+11,340+2,120+120+3,560−430)
Less Opening capital	111,365	(60,000+36,000+12,600+1,650+135+1,450−470)
Retained profits	(2,255)	
Add Drawings	23,700	
	21,445	
Less Capital introduced	7,800	
Net profit for the year ended 31 March 20*9	13,645	

● EXAMINATION TIP

Always show your workings – they may gain you marks if part of your answer is incorrect.

QUESTION 1

Chesney supplies the following information:

Assets and liabilities	at 30 November 20*9 £	at 30 November 20*8 £
Machinery	48,000	40,000
Equipment	14,000	10,000
Vehicles	15,000	17,000
Stock	1,300	1,250
Debtors	700	500
Creditors	1,000	910
Long-term loan	30,000	20,000
Bank balance	2,000	1,750

During the year Chesney withdrew £13,500 cash from the business for private use.

Required

Calculate the profit or loss for the year ended 30 November 20*9.

QUESTION 2

Marion supplies the following information:

Assets and liabilities	at 31 May 20*9 £	at 31 May 20*8 £
Vehicles	19,000	12,000
Stock	610	140
Debtors	400	–
Creditors	160	–
Bank balance	1,270	730
Bank loan	7,500	–
Cash in hand	30	20

During the year Marion withdrew £8,400 cash from the business for private use.

Required

Calculate the profit or loss for the year ended 31 May 20*9.

QUESTION 3

Pat provides the following information:

Assets and liabilities	at 31 December 20*9 £	at 31 December 20*8 £
Premises	40,000	40,000
Machinery	14,000	10,000
Vehicles	12,000	16,000
Stock	2,500	2,400
Debtors	200	180
Creditors	1,000	930
Bank balance	2,840	1,650

During the year Pat withdrew £24,500 from the business for private use. She also paid a National Lottery win of £12,500 into the business bank account.

Required

Calculate the profit or loss for the year ended 31 December 20*9.

QUESTION 4

Nicky had net assets valued at £67,800 on 1 October 20*8; one year later, on 30 September 20*9, her net assets were valued at £72,450. During the year ended 30 September 20*9 she withdrew £18,950 cash from the business for private use. She also took £875 of goods from the business for her own use.

During the year an uncle gave her a gift of £25,000 which she paid into the business bank account.

Required

Calculate the profit or loss for the year ended 30 September 20*9.

PREPARATION OF FINAL ACCOUNTS OF A CASH-BASED BUSINESS

We have seen how we can calculate the profit or loss by comparing closing and opening capital values. In real life this is usually not sufficient to satisfy HM Revenue and Customs for taxation and VAT purposes.

This government department would probably require more detailed records to be kept.

These records do not have to be a full set of double-entry records – there is no statutory requirement that sole traders or partnerships should maintain a full set of accounting records.

To satisfy the authorities, most traders would keep a record of all cash and bank transactions. They would also keep all source documents received and copies of those sent.

QUESTION

Identify **four** source documents kept by a sole trader who does not keep a full set of accounting records.

Answer

Your answer should have identified: purchases invoices; copies of sales invoices; bank statements; cheque book counterfoils; paying-in counterfoils; till rolls; invoices from the utilities (gas, electricity, water) – the list could go on. The source documents are a record of all monies received and paid out.

These source documents will:

- help us build up a picture of the financial transactions that have taken place throughout the financial year
- verify the receipts and payments made
- be necessary if the business is VAT registered. A record of VAT paid to suppliers and charged to customers is essential to determine whether VAT has to be paid to HM Revenue and Customs or claimed back from them.

In an examination any question that asks for the preparation of an income statement and a balance sheet will require the following procedures. So we must read the question very carefully.

In order to be able to use this second method it is essential that we have the following information to hand:

- valuations of assets and liabilities at the start of the financial year
- totals of trade receivables and trade payables at the start of the financial year
- accrued expenses at the start of the year
- pre-payments made at the start of the financial year
- payments made by debtors during the financial year
- payments made to creditors during the financial year
- cash payments made during the financial year
- cash receipts during the financial year
- valuations of assets and liabilities at the end of the financial year
- totals of trade receivables and trade payables at the end of the financial year
- accrued expenses at the end of the financial year
- pre-payments made at the end of the financial year.

There are five stages to preparing the final accounts from a set of records that are incomplete:

- Stage 1: Prepare an opening statement of affairs. You may have to calculate the capital figure if it is not given in the question.
- Stage 2: Compile a summary of bank transactions.
- Stage 3: Compile a summary of cash transactions.
- Stage 4: Construct adjustment accounts (some teachers call these 'control accounts').
- Stage 5: Prepare the financial statements by using all the information gained from Stages 1, 2 and 3.

REVISION TIP

Learn these five stages – they are so important.

It is essential to follow these stages methodically each time you are asked to produce a set of final accounts from incomplete records.

The stage that gives most people a problem is Stage 4. Stage 4 is necessary because most of the records kept by traders who keep less than a full set of books of account are records of cash spent to acquire the necessary resources to carry on business or records of cash when it is received.

As accountants we must be aware of and apply the **accruals concept** – the payment to acquire a resource is not the same as the use of that resource.

Consider two examples:

EXAMPLE

Jack receives £120 on 15 February 20*9 for a sale of goods that took place on 21 December 20*8.

Cash was recorded in February – the profit was earned in December (realisation concept which is part of the accruals concept).

Electricity meter was read on 28 July for electricity used in May, June and July.

The electricity bill was received on 13 August and the amount was paid (very late!) on 12 October.

Electricity (a resource) was used in May, June and July – even though the payment was not paid until October.

Stage 4 sounds very complicated, but if we rely on first principles that we learned in our AS year it should be simplified.

Rely on your knowledge of double entry.

Rely on using 'T' accounts.

We will concentrate on Stage 4 since this is the stage that seems to cause the main problem.

WORKED EXAMPLE

Saleem Zain does not keep full accounting records. He is able to provide the following information for the year ended 28 February 20*9:

Summarised bank account	£		£
Balance at 1 March 20*8	1,456	Payments to creditors	43,675
Receipts from debtors	86,494	General expenses	24,911
		Purchase of fixed asset	17,500
		Balance at 28 February 20*9	1,864
	87,950		87,950

Additional information

	at 28 February 20*9 £	at 1 March 20*8 £
Debtors	918	752
Creditors	633	857
Inventory	2,779	2,152

Required

Prepare an extract from the income statement for the year ended 28 February 20*9.

Answer

We must prepare an adjustment account to determine the amount of sales for the year (remember that this may be different to the cash received from debtors during the year).

We also need to construct a similar account to determine the amount of the purchases for the year.

'Missing figures' for sales and purchases are italicised

Debtors				Creditors			
Balance b/d	752	Cash received	86,494	Cash paid	43,675	Balance b/d	857
Sales	*86,660*	Balance c/d	918	Balance c/d	633	*Purchases*	*43,451*
	87,412		87,412		44,308		44,308
Balance b/d	918					Balance b/d	633

continued ➤

To avoid making an error with your debtors and creditors, always put the closing balances under the account totals and 'bring them up'.

Debtors on the debit *under the account*. Creditors on the credit *under the account*.

WORKED EXAMPLE *continued*

Saleem Zain
Income statement extract for the year ended 28 February 20*9

	£	£
Sales		86,660
Less Cost of sales		
Inventory at 1 March 20*8	2,152	
Purchases	43,451	
	45,603	
Inventory at 28 February 20*9	2,779	42,824
Gross profit		43,836

QUESTION 5

Tamsin Rook does not keep a full set of accounting records. She is able to provide the following information for the year ended 31 August 20*9:

Summarised bank account

	£		£
Balance at 1 September 20*8	2,963	Payments to creditors	59,846
Receipts from debtors	121,367	General expenses	60,957
		Balance at 31 August 20*9	3,527
	124,330		124,330

Additional information

	at 31 August 20*9	at 1 September 20*8
	£	£
Stock	9,566	8,467
Debtors	2,468	1,792
Creditors	1,067	815

Required

Prepare an income statement extract for the year ended 31 August 20*9.

QUESTION 6

Barbara Vun does not keep a full set of accounting records. She provides the following information for the year ended 31 March 20*9:

Summarised bank account

	£		£
Receipts from debtors	68,499	Balance at 1 April 20*8	852
Balance at 31 March 20*9	2,467	Payments to creditors	32,814
		General expenses	37,300
	70,966		70,966

Additional information

	at 31 March 20*9	at 1 April 20*8
	£	£
Inventory	637	488
Debtors	376	214
Creditors	2,841	1,496

Required

Prepare an income statement extract for the year ended 31 March 20*9.

We can use the same approach to determine the amount of any expenses to be debited to the income statement if we know the cash paid and the amount of any accruals and pre-payments outstanding at the end of each financial year.

WORKED EXAMPLE

Harry Cary does not keep a full set of accounting records but he is able to provide the following information for the year ended 31 July 20*9:

Amounts paid for staff wages	£21,387
Amounts paid to landlord for rent	£3,400
Amounts paid for electricity	£2,162
Amounts paid for insurances	£3,467

Additional information

Amounts owed	at 1 August 20*8 £	at 31 July 20*9 £
for staff wages	212	297
for rent	118	136
for electricity	167	48
Amount paid in advance for insurances	196	346

Required

Calculate the amounts for wages and rent to be included in the income statement for the year ended 31 July 20*9.

Answer

Wages	£21,472
Rent	£3,418
Electricity	£2,043
Insurances	£3,317

Workings
Use the same procedure that was used to determine sales and purchases earlier.

Wages			
Cash	21,387	Balance at 1 August 20*8	212
Balance at 31 July 20*9	297	*Inc. statement*	*21,472*
	21,684		21,684
		Balance at 1 August 20*9	297

continued ➤

WORKED EXAMPLE *continued*

Rent

Cash	3,400	Balance at 1 August 20*8	118
Balance at 31 July 20*9	136	Inc. statement	3,418
	3,536		3,536
		Balance at 1 August 20*9	136

Electricity

Cash	2,162	Balance at 1 August 20*8	167
Balance at 31 July 20*9	48	Inc. statement	2,043
	2,210		2,210
		Balance at 1 August 20*9	48

Insurances

Balance at 1 August 20*8	196	Inc. statement	3,317
Cash	3,467	Balance at 31 July 20*9	346
	3,663		3,663
Balance at 1 August 20*9	346		

Notice that the balances have been brought down. This is important since often there are marks in an examination for these balances.

QUESTION 7

Eric provides the following information for the year ended 31 January 20*9:

	at 31 January 20*9 £	at 1 February 20*8 £
Amount owed for motor expenses	461	78
Amount paid in advance for rates	145	120
Cash paid during the year ended 31 January 20*9 for motor expenses		£8,166
Cash paid during the year ended 31 January 20*9 for rates		£1,534

Required

Calculate the amounts to be entered in the income statement for the year ended 31 January 20*9.

QUESTION 8

Tanya provides the following information for the year ended 30 September 20*9:

	at 30 September 20*9 £	at 1 October 20*8 £
Amount owed for advertising	88	467
Amount paid in advance for rent	360	200
Cash paid during the year ended 30 September 20*9 for advertising		£2,784
Cash paid during the year ended 30 September 20*9 for rent		£6,160

Required

Calculate the amounts to be entered in the income statement for the year ended 30 September 20*9.

We shall now work through an example that incorporates the techniques outlined above.

Work carefully through this example. We will be using the five stages outlined at the start of this section.

Can you remember the five stages?

WORKED EXAMPLE

Roger Guillaume owns a florist's shop. He does not maintain proper books of account.

He provides the following information for the year ended 30 April 20*9:

	Summarised bank account		
	£		£
Balance at 1 May 20*8	1,793	Payments to creditors	22,497
Takings banked	74,887	Rates	2,430
		Rent	2,800
		Other expenses	20,075
		Drawings	8,409
		Purchase of vehicle	17,000
		Balance at 30 April 20*9	3,469
	76,680		76,680

All takings were paid into the bank account with the exception of the following:

Wages £14,280
Drawings £12,000

Additional information

Assets and liabilities	at 30 April 20*9 £	at 1 May 20*8 £
Stock	164	212
Debtors	130	48
Creditors	328	467
Cash in hand	237	142
Rates paid in advance	1,340	1,080
Rent owed	120	102
Fixtures at valuation	648	720
Vehicles at valuation	16,500	4,200

Required

Prepare an income statement for the year ended 30 April 20*9 and a balance sheet at that date.

Note that because the question asks for the preparation of a set of final accounts, we must go carefully and methodically through each of the five stages outlined earlier.

If the question had asked for a calculation of the profit or loss, we could have used the much quicker net asset method.

Both methods will give us the same profit figure but the net asset method would not give us the same amount of detail that a full set of financial statements will.

continued ➤

Answer

Stage 1: Prepare an opening statement of affairs

As an Advanced Level student you should be able to do this almost as quickly as you can write the items down.

Do not be concerned with categories of assets and liabilities.

Stage 1 is part of your workings **BUT** do write the figures down neatly as well as quickly.

	Statement of affairs at 1 May 20*8		
		£	
Assets	Inventory	212	
	Trade receivables	48	
	Rates in advance	1,080	
	Cash	142	
	Fixtures	720	
	Vehicles	4,200	
Don't forget …	Bank balance	1,793	
		8,195	
Liabilities	Trade payables	467	
	Rent owed	102	
		569	
	Net assets	7,626	This is also Roger's capital

Note that the assets have been written down in the order that they have appeared in the question; no attempt has been made to categorise them.

Do take care to include the bank balance if it is not included in the list of assets and liabilities given in the question.

● EXAMINATION TIP

Do not just key the assets and liabilities into your calculator. If you do make an error then you cannot be rewarded for the parts that you got correct. Write the items down before you key them in.

Stages 2 and 3: Compile summarised cash and/or bank accounts

A bank summary has been given in the question (one less task to be done!). But we do need to prepare a cash summary.

	Cash account		
Balance at 1 May 20*8 (from list of assets)	142	Takings banked (from bank summary)	74,887
Total takings for year (missing figure)	101,262	Wages paid	14,280
		Drawings	12,000
		Balance at 30 April 20*9 (from list of closing balances)	237
	101,404		101,404

Stage 4: Construct adjustment accounts

You may be uncertain how many adjustment accounts to use. Initially you may not be confident enough to decide which accounts to open and which items do not need to be adjusted.

If you are not confident, then open an account for every item listed in your statement of affairs.

Inventory – we will adjust the inventory in a special account in Stage 5. The special account is the income statement! You are well used to adjusting stock – you have done this in every trading account that you have ever done!

Open an adjustment account for each of:

trade receivables; rates; (not cash – we adjusted our cash figures in Stage 3); fixtures; (not bank – this has been adjusted for us in the question); trade payables, and finally rent.

Do each adjustment in turn.

Open a 'T' account for each:

1. Enter the opening balance (debit for an asset; credit for a liability).
2. Enter the closing balance under your 'T' account.
3. Take the closing balance up diagonally into the body of the account.
4. Debit cash paid from the bank or cash account.
5. Credit cash received into the bank or cash account.
6. Total the account.
7. Calculate the *missing figure* to be posted to the trading account or profit and loss account.

Let us prepare the adjustment accounts. Numbers are given as a guide to the order in which the entries are made.

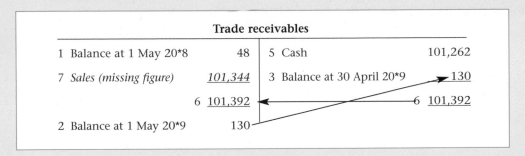

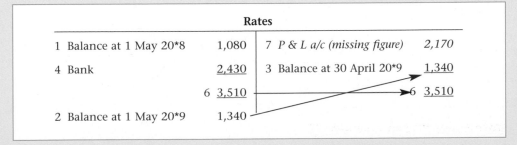

continued ➣

Fixtures

Balance at 1 May 20*8	720	P & L a/c (missing figure) (depreciation)	72
		Balance at 30 April 20*9	648
	720		720
Balance at 1 May 20*9	648		

Vehicles

Balance at 1 May 20*8	4,200	P & L a/c (missing figure) (depreciation)	4,700
Bank	17,000	Balance at 30 April 20*9	16,500
	21,200		21,200
Balance at 1 May 20*9	16,500		

Trade payables

Bank	22,497	Balance at 1 May 20*8	467
Balance at 30 April 20*9	328	Purchases (missing figure)	22,358
	22,825		22,825
		Balance at 1 May 20*9	328

Rent

Bank	2,800	Balance at 1 May 20*8	102
Balance at 30 April 20*9	120	P & L a/c (missing figure)	2,818
	2,920		2,920
		Balance at 1 May 20*9	120

Generally at this point in an examination you will have scored no marks unless you have specifically been asked to prepare the opening statement of affairs or one or two of the adjustment accounts in detail. The question asked us to prepare an income statement and balance sheet and as yet we have not done that. All that we have done is the preparatory work – we have got all our information ready.

An accountant in practice would call all the workings that we have done 'working papers'.

It is now time for Stage 5 where we bring all our workings together to prepare the final accounts.

● EXAMINATION TIP

Show all your workings, no matter how trivial they seem to be. If you have made an error in compiling your final accounts or even in your workings, you will be rewarded for the parts that you have got correct. Every mark counts towards that final grade.

Stage 5: Preparation of the financial statements

Roger Guillaume
Income statement for the year ended 30 April 20*9

	£	£
Sales		101,344
Less Cost of sales		
Inventory	212	
Purchases	22,358	
	22,570	
Inventory	164	22,406
Gross profit		78,938
Less Expenses		
Rates	2,170	
Rent	2,818	
Wages	14,280	
Other expenses	20,075	
Depreciation Fixtures	72	
Vehicles	4,700	44,115
Profit for the year		34,823

Balance sheet at 30 April 20*9

	£	£	£
Non-current assets			
Fixtures at valuation			648
Vehicles at valuation			16,500
			17,148
Current assets			
Inventory		164	
Trade receivables		130	
Bank balance		3,469	
Cash		237	
Rates paid in advance		1,340	
		5,340	
Less Current liabilities			
Trade payables	328		
Rent accrued	120	448	4,892
			22,040
Capital			7,626
Add Profit for the year			34,823
			42,449
Less Drawings			20,409
			22,040

CALCULATION OF MISSING CASH

Examination questions sometimes indicate that cash has been stolen during the course of the year. Part of the question might require the candidate to calculate the amount of cash that is missing.

The procedure involves working out what the cash position would have been had the mishap not occurred, and comparing that position with the actual position.

Imagine that you receive £80 wages from a part-time job. On the way home you buy a DVD costing £14.99 and a magazine costing £2.30.

Later, you are in the shower when your brother asks you to lend him some money.

You call to him 'Help yourself from my wallet'.

How would you calculate the amount of cash he had taken?

Use the same technique in an accounting problem where cash has gone missing.

WORKED EXAMPLE

Adele owns a general store. At 1 January her cash in hand was £167. At the end of the year, on 31 December, cash in hand was £143. Her till rolls show her takings to be £53,788. During the year she banked £21,894 after taking £13,600 cash for private use and paying wages of £17,840.

Adele believes that some cash has been stolen in a burglary over the Christmas period.

Required

Calculate the amount of cash stolen.

Answer

Cash summary				
Cash in hand at 1 January	167	Cash banked		21,894
Takings	53,788	Drawings		13,600
		Wages		17,840
		Cash stolen (missing figure)		478
		Cash in hand at 31 December		143
	53,955			53,955

Note that the question asked for a calculation; it did not ask for an account. The answer has been given in account form but full marks could have been gained by other means.

There are a variety of ways of arriving at the correct answer; each would be acceptable. However, do show full workings if you choose another method of arriving at your answer.

The answer shows an account as this fits in with the workings used throughout the chapter.

CALCULATION OF MISSING INVENTORY

To calculate the value of inventory that has gone missing during a financial year, the cost of sales that uses *actual figures* is compared with the figures that ought to have applied.

WORKED EXAMPLE

Gary owns a hairdressing salon. Several boxes of expensive perms have been stolen. Gary is unsure of the value of the stolen perms. He provides the following information for the year ended 30 April 20*9:

inventory of perms at 1 May 20*8 £210; inventory of perms at 30 April 20*9 £70; purchases of perms during the year ended 30 April 20*9 £4,690; sales of perms during the year £7,080. (All perms carry a uniform mark-up of 50%.)

Answer

	Actual figures are		They should be	
	£	£	£	£
Sales		7,080		7,080
Less Cost of sales				
Inventory at 1 May 20*8	210		210	
Purchases	4,690		4,690	
	4,900		4,900	
Inventory at 30 April 20*9	70		180	4,720
Stolen perms *(missing figure)*	110	4,720		
Gross profit		2,360		2,360

Note: The closing inventory of £70 appears as a current asset on the balance sheet; the mark-up percentage was used to calculate the gross profit; the stolen perms, £110 must also appear as an expense in the income statement to complete the double entry.

Chapter summary

- Profit for the year can be calculated by comparing net assets at the start of a period (usually a year) with net assets at the end of the period.
- This is a very accurate way of determining profit but it has the major drawback that it does not show all the financial details of exactly how this profit was earned. These details are essential for stewardship and management purposes.
- If a set of financial statements is to be prepared then the five-step approach must be adopted:
  - prepare an opening statement of affairs
  - compile a bank summary
  - prepare a summary of cash transactions
  - construct adjustment accounts
  - prepare financial statements.

SELF-TEST QUESTIONS

- A statement of affairs is the same as a ——————.
- Total assets less total liabilities = ——————.
- Opening capital + profit for the year − drawings = ——————.
- Closing capital less opening capital = ——————.
- Profits retained in the business + drawings = ——————.
- Profits retained in the business —— drawings —— capital introduced = profit for the year.
- Opening balance in a vehicles account is £23,000; no purchases or sales of vehicles takes place over the year. The closing balance is £18,000. What does the difference in balances represent?
- Cash paid to credit suppliers during the year is credited to the trade payables adjustment account. True or false?
- Cash received from credit customers during the year is credited to the trade receivables adjustment account. True or false?
- Sole traders are required by law to keep a full set of double-entry books. True or false?

TEST QUESTIONS

QUESTION 9

Fatima Aakloo provides the following information for the year ended 30 April 20*9: Her net assets at 30 April 20*8 were £47,682; her net assets at 30 April 20*9 were £37,901. During the year ended 30 April 20*9 she withdrew goods to the value of £831 and cash amounting to £17,467 from the business for private use.

Required

Calculate the profit or loss for the year ended 30 April 20*9.

QUESTION 10

Fred Gray provides the following information for the year ended 31 March 20*9: his capital at 31 March 20*8 was £67,583; his capital at 31 March 20*9 was £37,901. During the year he withdrew £14,500 cash and £276 goods from the business for his own use.

Required

Calculate the profit or loss for the year ended 31 March 20*9.

QUESTION 11

Angus McToff provides the following information:

Assets and liabilities	at 31 August 20*9 £	at 1 September 20*8 £
Machinery at valuation	100,000	84,000
Vehicles at valuation	20,000	26,000
Inventory	1,472	1,278
Trade receivables	3,824	3,461
Trade payables	3,167	2,138
Bank balance	812	1,796
Cash in hand	472	232
Long-term loan	20,000	10,000

During the year ended 31 August 20*9 Angus withdrew £18,750 cash and goods to the value of £1,798 from the business for his own use.

In February 20*9 Angus paid a legacy of £21,000 into the business bank account.

Required

Calculate the profit or loss for the year ended 31 August 20*9.

QUESTION 12

Hoi Yin provides the following information:

Assets and liabilities	at 31 November 20*9 £	at 1 December 20*8 £
Premises at valuation	138,000	140,000
Machinery at valuation	36,000	48,000
Vehicles at valuation	42,000	28,000
Inventory	4,807	4,862

Assets and liabilities	at 31 November 20*9 £	at 1 December 20*8 £
Trade receivables	2,468	1,296
Trade payables	1,277	632
Bank balance	–	840
Bank overdraft	3,592	–
Cash in hand	210	148
Long-term loan	22,000	2,000

During the year ended 30 November 20*9 Hoi made drawings of £19,750. In August she paid £26,000 into the business from a premium bond win.

Required

Calculate the profit or loss for the year ended 30 November 20*9.

QUESTION 13

Jack Hay provides the following information for the year ended 30 June 20*9:

	at 31 June 20*9 £	at 1 July 20*8 £
Inventory	2,348	1,791
Trade receivables	512	840
Trade payables	3,790	3,461

During the year cash received from customers was £73,498; cash paid to suppliers was £38,910.

Required

Prepare an extract from the income statement for the year ended 30 June 20*9.

QUESTION 14

Selina Szeto provides the following information for the year ended 31 May 20*9:

	at 31 May 20*9 £	at 1 June 20*8 £
Inventory	12,347	14,887
Trade receivables	2,003	1,277
Trade payables	7,942	8,766

During the year cash received from customers was £146,781; cash paid to suppliers was £81,313.

Required

Prepare an extract from the income statement for the year ended 31 May 20*9.

QUESTION 15

Sandra May provides the following information for the year ended 31 December 20*9:

	at 1 January 20*8 £	at 31 December 20*9 £
Inventory	982	1,271
Trade receivables	146	287
Trade payables	1,999	1,871

During the year cash received from customers was £61,803; cash paid to suppliers was £28,718. Discounts allowed during the year were £310.

Required

Prepare an extract from the income statement for the year ended 31 December 20*9.

QUESTION 16

Jane Lopez provides the following information for the year ended 28 February 20*9:

	at 1 March 20*8 £	at 28 February 20*9 £
Inventory	477	528
Trade receivables	316	349
Trade payables	1,792	1,981

During the year cash received from customers was £48,777; cash paid to suppliers was £11,466. Discounts allowed during the year were £523; discounts received were £291.

Required

Prepare an extract from the income statement for the year ended 28 February 20*9.

QUESTION 17

Dai Johns did not keep a full set of accounting records for the year ended 31 December 20*9; however he is able to provide the following information:

Cash book summary

	£		£
Balance at 1 January 20*9	2,347	Payments to credit suppliers	23,457
Cash sales	64,534	General expenses	34,561
Receipts from credit customers	16,409	Drawings	17,900
		Purchase of equipment	4,500
		Balance at 31 December 20*9	2,872
	83,290		83,290

Additional information

	at 1 January 20*9 £	at 31 December 20*9 £
Premises at cost	65,000	65,000
Equipment at valuation	14,000	15,000
Inventory	2,519	2,331

	at 1 January 20*9 £	at 31 December 20*9 £
Trade receivables	1,339	1,570
Trade payables	2,910	2,341
General expenses accrued	145	276

Required

Prepare:

a   an income statement for the year ended 31 December 20*9
b   a balance sheet at 31 December 20*9.

QUESTION 18

Noel Neal did not keep a full set of accounting records for the year ended 30 September 20*9; however he is able to provide the following information:

Cash book summary

	£		£
Balance at 1 October 20*8	3,762	Payments to credit suppliers	27,884
Cash sales	63,711	Purchase of vehicle	23,560
Cash received from credit customers	12,674	Drawings	7,821
Rent received	3,000	Wages	13,759
Balance at 30 September 20*9	11,440	General expenses	21,563
	94,587		94,587

Additional information

	at 1 October 20*8 £	at 31 September 20*9 £
Land and buildings at valuation	64,000	60,000
Machinery at valuation	34,000	30,600
Vehicles at valuation	16,600	30,000
Inventory	2,892	3,007
Trade receivables	238	541
Trade payables	5,935	5,442
Wages accrued and unpaid	239	1,671
General expenses paid in advance	679	395

Required

Prepare:

a   an income statement for the year ended 30 September 20*9
b   a balance sheet at 30 September 20*9.

QUESTION 19

Andre Lefevre did not keep a full set of accounting records for the year ended 31 March 20*9 but he was able to provide the following information:

Cash book summary

	£		£
Cash sales	43,734	Balance at 1 April 20*8	452
Cash received from credit customers	46,880	Cash paid to credit suppliers	34,872
Commission receivable	2,000	Cash purchases	5,761
		Drawings	23,560
		Purchase of fixtures	4,800
		Rent	6,600
		Wages	24,797
Balance at 31 March 20*9	21,971	General expenses	13,743
	114,585		114,585

Additional information

	at 31 March 20*9 £	at 1 April 20*8 £
Premises at valuation	54,000	56,000
Fixtures at valuation	20,000	18,000
Vehicle at valuation	4,000	8,000
Inventory	1,744	1,638
Trade receivables	459	1,649
Trade payables	2,619	2,225
Rent paid in advance	2,200	600
General expenses owed	981	127
Commission receivable owing	1,000	–

Required

Prepare:

a an income statement for the year ended 31 March 20*9
b a balance sheet at 31 March 20*9.

QUESTION 20

Ravi Ollie did not keep proper accounting records for the year ended 28 February 20*9, but he is able to supply the following information:

Cash book summary

	£		£
Balance at 1 March 20*9	4,619	Drawings	34,600
Cash sales	25,890	Cash paid to credit suppliers	32,842
Cash received from credit customers	76,882	Cash purchases	16,931
Rents received	2,400	Wages	17,805
Capital introduced	5,000	General expenses	13,775
Balance at 28 February 20*9	1,162		
	115,953		115,953

Additional information

	at 28 February 20*9 £	at 1 March 20*8 £
Equipment at valuation	31,000	36,000
Vehicle at valuation	6,000	12,000
Inventory	9,106	8,467
Trade receivables	882	499
Trade payables	4,166	3,821
Rent received in advance	240	120
Wages owed	236	–
Wages paid in advance	–	341
General expenses owed	838	1,639

Required

Prepare:

a an income statement for the year ended 28 February 20*9
b a balance sheet at 28 February 20*9.

QUESTION 21

Joe Duff provides the following information:

	at 31 December 20*9 £	at 1 January 20*9 £
Inventory	18,501	17,993
Trade payables	15,491	16,381

During the year sales amounted to £240,000. All goods sold are subject to a mark-up of 33⅓%.

All goods are purchased on credit. Cash paid to suppliers during the year amounted to £189,373.

Just before the end of the financial year Joe's business was burgled and a significant amount of inventory was stolen. Joe is unsure of the exact amount of stolen inventory.

Required

Calculate the value of stolen inventory during the year ended 31 December 20*9.

QUESTION 22

Alice Band provides the following information.

	at 30 April 20*9 £	at 1 May 20*8 £
Inventory	1,249	10,411
Trade payables	16,427	18,791

During the year sales amounted to £361,920. All goods are sold at a margin of 20%.

All goods are purchased on credit. Cash paid to suppliers during the year amounted to £290,929.

During the final week of the financial year an amount of inventory was stolen. Alice is unsure of the exact amount.

Required

Calculate the value of the stolen inventory.

QUESTION 23

Akit Patel did not keep a full set of accounting records. However, he is able to provide the following information for the year ended 30 September 20*9:

Summary of bank account

	£		£
Balance at 1 October 20*8	1,764	Wages	23,761
Cash banked	102,250	Drawings	10,470
Receipts from credit customers	6,479	Purchases	1,328
		General expenses	37,328
		Purchases of equipment	2,600
		Payments to credit suppliers	34,107
		Balance at 30 September 20*9	899
	110,493		110,493

Akit's till rolls show his takings to be £120,698. Before banking any of the business takings, Akit paid the following:

	£
Wages	4,380
Rent	2,400

He also withdrew £8,460 for his own personal use.

Akit provides the following additional information:

	at 30 September 20*9 £	at 1 October 20*8 £
Equipment at valuation	11,000	9,700
Vehicle at valuation	1,000	3,000
Inventory	1,358	984
Trade receivables	211	126
Trade payables	1,086	1,477
Cash in hand	326	238

Akit knows that a dishonest casual worker stole some cash before leaving the business; he is uncertain of the precise amount. His insurance company has agreed to pay £3,000 compensation for the loss on 20 October 20*9.

Required

a   Calculate the amount of cash stolen.
b   Prepare an income statement for the year ended 30 September 20*9.
c   Prepare a balance sheet at 30 September 20*9.

QUESTION 24

Jane Seager did not keep proper books of account for the year ended 31 July 20*9. However, she provides the following information:

Summary of bank account

	£		£
Cash banked	118,739	Balance at 1 August 20*8	3,168
Received from credit customers	4,783	General expenses	12,792
Capital introduced	8,000	Motor expenses	8,461
		Insurance	2,170
		Purchase of vehicle	23,000
		Payments to credit suppliers	48,672
		Drawings	31,798
		Balance at 31 July 20*9	1,461
	131,522		131,522

Before banking her business takings which amounted to £133,432, Jane paid the following:

	£
Wages	9,461
Electricity	1,240

She also withdrew £3,560 for personal use.

Jane provides the following additional information:

	at 31 July 20*9 £	at 1 August 20*8 £
Premises at valuation	124,000	126,000
Equipment at valuation	15,300	17,000
Vehicles at valuation	19,000	2,400
Inventory	4,883	4,618
Trade receivables	637	422
Trade payables	3,066	3,419
Cash in hand	528	816
Electricity bill unpaid	–	171
Garage bill unpaid	355	–
General expenses paid in advance	–	217
General expenses owed	333	–
Insurance paid in advance	326	210

During the weekend before her financial year-end, Jane's business was burgled and cash was stolen. Jane is unsure of the exact amount.

Required

a   Calculate the amount of cash stolen.
b   Prepare an income statement for the year ended 31 July 20*9.
c   Prepare a balance sheet at 31 July 20*9.

CHAPTER
THREE

Partnership Accounts

Up to now we have concentrated much of our studies on the simplest form of business organisation, that is, sole traders.

Although being a sole trader does have many advantages, many people in business form partnerships.

> **Limited liability** means that the liability of shareholders, for the debts of a limited company of which they are members, is limited to the amount they agreed to subscribe. Sole traders and partners have **unlimited liability**: this means that they are fully responsible for any debts incurred by the business, even if this means using private assets to discharge business debts.

ADVANTAGES OF BEING A SOLE TRADER

- The sole trader has complete control over how the business is run, so success or failure is dependent on the trader.
- The business can be established with the minimum of legal formalities.
- The financial results of the business do not need to be divulged to other members of the general public.

DISADVANTAGES OF BEING A SOLE TRADER

- The sole trader has unlimited liability.
- May involve long hours of work.
- Illness or other reasons that cause absence may affect the running of the business.
- No one with whom to share problems or ideas.
- May be difficult to raise extra finance when it is needed.

Expansion of a business usually involves raising extra finance. Raising the necessary finance can be very difficult without involving other people. This generally means that a sole trader is faced with the choice of converting the business into either

- a partnership or
- a limited liability company.

We shall deal with limited companies later, in Chapter Six.

PARTNERSHIP ACCOUNTING

The Partnership Act of 1890 defines a partnership as 'the relationship which subsists between persons carrying on business with a view of profit'.

Forming a partnership overcomes some of the disadvantages associated with being in business as a sole trader.

ADVANTAGES OF BEING IN PARTNERSHIP

- Access to more capital.
- Partners can share the workload.
- Partners can pool ideas and share problems.

DISADVANTAGES OF BEING IN PARTNERSHIP

- Partners have less independence than sole traders. Decisions have to be agreed by all partners. So, a partner's ideas for development of the business may be frustrated by other partners.

> **Specification coverage:**
> AQA ACCN3;
> OCR: F012.

> **By the end of this chapter you should be able to:**
> - prepare partnership income statements
> - prepare partners' capital and current accounts and explain their uses.

- The number of partners is limited to 20 (as far as 'A' level examinations are concerned); there are exceptions to this limit (eg firms of solicitors, accountants etc).
- Partners have unlimited liability.

It is usual for a partnership to have a written partnership agreement (although it is possible that the agreement could be a verbal one); this will reduce the possibility of any disputes arising.

The agreement usually covers:

- the duties of the individual partners
- the amount of capital to be subscribed by each of the partners
- the ways in which profits are to be shared (see later)
- the financial arrangements if there are any changes to the structure of the partnership.

If there is no agreement, the Partnership Act of 1890 lays down the following rules which must apply:

- partners should contribute equal amounts of capital
- no partner should be entitled to interest on capital
- no partner is entitled to a salary
- no partner is to be charged interest on drawings
- residual profits or losses are to be shared equally
- any loan made to the partnership by a partner will carry interest at the rate of 5% per annum.

● EXAMINATION TIP

If no details of the way in which profits are to be shared are given in a question, you must assume that no partnership agreement exists and so the Partnership Act of 1890 applies to the question.

PARTNERSHIP INCOME STATEMENTS

The internal final accounts for all businesses are shown in the same way in most respects.

It is only after the calculation of profit for the year that a change in layout may take place. When you prepared the final accounts of a sole trader the profit (or loss) for the year was entered in the trader's capital account.

The profit (or loss) earned by a partnership has to be shared between the partners in accordance with any agreement (or according to the Partnership Act of 1890 if there is no agreement).

The profit sharing is shown in detail in the final section of the income statement.

Partners usually agree to share profits in ways that will reflect the:

- workload of each partner
- amount of capital invested in the business by each partner
- risk-taking element of being in business.

Residual profits (or losses) are the profits (or losses) that remain once all appropriations of profit for the year have been allocated to the appropriate partners.

Although partners, like all entrepreneurs, receive a share of profits, for convenience's sake the profit division is shown under the headings of:

- salaries
- interest on capital
- share of residual profits.

PARTNERSHIP SALARIES

WORKED EXAMPLE

Ash and Ben are in partnership, sharing residual profits in the ratio of 2:1 respectively. Their net profit for the year ended 31 July 20*9 was £36,450.

Required

An extract from the income statement for the year ended 31 July 20*9.

Answer

<table>
<tr><td colspan="3" align="center">Ash and Ben
Income statement extract for the year ended 31 July 20*9</td></tr>
<tr><td></td><td align="center">£</td><td align="center">£</td></tr>
<tr><td>Profit for the year</td><td></td><td>36,450</td></tr>
<tr><td>Share of profit</td><td></td><td></td></tr>
<tr><td> Ash</td><td>(24,300)</td><td></td></tr>
<tr><td> Ben</td><td><u>(12,150)</u></td><td><u>(36,450)</u></td></tr>
</table>

Note the heading – 'for the year ended'. Fairly straightforward!

If a partner is entitled to a partnership salary, this is taken from the profit for the year before the residual profit shares are calculated.

WORKED EXAMPLE

Charlie and Divya are in partnership, sharing residual profits in the ratio 3:2 respectively after crediting Divya with a partnership salary of £4,200.

The profit for the year ended 31 December 20*9 was £29,460.

Required

Prepare an extract from the income statement for the year ended 31 December 20*9.

Answer

Charlie and Divya		
Income statement extract for the year ended 31 December 20*9		
	£	£
Profit for the year		29,460
Less salary – Divya		(4,200)
		25,260
Share of profit		
Charlie	(15,156)	
Divya	(10,104)	(25,260)

Note:

■ Divya's salary is deducted before the sharing of residual profits.
■ Divya's share of profits is £14,304 (she does not earn a salary in the same way that employees earn a salary; she is a part owner of the business and as such she earns profits no matter how they are described).

INTEREST ON CAPITAL

WORKED EXAMPLE

Ed and Fred are in partnership. They maintain fixed capital accounts the balances of which are £30,000 and £20,000 respectively. Their partnership agreement provides that profits and losses are shared 2:1 after interest on capital is provided at 8% per annum.

The net profit for the year ended 31 March 20*9 was £32,269.

Required

Prepare an extract from the income statement for the year ended 31 March 20*9.

Answer

Ed and Fred		
Income statement extract for the year ended 31 March 20*9		
	£	£
Profit for the year		32,269
Less Interest on capital		
Ed	(2,400)	
Fred	(1,600)	(4,000)
		28,269
Share of profit		
Ed	(18,846)	
Fred	(9,423)	(28,269)

Note the use of the 'inset' to show clearly the individual appropriations and the total appropriation.

■ Ed's share of the profit is £21,246 (interest £2,400 and £18,846 share of residual profit).
■ Fred's share of the profit is £11,023.

WORKED EXAMPLE

Gervais and Hannah are in partnership. They maintain fixed capital accounts at £50,000 and £32,000 respectively. The net profit for the year ended 31 August 20*9 was £47,632.

The partnership agreement provides that:

- Hannah be credited with a partnership salary of £3,750 per annum
- interest at the rate of 7% per annum be credited for partners' capital account balances
- residual profits be shared in the ratio 4:1 respectively.

Required

Prepare an extract from the income statement for the year ended 31 August 20*9.

Answer

<table>
<tr><td colspan="3">**Gervais and Hannah**</td></tr>
<tr><td colspan="3">**Income statement extract for the year ended 31 August 20*9**</td></tr>
<tr><td></td><td>£</td><td>£</td></tr>
<tr><td>Profit for the year</td><td></td><td>47,632</td></tr>
<tr><td>*Less* Salary – Hannah</td><td></td><td>(3,750)</td></tr>
<tr><td></td><td></td><td>43,882</td></tr>
<tr><td>*Less* Interest on capital –</td><td></td><td></td></tr>
<tr><td>Gervais</td><td>(3,500)</td><td></td></tr>
<tr><td>Hannah</td><td>(2,240)</td><td>(5,740)</td></tr>
<tr><td></td><td></td><td>38,142</td></tr>
<tr><td>Share of profit –</td><td></td><td></td></tr>
<tr><td>Gervais</td><td>(30,514)</td><td></td></tr>
<tr><td>Hannah</td><td>(7,628)</td><td>(38,142)</td></tr>
</table>

Note that the residual profit shares have been rounded.

● EXAMINATION TIP

If figures do not divide exactly, quickly check that you have not overlooked an entry somewhere (do not spend too much time doing this. Remember: time = marks).

If nothing has been missed then 'round' your figures, unless the question asks you to work in pence.

QUESTION 1

Ian and Jenny are in partnership. The net profit for the year ended 31 January 20*9 was £26,900. Their partnership agreement provides that Ian be credited with a partnership salary of £5,000 and that residual profits or losses be shared in the ratio of 2:1 respectively.

Required

Prepare an extract from the income statement for the year ended 31 January 20*9.

QUESTION 2

Kelly and Larry are in partnership. The net profit for the year ended 30 November 20*9 was £48,270. Their partnership agreement provides that Larry be credited with a partnership salary of £2,500 and that residual profits or losses be shared in the ratio of 3:2 respectively.

Required

Prepare an extract from the income statement for the year ended 30 November 20*9.

QUESTION 3

Maria and Nelly are in partnership. They have fixed capital accounts of £40,000 and £60,000 respectively. Their partnership agreement provides that Maria be credited with a partnership salary of £4,800 and that partners be credited with 8% interest on capital. Any residual profits or losses are to be shared in the ratio 3:1 respectively.
The profit for the year ended 31 March 20*9 amounted to £74,868.

Required

Prepare an extract from the income statement for the year ended 31 March 20*9.

QUESTION 4

Ollie and Paul are in partnership. They have fixed capital accounts of £100,000 and £120,000 respectively. Their partnership agreement provides that Ollie be credited with a partnership salary of £8,000 and that partners be credited with interest on capital at 7% per annum. Any residual profits or losses are to be shared equally.
The profit for the year ended 31 December 20*9 was £123,671.

Required

Prepare an extract from the income statement for the year ended 31 December 20*9.

QUESTION 5

Queenie and Rusty are in partnership, sharing profits and losses equally after providing for interest on capital of 6% per annum. The partners maintain fixed capital accounts of £30,000 and £20,000 respectively. The partners have agreed that from 1 August 20*8 Rusty be credited with a salary of £5,000 per annum.
The profit for the year ended 28 February 20*9 was £63,842.

Required

Prepare an extract from the income statement for the year ended 28 February 20*9.

QUESTION 6

Steve and Tajinder are in partnership, sharing profits and losses in the ratio 3:2 respectively after providing for interest on capital of 9% per annum. The partners maintain fixed capital accounts of £40,000 and £60,000 respectively. The partners agreed that from 1 March 20*9 Steve be credited with a salary of £6,000 per annum.
The profit for the year ended 31 August 20*9 was £31,450.

Required

Prepare an extract from the income statement for the year ended 31 August 20*9.

QUESTION 7

Ursula and Vincent are in partnership. They maintain fixed capital accounts of £10,000 and £60,000 respectively. Their partnership agreement provides that Ursula be credited with a partnership salary of £6,000 and that partners be credited with interest on capital of 5% per annum. Any residual profits or losses are to be shared in the ratio 3:2 respectively.
The profit for the year ended 31 December 20*9 was £8,400.

Required

Prepare an extract from the income statement for the year ended 31 December 20*9.

QUESTION 8

Wanda and Yvonne are in partnership, sharing residual profits and losses in the ratio 3:1 respectively. They maintain fixed capital accounts of £60,000 and £70,000. Their partnership agreement provides that Yvonne be credited with a salary of £14,000 and that partners be credited with interest on capital of 7% per annum.
The profit for the year ended 30 April 20*9 was £22,780.

Required

Prepare an extract from the income statement for the year ended 30 April 20*9.

INTEREST ON DRAWINGS

Some partnership agreements provide that partners will be charged interest on any drawings made during the financial year. This is supposed to deter partners from drawing cash from the business in the early part of the financial year.

We say 'supposed' since, if a partner needs to draw cash from the business, an interest charge is hardly likely to deter him or her.

WORKED EXAMPLE

The partnership agreement of Arbuthnot and Brennan provides that interest be charged on drawings, at 5% per annum. The business year-end is 31 December.

During the year, the partners made drawings as follows:

	Arbuthnot £	Brennan £
31 March	3,000	2,000
30 June	5,000	6,500
30 September	4,300	5,600
31 December	7,900	4,000

Required

Calculate the amount of interest to be charged to each partner for the year.

Answer

Arbuthnot will be charged **£291.25** interest on drawings.

Workings   £3,000 × 5% × ¾ year = £112.50
£5,000 × 5% × ½ year = £125.00
£4,300 × 5% × ¼ year = £53.75

Brennan will be charged **£307.50** interest on drawings.

Workings   £2,000 × 5% × ¾ year = £75.00
£6,500 × 5% × ½ year = £162.50
£5,600 × 5% × ¼ year = £70.00

Note that no interest has been charged for drawings made on the last day of the year.

The entries in the partnership accounts are:

   Credit the income statement and

   Debit the partners' current accounts.

The debit entry in the partners' current accounts has the effect of increasing the amount withdrawn during the year. It is, in effect, an additional amount of drawings.

○ EXAMINATION TIP

The amount of interest on drawings will generally be given in the question, so you will not be required to calculate the amounts to be charged to each partner.

WORKED EXAMPLE

Greta and Hanif are in partnership. They supply the following information for the year ended 31 August 20*9.

The partnership agreement provides that:

- Greta be credited with a partnership salary of £5,600
- partners be credited with interest on capital of 8% per annum
- partners be charged interest on their drawings at 5% per annum
- residual profits be shared equally
- Greta's fixed capital account stands at £42,000 while Hanif's fixed capital account stands at £50,000.
- The profit for the year before appropriations was £56,934.
- During the year Greta made drawings of £32,900 and Hanif's drawings were £21,750.
- Interest on drawings was calculated at £348 for Greta and £180 for Hanif.

Required

Prepare an extract from the income statement for the year ended 31 August 20*9.

Answer

Greta and Hanif
Income statement extract for the year ended 31 August 20*9

	£	£
Profit for the year		56,934
Add Interest on drawings – Greta	348	
Hanif	180	528
		57,462
Less Salary – Greta		(5,600)
		51,862
Less Interest on capital – Greta	(3,360)	
Hanif	(4,000)	(7,360)
		44,502
Share of profit – Greta	(22,251)	
Hanif	(22,251)	(44,502)

QUESTION 9

Gareth and Darius are in partnership. The partnership agreement provides that partners are to be charged interest on drawings and that residual profits or losses are to be shared equally.
The following information is available for the year ended 31 January 20*9:

	£
Profit for the year	27,362
Interest on drawings for the year – Gareth	146
Darius	238

Required

Prepare an extract from the income statement for the year ended 31 January 20*9.

QUESTION 10

Ali and Brenda are in partnership. They share profits and losses equally. They have also agreed that interest be charged on any drawings made during the financial year.
They provide the following information for the year ended 31 December 20*9:

	£
Profit for the year	17,614
Interest on drawings for the year – Ali	542
Brenda	104

Required

Prepare an extract from the income statement for the year ended 31 December 20*9.

QUESTION 11

Tramp and Hobo are in partnership, sharing profits and losses in the ratio 3:2 respectively. They have also agreed that Hobo be credited with a partnership salary of £2,000 and that interest be charged on drawings made during the financial year.
They provide the following information for the year ended 30 June 20*9:

	£
Profit for the year	25,570
Interest on drawings for the year – Tramp	267
Hobo	303

Required

Prepare an extract from the income statement for the year ended 30 June 20*9.

QUESTION 12

Jacques and Gillian are in partnership. Their partnership agreement provides that profits and losses be shared in the ratio 4:1 respectively. It also provides that Jacques be credited with a partnership salary of £3,500 and that partners be charged interest on drawings made during the financial year.
The following information is available for the year ended 31 October 20*9:

	£
Profit for the year	11,810
Interest on drawings for the year – Jacques	234
Gillian	901

Required

Prepare an extract from the income statement for the year ended 31 October 20*9.

QUESTION 13

Mark, Noreen and Oswald are in partnership, sharing profits and losses 3:2:1 respectively. They have agreed that interest be charged on drawings made during the financial year.
The following information is available for the year ended 31 March 20*9:

	£
Loss for the year	818
Interest on drawings for the year – Mark	261
Noreen	38
Oswald	279

Required

Prepare an extract from the income statement for the year ended 31 March 20*9.

QUESTION 14

Wilkinson, Sword and Cutlass are in partnership, sharing profits and losses 2:2:1 respectively. Their partnership agreement provides that they be charged interest on drawings.
The following information is available for the year ended 28 February 20*9:

	£
Net loss for the year	834
Interest on drawings for the year – Wilkinson	240
Sword	732
Cutlass	182

Required

Prepare an extract from the income statement for the year ended 28 February 20*9.

PARTNERSHIP CAPITAL AND CURRENT ACCOUNTS

> Partners' **capital accounts** show deliberate injections of capital into the business; plus any adjustments of a capital nature, eg goodwill adjustments; plus any profits or losses arising on a revaluation of assets (generally on the admission or the retirement of a partner).

> Partners' **current accounts** record entries relating to each partner's share of the profits of the business in the current year. The current account would also be used to adjust for any errors made in the profit share in previous years.

The balance sheet of a partnership differs from that of a sole trader in that, since there is more than one owner, there must be more than one capital account (and possibly current account), showing the financial commitment of each partner to the business.

Indeed, the capital employed in the business is usually divided into partners' capital accounts and partners' current accounts.

Capital accounts may change each year if current accounts are not maintained and they would resemble the capital accounts that you have already prepared in your studies. It is more usual for partnerships to maintain fixed capital accounts. However, some examination questions state that only capital accounts are maintained.

WORKED EXAMPLE

An extract from the income statement for the year ended 30 June 20*9 of Tessa and Alexia is shown. They share profits and losses in the ratio 2:3 respectively.

	£	£
Profit for the year		34,745
Less salary – Tessa		(6,000)
		28,745
Interest on capital –		
Tessa	(2,400)	
Alexia	(3,000)	(5,400)
		23,345
Share of profit –		
Tessa	(9,338)	
Alexia	(14,007)	(23,345)

The capital account balances at 1 July 20*8 were £40,000 and £50,000 respectively.

Drawings for the year were £22,350 (Tessa) and £26,850 (Alexia).

Required

Prepare the capital accounts of Tessa and Alexia at 30 June 20*9.

Answer

	Tessa £	Alexia £		Tessa £	Alexia £
Drawings	22,350	26,850	Balance b/d	40,000	50,000
Balance c/d	35,388	40,157	Salary	6,000	
			Interest on capital	2,400	3,000
			Share of profit	9,338	14,007
				57,738	67,007
	57,738	67,007			
			Balances b/d	35,388	40,157

continued ➤

Notice that a columnar layout has been used. This saves time and space. Do try it. It may be difficult the first time or two that you use it but it does mean that you don't have to repeat the descriptions used in each account.

The capital accounts would generally be shown on the balance sheet of the partnership as follows:

Capital accounts at 30 June 20*9	Tessa	Alexia	
	£	£	£
Balance	40,000	50,000	
Add Salary	6,000		
Interest on capital	2,400	3,000	
Share of profit	9,338	14,007	
	57,738	67,007	
Less Drawings	22,350	26,850	
	35,388	40,157	75,545

Both the capital accounts and the layout used above give the same result.

● EXAMINATION TIP

If a question asks you to prepare capital accounts, you must produce the information in account form as shown. If you do not, then you will most probably forfeit some marks. If a question asks for a 'calculation' or does not ask for 'accounts' then the second approach is acceptable.

The use of the accounts will save space in an answer so in many ways it is preferable to draw up the ledger accounts and merely insert the totals of the ledger accounts in the balance sheet.

So, in the above example the balance sheet might be drawn up showing only:

Capital accounts	£	£
Tessa	35,388	
Alexia	40,157	75,545

It is more usual for a partnership to maintain fixed capital accounts and showing all appropriations in the partnership current accounts.

All entries relating to profits earned and profits withdrawn are entered in the current accounts.

WORKED EXAMPLE

Terry and June are in partnership. They provide the following information for the year ended 31 August 20*9.

	Terry	June
	£	£
Capital account balances at 1 September 20*8	30,000	45,000
Current account balances at 1 September 20*8	1,542 Cr	238 Cr
Drawings for the year were	20,653	16,234
Interest to be charged on drawings	541	452

An extract from the income statement shows.

	£
Salary – Terry	4,800
Interest on capital – Terry	2,100
June	3,150
Share of residual profits – Terry	18,000
June	9,000

Required

Prepare detailed capital accounts and current accounts for the partnership at 31 August 20*9.

Answer

Current accounts				Terry	June
	Terry £	June £		£	£
			Balances b/d	30,000	45,000

Current accounts					Terry	June
	Terry £	June £			Terry £	June £
Drawings	20,653	16,234		Balances b/d	1,542	238
Interest on drawings	541	452		Salary	4,800	
				Interest on capital	2,100	3,150
				Share of profits	18,000	9,000
Balance c/d	5,248			Balance c/d		4,298
	26,442	16,686			26,442	16,686
Balance b/d		4,298		Balance b/d	5,248	

The capital accounts have remained 'fixed' and the profits earned and profits withdrawn from the business (drawings) and interest on drawings are recorded in the current account.

It is, of course, possible that a partner may withdraw more profits from the business than he or she has earned. In such a case the partner's current account will show a debit balance. In this example June has earned £12,150 and withdrawn £16,686.

WORKED EXAMPLE

Vikram and Walter provide the following information for their partnership for the year ended 30 April 20*9:

	Vikram £	Walter £
Current account balances	164 Cr	298 Cr
Interest on capital for the year	500	700
Share of residual profits	25,300	12,650
Drawings for the year	20,000	15,000
Interest on drawings	270	460

continued ➤

Required

Prepare:

a an extract from the income statement for the year ended 30 April 20*9
b current accounts at 30 April 20*9.

Answer

a

Vikram and Walter
Income statement extract for the year ended 30 April 20*9

	£	£
Net profit		38,420 *missing figure*
Add Interest on drawings – Vikram	270	
Walter	460	730
		39,150
Less Interest on capital – Vikram	(500)	
Walter	(700)	(1,200)
		37,950
Share of profits – Vikram	(25,300)	
Walter	(12,650)	(37,950)

b

Current accounts

	Vikram	Walter		Vikram	Walter
Drawings	20,000	15,000	Balances b/d	164	298
Interest on drawings	270	460	Interest on capital	500	700
			Share of profits	25,300	12,650
Balance c/d	5,694		Balance c/d		1,812
	25,964	15,460		25,964	15,460
Balance b/d		1,812	Balance b/d	5,694	

Chapter summary

- A partnership exists when two or more people are engaged in business with the aim of making profits.
- A partnership should have a partnership agreement. If there is no agreement then the Partnership Act 1890 lays down the rules by which the partnership is governed.
- Financial statements contain a section of the income statement that shows how profits (and losses) are shared between the partners.
- Partnerships can maintain fixed or fluctuating capital accounts.
- Most partnerships maintain fixed capital accounts. In such cases all transactions involving appropriations of profits and drawings of profits are entered in current accounts.
- Entries in capital accounts involve capital transactions only.

SELF-TEST QUESTIONS

- What is limited liability?
- A sole trader has limited liability. True or false?

- Partners have unlimited liability. True or false?
- Explain two advantages of being in partnership.
- Give the date of the Partnership Act that governs the basic rules that apply if a partnership does not have a partnership agreement.
- List four rules that apply if a partnership does not have a partnership agreement.
- A partnership cannot have both interest on drawings and interest on capital shown in the income statement. True or false?
- Give an example of an entry in a partner's capital account.
- Give two examples of debit entries in a partner's current account.
- Give two examples of credit entries in a partner's current account.

TEST QUESTIONS

QUESTION 15

Rooney and Timms are in partnership. Their profit for the year ended 31 May 20*9 was £27,967.

The partnership agreement provides that Rooney be credited with a partnership salary of £3,000 per annum; that interest on capital be credited to the partners at the rate of 10% per annum on fixed capital accounts; and that residual profits and losses be shared equally. The agreement also provides that interest be charged on drawings.

The following information is available:

	Rooney £	Timms £
Capital account balance at 1 June 20*8	12,000	10,000
Interest on drawings	82	179

Required

Prepare an extract from the income statement for the year ended 31 May 20*9.

QUESTION 16

Ramtochan and Welsh are in partnership. Their profit for the year ended 30 November 20*9 was £46,784.

The partnership agreement provides that:

- Welsh be credited with a partnership salary of £8,000 per annum
- interest on capital be provided at 10% per annum
- residual profits be shared 3:2 respectively
- interest be charged on drawings.

Additional information

	Ramtochan £	Welsh £
Capital account balances at 1 December 20*8	23,000	27,000
Interest on drawings	480	106

Required

Prepare an extract from the income statement for the year ended 30 November 20*9.

QUESTION 17

Gray and Pink are in partnership. Their partnership agreement provides that:

- Gray be credited with a partnership salary of £4,000 per annum
- interest on capital be credited to partners at 8% per annum
- residual profits and losses be shared in the ratio 4:1 respectively
- interest be charged on drawings.

Additional information

The profit for the year ended 30 November 20*9 was £37,951.

	Gray £	Pink £
Capital account balance at 1 December 20*8	30,000	70,000
Interest on drawings	171	298

Required

Prepare an extract from the income statement for the year ended 30 November 20*9.

QUESTION 18

Hunter and Carrier are in partnership. Their net profit for the year ended 31 December 20*9 was £5,195.

Their partnership agreement provides that Hunter be credited with a partnership salary of £1,500; that partners be credited with interest on capital of 7% per annum on fixed capital account balances; that interest be charged on drawings; and that residual profits or losses be shared in the ratio 3:2 respectively.

The following information was also available:

	Hunter £	Carrier £
Capital account balance at 1 January 20*9	20,000	30,000
Drawings for the year	17,500	16,750
Interest on drawings	212	193

Required

Prepare an extract from the income statement for the year ended 31 December 20*9.

QUESTION 19

Naylor, Niall and Norbert are in partnership. Their profit for the year ended 31 May 20*9 was £71,560.

The partnership agreement provides that:

- Niall be credited with a partnership salary of £7,500
- partners be credited with interest on capital at the rate of 6% per annum
- residual profits and losses be shared 3:2:2 respectively
- interest be charged on drawings.

Additional information

	Naylor £	Niall £	Norbert £
Drawings for the year	27,200	17,450	19,350
Interest on drawings	460	320	411
Fixed capital account balances at 1 June 20*8	50,000	35,000	40,000
(On 1 December Niall introduced £10,000 additional capital into the business)			
Current account balances at 1 June 20*8	85 Cr	162 Dr	131 Cr

Required

Prepare:

a an extract from the income statement for the year ended 31 May 20*9
b current accounts at 31 May 20*9.

QUESTION 20

Budgert, Grouper and Singh are in partnership. Their profit for the year ended 30 November 20*9 was £94,082.

The partnership agreement provides that:

- Budgert and Singh be credited with partnership salaries of £1,000 and £2,500 respectively
- interest on fixed capital accounts be credited at 5% per annum
- residual profits be shared 3:2:1 respectively
- interest be charged on drawings.

Additional information

	Budgert £	Grouper £	Singh £
Drawings for the year	38,000	23,000	21,000
Interest on drawings	210	440	316
Fixed capital account balances at 1 December 20*8	30,000	20,000	70,000
Current account balances	2,716 Dr	81 Cr	236 Cr

Required

Prepare:

a an extract from the income statement for the year ended 30 November 20*9
b current accounts at 30 November 20*9.

CHAPTER FOUR

Partnership Accounts – Structural Changes

Obviously, during the lifetime of any business there could be changes in the ownership.

Colin, a sole trader, may decide that he no longer wishes to trade as a farmer and that he will sell his business to Jayne on 31 July.

The ownership of a partnership could change because:

■ partners may decide to terminate the partnership
■ partners may decide to admit another partner
■ they may decide to alter their profit-sharing ratios.

When there is any kind of change to the structure of a partnership, the treatment is the same: one business ceases to exist at the date of the change and immediately after the date of the change a new business comes into being.

Specification coverage:
AQA: ACCN3;
OCR: F012.

By the end of this chapter you should be able to:
■ account for changes in profit-sharing ratios
■ account for the retirement and admission of partners
■ account for the dissolution of a partnership
■ account for the revaluation of assets and goodwill.

EXAMPLE

1. When Art and Bart admitted Carl as a partner on 1 April 20*9 there were two businesses involved:

Up to 31 March 20*9	**From 1 April 20*9**
Owners are Art and Bart	Owners are Art, Bart and Carl

2. When Iain retired from the partnership of Iain, Janet and Keith on 30 September 20*9 there were two businesses involved:

Up to 30 September 20*9	**From 1 October 20*9**
Owners are Iain, Janet and Keith	Owners are Janet and Keith

3. Dierdre and Ethel were in partnership sharing profits and losses equally. When they changed their profit sharing ratio to 3:2 on 30 June 20*9 there were two businesses involved:

Up to 30 June 20*9	**From 1 July 20*9**
Owners are Dierdre and Ethel	Owners are Dierdre and Ethel
(profit share equal)	(profit share 3:2)
different profit share =	= different business

● EXAMINATION TIP

When there is a structural change to a partnership, treat the information relating to the business before the change separately from the information relating to the business after the change.

THE ADMISSION OF A NEW PARTNER

WORKED EXAMPLE

Adele and Gloria are in partnership, sharing profits and losses equally. Their financial year-end is 31 December. They admit Carolyn as a partner on 1 July 20*9. They all agree that Adele, Gloria and Carolyn will share profits 3:2:1 respectively.

The profit for the year ended 31 December 20*9 was £40,000. The profit accrued evenly throughout the year.

Required

Prepare extracts from the income statements for the year ended 31 December 20*9.

Answer

Remember that we are dealing with two businesses:

Up to 30 June 20*9	From 1 July 20*9
Owners were Adele and Gloria	Owners are Adele, Gloria and Carolyn

So:

Adele and Gloria
Income statement extract for the six months ended 30 June 20*9

	£	£
Net profit		20,000
Profit share – Adele	(10,000)	
Gloria	(10,000)	(20,000)

Adele, Gloria and Carolyn
Income statement extract for the six months ended 31 December 20*9

	£	£
Net profit		20,000
Profit share – Adele	(10,000)	
Gloria	(6,667)	
Carolyn	(3,333)	(20,000)

Note that the profit share has been rounded. Do not work using pence unless you are instructed to do so in the question.

The worked example shown was fairly straightforward (I hope you agree!).

However, common sense would tell us that Adele and Gloria would not simply have allowed Carolyn to become a partner without her contributing some capital to the business.

Common sense would also suggest that Adele and Gloria would have considered the value of their business assets before allowing Carolyn to become a part-owner of those business assets.

Imagine that your grandparents have been in business for 40 years. Their business assets are recorded on the business balance sheet as follows:

	£	
Premises (book value)	18,500	Remember that we value assets at cost,
Equipment (book value)	5,500	not at what they could be sold for –
Other net assets	2,000	the 'going concern' concept.
	26,000	
Capital – Grandpa	11,000	
Grandma	15,000	
	26,000	

continued ➤

WORKED EXAMPLE *continued*

Now imagine that your grandparents admit Willy Fox as a partner into their business.

They ask him to provide £20,000 capital. He agrees and enters the business.

What would the balance sheet look like now?

	£	
Premises (book value)	18,500	Simple!
Equipment (book value)	5,500	Your grandparents are simple if
Other net assets	22,000	they agree to what has taken place!
	46,000	Remember that they have been in
Capital – Grandpa	11,000	business for 40 years.
Grandma	15,000	How much must the premises be
Willy Fox	20,000	worth now? Surely they are worth
	46,000	more than the book value shown?

Can you see your likely future inheritance disappearing into Willy Fox's pocket?

I can!

In fact, what needs to happen when any kind of structural change takes place is that the business assets have to be revalued. The increase in value (or decrease in value) belongs to the **original** partners.

WORKED EXAMPLE

Mike and Jeanette have been in partnership for many years, sharing profits and losses equally. The financial year-end for the business is 31 December. They decide to admit Kiri into the partnership, with effect from 1 May 20*9. Kiri will pay £25,000 capital into the business bank account. The partnership balance sheet at 30 April 20*9 was:

Mike and Jeanette
Balance sheet at 30 April 20*9

	£	£
Non-current assets		
Premises at cost		28,000
Vehicles at cost		16,000
		44,000
Current assets		
Inventory	3,500	
Trade receivables	4,300	
Cash and cash equivalents	1,560	
	9,360	
Less **Current liabilities**		
Trade payables	3,360	6,000
		50,000
Capital accounts – Mike		25,000
Jeanette		25,000
		50,000

Over the years, property prices have risen. The premises were valued at £70,000 at the end of April 20*9.

Required

Prepare a balance sheet at 1 May 20*9, after the admission of Kiri.

WORKED EXAMPLE *continued*

Answer

Mike, Jeanette and Kiri
Balance sheet at 1 May 20*9

	£	£
Non-current assets		
Premises at valuation		70,000
Equipment at cost		16,000
		86,000
Current assets		
Inventory	3,500	
Trade receivables	4,300	
Cash and cash equivalents	26,560	
	34,360	
Less **Current liabilities**		
Trade creditors	(3,360)	31,000
		117,000
Capital accounts – Mike		46,000
Jeanette		46,000
Kiri		25,000
		117,000

The rise in the value of the premises (by £42,000) has taken place while Mike and Jeanette have been the only proprietors, so any profits (because of inflation) belong to them. The increase in the value of the premises did not occur when Kiri was a partner, so she should not benefit. As they are equal partners, the increase has been divided equally between Mike and Jeanette.

QUESTION 1

Pat and Danny have been in partnership for a number of years, sharing profits and losses in the ratio of 2:1 respectively. Their balance sheet at 31 December 20*8 showed:

	£	£
Non-current assets (book value)		110,000
Current assets	15,000	
Current liabilities	(10,000)	5,000
		115,000
Capital accounts – Pat	60,000	
Danny	55,000	115,000

Before the start of business on 1 January 20*9 Pat and Danny admitted Janice as a partner. She introduced £25,000 as her capital. They agree that the non-current assets are to be valued at £155,000.

Required

Prepare a balance sheet at 1 January 20*9, immediately after Janice was admitted as a partner.

QUESTION 2

Bert and Vanessa have been in partnership for several years. They share profits and losses equally. The business balance sheet at 31 January 20*9 showed:

	£	£
Non-current assets (book value)		21,000
Current assets	4,500	
Current liabilities	(2,350)	2,150
		23,150
Capital accounts – Bert		10,950
Vanessa		12,200
		23,150

On 1 February 20*9 it was agreed to admitted Ellie as a partner. She introduced £12,500 as her capital. It was further agreed that the non-current assets be valued at £50,000.

Required

Prepare a partnership balance sheet at 1 February 20*9, after Ellie was admitted as a partner.

It is more usual to find a balance sheet showing details of all assets and liabilities. When a structural change takes place in such instances we use an account to record any changes to the values of assets and liabilities shown on the balance sheet and hence to calculate the (inflationary) profit or loss resulting from the changes.

A temporary account is opened and it is only used to record adjustments to the account balances from the ledgers shown on the balance sheet.

This is how the temporary account works:

WORKED EXAMPLE

Sandie and Ian are in partnership, sharing profits and losses in the ratio 4:3 respectively. They admit Laura as a partner before the start of business on 1 August 20*9; she pays £35,000 to the partnership as her capital.

The partnership balance sheet at 31 July 20*9 was:

	£	£
Non-current assets		
Premises at cost		48,000
Equipment (book value)		12,000
Vehicle (book value)		15,000
		75,000
Current assets		
Inventory	2,400	
Trade receivables	1,750	
Cash and cash equivalents	2,200	
	6,350	
Current liabilities		
Trade payables	(2,790)	3,560
		78,560
Capital accounts – Sandie	40,000	
Ian	30,000	70,000
Current accounts – Sandie	3,410	
Ian	5,150	8,560
		78,560

It was agreed that the assets on 31 July 20*9 be revalued as follows:

	£
Premises	100,000
Equipment	4,500
Vehicle	6,000
Inventory	2,000
Trade receivables	1,650

Required

Prepare a balance sheet at 1 August 20*9, after the admission of Laura as a partner.

WORKED EXAMPLE *continued*

Answer
Workings

We open an account for each asset that is to be revalued:

Premises

Bal b/d	48,000	Bal c/d	100,000
Revaluation	52,000		
	100,000		100,000
Bal b/d	100,000		

Equipment

Bal b/d	12,000	Revaluation	7,500
		Bal c/d	4,500
	12,000		12,000
Bal b/d	4,500		

Vehicle

Bal b/d	15,000	Revaluation	9,000
		Bal c/d	6,000
	15,000		15,000
Bal b/d	6,000		

Inventory

Bal b/d	2,400	Revaluation	400
		Bal c/d	2,000
	2,400		2,400
Bal b/d	2,000		

Trade receivables

Bal b/d	1,750	Revaluation	100
		Bal c/d	1,650
	1,750		1,750
Bal b/d	1,650		

The revaluation account is used to adjust the asset accounts and to calculate any profit or loss on revaluation. The profit or loss is transferred to the existing partners' capital accounts **before** the new partner is admitted.

Revaluation account

Equipment	7,500	Premises	52,000
Vehicle	9,000		
Inventory	400		
Trade receivables	100		
Capital – Sandie	20,000		
Ian	15,000		
	52,000		52,000

continued ➤

Capital – Sandie

Bal c/d	60,000	Bal b/d		40,000
	60,000	Revaluation a/c		20,000
				60,000
		Bal b/d		60,000

Capital – Ian

		Bal b/d		30,000
Bal c/d	45,000	Revaluation a/c		15,000
	45,000			45,000
		Bal b/d		45,000

Sandie, Ian and Laura
Balance sheet at 1 August 20*9

	£	£
Non-current assets		
Premises at valuation		100,000
Equipment at valuation		4,500
Vehicle at valuation		6,000
		110,500
Current assets		
Inventory	2,000	
Trade receivables	1,650	
Cash and cash equivalents	37,200	
	40,850	
Current liabilities		
Trade payables	(2,790)	38,060
		148,560
Capital accounts – Sandie	60,000	
Ian	45,000	
Laura	35,000	140,000
Current accounts – Sandie	3,410	
Ian	5,150	8,560
		148,560

Note that the changes to the capital structure of the business are entered in the partners' capital accounts. The current accounts have not been used. The current accounts will change only when trading profits or losses are shared between partners or as partners make drawings.

Notice that the non-current assets are now labelled 'at valuation' since they do not now appear 'at cost'.

When you get used to making adjustments to the partnership balance sheet because of a structural change you may find that you do not have to open an account for each asset and liability. However, it will be safer for you always to open a revaluation account to 'collect' the changes that have been implemented.

QUESTION 3

Umair and Tim are in partnership, sharing profits and losses in the ratio 3:2 respectively. Their balance sheet at 30 September 20*9 was as follows:

	£	£	£
Non-current assets			
Premises at cost			30,000
Equipment at cost			8,900
Vehicles at cost			14,100
			53,000
Current assets			
Inventory		4,500	
Trade receivables		6,500	
		11,000	
Current liabilities			
Trade payables	(2,700)		
Bank overdraft	(1,300)	(4,000)	7,000
			60,000
Capital accounts – Umair			30,000
Tim			30,000
			60,000

Eddie was admitted as a partner at the start of business on 1 October 20*9; he paid £10,000 as his capital. It was agreed that the following assets be revalued at 30 September 20*9:

	£
Premises	100,000
Equipment	1,400
Vehicles	12,000
Inventory	4,200
Trade receivables	6,400

Required

Prepare a balance sheet at 1 October 20*9, after the admission of Eddie as a partner.

QUESTION 4

George and Bernard are in partnership, sharing profits and losses 2:1 respectively. Their balance sheet at 31 March 20*9 was as follows:

	£	£
Non-current assets		
Premises at cost		36,000
Equipment at cost		23,900
Vehicles at cost		34,700
		94,600
Current assets		
Inventory	9,870	
Trade receivables	4,670	
Cash and cash equivalents	850	
	15,390	
Current liabilities		
Trade creditors	9,990	5,400
		100,000
Capital accounts – George		50,000
Bernard		50,000
		100,000

Shore was admitted to the partnership at the start of business on 1 April 20*9; he paid £40,000 as his capital. It was agreed that the following assets be revalued as follows:

	£
Premises	110,000
Equipment	16,000
Vehicles	20,000
Inventory	9,800
Trade receivables	4,340

Required

Prepare a balance sheet at 1 April 20*9, after the admission of Shore.

> Goodwill is the cost of acquiring a business less the total value of the assets and liabilities that have been purchased.

Goodwill is an **intangible asset**. It cannot be seen; it has no physical presence, unlike tangible assets such as premises or machinery or vehicles.

When a successful business is sold, the vendor will generally price the business at a level greater than the total of the net assets being sold.

The balance sheet of a local fish and chip shop might be as follows:

	£	£
Non-current assets		
Equipment		34,000
Fixtures and fittings		8,400
		42,400
Current assets		
Inventory	840	
Bank balance	2,345	
Cash in hand	455	
	3,640	
Current liabilities		
Payables	(1,420)	2,220
		44,620
Capital – Terri		44,620

Terri decided to sell her business. She advertised it at £90,000.

Henry bought the business for £90,000.

Two points emerge:

- Terri sold her business at a profit of £48,180. (She would not sell the bank balance or cash in hand.) She sold non-current assets of £42,400 and inventory of £840 less current liabilities of £1,420 for £90,000.
- Henry purchased the business net assets for £90,000. He has purchased net tangible assets for £41,820 and an intangible asset (goodwill) for £48,180.

● EXAMINATION TIP

> Goodwill is not sold; it is only purchased. The seller makes a profit; the purchaser buys net assets including goodwill.

We have already said that when there is a structural change to a partnership the change involves **two** businesses:

- the business that existed before the change and
- the business that comes into existence **because** of the change.

When a new partner is admitted to a partnership we have already seen that the assets need to be revalued. We also need to place a value on the intangible asset goodwill.

THE VALUATION OF GOODWILL

We cannot give a definitive method that can be used in every type of business when goodwill has to be valued. If a business were being purchased then goodwill would represent how much would be paid in excess of the value of the net assets being purchased. We have already seen this when Terri sold her fish and chip shop to Henry in the example used above.

How can we value goodwill when there is a structural change to a partnership; when no one is actually purchasing the business?

The value placed on goodwill has to be acceptable to the partners in the 'old' partnership as well as being acceptable to the new partner(s).

The following are the most commonly used methods of determining the value of goodwill.

Goodwill is valued at a multiple of the:

- average profits generated over the past few years
- average weekly sales generated over the past financial year
- average of 'gross fees' earned over a number of years
- 'super profits' earned by the business.

1. **A multiple of average profits generated over the past few years.**

WORKED EXAMPLE

It has been agreed that goodwill be valued at two years' purchase of the average profits taken over the past five years.

Profits for the past five years were:

Year	£
1	12,450
2	12,560
3	14,890
4	8,450
5	11,650

Required
Calculate the value to be placed on goodwill.

Answer
Goodwill is valued at £24,000.

Workings Total profits for 5 years £60,000/5 = £12,000 × 2 = £24,000

2. **A multiple of average weekly sales generated over the past financial year.**

WORKED EXAMPLE

It has been agreed that goodwill be valued at four weeks' purchase of average weekly sales over the past financial year.

Last year's annual sales were:

£
322,400

Required
Calculate the value to be placed on goodwill.

Answer
Goodwill is valued at £24,800.

Workings £322,400/52 = £6,200 × 4 = £24,800

3. **A multiple of an average of the gross fees earned over a number of years.**

This method is used by many professional businesses, such as accountants, doctors, solicitors and vets etc, when a partner retires or a new partner enters the business.

WORKED EXAMPLE

It has been agreed that goodwill be valued at two years' purchase of the average gross fees over the past four years.

Gross fees are the equivalent of sales income for a professional business.

Fees for the past four years were:

Year	£
1	98,000
2	77,000
3	72,000
4	69,000

Required

Calculate the value to be placed on goodwill.

Answer

Goodwill is valued at £158,000.

Workings   £98,000 + £77,000 + £72,000 + £69,000 = £316,000
£316,000/4 = £79,000 × 2 = £158,000

4. **A multiple of 'super profits' earned by the business.**

Opportunity cost is the cost of making a decision in terms of the benefit lost by not using a resource in the next best alternative.

Super profits are calculated using the principle of opportunity cost.

WORKED EXAMPLE

Dirgen, an estate agent, has £50,000 capital invested in his business. If he were working for another estate agent he could earn £23,000 salary per annum. His business is presently earning profits of £38,000.

Required

Calculate the amount of super profits earned by Dirgen's business.

Answer

Super profits earned were £12,500.

Workings	£
If Dirgen worked for another estate agent he could earn:	23,000
If Dirgen invested his capital outside his business he could earn (say) 5%:	2,500
	25,500

By carrying on as a self-employed estate agent he earns £12,500 more than he would earn by using his capital and talents in the next best alternative.

Homer owns and runs a small plumbing business. Profits for the past few years have averaged £18,000. Homer has £14,000 capital invested in his business. He could earn £12,000 as a plumber working locally. He currently earns 5% per annum on a building society account. Goodwill is to be valued at three years' super profits.

Required

Calculate the value to be placed on goodwill.

Answer

Goodwill is valued at £15,900.

Workings

£18,000 − £12,700 = £5,300 × 3= £15,900
(£12,000 earnings + £700 interest on the £14,000 invested)

FACTORS THAT CONTRIBUTE TO THE ESTABLISHMENT OF GOODWILL

The factors that determine the value of goodwill placed on business are varied. They include:

- a good reputation because of the quality of a product
- a good reputation because of good service
- a good reputation for the helpfulness of staff
- a good after-sales service
- a prominent physical position of premises
- popularity among customers.

No doubt you can think of one or two other factors that might contribute to the establishment of goodwill.

So, why might you pay £30,000 more than the net asset value placed on a business in order to purchase it?

- You cannot purchase a good reputation – you could destroy that overnight.
- You cannot buy popularity.
- You certainly cannot purchase customers.

The reason you might pay the 'extra' £30,000 is because you can see the prospect of earning high profits in the future – you can envisage yourself earning lots of profits.

Goodwill is paid by the purchaser of a business in order to gain access to future profits that may be generated by that business.

Let us see how goodwill is dealt with when a partner is **admitted** into a business.

Issmail and Gary are in partnership as door-to-door salesmen selling cleaning materials. They share profits and losses in the ratio 3:1 respectively. Their balance sheet at 31 August 20*9 showed:

continued ➤

WORKED EXAMPLE *continued*

	£
Bank balance	370
Capital accounts – Issmail	200
Gary	170
	370

Issmail and Gary admit June to the partnership, with effect from 1 September 20*9. June contributes £2,000 as her capital. They agree that goodwill be valued at £8,000.

Required

A balance sheet at 1 September 20*9, immediately after June was admitted to the partnership.

Answer

Issmail, Gary and June
Balance sheet at 1 September 20*9 (after admission of June)

	£
Bank balance	2,370
Goodwill	8,000
	10,370
Capital accounts – Issmail	6,200
Gary	2,170
June	2,000
	10,370

Notice that a new asset has appeared on the balance sheet: an asset (intangible) that has built up over the years while Issmail and Gary have been in business as partners. The two original partners have been responsible for creating the goodwill through their personality, products, after-sales service etc, so it is only *their* capital accounts that have been credited in the profit-sharing ratios.

The book-keeping entries to record the introduction of goodwill into the partnership books would look like this:

Capital (Issmail)

Balance c/d	6,200	Balance b/d	200
	6,200	Goodwill	6,000
			6,200
		Balance b/d	6,200

Capital (Gary)

Balance c/d	2,170	Balance b/d	170
	2,170	Goodwill	2,000
			2,170
		Balance b/d	2,170

Goodwill		
Capital – I	6,000	
Capital – G	2,000	

QUESTION 5

Mo and Doug are in partnership, sharing profits and losses in the ratio 2:1 respectively. They provide the following information:

Balance sheet at 31 March 20*9	
	£
Bank balance	1,760
Capital accounts – Mo	1,010
Doug	750
	1,760

They admit Tracey to the partnership, with effect from 1 April 20*9. Tracey pays £3,000 into the business bank account as capital. It was agreed that goodwill be valued at £12,000.

Required

Prepare a balance sheet at 1 April 20*9, after the admission of Tracey as a partner.

QUESTION 6

Meena and Talha are in partnership, sharing profits and losses in the ratio of 3:2 respectively. They provide the following information:

Balance sheet at 31 October 20*9	
	£
Bank balance	7,500
Capital accounts – Meena	5,000
Talha	2,500
	7,500

Divya is admitted to the partnership, with effect from 1 November 20*9. She pays £1,000 into the business bank account as her capital. It was agreed that goodwill be valued at £10,000.

Required

Prepare a balance sheet at 1 November 20*9, after the admission of Divya as a partner.

Goodwill only appears in a balance sheet when it is purchased. If you see the asset on any balance sheet you can say with some certainty that:

- either the ownership has changed recently
- or the business has recently purchased another business.

This applies no matter what type of business balance sheet you are examining.

Inherent goodwill is the goodwill that has been generated internally, it has not been purchased, it is the goodwill that is enjoyed by a business while it is still ongoing.

Inherent goodwill is not entered in the books of account so it is never shown on a balance sheet.

Well-established businesses such as Marks and Spencer plc or McDonald's enjoy much inherent goodwill but this will not be shown on their balance sheets. Both these businesses are going concerns.

The going concern concept tells us that assets should be shown at cost price, not at what they would fetch if sold. Neither of the businesses is due to be sold in the next few days so as a going concern they would not show inherent goodwill.

Goodwill can appear in the books of any business when it is purchased.

Goodwill is generally written off immediately after purchase in examination questions involving partnerships.

[But see Chapter Five on IAS 38 *Intangible assets*.]

WORKED EXAMPLE

Arthur and Bruce are in partnership, sharing profits and losses equally. They provide the following information:

Balance sheet at 31 July 20*9

	£
Bank balance	6,500
Capital accounts – Arthur	3,500
Bruce	3,000
	6,500

They admit Ches as a partner, with effect from 1 August 20*9. Ches pays £5,000 into the partnership bank account as his capital. They agree that goodwill be valued at £18,000 and that the account will not appear in the balance sheet. They further agree to share profits 3:2:1 respectively.

Required

Prepare a balance sheet at 1 August 20*9, after the admission of Ches as a partner.

Answer

Arthur, Bruce and Ches
Balance sheet at 1 August 20*9 (after the admission of Ches)

	£
Bank balance	11,500
Capital accounts – Arthur	3,500
Bruce	6,000
Ches	2,000
	11,500

The book-keeping entries showing the above transactions are:

Bank

Balance b/d	6,500		
Capital – Ches (3)	5,000		

Capital (Arthur)

Goodwill (4)	9,000	Balance b/d	3,500
Balance c/d	3,500	Goodwill (1)	9,000
	12,500		12,500
		Balance b/d	3,500

Capital (Bruce)

Goodwill (5)	6,000	Balance b/d	3,000
Balance c/d	6,000	Goodwill (2)	9,000
	12,000		12,000
		Balance b/d	6,000

Capital (Ches)

Goodwill (6)	3,000	Bank (3)	5,000
Balance c/d	2,000		
	5,000		5,000
		Balance b/d	2,000

Goodwill account

Capital – Arthur (1)	9,000	Capital – Arthur (4)	9,000
Bruce (2)	9,000	Bruce (5)	6,000
		Ches (6)	3,000
	18,000		18,000

Numbers in brackets have been placed next to each entry so that you can trace each entry individually to each account.

Notice that the goodwill account has disappeared and is not shown in the final balance sheet.

QUESTION 7

Victor and Ffiona are in partnership, sharing profits and losses in the ratio 3:1 respectively. They provide the following information:

Balance sheet at 30 September 20*9

	£
Bank balance	1,500
Capital accounts – Victor	800
Ffiona	700
	1,500

They agree to admit Eric as a partner, with effect from 1 October 20*9. The new profit-sharing ratio would be 2:2:1 respectively. Eric will provide £7,500 as his capital. The partners agreed that profits in future would be shared equally. It was further agreed that goodwill be valued at £10,000 and that it would not appear on the balance sheet.

Required

Prepare a balance sheet at 1 October 20*9, after the admission of Eric to the partnership.

QUESTION 8

Clarissa and Gareth are in partnership, sharing profits and losses equally. They provide the following information:

Balance sheet at 28 February 20*9

	£
Bank balance	6,000
Capital accounts – Clarissa	4,000
Gareth	2,000
	6,000

They admit Hugo to the partnership, with effect from 1 March 20*9. The new partnership agreement provides that profits and losses will be shared equally. Goodwill is valued at £7,500 and will not appear in the balance sheet.

Required

Prepare a balance sheet at 1 March 20*9, after Hugo was admitted to the partnership.

Clearly, it is very unusual for a business to have a bank balance as its only asset. The above examples were used to highlight the way goodwill is treated when it does not remain in the books of account.

Let us put together a more realistic scenario – a situation where the assets are revalued and a value is placed on goodwill.

WORKED EXAMPLE

Len, Don and Ben are in partnership, sharing profits and losses in the ratio 3:2:1 respectively. They provide the following information:

Balance sheet at 31 May 20*9		
	£	£
Non-current assets at cost		26,000
Current assets	9,000	
Current liabilities	(2,000)	7,000
		33,000
Capital accounts – Len		10,000
Don		15,000
Ben		8,000
		33,000

They agree that Cat be admitted as a partner, with effect from 1 June 20*9. Profits in future will be shared equally. They further agree that non-current assets be revalued at £28,000 and that goodwill be valued at £10,000. Goodwill should not remain in the business books of account.

Cat is to pay £5,000 into the business bank account as capital.

Required

Prepare:
a   a revaluation account
b   a goodwill account
c   capital accounts for each partner
d   a balance sheet at 1 June 20*9, after the admission of Cat as a partner.

Answer

Revaluation account				
Capital – Len	6,000	Non-current assets	2,000
Don	4,000	Goodwill	10,000
Ben	2,000		
	12,000		12,000

Goodwill account

Revaluation a/c	10,000	Capital – Len		2,500
		Don		2,500
		Ben		2,500
		Cat		2,500
	10,000			10,000

Capital accounts

Note: All figures are in £000

	Len	Don	Ben	Cat		Len	Don	Ben	Cat
Goodwill	2.5	2.5	2.5	2.5	Balances b/d	10	15	8	
Balances c/d	13.5	16.5	7.5	2.5	Revaluation a/c	6	4	2	
					Bank				5
	16	19	10	5		16	19	10	5
					Balances b/d	13.5	16.5	7.5	2.5

Len, Don, Ben and Cat
Balance sheet at 1 June 20*9 (after the admission of Cat)

	£	£
Non-current assets at valuation		28,000
Current assets	14,000	
Current liabilities	(2,000)	12,000
		40,000
Capital accounts – Len		13,500
Don		16,500
Ben		7,500
Cat		2,500
		40,000

Note the use of columnar capital accounts; this technique saves a little time. Four partners have been involved in the partnership, to show that the techniques do not change when a question has more than three partners. Examination questions usually have two or three partners.

Note the heading too. All accounting statements need a heading which includes the name of the business.

● EXAMINATION TIP

Write figures out in full. Many examination candidates make errors when they forget that they are using thousands and put a figure in their answers as, say, £13.5 when it should say £13,500. Careless mistakes cost valuable marks – do not throw marks away.

QUESTION 9

Shubratha and Ciaran are in partnership, sharing profits and losses in the ratio 4:1. Their balance sheet is shown.

Balance sheet at 31 December 20*8

	£	£
Non-current at cost		34,000
Current assets	11,000	
Current liabilities	(10,000)	1,000
		35,000
Capital accounts – Shubratha		20,000
Ciaran		15,000
		35,000

Jim was admitted to the partnership on 1 January 20*9. The following terms have been agreed:

	£
Non-current assets to be revalued at	50,000
Goodwill to be valued at	24,000
Jim introduces capital of	15,000

It was further agreed that goodwill should not remain in the books of account, and that in future profits and losses would be shared equally.

Required

Prepare:

a a revaluation account
b a goodwill account
c partners' capital accounts (in columnar form)
d a balance sheet at 1 January 20*9.

QUESTION 10

Therese and Jean-Luc are in partnership; they share profits and losses equally.
Their balance sheet shows:

Balance sheet at 31 January 20*9

	£	£
Non-current assets at cost		46,000
Current assets	9,450	
Current liabilities	(5,450)	4,000
		50,000
Capital accounts – Therese		35,000
Jean-Luc		15,000
		50,000

They admitted Frebus to the partnership, with effect from 1 February 20*9, under the following terms:

	£
Frebus introduced capital of	25,000
Non-current assets were revalued at	60,000
Goodwill was valued at	26,000

Goodwill was not to remain in the business books of account.
Profits and losses were to be shared Therese ¼; Jean-Luc ½; Frebus ¼.

Required

Prepare:

a a revaluation account
b a goodwill account
c partners' capital accounts
d a balance sheet at 1 February 20*9.

If we consider a more detailed balance sheet, the principles for dealing with the introduction of another partner are just the same as those already used.

Do you remember that we collect all the detailed changes to assets and liabilities in the revaluation account?

WORKED EXAMPLE

Gwen and David are in partnership, sharing profits and losses in the ratio 3:2 respectively. The following information is provided:

Gwen and David
Balance sheet at 30 June 20*9

	£	£
Non-current assets		
Premises at cost		45,000
Equipment at cost		23,000
Vehicles at cost		17,000
		85,000
Current assets		
Inventory	11,000	
Trade receivables	4,500	
Cash and cash equivalents	1,500	
	17,000	
Current liabilities		
Trade payables	(2,000)	15,000
		100,000
Capital accounts – Gwen		60,000
David		40,000
		100,000

Anne was admitted to the partnership on 1 July 20*9. It was agreed that she paid £30,000 into the business bank account as her capital and share of the goodwill.

It was agreed that the assets of the business be valued at:

	£
Premises	80,000
Equipment	15,000
Vehicles	8,000
Inventory	10,800
Trade receivables	4,400
Goodwill	40,000

It was further agreed that in future profits and losses be shared equally and that goodwill should not remain in the books of account.

Required

Prepare:
a   a revaluation account
b   a goodwill account
c   partners' capital accounts
d   a balance sheet at 1 July 20*9, after the admission of Anne as a partner.

continued ➤

WORKED EXAMPLE *continued*

Answer

Revaluation account

Equipment	8,000	Premises	35,000
Vehicles	9,000	Goodwill	40,000
Inventory	200		
Trade receivables	100		
Capital – Gwen	34,620		
David	23,080		
	75,000		75,000

Goodwill account

Revaluation account	40,000	Capital – Gwen	13,334
		David	13,333
		Anne	13,333
	40,000		40,000

Capital accounts

	Gwen	David	Anne		Gwen	David	Anne
Goodwill	13,334	13,333	13,333	Balance b/d	60,000	40,000	
				Revaluation a/c	34,620	23,080	
Balances c/d	81,286	49,747	16,667	Bank			30,000
	94,620	63,080	30,000		94,620	63,080	30,000
				Balances b/d	81,286	49,747	16,667

Gwen, David and Anne
Balance sheet at 1 July 20*9 (after the admission of Anne)

	£	£
Non-current assets		
Premises at valuation		80,000
Equipment at valuation		15,000
Vehicles at valuation		8,000
		103,000
Current assets		
Inventory	10,800	
Trade receivables	4,400	
Cash and cash equivalents	31,500	
	46,700	
Current liabilities		
Trade payables	(2,000)	44,700
		147,700
Capital accounts – Gwen		81,286
David		49,747
Anne		16,667
		147,700

QUESTION 11

Chuck and Todd are in partnership, sharing profits and losses in the ratio 2:1 respectively. They provide the following information:

Balance sheet at 31 March 20*9

	£	£	£
Non-current assets			
Land and buildings at cost			65,000
Equipment at cost			34,000
Vehicles			56,000
			155,000
Current assets			
Inventory		4,800	
Trade receivables		6,200	
		11,000	
Current liabilities			
Trade payables	(4,570)		
Bank overdraft	(2,430)	(7,000)	4,000
			159,000
Non-current liability			
Loan – Mellerby Building Society			(29,000)
			130,000
Capital accounts – Chuck			80,000
Todd			50,000
			130,000

On 1 April 20*9 Buzz was admitted to the partnership. The following terms were agreed.
Buzz would pay £25,000 as his capital and share of goodwill. Profits and losses in future would
be shared Chuck ½; Todd ¼; and Buzz ¼.
The following asset values were agreed:

	£
Land and buildings	140,000
Equipment	10,000
Vehicles	26,000
Inventory	4,100
Trade receivables	6,000
Goodwill	60,000

It was also agreed that a goodwill account would not be maintained in the books of account.

Required

Prepare:

a   a revaluation account
b   a goodwill account
c   partners' capital accounts
d   a balance sheet at 1 April 20*9 (after the admission of Buzz as a partner).

QUESTION 12

Paddy and Mick are in partnership, sharing profits and losses in the ratio 4:1 respectively. They
provide the following information:

Balance sheet at 30 November 20*9

	£	£	£
Non-current assets			
Equipment at cost			26,500
Vehicles at cost			23,500
			50,000
Current assets			
Inventory		4,000	
Trade receivables		3,000	
		7,000	
Current liabilities			
Trade payables	(2,600)		
Bank overdraft	(2,400)	(5,000)	2,000
			52,000
Non-current liability			
Mortgage			(25,000)
			27,000

Capital accounts – Paddy	£	£	£
			12,000
Mick			15,000
			27,000

On 1 December 20*9 Declan was admitted to the partnership, under the following terms. Declan would contribute £20,000 as his capital and share of goodwill. The new profit-sharing ratio would be Paddy ½; Mick ⅓ and Declan ⅙.
The following asset values were agreed:

	£
Equipment	8,000
Vehicles	12,000
Inventory	3,100
Trade receivables	2,900
Goodwill	12,500

It was agreed that a goodwill account would not be maintained in the books of account.

Required

Prepare:

a a revaluation account
b a goodwill account
c partners' capital accounts
d a balance sheet at 1 December 20*9, after Declan was admitted to the partnership.

THE RETIREMENT OF A PARTNER

We have dealt with the admission of a new partner in some detail. The same principles apply when a partner leaves a partnership. The business assets (and liabilities) need to be examined in order to determine whether they reflect the true worth of the business.

Imagine that you have been a partner in a business for many, many years and the following is the summarised balance sheet:

	£	
Non-current assets (NBV)	12,000	These fixed assets include your premises that were purchased many years ago. Property prices in general have risen over your years of ownership and these premises could now be sold for, say, £80,000! Would you settle for a payout of £10,000 – your worth (capital) shown on the balance sheet? I think not!
Net current assets	8,000	
	20,000	
Capital – You	10,000	
Your partner	10,000	
	20,000	

You would have the business assets revalued so that you could retire (or perhaps start a new business) and receive the true value of your worth represented by the net assets of the business.

As Del Boy would say: 'You know it makes sense!'

WORKED EXAMPLE

Gertie, Bertie and Jon are in partnership, sharing profits and losses in the ratio 3:2:1 respectively. They supply the following information:

Balance sheet at 30 September 20*9

	£	£
Non-current assets (book value)		45,000
Current assets		
Inventory	4,300	
Trade receivables	3,700	
Cash and cash equivalents	4,000	
	12,000	
Current liabilities – trade payables	(8,000)	4,000
		49,000
Capital accounts – Gertie		20,000
Bertie		15,000
Jon		14,000
		49,000

Jon has decided to retire with effect from close of business on 30 September 20*9.

The partners have agreed that:

- non-current assets be revalued at £100,000
- inventory be valued at £4,000
- receivables be valued at £3,000
- goodwill be valued at £12,000 and goodwill should not appear in the business books of account
- any amount due to Jon would be paid from the business bank account (assume that overdraft facilities have been agreed with the business bank)
- in the future, Gertie and Bertie will share profits and losses equally.

Required

Prepare:

a a revaluation account
b a goodwill account
c partners' capital accounts
d a balance sheet at 30 September 20*9, after the retirement of Jon.

Answer

Revaluation account

Inventory	300	Non-current assets	55,000
Receivables	700	Goodwill	12,000
Capital – Gertie	33,000		
Bertie	22,000		
Jon	11,000		
	67,000		67,000

Goodwill account

Revaluation a/c	12,000	Capital – Gertie	6,000
		Bertie	6,000
	12,000		12,000

continued ➤

Capital accounts

	Gertie	Bertie	Jon		Gertie	Bertie	Jon
Bank			25,000	Bals b/d	20,000	15,000	14,000
Goodwill	6,000	6,000		Revaluation	33,000	22,000	11,000
Bals c/d	47,000	31,000					
	53,000	37,000	25,000		53,000	37,000	25,000
				Bals b/d	47,000	31,000	

Gertie and Bertie
Balance sheet at 30 September 20*9 (after the retirement of Jon)

	£	£	£
Non-current assets at valuation			100,000
Current assets			
Inventory		4,000	
Trade receivables		3,000	
		7,000	
Current liabilities			
Trade payables	(8,000)		
Bank overdraft	(21,000)	(29,000)	(22,000)
			78,000
Capital accounts – Gertie			47,000
Bertie			31,000
			78,000

Note that the question is dealt with in two parts because it involves two businesses:

Up to midnight on 30 September 20*9	From a microsecond after midnight (on 1 October 20*9)
Owners were Gertie, Bertie, Jon	Owners are Gertie and Bertie

We credited the capital accounts with the increase in the value of the net assets in order that Jon can receive his just dues before his retirement. After all, he has presided over the increase in the value of the assets as well as contributing to the value of the goodwill of the business.

We debited the two capital accounts (there are only two partners – Gertie and Bertie – in this new business) with the writing-off of the asset of goodwill. Notice that when we wrote off the goodwill there were only two partners in the 'new' business – Jon is now no longer involved in the running of the business.

HOW CAN A RETIRING PARTNER BE PAID OUT WHEN HE OR SHE LEAVES THE BUSINESS?

This can pose problems to a partnership. A retiring partner could have a considerable amount standing to the credit of his or her capital (and current) account. If a large sum were to be paid out, the withdrawal could deprive the business of a great deal of liquid resources.

How can the problem be resolved?

- The retiring partner's capital account balance could be transferred to a loan account and an amount could be paid each year to the partner who had retired
- A new partner could join the business and the payment made by the new partner could be used to pay off the 'old' partner.

- The cash to pay off the 'old' partner could be borrowed from a bank or other financial institution.
- Remaining partners could inject sufficient further capital into the business to allow the payment to be made.
- An investment could be made which, on maturity, would pay for the retirement.

QUESTION 13

Gordon, Frances and Jacqui are in partnership, sharing profits and losses in the ratio 2:2:1. They provide the following information:

Balance sheet at 31 March 20*9

	£	£
Non-current assets		34,000
Current assets	12,000	
Current liabilities	(9,000)	3,000
		37,000
Capital accounts – Gordon		20,000
Frances		10,000
Jacqui		7,000
		37,000

Frances decided to retire at the close of business on 31 March 20*9.
The partners have agreed that:

- Non-current assets be valued at £84,000
- goodwill be valued at £20,000
- any balance owed to Frances be temporarily transferred to a loan account
- a goodwill account should not remain in the books of account
- from 1 April 20*9 profits and losses be shared equally.

Required

Prepare:

a a revaluation account
b a goodwill account
c partners' capital accounts
d a balance sheet at 31 March 20*9 (after Frances's retirement).

QUESTION 14

Daisy, Dot and Dora are in partnership, sharing profits and losses in the ratio 3:3:1 respectively. The following information is available:

Balance sheet at 31 December 20*9

	£	£
Non-current assets		125,000
Current assets	65,000	
Current liabilities	(50,000)	15,000
		140,000
Capital accounts – Daisy		60,000
Dot		55,000
Dora		25,000
		140,000

Daisy retired at the close of business on 31 December 20*9. It was agreed that the non-current assets be valued at £200,000 and that goodwill was valued at £60,000.
Dot and Dora are to continue in business. They will share profits in the ratio of 3:2 respectively. They agree that a goodwill account would not be maintained in the business books of account. An balance due to Daisy should be transferred temporarily to a loan account.

Required

Prepare:

a a revaluation account
b a goodwill account
c partners' capital accounts
d a balance sheet at 31 December 20*9, after Daisy's retirement.

QUESTION 15

Ruairi, Gareth and Jock were in partnership, sharing profits and losses in the ratio 3:2:1 respectively. The following information is available:

Balance sheet at 31 August 20*9

	£	£	£
Non-current assets			
Premises			45,000
Equipment			23,000
Vehicles			34,000
			102,000
Current assets			
Inventory		11,250	
Trade receivables		5,800	
Cash and cash equivalents		1,480	
		18,530	
Current liabilities			
Trade payables		(6,530)	12,000
			114,000
Capital accounts			
Ruairi			60,000
Gareth			40,000
Jock			14,000
			114,000

Gareth retired from the partnership with effect from the close of business on 31 August 20*9. It was agreed that the following valuations would apply on that date:

	£
Premises	110,000
Equipment	5,000
Vehicles	18,000
Inventory	10,250

It was further agreed that goodwill be valued at £36,000.

Ruairi and Jock carried on in business, sharing profits and losses equally. They agreed that goodwill would not be maintained in the business books of account and that any amount due to Gareth be transferred to a loan account.

Required

Prepare:

a a revaluation account
b a goodwill account
c partners' capital accounts
d a balance sheet at 31 August 20*9, after Gareth's retirement.

QUESTION 16

George, Mildred and Michelle were in partnership, sharing profits and losses in the ratio 4:4:1 respectively. The following information is available:

Balance sheet at 31 December 20*9

	£	£	£
Non-current assets			
Land and buildings			68,000
Equipment			54,000
Vehicles			48,000
			170,000
Current assets			
Inventory		64,300	
Trade receivables		17,800	
		82,100	
Current liabilities			
Trade payables	(14,700)		
Bank overdraft	(7,400)	(22,100)	60,000
			230,000

Capital accounts	£
George	90,000
Mildred	90,000
Michelle	50,000
	230,000

George retired from the partnership with effect from the close of business on 31 December 20*9. It was agreed that certain assets be revalued:

	£
Land and buildings	208,000
Equipment	44,000
Vehicles	39,000
Inventory	63,300

It was further agreed that goodwill be valued at £60,000.

Mildred and Michelle carried on in business, sharing profits in the ratio 3:2 respectively. They agreed that a goodwill account would not be maintained in the business books of account and that any amount due to George on his retirement be transferred to a loan account.

Required

Prepare:

a a revaluation account
b a goodwill account
c partners' capital accounts
d a balance sheet at 31 December 20*9, after George's retirement.

A CHANGE TO THE PROFIT-SHARING RATIOS

Any change to the profit-sharing ratios must be treated in much the same way as other structural changes.

View the change as dealing with two distinct businesses.

The 'first' business must be revalued in order that the 'old' owners can be credited with any increase in the value of their business.

If goodwill is not to be maintained in the 'second' business's books of account it must be deleted and the 'new' partners debited in their profit-sharing ratios.

WORKED EXAMPLE

Jean and Sean are in partnership, sharing profits and losses in the ratio of 3:1 respectively. From 1 January 20*9 they will share profits and losses equally.

Their summarised balance sheet at 31 December 20*8 showed:

	£	£
Non-current assets		48,000
Current assets	12,000	
Less **Current liabilities**	(8,000)	4,000
		52,000
Capital accounts – Jean		30,000
Sean		22,000
		52,000

continued ➤

The partners agreed that non-current assets be revalued at £70,000 and that goodwill be valued at £28,000. They further agreed that a goodwill account would not be maintained in the business books of account.

Required

Prepare a balance sheet at 31 December 20*9, after the change to the new profit-sharing ratio has been implemented.

Answer

Balance sheet at 31 December 20*9

	£	£	
Non-current assets		70,000	
Current assets	12,000		
Less Current liabilities	8,000	4,000	
		74,000	
Capital accounts – Jean		53,500	(30,000 + 37,500 − 14,000)
Sean		20,500	(22,000 + 12,500 − 14,000)
		74,000	

PARTNERSHIP DISSOLUTION

A partnership may be dissolved, that is it may cease to be a partnership, under the following circumstances:

- on the death of a partner
- on the retirement of a partner
- when a partner is declared bankrupt
- by mutual agreement of the partners.

When a partnership is dissolved, the assets of the business are disposed of and any liabilities are then settled. The order of settling any debts (liabilities) is:

1. creditors
2. partners' loan accounts
3. partners' capital accounts.

The assets can be disposed of in a variety of ways:

- some assets may be sold for cash
- some assets may be sold to a limited company for shares, or debentures or a combination of cash, debentures and shares
- some assets may be taken over by one or more partners.

The way we tackle the closing down of the partnership is by preparing a realisation account. This is rather like an income statement.

On the debit side of the account, we find the assets that are disposed of and any expenses incurred in the dissolution. On the credit side, we find what the assets have realised.

Income statement	
What has been sold (purchases)	What has been realised (sales)
Costs of running the business (expenses)	Other incomes or benefits
Profit	Loss

Realisation account	
The book value of the assets	The proceeds from the sale of the assets shown opposite
Costs of the dissolution	Other incomes or benefits
Discounts allowed	Discounts received
Profit on realisation	Loss on realisation

Unless you are told differently in a question, assume that the partnership will collect any outstanding monies from debtors and pay off outstanding creditors.

Try to think what you will be doing in the circumstances when a partnership is dissolved.

All the assets to be disposed of are entered on the debit side of the realisation account.

All the proceeds of the disposals are entered on the credit side.

Any **profit** resulting from the realisation of the assets will appear on the debit side of the realisation account. It is posted from here to the credit side of the partners' capital accounts in their profit-sharing ratios.

Any **loss** will be shown on the credit side of the realisation account and it will be posted to the debit side of the partners' capital accounts in their profit-sharing ratios.

If partners take over any of the assets, treat these as a 'sale' to the partner.

If a question states that a partner takes over the inventory of the partnership, the entries would be:

Dr Partner – Capital account   Cr Realisation account
                          with the agreed value of the inventory.

So if Jim, a partner, takes a business-owned car at an agreed valuation of £4,700, this would be entered as:

Dr Capital – Jim £4,700   Cr Realisation account £4,700

WORKED EXAMPLE

Barbara and Ben are in partnership, sharing profits and losses in the ratio 2:1 respectively. They agree to dissolve their partnership on 30 November 20*9. They provide the following information:

Balance sheet at 30 November 20*9

	£	£
Non-current assets		80,000
Current assets	17,000	
Cash and cash equivalents	3,000	
	20,000	
Current liabilities	(14,000)	6,000
		86,000
Capital – Barbara		50,000
Ben		36,000
		86,000

- The current liabilities were paid their due amounts.
- The non-current assets were sold for £100,000 cash.
- The current asset fetched £15,000.

Required

Prepare:

a a realisation account
b a bank account
c partners' capital accounts.

continued ➤

Answer

Realisation account

	£		£
Non-current assets	80,000	Bank	100,000
Current assets	17,000	Bank	15,000
Capital – Barbara	12,000		
Ben	6,000		
	115,000		115,000

Bank

	£		£
Balance	3,000	Payables	14 000
Realisation – Non-current assets	100,000	Barbara – Capital	62 000
Current assets	15,000	Ben – Capital	42 000
	118,000		118,000

Capital accounts

	Barbara	Ben		Barbara	Ben
	£	£		£	£
Bank	62,000	42,000	Bal b/d	50,000	36,000
			Realisation	12,000	6,000
	62,000	42,000		62,000	42,000

In order to show the sequence of entries shown above, the entries have been journalised:

Dr	Payables	14,000	
	Bank a/c		14,000

Paying creditors

Realisation	80,000	
Non-current assets		80,000

Clearing the partnership books of the non-current assets

Realisation	17,000	
Current assets		17,000

Clearing the partnership books of the current assets

Bank	100,000	
Realisation		100,000

Sale of non-current asset for cash

| Bank | 15,000 | |
| Realisation | | 15,000 |

Sale of current assets for cash

| Realisation account | 12,000 | |
| Capital – Barbara | | 12,000 |

Barbara's share of profit on realisation

| Realisation account | 6,000 | |
| Capital – Ben | | 6,000 |

Ben's share of the profit on realisation

| Capital – Barbara | 62,000 | |
| Bank | | 62,000 |

Payment from business bank account to clear Barbara's capital

---

| Capital – Ben | 42,000 | |
| Bank | | 42,000 |

Payment from business bank account to clear Ben's capital

Do not attempt to share the balance left in the bank account in any pre-determined ratio. The bank account is used to clear any outstanding balances left on the partners' capital accounts.

WORKED EXAMPLE

Dave and Dierdre are in partnership, sharing profits 3:2 respectively. They agree to dissolve their partnership on 28 February 20*9. They provide the following information:

Balance sheet at 28 February 20*9			
	£	£	
Non-current assets		40,000	
Current assets	8,000		
Bank	2,000		
	10,000		
Current liabilities	(6,000)	4,000	
		44,000	
Capital accounts – Dave		25,000	
Dierdre		19,000	
		44,000	

■ The non-current assets were taken over by Dave at an agreed value of £36,000.
■ The current assets realised cash of £7,000.
■ The current liabilities were settled at book value.

continued ➤

WORKED EXAMPLE *continued*

Required

Prepare:

a a realisation account
b a bank account
c partners' capital accounts.

Answer

Realisation account

Non-current assets	40,000	Capital – Dave		36,000
Current assets	8,000	Bank		7,000
		Capital – Dave		3,000
			Dierdre	2,000
	48,000			48,000

Bank

Balance	2,000	Creditors	6,000
Realisation	7,000	Dierdre	17,000
Dave	14,000		
	23,000		23,000

Capital accounts

	Dave	Dierdre		Dave	Dierdre
Realisation	36,000		Balance	25,000	19,000
Realisation	3,000	2,000	Bank	14,000	
Bank		17,000			
	39,000	19,000		39,000	19,000

Again, to show the sequence of events:

Payables	6,000	
Bank		6,000

Paying off payables

Realisation	40,000	
Non-current assets		40,000

Closing down non-current assets accounts

Realisation	8,000	
Current assets		8,000

Closing down current assets accounts

Capital – Dave   36,000
   Realisation   36,000
Dave 'buys' non-current assets from partnership

Bank   7,000
   Realisation   7,000
Sale of current assets

Bank   14,000
   Capital – Dave   14,000
Dave pays off the deficit on his capital account

Capital – Dierdre   17,000
   Bank   17,000
Dierdre withdraws sufficient cash to clear the amount the partnership owes her.

QUESTION 17

Eliza, Sze Hang and Hazel were in partnership, sharing profits and losses equally. They agree to dissolve their partnership on 31 October 20*9. They provide the following information:

Balance sheet at 31 October 20*9

	£	£
Fixed assets		
Premises		70,000
Equipment		30,000
Vehicles		18,000
		118,000
Current assets	16,000	
Cash and cash equivalents	3,000	
	19,000	
Current liabilities		
Trade payables	(7,000)	12,000
		130,000
Capital accounts – Eliza		60,000
Sze Hang		40,000
Hazel		30,000
		130,000

The following assets were sold for cash:

	£
Premises	100,000
Equipment	18,000
Current assets	15,000

- The vehicles were taken over by Hazel at an agreed valuation of £10,000.
- Trade payables were paid the amounts due.

Required

Prepare:

a a realisation account

b a bank account

c partners' capital accounts.

QUESTION 18

McStravich, Thomas and Henry were in partnership, sharing profits and losses 2:2:1 respectively. They agree to dissolve their partnership on 31 July 20*9. They provide the following information:

Balance sheet at 31 July 20*9

	£	£
Fixed assets		
Land and buildings		120,000
Equipment		80,000
Vehicles		30,000
		230,000
Current assets	26,000	
Cash and cash equivalents	4,000	
	30,000	
Current liabilities		
Trade payables	(10,000)	20,000
		250,000
Capital accounts – McStravich		100,000
Thomas		70,000
Henry		80,000
		250,000

The following assets were sold for cash:

	£
Land and buildings	150,000
Equipment	37,000
Current assets	23,000

- The vehicles were taken over by Henry at an agreed valuation of £8,000.
- Trade payables were paid the amounts due.

Required

Prepare:

a a realisation account

b a bank account

c partners' capital accounts.

Clearly, there are times when the debtors do not all pay the amounts that they owed to the business when the partnership is wound up. This may be because there may be some bad debtors or because the partnership offers cash discounts in order to get the cash in quickly.

Similarly, there may be times when the partnership is able to benefit from cash discounts available from creditors.

Any discounts received from creditors and discounts allowed to debtors are entered in the realisation account (as would any debtors who proved to be bad).

WORKED EXAMPLE

Alex, Bernard and Charlie decide to dissolve their partnership on 30 April 20*9. At that date debtors owed £7,450 and creditors were owed £3,950.

Debtors paid £7,250 in settlement and creditors accepted £3,800 in settlement.

Required

Prepare the entries to record these transactions on:

a the realisation account

b the bank account

c sundry debtors account
d sundry creditors account.

Answer

Realisation account			
Sundry debtors	200	Sundry creditors	150

Bank account			
Sundry debtors	7,250	Sundry creditors	3,800

Sundry debtors account			
Balance b/d	7,450	Bank	7,250
		Realisation	200
	7,450		7,450

Sundry creditors account			
Bank	3,800	Balance b/d	3,950
Realisation	150		
	3,950		3,950

Winding up the partnership will inevitably incur costs. These costs may be to advertise various assets to be sold; they may be paid to a solicitor who will tie up and formalise the legal side of the dissolution. Any costs should be:

debited to the **realisation account** … and … **credited** to the **bank account**.

Finally, remember to settle any partnership loans after you have dealt with debtors and creditors – very straightforward:

Dr Loan account   Cr Bank account.

WORKED EXAMPLE

Mary and Douglas were in partnership, sharing profit and losses equally. They agreed to dissolve their partnership on 31 July 20*9. They provide the following information:

continued ➤

Balance sheet at 31 July 20*9

	£	£
Non-current assets		40,000
Current assets		
Inventory	9,000	
Trade receivables	4,000	
Cash and cash equivalents	2,000	
	15,000	
Current liabilities		
Trade payables	(8,000)	7,000
		47,000
Less **Long-term loan** – Douglas		(2,000)
		45,000
Capital accounts:		
Mary		25,000
Douglas		20,000
		45,000

- The non-current assets were sold for £58,000 cash.
- Inventory was taken over by Mary at an agreed value of £7,700.
- Debtors paid £3,800 in settlement.
- Creditors were paid £7,500 in settlement.
- The costs incurred during the dissolution amounted to £3,400.

Required

Prepare:

a a realisation account for the partnership
b a bank account
c capital accounts.

Answer

Realisation account

Non-current assets	40,000	Discounts received	500
Inventory	9,000	Bank	58,000
Discount allowed	200	Capital – Mary	7,700
Costs	3,400		
Profit – capitals	13,600		
	66,200		66,200

Bank account

Balance	2,000	Loan – Douglas	2,000
Receivables	3,800	Payables	7,500
Realisation	58,000	Costs	3,400
		Capital – Mary	24,100
		Douglas	26,800
	63,800		63,800

Capital accounts

	Mary	Douglas		Mary	Douglas
Realisation	7,700		Balance	25,000	20,000
Bank	24,100	26,800	Realisation	6,800	6,800
	31,800	26,800		31,800	26,800

QUESTION 19

Bertram, Chipperfield and Mills were in partnership, sharing profits and losses 3:2:1 respectively. They agree to wind up their partnership with effect from 31 December 20*9. The following information is available:

Balance sheet at 31 December 20*9

	£	£
Non-current assets		
Premises		210,000
Equipment		84,000
Three vehicles		42,000
		336,000
Current assets		
Inventory	12,400	
Trade receivables	8,200	
Cash and cash equivalents	2,700	
	23,300	
Trade payables	(9,300)	14,000
		350,000
Less **Long-term loan**		
Chipperfield		(50,000)
		300,000
Capital accounts		
Bertram		150,000
Chipperfield		100,000
Mills		50,000
		300,000

The following assets were sold for cash:

	£
Equipment	57,000
Vehicle (1)	9,000
Inventory	10,800

- Premises were taken over by Bertram at an agreed value of £300,000.
- Vehicle (2) was taken over by Chipperfield at an agreed value of £5,000.
- Vehicle (3) was taken over by Mills at an agreed value of £6,000.
- Debtors paid £8,100 in settlement.
- Creditors accepted £8,900 in settlement.
- Costs incurred during the dissolution amounted to £6,450.

Required

Prepare:

a   a realisation account
b   a bank account
c   partners' capital accounts.

Tip: Do not panic over the treatment of the vehicles. Here are the journal entries. Enter them in the appropriate account in your answer.

Dr Realisation account	£42,000	
Cr Vehicles account		£42,000
Dr Bank	£9,000	
Cr Realisation account		£9,000
Dr Capital – Chipperfield	£5,000	
Cr Realisation account		£5,000
Dr Capital – Mills	£6,000	
Cr Realisation account		£6,000

QUESTION 20

Jason, Robert and Samuel are in partnership, sharing profits and losses 5:9:1 respectively. They agree to dissolve their partnership on 31 January 20*9. They provide the following information:

Balance sheet at 31 January 20*9

	£	£	£
Non-current assets			
Premises			190,000
Equipment			48,000
Vehicles (2)			33,000
			271,000
Current assets			
Inventory		14,780	
Trade receivables		3,960	
		18,740	
Current liabilities			
Trade payables	(4,120)		
Bank overdraft	(2,620)	(6,740)	12,000
			283,000
Long-term loan – Jason			(40,000)
			243,000
Capital accounts			
Jason			100,000
Robert			80,000
Samuel			63,000
			243,000

The following assets were sold for cash:

	£
Premises	350,000
Equipment	18,000
Inventory	14,500

- One car was taken over by Robert at an agreed value of £15,000.
- The other was taken over by Samuel at an agreed value of £8,000.
- Debtors paid £3,800 in full settlements.
- Creditors accepted £3,750 in settlements.
- Costs of dissolution amounted to £6,560.

Required

Prepare:

a a realisation account
b a bank account
c partners' capital accounts.

So far, all assets of the business have either been taken over by a partner or have been sold for cash. We must finally consider the situation where some assets are sold to a limited company. The limited company could settle the deal by paying:

- cash or
- cash and shares or
- cash and debentures or
- any combination of the three.

Sounds daunting, doesn't it?

WORKED EXAMPLE

Karl and Betty are in partnership, sharing profits and losses in the ratio 2:1 respectively. They agreed to sell their business to Tontong Ltd. The purchase consideration was £100,000, being made up of £20,000 cash and 50,000 ordinary shares of £1 each. The partners agreed that the shares be distributed to the partners in their profit-sharing ratios. The partnership balance sheet immediately prior to the takeover was:

Net assets	82,000		
Capital – Karl	50,000		
Betty	32,000		
	82,000		

Required

Prepare the account to close the books of Karl and Betty.

Answer

Realisation account

Net assets	82,000	Tontong Ltd	100,000
Capital – Karl	12,000		
Betty	6,000		
	100,000		100,000

Tontong Ltd

Realisation	100,000	Bank	20,000
		Capital – Karl	53,333
		Betty	26,667
	100,000		100,000

Bank account

Tontong Ltd	20,000	Capital – Karl	8,667
		Betty	11,333
	20,000		20,000

Capital accounts

	Karl	Betty		Karl	Betty
Ord. shares in Tontong	53,333	26,667	Balance	50,000	32,000
Cash	8,667	11,333	Realisation	12,000	6,000
	62,000	38,000		62,000	38,000

Journal entries to show the chronology of the entries:

Realisation	82,000	
Net assets		82,000

This closes down the asset accounts.

Tontong Ltd	100,000	
Realisation		100,000

Purchase consideration agreed between Tontong Ltd and the partners.

Realisation	18,000	
Capital – Karl		12,000
Betty		6,000

Profit on realisation is credited to the partners in their profit sharing ratios.

continued ➤

Bank   20,000

        Tontong Ltd   20,000

Cash paid by Tontong Ltd.

Capital – Karl   53,333

        Betty   26,667

        Tontong Ltd   80,000

Shares given to the partners in the agreed ratios – note that the ordinary shares are shared in value terms, not in nominal values.

Capital – Karl   8,667

        Betty   11,333

        Bank   20,000

Cash is issued to balance the capital accounts.

Talk yourself through this a couple of times. It is much easier than you think. The point at which most candidates go wrong is when the ordinary shares have to be given to the partners – simply divide the balance on the company's account by the ratios given in the question.

WORKED EXAMPLE

Ray and Rex are in partnership, sharing profits and losses in the ratio 3:2 respectively. They sell their business to Dorken Ltd for an agreed purchase consideration of £200,000. The purchase consideration being made up as follows:

	£
Cash	40,000
6% debentures	50,000
30,000 ordinary shares of £1 each	

[Remember that those £1 ordinary shares may be worth more than £1 or less than £1. Can you say how much they are worth?

£3.67 each. Did you get it right? Value £110,000/30,000.]

It was agreed that the partners would distribute the debentures in the last agreed capital account ratios and that the ordinary shares would be divided according to the profit- and loss-sharing ratio.

The partnership balance sheet immediately prior to takeover was:

	£
Net assets	120,000
Capital – Ray	80,000
Rex	40,000
	120,000

WORKED EXAMPLE *continued*

Required

Prepare the entries to close the partnership books of account.

Answer

Realisation account

Net assets	120,000	Dorken Ltd		200,000
Capital – Ray	48,000			
Rex	32,000			
	200,000			200,000

Dorken Ltd

Realisation	200,000	Bank	40,000
		Debentures	50,000
		Ordinary shares	110,000
	200,000		200,000

Bank

Dorken Ltd	40,000	Capital – Ray	28,667
		Rex	11,333
	40,000		40,000

Capital accounts

	Ray	Rex		Ray	Rex
Dorken (Debentures)	33,333	16,667	Balances	80,000	40,000
Dorken (Ordinary shares)	66,000	44,000	Realisation	48,000	32,000
Bank (to balance)	28,667	11,333			
	128,000	72,000		128,000	72,000

Journal entries:

Realisation	120,000	
Net assets		120,000

Dorken Ltd	200,000	
Realisation		200,000

Realisation	48,000	
Realisation	32,000	
Capital – Ray		48,000
Rex		32,000

Bank	40,000	
Dorken Ltd		40,000

continued ➤

Capital – Ray	33,333	
Rex	16,667	
Dorken Ltd (debentures)		50,000

Capital – Ray	66,000	
Rex	44,000	
Dorken Ltd (ordinary shares)		110,000

Capital – Ray	28,667	
Rex	11,333	
Bank		28,667
Bank		11,333

As a point of interest, the entries in the books of Dorken Ltd would show:

- bank reducing by £40,000
- debentures increasing by £50,000
- ordinary share capital increasing by £30,000 (share premium £80,000)
- net tangible assets increasing by £120,000
- and yes, you've guessed it – goodwill by £80,000.

QUESTION 21

Joan and Darby are in partnership, sharing profits and losses 4:1 respectively. They agree to sell their partnership assets to Agas Ltd for £210,000. The purchase consideration is made up of £25,000 cash and 60,000 ordinary shares of £1 each. The partners agree that the shares in Agas Ltd would be distributed according to the profit-sharing ratios.
Joan and Darby's balance sheet prior to the purchase was:

	£
Net assets	100,000
Capital – Joan	60,000
Darby	40,000
	100,000

Required

Prepare entries to close the partnership books of account.

QUESTION 22

Ned and Ted are in partnership, sharing profits and losses 3:1 respectively. They agree to sell their partnership assets to Tedden plc, the purchase consideration of £200,000 being made up of £30,000 cash; 60,000 6% debentures (to be shared equally between the partners) and 400,000 ordinary shares of 10p each (to be shared in profit-sharing ratios).
Ned and Ted's balance sheet prior to the purchase was:

	£
Net assets	140,000
Capital – Ned	100,000
Ted	40,000
	140,000

Required

Prepare entries to close the partnership books of account.

Occasionally, when the dissolution has been completed, a partner's capital account ends up with a debit balance, as in the case of Dave (Dave and Dierdre, earlier). Generally, the partner will pay an amount to clear the debt.

There are times when a partner may not be able to clear the balance.

In the case of *Garner v Murray*, the court ruled that such a deficiency was to be shared among the remaining partners in the ratio of the capital account balances shown in the balance sheet prepared at the end of the last financial year.

WORKED EXAMPLE

Doc, Grumpy and Bashful are in partnership, sharing profits and losses equally. At 31 December 20*9 their capital account balances were £30,000, £40,000 and £10,000 respectively. The partnership is dissolved. After closing all ledger accounts for the partnership, the following balances remain in the books of account:

	Dr £	Cr £
Capital		
Doc		17,000
Grumpy		6,000
Bashful	14,000	
Bank	9,000	

Bashful is unable to meet his liability to the partnership out of his personal funds.

Required

Prepare the entries to close the partnership books of account.

Answer

Capital							
	Doc	Grumpy	Bashful		Doc	Grumpy	Bashful
Balance			14,000	Balance	17,000	6,000	

Under normal circumstances, Bashful would pay £14,000 into the partnership bank account; Doc and Grumpy would receive £17,000 and £6,000 respectively; so . . .

Capital							
	Doc	Grumpy	Bashful		Doc	Grumpy	Bashful
Bank	17,000	6,000		Bank			14,000

Bashful cannot do this so the £14,000 debt to the partnership must be shared between the remaining partners in the ratio of the balance standing in the capital accounts in the balance sheet drawn up at the end of the last financial period.

Bashful's debt must be shared between the remaining two partners ⅗ to Doc and ⅖ to Grumpy.

So the closing entries are:

continued ➤

WORKED EXAMPLE *continued*

Capital account

	Doc	Grumpy	Bashful		Doc	Grumpy	Bashful
Balance			14,000	Balance	17,000	6,000	
Bashful	6,000	8,000		Doc			6,000
Bank	11,000			Grumpy			8,000
				Bank		2,000	
	17,000	8,000	14,000		17,000	8,000	14,000

Bank account

Balance b/d	9,000	Doc	11,000
Grumpy	2,000		
	11,000		11,000

Doc receives £11,000 while Grumpy pays £2,000 into the bank account.

QUESTION 23

Stephen, Asman and Shably are in partnership, sharing profits and losses equally. They agree to dissolve their partnership. They provide the following information:

Balance sheet at 31 May 200*9

	£
Net assets	40,000
Cash and cash equivalents	10,000
	50,000
Capital accounts	
Stephen	40,000
Asman	20,000
Shably	(10,000)
	50,000

The net assets were sold for £55,000 cash. Shably is unable to meet any liability to the partnership out of his personal funds.

Required

Prepare:

a a realisation account
b a bank account
c partners' capital accounts.

QUESTION 24

Kurt, Liam and Mike are in partnership, sharing profits and losses in the ratios 3:2:1 respectively. They agree to dissolve their partnership on 31 December 20*9. They provide the following information:

Balance sheet at 31 December 20*9

	£
Net assets	120,000
Bank overdraft	(8,000)
	112,000
Capital accounts	
Kurt	110,000
Liam	20,000
Mike	(18,000)
	112,000

The net assets were sold for £150,000 cash. Mike is unable to meet any liability to the partnership out of his personal funds.

Required

Prepare:

a   a realisation account
b   a bank account
c   the partners' capital accounts.

Chapter summary

- When a structural change takes place in a partnership, two appropriation accounts should be prepared – one before the change and one after the change.
- When a structural change takes place the business should be revalued and a value is placed on goodwill. This value is shared among the 'old' partners (who have helped to create it) in their profit-sharing ratios.
- When writing off goodwill it is the profit-sharing ratios of the 'new' partnership that are used to debit the partners' capital accounts.
- When a partnership is wound up, assets are transferred to a realisation account and any profit or loss is calculated. The profit (or loss) is then apportioned to the partners in their profit-sharing ratios.
- Capital accounts are closed by a transfer of cash to or from the bank account.
- If a partner is insolvent the balance on the capital account is shared between the remaining partners in a ratio that reflects the balance on the capital accounts as shown on the balance sheet at the end of the last financial year.

SELF-TEST QUESTIONS

- Give an example of a structural change to a partnership.
- Explain why it is necessary to revalue assets when a structural change takes place.
- Define 'goodwill'.
- Explain one method of placing a value on goodwill.
- Goodwill is the purchase of existing customers. True or false?
- Non-current assets £30,000; current liabilities £8,000; purchase price £50,000. Calculate the value of goodwill.
- Explain the term 'inherent goodwill'.
- Explain how inherent goodwill would be shown on a balance sheet.
- Explain the circumstances under which a partnership would be dissolved.
- Explain the ruling in *Garner v Murray*.

TEST QUESTIONS

QUESTION 25

Arbuthnot and Barton were in partnership, sharing profits and losses equally. They provide the following information:

Balance sheet at 30 June 20*9

	£	£
Non-current assets		
Premises		48,000
Equipment		23,000
Vehicles		34,000
		105,000
Current assets		
Inventory	8,900	
Trade receivables	4,600	
Cash and cash equivalents	2,500	
	16,000	
Trade payables	(6,000)	10,000
		115,000
Capital accounts – Arbuthnot		65,000
Barton		50,000
		115,000

On 1 July 20*9 Currock was admitted to the partnership under the following terms:

	£	£	£
Current liabilities:			
Trade payables	(14,300)		7,000
Bank overdraft	(9,100)	23,400	52,000
Capital accounts – Findlay			28,000
Forster			8,000
Farquar			16,000
			52,000

Findlay retired from the partnership at close of business on 31 January 20*9. The following asset values were agreed:

	£
Equipment	16,000
Vehicles	9,000
Goodwill	90,000

Forster and Farquar carried on in business, sharing profits in the ratio 3:2 respectively and they agreed that a goodwill account would not be maintained in the business books of account.

They agreed that any amount due to Findlay would be paid out of the business bank account. Their bank manager agreed to provide overdraft facilities if they were necessary.

Required

Prepare:

a a revaluation account
b a goodwill account
c partners' capital account
d a balance sheet at 31 January 20*9, immediately after Findlay's retirement.

QUESTION 29

Stan and Ollie are in partnership, sharing profits and losses equally. Their balance sheet at 30 April 20*9 is shown:

Balance sheet at 30 April 20*9

	£	£
Non-current assets		
Equipment		65,000
Vehicles		25,000
		90,000
Current assets		
Inventory	10,000	
Trade receivables	9,000	
Cash and cash equivalents	1,500	
	20,500	
Current liabilities		
Trade payables	(8,500)	12,000
		102,000
Capital accounts – Stan		70,000
Ollie		32,000
		102,000

They agree that from close of business on 30 April 20*9: they will share profits and losses ¾ to Stan and ¼ to Ollie. The following values have been agreed for business assets:

	£
Equipment	40,000
Vehicles	8,000
Goodwill	50,000

It has been agreed that a goodwill account will not be maintained in the business books of account.

Required

Prepare a balance sheet at 30 April 20*9, after the change to the profit-sharing ratios.

QUESTION 30

McMeel and Coary are in partnership, sharing profits and losses 2:1 respectively. The following information is available:

Balance sheet at 30 November 20*9

	£	£
Non-current assets:		
Premises		28,000
Equipment		87,000
Vehicles		35,000
		150,000
Current assets		
Inventory	2,100	
Trade receivables	1,800	
Cash and cash equivalents	800	
	4,700	
Trade payables	(4,200)	500
		150,500
Capital accounts – McMeel		75,500
Coary		75,000
		150,500

It has been agreed that from close of business on 30 November 20*9 partners would share profits and losses in the ratio 3:2 and that the following assets would be revalued:

	£
Premises	40,000
Equipment	60,000
Vehicles	20,000
Goodwill	70,000

It was further agreed that a goodwill account would not be maintained in the business books of account.

Required

Prepare a balance sheet at 30 November 20*9, after the change to the profit-sharing ratio.

QUESTION 31

Pritpal and Sukhdeep are in partnership, sharing profits and losses equally. They decide to dissolve their partnership on 28 February 20*9. Their balance sheet as at that date showed:

	£	£
Non-current assets		
Land and buildings		40,000
Equipment		30,000
Vehicle		10,000
		80,000
Current assets		
Inventory	3,400	
Trade receivables	18,400	
Cash and cash equivalents	2,700	
	24,500	
Trade payables	(6,400)	18,100
		98,100
Long-term loan – Pritpal		(25,000)
		73,100
Capital accounts – Pritpal		48,300
Sukhdeep		24,800
		73,100

The receivables realised £18,000. Equipment was sold for £17,000 cash. Inventory was sold for £2,000 cash. The vehicle was taken over by Sukhdeep at an agreed value of £6,000. Dissolution expenses were £4,300 and discounts of £300 were received from creditors. The land and buildings were sold to Divya Ltd for a purchase consideration of £60,000, consisting of 40,000 ordinary shares of 50p each, to be divided between the partners in their profit-sharing ratio, and £30,000 cash.

Required

Prepare:

a a realisation account
b a cash account
c partners' capital accounts.

QUESTION 32

McTavish and McGonagle have been in partnership for many years, sharing profits and losses in the ratio 3:2 respectively. Their balance sheet at 31 January 20*9 is as follows:

Balance sheet at 31 January 20*9

	£	£	£
Non-current assets			38,000
Current assets			
Inventory		4,800	
Trade receivables		6,000	
		10,800	
Current liabilities			
Trade payables	(4,900)		
Bank overdraft	(1,400)	(6,300)	4,500
			42,500
Capital accounts – McTavish			25,000
McGonagle			17,500
			42,500

McTavish and McGonagle decide to dissolve their partnership.

- The inventory was sold for £4,000 cash.
- Trade receivables paid £5,700 in settlement.
- Trade payables accepted £4,750 in settlement.
- Dissolution costs amounted to £5,700.
- The non-current assets were sold to Ripov Ltd for £100,000.

The purchase consideration consisted of £30,000 cash; £40,000 5% debentures, to be shared in profit-sharing ratio; and 10,000 ordinary shares of £1 each; to be shared equally between the partners.

Required

Prepare:

a a realisation account
b a cash account
c partners' capital accounts.

QUESTION 33

Jacques, Marcel and Guillaume, who share profits and losses in the ratio 3:2:1, decide to dissolve their partnership with effect from 30 June 20*9. They provide the following information:

Balance sheet at 30 June 20*9

	£	£
Non-current assets		
Equipment		42,000
Current assets		
Inventory	17,000	
Trade receivables	3,500	
Cash and cash equivalents	800	
	21,300	
Current liabilities		
Trade payables	(6,400)	14,900
		56,900
Long-term loan – Guillaume		(30,000)
		26,900
Capital accounts – Jacques		15,000
Marcel		1,900
Guillaume		10,000
		26,900

- The equipment was sold for £25,000 cash.
- Inventory was taken over by Jacques at an agreed valuation of £15,000.
- Trade receivables were allowed discounts of £300 and discounts received from creditors amounted to £140.
- Costs of dissolution amounted to £8,300.
- Marcel is unable to meet any liability to the partnership out of private funds.

Required

Prepare:

a a realisation account
b a cash account
c partners' capital accounts.

QUESTION 34

Tom, Dick and Mary have been in partnership for many years, sharing profits and losses 4:2:1 respectively. They decide to dissolve their partnership with effect from the close of business on 31 March 20*9. They provide the following information:

Balance sheet at 31 March 20*9

	£	£	£
Non-current assets			
Premises			40,000
Equipment			30,000
Vehicles (3)			20,000
			90,000
Current assets			
Inventory		10,000	
Trade receivables		7,000	
		17,000	
Current liabilities			
Trade payables	(6,000)		
Bank overdraft	(5,000)	(11,000)	6,000
			96,000
Long-term loan – Tom			36,000
			60,000
Capital accounts – Tom			40,000
Dick			15,000
Mary			5,000
			60,000

- Premises were sold for £50,000 cash.
- Equipment was taken over by Tom at an agreed value of £18,000.
- One vehicle was taken over by Tom at an agreed value of £8,000.
- Another vehicle was taken over by Dick at an agreed value of £6,000.
- The third vehicle was sold for scrap for £500 cash.
- Inventory realised £9,500.
- A trade debtor who owed £2,000 was written off as a bad debt; the remainder paid what they owed.
- Trade creditors allowed £400 cash discount.
- Dissolution expenses amounted to £7,450.

Required

Prepare:

a a realisation account
b a bank account
c partners' capital accounts.

CHAPTER
FIVE

Accounting Standards

Limited companies must prepare their final accounts within a regulatory framework.

This framework consists of:

- the Companies Act 1985, as amended by the Companies Act 1989
- international accounting standards (IAS and IFRS)
- regulations required by the Stock Exchange (these will not be discussed here since none of the major UK examinations boards examines these regulations).

Nowadays, limited companies must adhere to the Companies Act 1985, as amended by the Companies Act 1989, as well as to accounting standards.

Why is there a need to have standards?

The standards seek to:

- iron out areas of difference in the preparation and presentation of accounting information
- recommend disclosure of accounting bases
- identify any departure from the standards
- improve existing disclosure requirements.

So the standards are the 'ground rules' that apply to the preparation of the accounts of limited companies and the audit of their accounts. These ensure that the standards that are applied in Carlisle are the same as those being applied in Cheltenham.

At the moment there are over 30 IAS and 6 IFRS in operation.

Fortunately for you, not all of the standards are examined.

HEALTH WARNING!
- It is important to stress that you will not be required to have a detailed knowledge of the standards that are examinable.
- However, you should know the number, for example 'IAS 7 *Statement of cash flows*' and the broad outline of what the standard says.
- Different examination boards examine different standards.

Health Warning

Since 1 January 2005 it has been mandatory for all limited companies listed on a regulated stock market within the European union to prepare their financial statements in accordance with international accounting standards (IAS).

International standards (IAS) are gradually being replaced with international financial reporting standards (IFRS). At present the AQA A-level examining board requires knowledge and understanding of 10 IAS.

Although it is not yet mandatory for the financial statements of private limited companies (Ltd) to be prepared in accordance with the IAS it seems inevitable that in time the standards will apply to all limited companies.

Consequently in this book appropriate standards will be applied to the preparation of the financial statements of all limited companies.

The Companies Act 1989 introduced a requirement that the financial statements of companies must be prepared in accordance with the standards in force and that any material deviations from these should be identified and reasons given for any such deviation.

Specification coverage:
AQA ACCN 3;
OCR F013.

By the end of this chapter you should be able to:
- demonstrate a basic knowledge of IAS 1; IAS 2; IAS 8; IAS 10; IAS 16; IAS 18; IAS 36; IAS 37; IAS 38.

Although the adherence to international accounting standards is not embodied in law, the Companies Act 1989 requires that directors of a company using the standards to prepare the company's financial statements must state this fact.

In 1989 'Framework for the preparation of financial statements' was issued by the International Standards Committee. It sets out the underlying principles for the preparation and presentation of financial statements.

The Framework states that '... financial statements ... provide information about the financial position, performance and changes in financial position of an entity ...'.

It can be assumed that all financial statements have been prepared using two concepts that you came across in Chapter 19 of *Introducing Accounting for AS*:

- The accruals concept. This records the value of the resources used by the business and the benefits derived from the use of those resources in the financial year of use, and not when cash is paid or received.
- The going concern concept. This means that unless we have knowledge to the contrary, we assume that the company will continue to trade in its present form for the foreseeable future.

Financial statements should be useful to all the people who use the statements. The Framework identifies four characteristics of financial statements that are meant to ensure their usefulness to the users:

- Understandability. Information should be capable of being understood by people with a reasonable knowledge of business and accounting. This may require 'study with reasonable diligence on behalf of the user'.
- Relevance. The statements must contain information that is able to influence the decisions of users and, if provided in time, influence those decisions.
- Reliability. The statements must contain information that can be relied on as a faithful representation of the substance of what has taken place. The information should be unbiased, prudent, completely free from material errors and record the effect of a transaction (accurate representation; substance over form).
- Comparability. The users of financial statements must be confident that they can compare data from one time period to another. This is achieved by the financial statements being prepared on a consistent basis and by accounting policies used in the preparation of the financial statements being disclosed. This will enable users to identify and evaluate differences and similarities.

The framework states that if the four characteristics are present in the preparation of financial statements then, under normal circumstances, the statements will show a true and fair view of the financial position.

There are a number of concepts (Chapter 19 *Introducing Accounting for AS*) which form the major influences in preparing the financial statements.

- Business entity. Only the expenses and revenues relating to the business are recorded in the business books of account. Transactions involving the private affairs of the owner(s) or director(s) should not be included in the business books.
- Materiality. If the inclusion or exclusion of information would mislead the users of financial statements, then that information is material. This concept recognises that some types of expenditure are less important in a business context than others. So absolute precision is not essential.
- Prudence. This requires that revenues and profits are included in the accounts only when they are realised or where their realisation is reasonably certain. The concept does allow for provisions to be made for known expenses or losses when they become known (characteristic of reliability).
- Consistency. This requires that once a method of treating information has been established, the method should be used in subsequent years' accounts. If information is treated differently each year, then inter-year results cannot be easily compared and trends determined (characteristic of comparability).
- Historical cost. This is an objective valuation. Values based on what any asset(s) might be sold for if the business were to liquidate are irrelevant to the business's ability to generate profits or cash.
- Duality. The assets of a business are always equal to the liabilities of the business. So every financial transaction has a double impact on the financial records of the business.

Examination candidates are required to 'explain and comment on the purpose and importance of the following international accounting standards'. However, remember that you do not need a detailed knowledge of any of the IAS, with the exception of IAS 7 *Statement of cash flows*. You should, however, know their number and heading, e.g. IAS 18 *Revenue*.

IAS 1 *PRESENTATION OF FINANCIAL STATEMENTS*

The standard sets out the ground rules of how financial statements should be presented. Adherence to the standard means that comparisons can be made with previous accounting periods and with other companies.

The standard identifies five components that make up a complete set of financial statements. These are:

- an income statement
- a statement of changes in equity
- a balance sheet
- a statement of cash flows
- a statement of accounting policies and explanatory notes to the accounts.

The standard requires that the financial statements should contain an explicit and unreserved statement that they comply with international standards. This should mean that the statements achieve a fair presentation.

The standard requires that the statements comply with accounting concepts.

In order to facilitate comparison, there is a requirement that the figures from previous periods must be published.

The name of the company should be given along with the time period covered by the financial statements.

THE INCOME STATEMENT

Although much of the detail of all expenses does not need to be shown in the income statement, certain items must be disclosed:

- revenue
- finance costs
- tax expense
- profit (or loss) for the period attributable to equity holders.

In reality, examination questions would require you to show more detail. Indeed, more information is needed to make the income statement understandable.

An income statement prepared in answer to an examination question is likely to require more detail than that prescribed by the standard.

WORKED EXAMPLE

The following information is available for Sonuk plc for the year ended 31 August 20*9:

	£000
Administrative expenses	173
Debenture interest paid	28
Distribution costs	158
Dividends paid	48
Inventories 1 September 20*8	32
31 August 20*9	28
Purchases	243
Retained earnings at 1 September 20*8	623
Revaluation reserve	470
Sales	900
Sales returns	12

The directors wish to make a provision for corporation tax of £69,000.

Required

Prepare an income statement for the year ended 31 August 20*9.

WORKED EXAMPLE *continued*

Answer

```
                          Sonuk plc
        Income statement for the year ended 31 August 20*9
                          £000
Revenue                   888      Sales less sales returns
Cost of sales            (247)     Opening inventory plus purchases less closing
                                   inventory
Gross profit              641
Distribution costs       (158)     Warehouse costs plus cost of getting goods to
                                   customers
Administrative expenses  (173)     Costs of maintaining and running the offices
Profit from operations    310
Finance costs             (28)     Interest paid
Profit before tax         282
Tax                       (69)
Profit for the year       213
```

STATEMENT OF CHANGES IN EQUITY

IAS 1 requires that a statement of changes in equity is included as part of the financial statements.

This statement shows the changes that have affected the shareholders' stake in the company.

WORKED EXAMPLE

Use the same information given in the previous worked example.

Additional information

During the year ended 31 August 20*9 non-current assets have been revalued from a cost price of £340,000 to a value of £450,000.

Required

Prepare a statement showing the changes in equity for the year ended 31 August 20*9.

Answer

```
                    Statement of changes in equity
                              £000
Retained earnings
Balance at 1 September 20*8        623
Profit for the year                213
                                   836
Dividends paid                      48
Balance at 31 August 20*9          788

Revaluation reserve
Balance at 1 September 20*8        470
Revaluation of non-current assets  110
Balance at 31 August 20*9          580
```

THE BALANCE SHEET

IAS 1 states the items that must be shown as a minimum in the balance sheet. These include:

- intangible assets
- property, plant and equipment
- investment property
- financial assets
- investments
- inventories
- trade and other receivables
- cash and cash equivalents
- trade and other payables
- provisions
- financial liabilities
- tax liabilities
- issued capital
- reserves.

CURRENT ASSETS

These comprise:

- cash and cash equivalents
- assets that will be disposed of within the next normal operating cycle (usually the next financial year); examples are inventories and trade receivables.

All other assets are classified as **non-current assets**.

CURRENT LIABILITIES

These comprise liabilities that are expected to be settled within the next normal operating cycle (usually the next financial year); examples are trade payables, tax liabilities and bank overdrafts (shown as negative cash and cash equivalents).

All other liabilities are **non-current liabilities**.

SHARE CAPITAL

The following detail must be shown either as part of the balance sheet or in the notes to the financial statements:

- the number of shares authorised
- the number of shares issued and fully paid
- the number of shares issued and not fully paid
- the par value of the shares.

RESERVES

A list of all the reserves created is shown either on the face of the balance sheet or as a note to the financial statements. If the detailed list of reserves is shown as a note, then the total of all reserves is shown on the face of the balance sheet.

Generally an examination answer would require you to list the reserves given in the question.

WORKED EXAMPLE

The directors of Nivlan plc provide the following information at 31 July 20*9:

	£000
Cash and cash equivalents	142
Goodwill	150
Inventories at 31 July 20*9	896
Issued share capital	3,000
Property plant and equipment	8,760
Retained earnings	2,298
Revaluation reserve	1,500
Share premium account	1,000
Trade and other payables	587
Trade and other receivables	779
9% Debentures (2027)	2,000

The directors have made a provision for corporation tax of £342,000.

Required

Prepare a balance sheet at 31 July 20*9.

Answer

Nivlan plc
Balance sheet at 31 July 20*9

	£000	£000
Non-current assets		
Goodwill	150	
Property, plant and equipment	8,760	8,910
Current assets		
Inventories	896	
Trade and other receivables	779	
Cash and cash equivalents	142	
	1,817	
Current liabilities		
Trade and other payables	(587)	
Tax liability	(342)	
	(929)	
Net current assets		888
		9,798
Non-current liabilities		
9% debentures (2027)		(2,000)
Net assets		7,798
Equity		
Issued share capital		3,000
Share premium account		1,000
Revaluation reserve		1,500
Retained earnings		2,298
Total equity		7,798

DIVIDENDS

Dividends are distributions to shareholders of profits earned by a limited company. Dividends are paid annually but most limited companies will pay an interim dividend approximately halfway through their financial year.

Interim dividends are based on the profits earned for the first half of the financial year. The final dividend is based on the reported profits for the full year.

Since directors do not have the authority to pay dividends without the approval of the owners of the company (i.e. the shareholders), the final dividend can only be proposed after the financial

year-end. Shareholder approval should occur two or three months later at the company annual general meeting.

Only dividends actually paid during a financial year can be recorded in the financial statements.

WORKED EXAMPLE

The following information is available for Engary plc for the financial year ended 31 December 20*9:

January 20*9	Directors propose a final dividend of £34,000 on ordinary shares based on reported profits for the year ended 31 December 20*8.
March 20*9	Shareholders approve the final dividend for the year ended 31 December 20*8.
May 20*9	Final dividend of £34,000 for the year ended 31 December 20*8 paid to shareholders.
August 20*9	Interim dividend of £19,000 paid to shareholders based on reported profits for the half-year ended 30 June 20*9.
January 20*0	Directors propose a final dividend of £41,000 based on reported profits for the year ended 31 December 20*9.

Required

Prepare a statement detailing the total entry in the financial statements for the year ended 31 December 20*9 for dividends.

Answer

Dividend entry in financial statements for the year ended 31 December 20*9	
	£
Final dividend for year ended 31 December 20*8	34,000
Interim dividend for half year ended 30 June 20*9	19,000
Total entry for dividends	53,000

The details of dividends paid during the financial year are shown in a note to the published accounts. The above information for Engary plc would be shown as follows.

WORKED EXAMPLE

Dividends	
	£
Equity dividends on ordinary shares	
Amounts recognised during the year	
Final dividend for the year ended 31 December 20*8 of 3.4p	34,000
Interim dividend for the year ended 31 December 20*9 of 1.9p	19,000
	53,000
Proposed final dividend for the year ended 31 December 20*9 of 4.1p	41,000

The proposed final dividend is subject to approval by shareholders at the annual general meeting and accordingly has not been included as a liability in the financial statements.

The financial statements must contain a directors' report and an auditors' report.

The directors' report is rather like your school/college report. The report contains:

- a statement of the principal activities of the company
- a review of performance over the preceding year
- a review of likely future developments
- the names of directors and their shareholdings
- details of dividends
- differences between book value and market value of land and buildings
- political and charitable donations
- a statement on employees and employment policies (i.e. equal opportunities policy, policies with regard to the disabled, and to health and safety of employees)
- policy of opportunities and participation of employees
- suppliers' payment policy.

The auditors' report contains three sections:

- Respective responsibilities of directors and auditors. The directors' responsibilities are to prepare the annual report and financial statements in accordance with law and international reporting standards.
- Basis of audit opinion. The audit should be conducted in accordance with international accounting standards. The auditors should obtain all the information and explanations that are necessary to provide sufficient evidence to allow them to assure the shareholders that the financial statements are free from material misstatement.
- Opinion. The auditors' view of the financial statements and their opinion as to whether they give a true and fair view, in accordance with international financial reporting standards and international accounting standards, of the state of the company's affairs and of its profit/loss for the period covered by the audit.

The report should also express an opinion as to whether or not the financial statements have been properly prepared in accordance with the Companies Act 1985.

NOTES TO THE FINANCIAL STATEMENTS

The standard requires that notes to the financial statements be included. These notes:

- give additional detail to items that may be summarised in the main body of the financial statements
- provide additional information to help the users understand the financial statements
- are also used to explain the particular treatment of items contained in the main body, i.e. the bases used in the preparation (see IAS 8, below).

IAS 2 *INVENTORIES*

This standard is one of the most frequently tested.

'Inventories' are defined as:

- goods or other assets purchased for resale
- consumable stores
- raw materials and components purchased for incorporation into products for sale
- products and services in intermediate stages of completion
- finished goods.

'Cost' is defined as 'expenditure which has been incurred in the normal course of business in bringing the product or service to its present location and condition'.

Cost of purchase comprises purchase price including import duties, transport and handling costs and any other directly attributable costs less trade discounts, rebates and subsidies.

Production overheads: overheads incurred in respect of materials, labour or services for production, based on the normal level of activity, taking one year with another.

Cost of conversion comprises:

- costs which are specifically attributable to units of production, eg direct labour, direct expenses and sub-contracted work

- production overheads
- other overheads, if any.

> **Net realisable value** is the actual or estimated selling price (net of trade discount but before cash discount) less all further costs to completion and all marketing, selling and distribution costs.

The standard states that inventory should be valued at the lower of cost or net realisable value of the separate items of inventory or of groups of similar items.

The inventories should be categorised in the balance sheet as raw materials, work in progress or finished goods.

The standard accepts inventories valued using:

- FIFO ('first in, first out')
- AVCO (weighted average cost)
- standard cost (if it bears a reasonable relationship to actual costs obtained during the period).

> **Base cost** is 'the calculation of the cost of inventories on the basis that a fixed unit value is ascribed to a pre-determined number of units of inventory ...'

The standard does not accept:

- LIFO ('last in, first out')
- base cost
- replacement cost (unless it provides the best measure of net realisable value and this is less than cost).

Work in progress should be valued at total cost of production.

Prime cost is not acceptable as a basis.

IAS 7 *STATEMENT OF CASH FLOWS*

This topic is dealt with in detail in Chapter Seven.

IAS 8 *ACCOUNTING POLICIES, CHANGES IN ACCOUNTING ESTIMATES, AND ERRORS*

IAS 1 requires companies to include details of specific accounting policies used in the preparation of financial statements. IAS 8 gives more detail. It defines accounting policies as '... the specific principles, bases, conventions, rules and practices applied ... in preparing and presenting financial statements'.

The principles are the concepts that you have already learned (I hope). They apply to all the financial statements that you have prepared in your studies so far. They are the going concern concept, the accruals concept, prudence, consistency and materiality.

The bases are the individual methods of treatment used when applying accounting principles to particular situations – for example, the application of cost value or net realisable value to certain items of inventory.

Accounting bases are selected by directors, eg method of selecting and applying the methods of depreciation to be used in preparing the financial statements.

Where an accounting policy is given in a standard, that policy must be applied. If there is no standard to provide guidance, the directors must use their judgement in selecting a policy to follow, bearing in mind that any information provided in the financial statements should be relevant and reliable.

Accounting policies should be applied consistently in similar situations.

IAS 8 also deals with the effect of errors on financial statements. Once a material error is discovered, it should be corrected in the next set of financial statements by adjusting the comparative figures.

IAS 10 *EVENTS AFTER THE BALANCE SHEET DATE*

These are events that occur after the balance sheet date but before the financial statements are authorised for issue. The events may be:

- adjusting events – this is evidence that certain conditions arose at or before the balance sheet date that have not been taken into account in the financial statements. If the financial implications are material, then changes should be made in the financial accounts before they are authorised. An example is where a customer that owed a material debt at the financial year-end becomes insolvent after the end of the financial year. It would be necessary to make a change to the amount recorded as trade payables.
- non-adjusting events arise after the balance sheet date; no adjustments to the financial statements are necessary. However, if they are material they should be disclosed by way of a note to the accounts. An example would be a large purchase of non-current assets.

Proposed dividends at the financial year-end are non-adjusting events and so are not recorded as a current liability on the balance sheet. They are recorded as a note to the accounts.

See the example of Engary plc, above.

IAS 16 *PROPERTY, PLANT AND EQUIPMENT*

The objective of the standard is to ensure that accounting principles regarding non-current assets are applied consistently and that the company's treatment of the assets is understood by the users of the financial statements.

Property, plant and equipment (PPE) comprises all non-current tangible assets from which economic benefits flow. They are held for more than one time period for use in the production process or the supply of goods and services. Examples would include land and buildings, plant and machinery, office equipment, vehicles etc.

Depreciation is the apportioning of the cost or valuation of an asset over its useful economic life.

Residual value is the amount that the company expects to obtain for an asset less any disposal costs at the end of its useful life.

Fair value is the amount for which an asset could be exchanged between knowledgeable, willing parties in an arm's-length transaction.

Carrying amount is the amount shown on the balance sheet after the deduction of accumulated depreciation or impairment losses.

PPE should initially be valued at cost in the balance sheet. Cost includes expenditure directly attributable to bringing the asset into a usable condition. Costs could include import duties, delivery charges, the costs of preparing the site and other installation costs.

After acquisition of PPE the company must show the carrying amount assets at either:

- cost less accumulated depreciation and impairment losses, or
- revaluation based on fair value less subsequent depreciation and impairment losses (see IAS 36 *Impairment of assets*, below).

Fair values based on the revaluation model for land and buildings would generally be based on market value calculated by professional valuers. In the case of plant and equipment the fair value would usually be based on market value.

DEPRECIATION

The objective of providing depreciation is to reflect the cost of using an asset.

The depreciation for a financial period is shown in the income statement and should reflect the cost of using the asset over the financial period under review. It should reflect the pattern in which the economic benefits derived from the asset are consumed.

When determining the useful life of an asset, several factors should be taken into account:

- the expected use of the asset
- the expected wear and tear on the asset
- economic and technical obsolescence
- legal or similar restraints.

Depreciation policy is not affected by repairs and/or maintenance. However, the residual value and the useful life of the asset are to be reviewed on an annual basis to determine if any change is to be made in the depreciation policy.

Generally, land and buildings should be treated separately since land is not depreciated. It has an infinite economic life, unlike other non-current assets, which have a finite economic life. Note that leasehold land does have a finite life – i.e. the duration of the lease – and should therefore be depreciated.

There is a variety of methods that can be used to calculate the annual depreciation charge. Only two are examined at A level:

- the straight-line method: this charges a constant annual amount over the life of the asset
- the reducing balance method: this charges a decreasing annual amount over the life of the asset.

When the pattern of use of an asset is uncertain, the straight-line method is usually adopted.

Changing the basis of calculating the annual charge is permissible only when the new method gives a fairer representation of the use of the asset. The change must be documented in a note to the financial statements. Any change to methods must be a permanent change.

Derecognition occurs when an asset is disposed of or is incapable of yielding any further economic benefits.

Derecognition means that the asset will no longer be recognised on the balance sheet. If the asset is sold, then the profit or loss on disposal is shown in the profit and loss account.

For each asset the financial statements must show (generally in the notes to the financial statements):

- the basis for determining the carrying amount
- the depreciation method used
- the duration of the useful economic life or the rates of charging depreciation
- the carrying amount
- the accumulated depreciation and impairment losses at the start and end of the accounting period
- a reconciliation of the carrying amount at the start and end of the accounting period that shows:
  - additions
  - disposals
  - revaluations
  - impairment losses
  - depreciation.

IAS 18 *REVENUE*

The standard states that revenue is the fair value of consideration received or receivable, that is, the inflows of economic benefits that arise through the normal activities of the business; they are revenue incomes.

Revenue therefore comprises:

- income derived from the sale of goods
- income from providing a service

- income from royalties
- interest or dividend income etc.

Revenue is recognised when the seller of the goods has transferred to the buyer significant risks and rewards of ownership.

Revenue should only be recorded in the business books of account when the goods have been replaced by a debtor or by cash.

IAS 36 *IMPAIRMENT OF ASSETS*

Recoverable amount is the higher of an asset's fair value (the amount for which it could be sold less selling costs) and its value in use (calculated by discounting all the future cash flows generated by using the asset).

Impairment applies to nearly all non-current assets (at A level it is unlikely that you would be tested on impairment of the exceptions).

Impairment occurs when the recoverable amount is less than the assets carrying amount (the value shown in the balance sheet after deduction of accumulated depreciation).

The values of assets shown on the balance sheet need to be reviewed at each balance sheet date to determine if there is any indication of impairment.

Evidence of impairment could be:

- a significant fall in the market value of the asset
- a significant fall in the value of an asset due to a change in technology
- a significant fall in the value of an asset due to an economic downturn
- a significant fall in the value of an asset due to it being damaged, resulting in the fair value of the asset falling or its future cash-generating ability falling
- a significant fall in the value of an asset due to a restructuring of the business.

An impairment loss is recognised when the recoverable amount is less than the carrying amount. The amount of the loss is to be shown in the income statement.

IAS 37 *PROVISIONS, CONTINGENT LIABILITIES AND CONTINGENT ASSETS*

A **provision** is an amount set aside out of profits for a known expense, the amount of which is uncertain.

A **contingent liability** is a potential liability which exists when the balance sheet is drawn up, the full extent of which is uncertain.

A **contingent asset** is a potential asset which exists when the balance sheet is drawn up. The inflow of economic benefit is uncertain.

The standard seeks to ensure that there is sufficient information given to enable the users of the financial statements to understand the effects of provisions, contingent liabilities and contingent assets.

Provisions are to be recognised as a liability in the financial statements if the company has an obligation because of a past event and it is probable that the obligation requires settlement (ie more than 50% chance of occurrence). It is also necessary that a reliable estimate of the amount of the liability can be made.

Provisions should be detailed in a note to the financial statements.

Contingent liabilities are possible obligations (ie less than a 50% chance of occurrence). If the liability is possible, the contingent liability should be disclosed as a note to the financial statements, but no disclosure is necessary in the main body of the statements. If there is only a remote chance of the occurrence, then no reference needs to be made in either the financial statement or the notes.

Contingent assets are possible assets arising from past events with the possibility that economic benefit could accrue in the future.

If there is a probable economic benefit in the future deriving from the past event, then a note to the financial statements should be made. If the future economic benefits are only possible or remote, no reference needs to be made.

IAS 38 *INTANGIBLE ASSETS*

Intangible assets do not have physical substance. They are identifiable and are controlled by the company. They include licences, quotas, patents, copyrights, franchises, trademarks etc.

Goodwill is not covered in this standard.

Goodwill is the difference between the fair value of the assets and liabilities acquired in the combination and the cost of acquisition. Goodwill must be tested annually for impairment.

IFRS 3 *Business combinations* deals with goodwill. This IFRS is not part of the AQA specification.

Intangible assets are either purchased or internally generated.

Internally generated assets cannot be recognised in the financial statements.

Like PPE, intangible assets are initially shown at cost in the balance sheet.

After acquisition they can be shown at:

■ cost less accumulated depreciation and impairment losses, or
■ revaluation based on fair value less subsequent amortisation and impairment losses.

Revaluations are to be made regularly to ensure that the carrying value does not differ materially from the fair value at the balance sheet date.

Any increase in value should be recognised in the statement of changes in equity and shown as part of any revaluation reserve.

Any reduction in value will be recognised as an expense in the income statement.

An intangible asset with a finite life is amortised over its useful economic life, whereas an intangible asset with an infinite life is not amortised.

Research and development is the exploration of new scientific methods of manufacturing, the results being used to produce an end product. The research can be:

■ pure research, where no end result was foreseen when it was first undertaken, the main aim being to further knowledge in the field
■ applied research directed towards a practical application, eg a cure for cancer.

Development is the application of knowledge gained from research to produce or improve a product or process before it is marketed commercially.

The standard requires that a distinction is made between revenue expenditure and capital expenditure on research.

Revenue expenditure is entered in the income statement, while capital expenditure on non-current assets is recorded as non-current assets and is depreciated over its useful life.

Development costs are treated as an expense in the income statement when they are incurred, or they may be capitalised as an intangible asset if the directors can demonstrate that they can establish the result as an asset that is capable of being used and sold.

Research costs are to be treated as revenue expenditure.

Chapter summary

- International accounting standards provide the basic ground rules by which all accounting records are produced.
- It is important that you know the number and title of each standard.
- You need not know the content of each standard by heart – you just need to understand their broad outlines.
- The broad general principles of each standard must be thoroughly understood so that you can apply them to a variety of business problems.

SELF-TEST QUESTIONS

- Why is there a need for international accounting standards?
- What does IAS 7 deal with?
- Which standard deals with depreciation of non-current assets?
- What does IAS 2 deal with?
- Which standard deals with the treatment of research and development costs?
- Which standard deals with intangible fixed assets?
- Which standard says that financial statements should be understandable?
- Which objective in the preparation of financial statements is missing: relevance, comparability, understandability?
- What is the overriding principle in the valuation of inventories?
- What are the six components of a complete set of financial statements?

TEST QUESTIONS

QUESTION 1

A company has spent £25 million establishing a brand name. The finance director plans to include the brand name as an intangible asset on the next balance sheet. It will be amortised over the next five years.

Required

Comment on the finance director's proposal.

QUESTION 2

Khana plc purchased a machine seven years ago at a cost of £80,000. It has been depreciated to date by £56,000. A new machine has recently been purchased, so the older machine will now only be used as back-up when the new machine needs major maintenance. Khana estimates that the present value of future economic benefits will be £4,000. The old machine could be sold for £5,000.

Required

State the amount to be shown in the balance sheet for the old machine. Justify your valuation.

QUESTION 3

Yew plc recently purchased a new delivery vehicle at a cost of £45,000. The depreciation at the end of the financial year will be £15,000. The vehicle has a trade-in price of £27,500. The directors estimate that the present value of future economic benefits will be £90,000.

Required

State the amount to be shown in the balance sheet for the delivery vehicle. Justify your valuation.

QUESTION 4

Inventories which cost £50,000 can now be replaced for £40,000. The estimated net realisable value of the inventories is £37,500. The directors of Attled plc are to include the inventories in the balance sheet at £37,500.

Required

Comment on the directors' proposed treatment of inventories.

QUESTION 5

Ng, Tripp and Co plc purchased new premises in 1991. The market value of local properties fell for the first five years of ownership, so the directors depreciated the premises. Since 20*8 property prices have risen substantially; the directors propose to revalue the premises and discontinue the practice of depreciating them.

Required

Comment on the directors' proposal.

QUESTION 6

Sadleigh plc has undertaken pure research which has cost £1.3 million this year. It is proposed to capitalise the research since this is such a large amount.

Required

Comment on the proposal.

QUESTION 7

Gougham and Kram plc purchased a piece of machinery costing £560,000 from Switzerland. The transportation costs from Switzerland cost £4,600 and installation costs amounted to £7,400.

The finance director wishes to capitalise £572,000: the whole amount.

The managing director wishes to capitalise £560,000 and include the £12,000 expenses on the profit and loss account.

Required

Advise the board of directors as to which treatment is correct.

QUESTION 8

After preparing the final accounts of Tryodge plc, the directors are disappointed at the level of the profits revealed. They plan to rearrange the way the financial statements are presented, to disguise the poor results.

Required

Comment on the directors' plan.

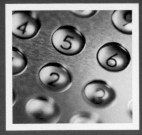

CHAPTER
SIX

The Accounts of Limited Companies

A **limited company** is an organisation that has a legal identity that is separate from that of its owners. The owners of a limited company are called **shareholders** (or members); their liability is limited to the amount that they have agreed to pay the company for their shares.

A limited company can be a very small business, or a giant multinational business with branches and/or subsidiary companies trading throughout the world.

The majority of businesses are sole traders or partnerships. The major drawback of these two types of business is that their owners have unlimited liability.

As we have already seen, a sole trader is responsible for all debts incurred by him or her in the course of running their business.

If Mona, a sole trader, runs up business debts of £25,000, she may have to settle these debts from her private building society account or she may have to sell her house or car to clear the debts. Mona has unlimited liability.

Similarly, if the business partnership of Clint and Dyke has debts of £30,000, both partners are 'jointly and severally responsible' for the debts of the business and between them they may have to raise the money privately to pay off the amount that is owed. Clint and Dyke have unlimited liability.

However, Blinva plc has debts of £345,000. Jemma, a shareholder in the company (she owns 500 ordinary shares of £1 each), could not be asked to contribute further funds in order to help pay off the debts of the company. She could lose her investment but that is all she would lose. Her personal possessions are safe. Jemma has limited liability.

So unlimited liability means that the owners of a business have responsibility for all the debts incurred by their business.

In the vast majority of cases unlimited liability is of little significance. However, if a business is making losses on a regular basis then the continued existence of the business may well be in doubt.

So a major drawback of being a sole trader or a partner in a business is unlimited liability for the owners.

As a consequence of unlimited liability there is another major drawback for unlimited businesses. There are fewer opportunities to find extra capital that may be necessary for an expansion programme. Prospective investors may not wish to take the risk of losing their private assets as well as their investment.

Specification coverage:
AQA ACCN3;
OCR F013.

By the end of this chapter you should be able to:
- prepare a set of final accounts for internal use
- distinguish between different types of shares
- account for and distinguish between different types of reserves
- account for right issues and bonus issues of shares.

THE MAIN FEATURES OF PARTNERSHIPS AND PRIVATE LIMITED COMPANIES

Partnerships	Private limited companies (Ltd)
2–20 partners	At least 1 member, no maximum
Unlimited liability of partners	Limited liability of shareholders
Profits credited to partners' current accounts according to partnership agreement	Profits distributed by dividends
No tax on business profits*	Corporation tax charged on company profits
Partners run the business	Shareholders delegate running of the business to directors
*Partnerships are not taxed on their business profits. The partners pay tax on their earnings as partners.	

THE MAIN FEATURES OF PRIVATE LIMITED COMPANIES AND PUBLIC LIMITED COMPANIES

Private limited companies	Public limited companies
'Ltd' appears after company name	'plc' appears after company name
Minimum of 1 shareholder to the limit of authorised share capital and at least 1 director	Minimum of 2 shareholders to the limit of authorised share capital and at least 2 directors
Share trading restricted	No restriction to share trading
No minimum to issued capital	£50,000 minimum issued capital
No stock market listing	Usually listed on recognised stock market

Private limited companies do not sell their shares to the general public at large, so if a private limited company wishes to raise additional finance through a share issue, the directors must find other people who might be willing to invest in the company.

This is why many private limited companies are often family businesses, with members of the family or close friends owning all the shares.

On the other hand, if the directors of a public limited company wish to raise additional finance, the directors may well advertise the fact in the financial sections of daily newspapers in order that the general public at large may subscribe to the offer.

The advantages of limited liability status and the ability to raise large amounts of finance are offset by certain legal obligations:

- annual accounts must be audited by professionally qualified personnel (this is not the case with partnerships or with sole traders)
- annual returns must be completed and filed with the Registrar of Companies. These filed accounts may be inspected by the general public at Companies House
- companies are regulated by the Companies Act 1985, as amended by the Companies Act 1989
- copies of the company's annual audited accounts must be sent to each shareholder and debenture holder.

All business organisations produce accounts for two main purposes.

Can you remember them? Of course you can.

- Accounts are produced for **management** purposes. The accounts are used by management to highlight areas of good practice and to find areas within the business that could benefit from improvement.
- Accounts are also produced for **stewardship** reasons. The accounts show the providers of finance how the funds that they provided are being used. Are the funds being used wisely or is the finance being squandered?

Under the stewardship umbrella we also find the need to provide accounts that comply with:

- the Companies Act 1985
- accounting standards
- Stock Exchange regulations
- tax legislation.

In this chapter we are going to concentrate on the first of these.

It was pointed out in *Introducing Accounting* that the financial statements prepared for all business organisations are broadly similar.

If the heading was covered over, the set of financial accounts prepared for a limited company would look similar to a set of financial statements prepared for a sole trader.

Who are the users of the final accounts of a limited company?

They include:

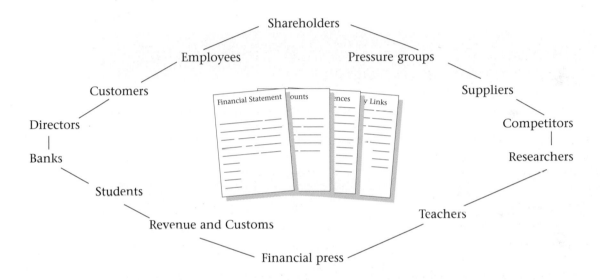

THE INCOME STATEMENT OF A LIMITED COMPANY

Income statements identify gross profit and net profit.

Revenue comprises the receipts from the sales of goods by the company.

Overheads are the expenses incurred by the company during the financial year.

Profit from operations is the profit of the company before deducting finance costs and taxation.

Finance costs comprise interest paid on all debt.

Dividends are the rewards paid to shareholders out of the profits earned by a limited company. The dividends are paid to individual shareholders in proportion to the number of shares they own. Dividends are paid annually, but most limited companies will pay an **interim dividend** half way through their financial year.

Ordinary dividends are variable in nature. The dividend will vary according to the level of profits earned by the company

Preferred dividends are usually a fixed amount. Generally, half of the total dividend is paid as an interim dividend, the balance being paid at the year-end.

Debenture interest is paid to investors who have loaned money to a company. The interest is usually paid in two equal instalments during the year.

Note: These definitions will be expanded later, when shares and debentures are discussed more fully.

Here is an example of an income statement of a limited company:

EXAMPLE

Nedert Ltd
Income statement
for the year ended 31 December 20*9

	£000	£000	Looks
Revenue		3,434	similar
Less Cost of sales			to
Inventories at 1 January 20*9	632		'other'
Purchases	1,578		sets of
	2,210		final
Inventories at 31 December 20*9	(711)	(1,499)	accounts
Gross profit		1,935	so
Overheads			far,
Wages	(451)		doesn't
Other general expenses	(349)		it?
Depreciation	(56)	(856)	
Profit before tax		1,079	
Tax		(223)	
Profit/(loss) for the year		856	

> **Operating profit** is the profit earned by a limited company after deducting all operating expenses but before deducting any interest payable.

Why is it important to identify the operating profit? Consider this simple example.

EXAMPLE

Ken is a sole trader. His wealthy father set him up in business a number of years ago. His business earns a gross profit of £100,000 per annum.

Kath is a sole trader who is in the same business sector as Ken. Their businesses are a similar size. She has no wealthy relatives and she borrowed money from the bank to help finance her business. Her business also earns a gross profit of £100,000 per annum.

Ken's business expenses for the year are £60,000. Kath's business expenses for the year are £70,000 of which £20,000 is interest payments to the bank.

Which of the two business owners runs a more efficient business?

Ken's operating profit is £40,000 while Kath's is £50,000.

If Kath had been blessed with a rich daddy, her profits would have been the greater of the two. She appears to be running her business more efficiently than Ken.

After the deduction of interest payable from the operating profit we have ... profit before taxation.

One other point.

It is usual to group certain types of expenses together. The reason for this is that it makes the production of published accounts easier. We will consider published accounts a little later.

WORKED EXAMPLE

The directors of Treadle plc provide the following information at 31 October 20*9:

	£
Revenue	956,230
Purchases	438,920
Inventories at 1 November 20*8	43,310
Inventories at 31 October 20*9	41,760
Directors' fees	106,900
Salaries – sales personnel	54,970
administrative	67,830
Depreciation – delivery vehicles	54,000
premises	20,000
Other expenses – selling and distribution	31,140
administrative	34,800
Audit fees	23,000
Debenture interest	40,000
Corporation taxation	21,000
Ordinary dividends paid	24,000
Retained earnings at 31 October 20*8	127,600

Required

Prepare an income statement for the year ended 31 October 20*9.

continued ➢

WORKED EXAMPLE *continued*

Answer

Treadle plc
Income statement for the year ended 31 October 20*9

	£	£
Revenue		956,230
Less Cost of sales		
Inventories at 1 November 20*8	43,310	
Purchases	438,920	
	482,230	
Inventories at 31 October 20*9	(41,760)	(440,470)
Gross profit		515,760
Overheads		
Selling and distribution expenses		
Salaries	(54,970)	
Directors' fees	(106,900)	
Other expenses	(31,140)	
Depreciation – delivery vehicles	(54,000)	(247,010)
Administrative expenses		
Salaries	(67,830)	
Audit fees	(23,000)	
Other expenses	(34,800)	
Depreciation – premises	(20,000)	(145,630)
Profit from operations		123,120
Finance costs		(40,000)
Profit before tax		83,120
Corporation tax		(21,000)
Profit for the year		62,120

Statement of changes in equity

	£
Retained earnings at 1 November 20*8	127,600
Profit for the year	62,120
	189,720
Dividends paid	(24,000)
Balance of retained earnings at 31 October 20*9	165,720

Revenue reserves are profits that are retained in the company.

Dividends are the part of the profits of a company that are paid to the shareholders (owners). Any part of the profit that is not paid out to the shareholders as dividends is retained within the company as a revenue reserve.

The portion of the profits retained in the business is sometimes said to be 'ploughed back'. These retained profits may be described on the balance sheet as retained earnings.

All profits (after taxation and preference dividends) belong to the ordinary shareholders (owners), so the amount of profit retained within the company will, generally, have a positive effect on the price of second-hand shares in the (stock) market place.

The retained earnings are a revenue reserve.

Traditionally, many companies transferred part of the retained profits into a general reserve in order to strengthen the financing of the company. These transfers do not often take place nowadays but we will transfer amounts to the general reserve since this procedure is still tested on some occasions.

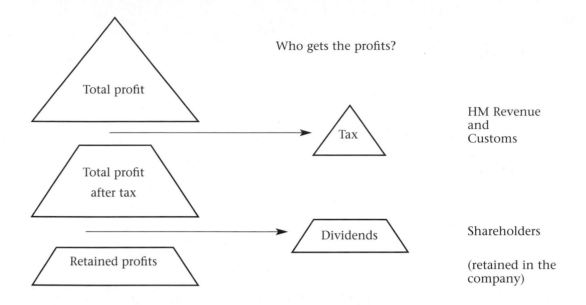

Who gets the profits?

Total profit

Tax → HM Revenue and Customs

Total profit after tax

Dividends → Shareholders

Retained profits

(retained in the company)

WORKED EXAMPLE

The following information is available at 31 March 20*9 for Evahline plc:

Profit before tax	746
Tax	218
Ordinary dividends paid	146
Preferred dividends paid	70
Retained earnings at 1 April 20*8	814

The directors recommend a transfer to general reserve of £60,000.

Required

Prepare

a an income statement extract for the year ended 31 March 20*9
b a statement showing changes in equity.

Answer

Evahline plc
Extract from income statement for the year ended 31 March 20*9

	£000
Profit before tax	746
Tax	(218)
Profit after tax	528
Transfer to general reserve	(60)
Profit for the year	468

Statement of changes in equity

	£000
Retained earnings	
Balance at 1 April 20*8	814
Profit for the year	468
	1,282
Dividends paid	(216)
Balance at 31 March 20*9	1,066

QUESTION 1

The following information is available for Purlin plc at 30 November 20*9:

	£000
Profit before tax	786
Directors' fees	144
Preferred dividends paid	35
Ordinary dividends paid	95
Tax	120
Retained earnings at 1 December 20*8	997

The directors recommend a transfer to general reserve of £100,000.

Required

Prepare

a an income statement for the year ended 30 November 20*9
b a statement showing changes in equity.

QUESTION 2

The following information is available for Vestov and Freaze plc at 28 February 20*9:

	£000
Profit before tax	409
Directors' fees	97
Preferred dividends paid	18
Ordinary dividends paid	46
Tax	88
Retained earnings at 1 March 20*8	704

The directors recommend a transfer to general reserve of £75,000.

Required

Prepare

a an income statement for the year ended 28 February 20*9
b a statement showing changes in equity.

WORKED EXAMPLE

The following information is provided for the year ended 31 December 20*9 for Dohoma plc:

	£000
Sales	3,160
Purchases	211
Inventories: 1 January 20*9	87
31 December 20*9	91
Salaries and general expenses	531
Directors' fees	312
Rent and rates	80
Depreciation of delivery vehicles	75
Salespersons' salaries	612
Advertising	147
Ordinary share dividend paid	200
Preferred share dividend paid	180
Tax	312
Depreciation – office equipment	28
Debenture interest	50
Retained earnings at 1 January 20*9	4,106

Required

Prepare

a an income statement for the year ended 31 December 20*9
b a statement showing changes in equity.

Answer

Dohoma plc income statement for the year ended 31 December 20*9

	£000	£000
Revenue		3,160
Less Cost of sales		
Inventories	87	
Purchases	211	
	298	
Inventories	(91)	207
		2,953
Selling and distribution expenses		
Salaries	(612)	
Advertising	(147)	
Depreciation – delivery vehicles	(75)	(834)
Administration expenses		
Salaries and general expenses	(531)	
Directors' fees	(312)	
Rent and rates	(80)	
Depreciation – office equipment	(28)	(951)
Profit from operations		1,168
Finance costs		(50)
Profit before tax		1,118
Tax		(312)
Profit for the year		806

Statement of changes in equity

	£000
Retained earnings	
Balance at 1 January 20*9	4,106
Profit for the year	806
	4,912
Dividends paid	(380)
Balance at 31 December 20*9	4,532

Note the way that the expenses are categorised. You should be able to tell quite easily which expense goes under which heading.

Make sure that you use the correct labels, eg:

continued ➤

QUESTION 3

The following information is given for Sleerock plc at 31 July 20*9:

	£000
Ordinary dividends paid	70
Preferred dividends paid	40
Sales	757
Purchases	312
Inventories: 1 August 20*8	83
31 July 20*9	74
Selling and distribution expenses	89
Administration expenses	112
Finance costs	36
Tax	39
Retained earnings at 1 August 20*8	844

Required

Prepare

a an income statement for the year ended 31 July 20*9
b a statement of changes in equity.

QUESTION 4

The following information is available for Aromability plc at 31 July 20*9:

	£000
Ordinary dividends paid	210
Preferred dividends paid	120
Sales	2,746
Purchases	1,874
Inventories: 1 February 20*8	163
31 January 20*9	148
Selling and distribution costs	106
Finance costs	45
Tax	135
Retained earnings at 1 February 20*8	1,178

Required

Prepare

a an income statement for the year ended 31 January 20*9
b a statement of changes in equity.

CAPITAL STRUCTURE

A limited company raises capital in order to provide finance for the purchase of the fixed assets (and initially to provide working capital). It raises capital in a variety of ways.

A company can:

- issue shares
- issue debentures
- borrow from financial institutions.

> **Liquidation** is a legal procedure applied to a limited company when it is unable to discharge its liabilities.

> **Nominal value**, also known as the par value, is the face value of shares. Once the shares have been issued, their market price can rise or fall. Any change in the market price is not reflected in the company's books of account.

Shares are divided into:

ORDINARY SHARES

Ordinary shares are the most common type of share. The holders of ordinary shares are part-owners of the company. At meetings in which voting is required, each share has one vote, so ordinary shareholders can appoint the directors and can influence the policies that the directors and managers wish to follow. They may receive a variable dividend in years when the company is profitable. They may receive an interim dividend during the year and a final dividend shortly after the financial year-end.

PREFERRED SHARES

Preferred shareholders are entitled to a fixed dividend (if profits and cash are available). The percentage is calculated on the nominal value of the shares. In the event of a liquidation, the preferred shareholders are entitled to be repaid the nominal value of their shares before the ordinary shares are repaid.

Preferred shares may be **cumulative** or **non-cumulative**. The dividends due on **cumulative** preferred shares will accumulate if the company is unable to pay a dividend in any particular year, eg on 6% cumulative preferred shares for three years, the holder would receive the 18% arrears of dividend in Year 4 if sufficient profits were made. Most preferred shares are cumulative.

If the preferred shares are **non-cumulative**, any dividends not paid are forfeit.

Redeemable preferred shares may be bought back by the company on a specified date. The date is shown on the balance sheet or as a note to the balance sheet.

Debentures are not shares (repeat after me: 'Debentures are not shares'!) – they are bonds recording a long-term loan to a company. The document is evidence of the loan and the holder is entitled to a fixed rate of interest each year. They may be repayable at some future date or they may be irredeemable, that is the holder will be repaid only if the company goes into liquidation.

Some debentures have the loan secured against specific assets or against all the company's assets. These are known as **mortgage debentures**.

If the company is wound up or fails to pay the interest due, the holders of mortgage debentures can sell the assets of the company and recoup any outstanding amounts.

CHARACTERISTICS OF LONG-TERM FINANCE AVAILABLE TO LIMITED COMPANIES

Ordinary shares	Preferred shares	Debentures
Shares	Shares	Long-term loans (Creditor)
Part-owners of company	Not owners	Not owners
Voting rights	(Usually) no voting rights	No voting rights
Paid out last in case of liquidation	Paid out before ordinary shareholders in case of liquidation	Paid out before preferred shareholders in case of liquidation
Dividends	Dividends	Interest
Variable dividend	Fixed dividend	Fixed rate of interest
Part of capital employed	Capital employed	Capital employed

Authorised share capital identifies the amount of share capital that a company is allowed to issue in accordance with its memorandum and articles of association.

Current syllabuses at A Level do not require a detailed knowledge of the book-keeping entries that would be used to record the issue of shares. This technique will be necessary if you continue your studies to a professional level.

Issued share capital is the amount of share capital that has actually been issued by the company. The issued share capital can never exceed the authorised share capital.

Called-up share capital is the amount of issued share capital that the shareholders have been asked to pay to date. It may be less than the value of the issued share capital.

Paid-up capital is the amount of share capital that appears on the balance sheet and is the amount of cash that the company has actually received from the shareholders.

The balance sheet of a limited company is very similar to the balance sheets that you have already prepared many times before. There are differences but if you follow the same pattern that you have previously used, you will soon master the technique again.

There are some important differences in layout and in the accounting terms used. It is very important that you start to learn these differences now.

Equity is the heading covering share capital and reserves.

Non-current assets (formerly known as fixed assets) are assets that are held for more than one financial period. They are not purchased primarily for resale; they are held to help generate profits for the company.

Inventories are goods held for resale, raw materials, components or work in progress held by a company that have not been disposed of during the financial period.

Trade receivables are persons or organisations that owe money to a company.

Trade payables are persons or organisations that are owed money by a company.

Cash and **cash equivalents** comprise cash in hand and other short-term highly liquid investments that can be converted into cash within three months of their acquisition. Bank balances and bank overdrafts are part of cash and cash equivalents.

Current liabilities are short-term debts that a company has to pay within the following accounting period.

Non-current liabilities are longer-term liabilities, i.e. amounts that do not necessarily have to be repaid within the following accounting period.

The 'top' section of a vertical balance sheet for sole traders and partnerships looks like this:

	£000	£000
Non-current (fixed) assets		100
Current assets	30	
Less **Current liabilities**	(10)	20
		120
Non-current liabilities		(50)
		70

Figures are included for illustrative purposes only.

It is only the lower part that looks different:

Sole Trader

	£000
Capital	70

Partnership

		£000	£000
Capital account – Doe			40
Ray			25
			65
Current accounts – Doe		3	
Ray		2	5
			70

The lower part of the balance sheet of a limited company might look like this:

	£000
Equity	
Ordinary shares of £1 each	35
6% Preferred shares of 50p each	25
Reserves	10
	70

Let us look initially at the lower section of a company balance sheet.

The section should be headed 'Equity'.

Examination questions often give figures for authorised share capital. This should be shown somewhere in an answer. In real life the details will generally be shown as a note to the accounts, not actually in the main 'body' of the balance sheet, although legally both methods are acceptable.

● EXAMINATION TIP

Show the authorised share capital at the start of the lower section of the balance sheet; rule it off but do not add it to the remainder of the section.

Both the authorised and issued share capital can have preferred and ordinary shares. Each should be described fully, for example:

Authorised share capital	£m
120,000,000 ordinary shares of £1 each	120.00
1,750,000 7% preferred shares of £1 each	1.75
	121.75
Equity	
Ordinary shares of £1 each	50.00
7% preferred shares of £1 each	1.00

The balance sheet extract shows that the nominal value of each class of share is £1 and that the company could issue 120 million ordinary shares and 1.75 million preferred shares. It further shows that 50 million ordinary shares have actually been issued and 1 million preferred shares have actually been issued.

Any ordinary dividend to be paid will be expressed as a percentage of the nominal value or as an amount per share. So a dividend may be declared as 5% (ie 5% of £1 nominal value) or as an amount of, say, 6.3 pence (ie the holder of 100 shares would receive £6.30 as a dividend).

The preferred shareholder will receive a dividend of 7% (ie 7 pence for every share held).

The issued share capital may be the same as the authorised share capital. If this is the case, it is acceptable to combine the headings so:

Authorised and issued share capital	£
30,000 ordinary shares of £1 each	30,000

Do be very careful when using millions and thousands – many errors are caused when candidates put decimal points in the wrong place, for example:

Correct answer	Wrong answer
£000	£000
30	30
1.6	1,600

Errors like this cost marks. If you are not confident, then write the figures in full, for example:

£
30,000
1,600

RESERVES

The profits earned by a sole trader or by the partners belong to them (the owners) but the profits earned by a limited company belong to the ordinary shareholders (the owners).

Some profits are taken out of the business by the owners as drawings (in the case of a sole trader or partnership) or as dividends (in the case of limited companies). The profit that remains in the business increases the capital structure of the business.

EXAMPLE

	Sole trader	Partnership	Limited company
Profit £26,000	Drawings £12,000	Drawings, say, £8,000 and £4,000	Dividends £12,000
Retained profit	£14,000	£14,000	£14,000
	Part of capital	Part of capital	Part of reserves

RETAINED PROFITS AND RESERVES

Do not say that reserves are cash. Some of the profits will already have been used to replace fixed and other assets.

There are two types of reserves:
- **Revenue reserves** are 'normal' trading profits that have been retained in (ploughed back into) the company. They are debited to the income statement, thus reducing the amount of profits available for dividend purposes.
  Revenue reserves are the most flexible form of reserve. If in the future the revenue reserves are found to be excessive or are unnecessary they can be added back to current profits and used for dividend purposes.
  The revenue reserves can either be set aside for a specific purpose, such as the expansion of the company or replacement of fixed assets, or generally in order to strengthen the financial postion of the company.
  The main revenue reserves that you might encounter are:
  - retained earnings
  - general reserve (less commonly seen in practice nowadays)
  - asset replacement reserve.
- **Capital reserves** arise from capital transactions and adjustments to the capital structure of the company. Since they do not arise through 'normal' trading activities, they are not available for the payment of cash dividends. Any distribution to shareholders of these reserves will take the form of bonus shares.

The three main capital reserves that you might encounter are:

- share premium account
- revaluation reserve
- a capital redemption reserve.

SHARE PREMIUM ACCOUNT

A share premium account arises when a company issues shares at any price that is greater than the nominal value of the shares.

● EXAMINATION TIP

A share premium account only arises when the company issues the shares.

If Maggie sells her £1 shares in Placton plc to Moira for more than the nominal value (or the price that she paid for them) there is no share premium. This is a private financial transaction and will not be recorded in the company's books of account. [Maggie's name will be taken out of the company share register and Moira's name will be included.]

The book-keeping entries are fairly straightforward.

WORKED EXAMPLE

Premsha plc offers 100,000 ordinary shares of 50p each for sale at £1.50 each. All monies were received on application.

Required

Prepare the ledger accounts to record the share issue.

Answer

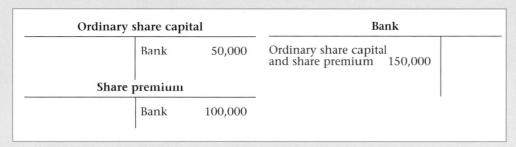

Ordinary share capital			Bank	
	Bank	50,000	Ordinary share capital and share premium	150,000
Share premium				
	Bank	100,000		

More often than not, the ledger accounts will not be required. Candidates may be asked to show the effect on the company balance sheet.

Answer

	£
Current assets	
Bank	+150,000
Equity	
Ordinary shares of 50p each	+50,000
Share premium account	+100,000

A share premium account may be used to:

- pay up unissued shares to issue as bonus shares
- write off preliminary expenses (expenses incurred in the formation of the company)

- write off any expenses incurred in the issue of shares
- provide any premium payable on the redemption of shares or debentures.

> A **revaluation reserve** is created when a fixed asset is revalued in order to reflect an increase in the value of the asset. It ensures that the balance sheet shows the permanent increase in value.

Once again, the book-keeping entries are fairly straightforward.

WORKED EXAMPLE

The summarised balance sheet of Kato plc is shown:

Kato plc
Balance sheet at 31 December 20*9

	£000
Non-current assets at cost	40,000
Net current assets	8,000
	48,000
Equity	
Ordinary shares	25,000
Retained earnings	23,000
	48,000

The directors of the company revalue the non-current assets on 31 December 20*9 at £51,000,000.

Required

Prepare a balance sheet at 31 December 20*9, after revaluation of the fixed assets.

Answer

Kato plc
Balance sheet at 31 December 20*9

	£000	
Non-current assets at valuation	51,000	*(increase of £11 million)*
Net current assets	8,000	
	59,000	
Equity		
Ordinary shares	25,000	
Revaluation reserve	11,000	
Retained earnings	23,000	
	59,000	

The book-keeping entries would be:

Fixed assets

Balance	40,000,000
Revaluation reserve	11,000,000

Revaluation reserve

	Non-current assets	11,000,000

If the non-current asset to be revalued has been depreciated then any depreciation needs to be written off.

WORKED EXAMPLE

Heret plc shows the following accounts:

Premises		Provision for depreciation of premises	
Bal b/d 200,000			Bal b/d 120,000

The directors revalue the premises at £350,000.

Required

Prepare:

a book-keeping entries to record the revaluation of premises
b journal entries to record the revaluation.

Answer

a

Premises			Provision for depreciation of premises			
Bal b/d	200,000		Revaluation reserve	120,000	Bal b/d	120,000
Revaluation reserve	150,000					

Revaluation reserve		
	Premises	150,000
	Depreciation	120,000

b

Premises	150,000	
Provision for depreciation of premises	120,000	
Revaluation reserve		270,000
Revaluation of premises to a value of £350,000.		

A revaluation reserve may be used to pay up unissued shares to issue as bonus shares.

RIGHTS ISSUES AND BONUS ISSUES OF SHARES

Rights issues and bonus issues of shares are frequently mixed up by students. They are frequently the subject of examination questions.

THE CHARACTERISTICS OF A RIGHTS ISSUE AND A BONUS ISSUE

Rights issue	Bonus issue (scrip issue)
Issue is offered to existing shareholders	Issued to existing shareholders
Issue based on present holding	Issue based on present holding
The control of the company does not change; it remains with the existing shareholders	The control of the company does not change; it remains with the existing shareholders
Specified price is usually cheaper than present market price since the company saves on widely advertising the issue and preparing a full prospectus	No charge to shareholders
If shareholder does not wish to exercise his or her right it may be sold to a third party	

Bonus shares are issued when the directors of a company feel that the ordinary share capital account does not adequately reflect the net asset base of the company.

Consider the two scenarios:

Balance sheet many years ago		Balance sheet today	
	£		£
Net assets	800	Net assets	25,000
Equity	800	Equity	800
		Reserves	24,200

You can see that over the years the ordinary share capital has remained unchanged whereas the asset base of the company has increased, with retained revenue reserves and capital reserves.

The directors may redress this imbalance, if the shareholders agree, by transferring some of the balances on reserve accounts to the ordinary share capital account.

Again, the process is fairly straightforward:

Dr Reserve(s) account

    Cr Share capital account.

WORKED EXAMPLE

The following balance sheet is given for Blazet plc:

	£
Net assets	13,000
Ordinary share capital (£1 shares)	4,000
Share premium account	2,000
Retained earnings	7,000

A bonus issue is made on the basis of one new share for every share already held.

It is the directors' policy to maintain reserves in their most flexible form.

Required

Prepare a balance sheet after the bonus issue has been completed.

Answer

Blazet plc
Balance Sheet

	£
Net assets	13,000
Ordinary share capital	8,000
Retained earnings	5,000

Notice that the share premium account has been fully used and the remainder of the issue has come from the retained earnings.

The instruction re 'maintaining the reserves in their most flexible form' means that you should use capital reserves before using revenue reserves.

QUESTION 5

The following balance sheet has been prepared for Typleat plc:

Balance sheet at 28 February 20*9

	£000	£000
Non-current assets		1,836
Current assets	457	
Current liabilities	(349)	108
		1,944
Equity		
Ordinary shares of £1 each		900
Share premium account		450
Retained earnings		594
		1,944

On 28 February 20*9 Typleat plc made a rights issue of 100,000 ordinary shares at a premium of £1 each. Immediately after the rights issue a bonus issue of shares of one ordinary share for every two held was made (the rights issue of shares was eligible for the bonus issue). It is company policy to maintain reserves in their most flexible form.

Required

Prepare a balance sheet at 28 February 20*9, immediately after both share issues.

QUESTION 6

The following balance sheet for Omigosh plc is given:

Balance sheet at 31 October 20*9

	£000	£000
Non-current assets		2,176
Current assets	377	
Current liabilities	(283)	94
		2,270
Equity		
Ordinary shares of £1 each		1,000
Share premium account		500
Revaluation reserve		200
Retained earnings		570
		2,270

On 31 October 20*9 Omigosh plc made a rights issue of 1 million ordinary shares at a premium of £1 each. Immediately after the rights issue the company issued one bonus share for every two ordinary shares held (the rights issue of shares was eligible for the bonus issue). It is company policy to maintain reserves in their most flexible form.

Required

Prepare a balance sheet at 31 October 20*9, immediately after the rights issue and the bonus issue.

At this point it may be as well to highlight the differences between provision, reserves and liabilities.

Provision	Reserves	Liabilities
Amounts set aside out of profits for a known expense the amount of which is uncertain.	Any other amount set aside out of profits.	Amounts owed that can be determined with substantial accuracy.

NON-CURRENT ASSETS

Non-current assets should be shown under three headings:

- **intangible non-current assets** – these are non-physical assets such as goodwill, the ownership of a patent, a licence, a trade mark etc
- **tangible non-current assets** – these are assets that can be seen and touched: examples would include land and buildings, plant and machinery, fixtures and fittings, vehicles etc
- **investments** – like other assets, should be valued at cost. (Remember that these investments are long term, ie over one year. If the investment was for less than one year then it would be classified as a current asset.)

LIABILITIES

Liabilities are classified according to when payment is due.

The long-term liabilities that we encountered earlier in our studies are headed: '**Non-current liabilities**'. These would include debentures, mortgages, bank loans.

Current liabilities would include trade payables, current taxation due, bank overdrafts.

THE PUBLISHED ACCOUNTS OF LIMITED COMPANIES

The AQA Advanced level specification requires candidates to understand the contents of published accounts but candidates are not expected to be able to prepare income statements or balance sheets in a form suitable for publication.

The OCR specification also requires candidates to be able to prepare income statements and balance sheets according to the Companies Act 1985.

The financial statements that a limited company produces have to be used by the directors and managers for decision-making purposes. They need to contain much useful detail. If those same accounts were published in this useful form, competitors might gain access to information that could be used to undermine the company.

The Companies Act 1985 requires every company to send a copy of the company's financial statements to:

- every shareholder
- every debenture holder
- all other persons entitled to receive copies.

The financial statements must be sent not less than 21 days before the Annual General Meeting.

So, although legally the shareholders, lenders and others must be sent a copy of the financial statements, the law protects the company by allowing it to publish an 'abridged' version that contains much less detail.

The financial statements that are published are incorporated into an annual report.

IAS 1 states that a complete set of financial statements must include:

- income statement
- balance sheet
- statement of cash flows

- statement of changes in equity
- explanatory notes on:
  - accounting policies
  - items in the income statement:
    - turnover
    - interest
    - income from investments
    - rent from land
    - amounts payable for the hire of plant and machinery
    - the amount of auditors' expenses paid
    - details of the tax charged in the accounts
    - particulars of staff
    - wages and salaries paid (including the number of high-earning employees)
    - particulars of directors' emoluments
- items in the balance sheet
- a statement from the chairman
- directors' report
- auditors' report.

You may obtain copies of company reports by writing to the registered office of the company or you may visit the company's website.

Try:

- http://www.manutd.com
- http://www.tesco.com
- http://marks-and-spencer.co.uk
- The **notes on accounting policies** will explain the accounting policies used to prepare the accounting statements. It will cover items such as: turnover, depreciation policy, treatment of goodwill etc.
- **Explanatory notes** will show details of the figures published in the profit and loss account, balance sheet and cash flow statement.
- The statement from the chairman will give a brief review of the company's progress over the past years, highlighting sales, profits, dividends etc. It may indicate future developments in the company while evaluating current developments.
- The directors' report will cover a review of the period covered by the accounts, commenting on results and dividend policies. It will outline company employment policy, paying particular attention to equal opportunities and policies on the employment of people with disabilities. It provides a list of directors and their interest in the company, together with any share options. The report itemises political and charitable donations, sets out health and safety policy and provides an insight into future developments for the company.
- The auditors' report is a legal requirement. The report sets out the respective responsibilities of directors and auditors. The report makes a statement on the basis of the audit opinion and then gives an opinion stating whether the financial statements present a 'true and fair view' of the company's activities over the financial period covered by the accounts.

Chapter summary

- A limited company has a legal identity separate from that of its members.
- Shareholders have limited liability. They may receive dividends if the company is profitable and it has sufficient cash to pay the dividend.
- Directors of a company are not its owners. They run the company on behalf of the shareholders.
- Companies raise capital by issuing shares and debentures. Debentures are not part of the share capital.
- Profits are retained within the company in the form of reserves. Revenue reserves are trading profits that have been 'ploughed back' into the company and may be used to pay dividends. Capital reserves arise through capital profits and may not be used to issue dividends.
- Companies must send a copy of the financial statements to all shareholders and debenture holders. These published financial statements are produced in an abridged format in order to protect the company.

SELF-TEST QUESTIONS

- Define limited liability.
- A private limited company could have 35 shareholders. True or false?
- A public limited company could have 3,500 shareholders. True or false?
- Shareholders must own a minimum of 100 shares in order to have a vote at a company's AGM. True or false?
- Gross profit £30,000; administration expenses £10,000; interest payable £8,000. Calculate profit from operations and profit before tax.
- Profit after tax £120,000; transfer to general reserve £20,000; dividends paid £18,000. Calculate profit for the year.
- Explain the difference between revenue reserves and capital reserves.
- Bonus shares can be issued out of revenue reserves. True or false?
- Bonus shares can be issued out of capital reserves. True or false?
- Name one revenue reserve.
- Name one capital reserve.
- Explain the main difference between a rights issue of shares and a bonus issue of shares.

TEST QUESTIONS

QUESTION 7

The directors of Pitcherdy plc provide the following information at 31 December 20*9:

	£000
Ordinary shares of £1 each fully paid	1,000
6% preferred shares of £1 each fully paid	200
Gross profit	746
Administration expenses	124
Selling and distribution expenses	88
Dividends paid – preferred shares	12
ordinary shares	14
Interest paid	36
Retained earnings at 1 January 20*9	1,467

The directors wish the following to be taken into account:

- tax of £160,000 is to be provided on the year's profit
- a transfer of £50,000 to an asset replacement reserve is to be made.

Required

Prepare

a an income statement for the year ended 31 December 20*9
b a statement of changes in equity.

QUESTION 8

The directors of Brocknam plc provide the following information at 31 August 20*9:

	£000
7% preferred shares of £1 each fully paid	400
Ordinary shares of £1 each fully paid	500
Gross profit	1,347
Administration expenses	487
Selling and distribution expenses	391
Dividends paid – preferred shares	28
ordinary shares	32
Interest paid	76
Retained earnings at 1 September 20*9	796

The directors also wish the following to be taken into account:

- tax of £98,000 is to be provided on the profit for the year
- a transfer of £40,000 is to be made to general reserve.

Required

Prepare

a an income statement for the year ended 31 August 20*9
b a statement of changes in equity.

QUESTION 9

The following information is available for Masqik plc at 30 November 20*9:

	£000
Equity	
Ordinary shares of £1 each	1,500
8% preferred shares	400
Share premium account	412
Retained earnings	228
	2,540

On 30 November 20*9 a bonus issue of one ordinary share for every five held was made. It is company policy to maintain reserves in their most flexible form.

Required

Prepare the equity section of the balance sheet at 30 November 20*9, immediately after the share issue.

QUESTION 10

The following balances have been taken from the books of account of YTP plc at 31 January 20*9:

	£000
Ordinary shares of 50 pence fully paid	1,200
6% preferred shares of £1 each	400
Share premium account	600
Retained earnings	452
	2,652

On 31 January 20*9 a bonus issue of one ordinary share for every six held was made. The issue was funded by transferring equal amounts from all reserves.

Required

Prepare the equity section of a balance sheet at 31 January 20*9, immediately after the share issue.

QUESTION 11

The following is a summarised draft balance sheet of Klobule plc at 30 September 20*9:

	£000
Net assets (including bank)	2,973
Equity	
Ordinary shares of 25 pence	1,390
Share premium account	450
Retained earnings	1,133
	2,973

On 30 September 20*9 an issue of 1,000,000 ordinary shares was made at 40 pence per share.

Required

Prepare a summarised balance sheet at 30 September 20*9, immediately after the issue of shares.

QUESTION 12

The summarised draft balance sheet at 28 February 20*9 for Potyiat plc is shown:

	£000
Net assets (including bank)	2,450
Equity	
Ordinary shares of 50 pence each	1,600
Share premium account	340
Retained earnings	510
	2,450

On 28 February 20*9 an issue of 500,000 ordinary shares was made at 60 pence per share.

Required

Prepare a summarised balance sheet at 28 February 20*9, immediately after the share issue.

QUESTION 13

The following summarised balance sheet at 31 July 20*9 is available for Ardbeck plc:

	£000
Net assets	2,050
Equity	
Ordinary shares of 10 pence each	900
Share premium account	850
Retained earnings	300
	2,050

On 1 August 20*9 the net assets were revalued at £2,500,000.

After the revaluation, a bonus issue of ordinary shares was made, of one new share for every one already held. The issue was funded by transferring equal amounts from all capital reserves.

Required

Prepare a summarised balance sheet at 1 August 20*9, after all the above transactions have been taken into account.

QUESTION 14

The following summarised balance sheet at 31 August 20*9 is available for Harmark plc:

	£000
Net assets	4,250
Equity	
Ordinary shares of £5 each	2,000
Share premium account	1,100
Retained earnings	1,150
	4,250

On 1 September 20*9 the net assets were revalued at £5,000,000.

A bonus issue of one ordinary share for every four held was made. Equal amounts were transferred from all capital reserves.

Required

Prepare a summarised balance sheet at 1 September 20*9, after the above transactions have been taken into account.

QUESTION 15

The following balance sheet extract has been prepared at 31 March 20*9 for McTavish-Jones plc:

	£000
Equity	
Ordinary shares of £1 each	600
6% preferred shares of £1 each	120
Share premium account	130
Revaluation reserve	50
Retained earnings	238
	1,138

1. On 1 April 20*9 the company increased its ordinary share capital by an issue of bonus shares, one bonus share being issued for every three ordinary shares held. It is company policy to maintain reserves in their most flexible form.
2. On 2 April 20*9 a rights issue was made whereby all shareholders (including preferred shareholders) subscribed for five ordinary shares at £2.50 for every three shares of either class held. Bonus shares were excluded from the issue. The full amount was received on 2 April 20*9.

No other transactions took place.

Required

An extract from the balance sheet at 2 April 20*9, showing the equity section of the balance sheet.

QUESTION 16

The following is an extract taken from the balance sheet at 31 January 20*9 for Arkwright-Thoms plc:

	£000
Equity	
Ordinary shares of 25 pence each	200
7% preferred shares of £1 each	60
Share premium account	260
Asset replacement reserve	45
Retained earnings	345
	910

The following transactions took place on 1 February 20*9:

1. One bonus share was issued for every five ordinary shares held. It is company policy to maintain reserves in their most flexible form.
2. Both ordinary shareholders and preferred shareholders subscribed for one ordinary share for every share held (excluding bonus shares). 40 pence per share was received.

No other transactions took place.

Required

Prepare a balance sheet extract at 1 February 20*9, showing the equity section of the balance sheet.

QUESTION 17

Omerdoh plc has prepared the following draft balance sheet at 31 December 20*9:

	Cost £	Depreciation £	Net book value £
Non-current assets			
Premises	240,000	66,000	174,000
Equipment	86,000	56,000	30,000
Vehicles	112,000	84,000	28,000
	438,000	206,000	232,000
Current assets			
Inventories		64,000	
Trade receivables		47,000	
Cash and cash equivalents		51,000	
		162,000	
Current liabilities			
Trade payables		(21,000)	141,000
			373,000
Equity			
Ordinary shares of £1 each			300,000
Share premium account			40,000
Retained earnings			33,000
			373,000

No entries have been made in the final accounts for the following:

1. A bonus issue of one ordinary share for every five ordinary shares held was made in October 20*9. The share premium account was utilised for the issue.
2. On 31 December 20*9 the premises were revalued at £250,000.
3. Included in the inventory held at 31 December 20*9 was obsolete inventory with a cost value of £5,000. The inventory can only be sold for scrap at £1,000.
4. During August a vehicle that had cost £36,000 was involved in a road accident and had to be written off. The vehicle had a net book value of £9,000. The insurance company paid £7,000 in compensation for the loss.

Required

Prepare the balance sheet at 31 December 20*9 after taking notes 1–4 into account.

QUESTION 18

The following balance sheet has been prepared at 1 February 20*9 for Lisamarg plc:

	£000	£000
Non-current assets		
Land and buildings		650
Other fixed assets		215
		865
Current assets including bank balance	400	
Current liabilities	(120)	280
		1,145
Equity		
Ordinary shares of 25 pence each		500
4% preferred shares £1 each		400
Share premium account		70
Retained earnings		175
		1,145

The following transactions took place in February 20*9:

1. On 2 February 20*9 a rights issue of one ordinary share for every five shares of any class held was made at £1 per share. All shareholders took up their rights.
2. Land and buildings were revalued at £750,000 on 14 February 20*9.
3. On 20 February 20*9 a bonus issue was made of one ordinary share for every four held this was made by utilising the share premium account.

No other transactions took place during February 20*9.

Required

Prepare a balance sheet at 28 February 20*9 after the transactions in notes 1–3 are taken into account.

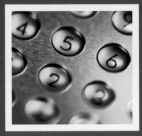

CHAPTER
SEVEN

Statement of Cash Flows – IAS 7

Throughout this chapter, reference will be made to companies. All but the smallest limited companies are required to prepare a cash flow statement.

Even though small companies, sole traders and partnerships do not have to produce a cash flow statement, they may find it in their best interests to prepare one.

IAS 7 requires that companies prepare a statement of cash flows in the format described in the standard.

It provides the following standard headings:

- operating activities
- investing activities
- financing activities.

Where different categories appear under the same heading, they must be shown separately.

The standard requires an adjustment to operating profit to calculate the cash flow from operating activities.

So, the cash flow statement should include all inflows and outflows involving cash. Any transactions that do not involve cash should not appear in the statement.

USES OF CASH FLOW STATEMENTS

The income statements concentrate on the determination of profits or losses over a period of time, since profits should ensure the long-term survival of the company. The balance sheet concentrates on the position of the company at a particular moment in time.

Cash flow statements:

- concentrate on cash inflows and cash outflows since cash is important for the short-term survival of all businesses
- reveal information that is not disclosed in the income statements. This helps in financial planning
- provide information that enables users to assess the efficiency (or inefficiency) or how cash and cash equivalents have been used during the year
- provide information that helps to assess the liquidity, viability and financial adaptability of the company
- allow comparisons to be made year on year or inter-firm. This is facilitated by a prescribed format (although a cash flow statement is a historical document (ie it is prepared using the figures from the last financial year)
- help to provide information that will assist in the projection of future cash flows.

We shall concentrate initially on the calculation of the figures to be used in a cash flow statement. We will then categorise the cash flows under the appropriate headings.

THE CALCULATIONS

Cash is money in notes and coins and deposits that are repayable on demand.

Cash equivalents are short-term investments that are convertible into cash without notice. They have less than three months to run when acquired. Overdrafts repayable in less than three months are deducted from cash equivalents.

In most examinations, information will be given in the form of two balance sheets; one prepared at the beginning of the financial year and one prepared at the end of the financial year. This is known as the **indirect method**.

The technique used to find cash flows is to compare the two sets of information.

WORKED EXAMPLE

The following balance sheets are available:

Bursil plc
Balance sheets at

	31 March 20*9		31 March 20*8	
	£000	£000	£000	£000
Non-current assets				
Premises at cost	11,377		7,065	
Less Depreciation	3,967	7,410	(3,112)	3,953
Machinery at cost	4,413		3,789	
Less Depreciation	(1,736)	2,677	(1,351)	2,438
Vehicles at cost	1,657		1,657	
Less Depreciation	(1,176)	481	(763)	894
		10,568		7,285
Current assets				
Inventory	918		734	
Trade receivables	323		330	
Cash and cash equivalents	145		112	
	1,386		1,176	
Current liabilities				
Trade payables	(338)		(312)	
Tax liabilities	(652)		(609)	
	(990)		(921)	
Net current assets		396		255
		10,964		7,540
Equity				
Issued share capital		3,850		2,570
Share premium account		2,375		1,735
Retained earnings		4,739		3,235
		10,964		7,540

Note:

1. No interim dividends have been paid during the year.
2. There have been no disposals of fixed assets during the year.

Required

Prepare a statement to identify the cash inflows and cash outflows.

Answer

Each calculation is done in turn, identifying the cash inflow or outflow. The summary appears at the end, when all the calculations have been completed. We are going to systematically take each item on the balance sheet and compare the opening figure with the closing figure. Any difference in the two figures will be because of a cash movement (with one notable exception!).

Premises on the first day of the financial year had cost £7,065,000; on the last day of the year the figure has risen to £11,377,000. Bursil plc must have purchased some additional premises during the year, at a cost of £4,312,000. The purchase must have entailed cash leaving the company. **Cash outflow £4,312,000.**

The next item on our way down the balance sheet is **depreciation of premises**.

Let us consider depreciation and how it affects cash. (Do you remember that in *Introducing Accounting* we said that depreciation does not have a direct influence on cash flows? – no one appears at my front door demanding that I pay the depreciation on my car or television set!)

To help clarify the situation, consider the following:

WORKED EXAMPLE *continued*

Dougie is a trader who deals only in cash.

During one particular week, Dougie drives his van to Manchester and purchases £400 worth of jeans and sells them over the next couple of days for £600.

He prepares his revenue account.
It looks like this:

His bank account would also show:

	£		£
Sales	600		
Less Purchases	(400)	Income from sales	600
	200	*Less* Cheque for jeans	(400)
Petrol	35	Cheque for petrol	(35)
Profit	165	Balance	165

Dougie's cash and profit are the same!

However, as an A Level accounting student, you explain to Dougie that the 'matching' concept required him to include the value placed on the use of any assets used to generate his profit. He should include in his revenue account an amount for the use of his van (ie depreciation on his van). You suggest £20.

His redrafted revenue statement now shows:

	£
Sales	600
Less Purchases	(400)
	200
Less Petrol	(35)
Less Depreciation	(20)
Profit	145

His profit now no longer matches his cash flow.

How can we reconcile the two figures?

We can reconcile the two figures by adding the depreciation charged to the profit and loss account to the profit figure.

Profit £145 + depreciation of van £20 = £165, which agrees with the bank balance.

So, in order to calculate any cash flows for the year, depreciation charges should be added to the net profit for the year.

Depreciation on premises at the start of the year is £3,112,000; at the end of the year it is £3,967,000. Change for the year is £855,000.

Although this is not really a cash inflow, we treated it as such, as we did with Dougie.

To be added to the **cash inflows: £855,000** for depreciation of premises.

The depreciation charged to the income statement for the other two non-current assets should be treated in the same way.

continued ➤

WORKED EXAMPLE *continued*

Add to cash inflow: ■ £385,000 for depreciation of machinery and
■ £413,000 for depreciation of vehicles.

Machinery purchased during the year amounted to £624,000.

Would this cause cash to flow out of the business or cash to flow into the business?

That's right, it is a cash outflow. **Cash outflow £624,000.**

There has been no change in the cost of vehicles during the year. As far as we can tell, no purchases have been made.

During the year, **inventories** have increased by £184,000.

In order to increase inventories, a cash outflow has to take place. **Cash outflow £184,000.**

Trade receivables at the start of the year were £330,000. At the end of the year the amount was £323,000, so trade receivables have fallen by £7,000. This is because of a net cash inflow. **Cash inflow £7,000.**

The next item, ie **cash and cash equivalents**, are overlooked at the moment. Why?

They are ignored because we are trying to amass information to explain why there is a change to the balance over the year.

Trade payables at the start of the year were owed £312,000. One year later they were owed £338,000. They have increased by £26,000. This increase in trade payables can be used to finance the company's activities and is therefore an inflow. **Cash inflow £26,000.**

We can see that at the end of the year Bursil plc owed **Revenue and Customs** £652,000. This amount has been entered in the company's income statement – it has reduced the year's retained earnings but it will not be paid to the tax authorities for some time yet. (This is why it appears as a current liability.) It has reduced the profit but has not yet become a cash outflow. This amount needs to be added back to the profit as a cash inflow. **Cash inflow £652,000.**

In last year's cash flow statement the same adjustment was made for tax. But last year's amount owed will have been paid in the year covered by the cash flow statement.

So:

Cash outflows for:

■ tax £609,000

The **issued share capital** has increased by £1,280,000. The company has made a further issue of shares during the year. **Cash inflow £1,280,000.**

The **share premium** has increased by £640,000. The new issue of shares has clearly been issued at a premium of 50% on nominal value. **Cash inflow £640,000.**

Finally, **retained earnings** increased by £1,504,000; the amount of unappropriated profit ploughed back into the company. **Cash inflow £1,504,000.**

A summary of all the differences deduced would look like this:

Cash inflows	£000	Cash outflows	£000
Depreciation: premises	855	Purchase of premises	4,312
machinery	385	Purchase of machinery	624
vehicles	413	Increase in inventories	184
Decrease in trade receivables	7	Tax paid	609
Increase in trade payables	26		
Tax owed	652		
Share issue	1,280		
Premium on share issue	640		
Profits	1,504		
	5,762		5,729

WORKED EXAMPLE *continued*

So you can see that, according to our calculations, Bursil plc received £33,000 more cash than it spent during the year.

This should be reflected in the cash and cash equivalent balances held by the company at the end of the year compared with those it held at the start of the year.

	£000
Net increase/(decrease) in cash and cash equivalents	33
Cash and cash equivalents at beginning of year	112
Cash and cash equivalents at end of year	145

QUESTION 1

The following information is available for Rao plc:

Rao plc
Balance sheets at 31 January

	£000	20*9 £000	£000	£000	20*8 £000	£000
Non-current assets			1,546			962
Current assets						
Inventories		159			146	
Trade receivables		198			212	
Cash and cash equivalents		46			39	
		403			397	
Current liabilities						
Trade creditors		(171)			(162)	
Tax		(123)			(108)	
		(294)	109		(270)	127
			1,655			1,089
Equity						
Share capital			600			500
Share premium			400			100
Retained earnings			655			489
			1,655			1,089

Required

Prepare a table showing cash inflows and cash outflows for the year ended 31 January 20*9.

QUESTION 2

The following information is given:

Rabadia plc
Balance sheets at 30 November

	£000	20*9 £000	£000	£000	20*8 £000	£000
Non-current assets			1,010			830
Current assets						
Inventories		486			479	
Trade receivables		318			337	
Cash and cash equivalents		104			86	
		908			902	
Current liabilities						
Trade payables		(230)			(246)	
Tax		(86)			(92)	
		(316)	592		(338)	564
			1,602			1,394
Equity						
Ordinary share capital			800			800
Retained earnings			802			594
			1,602			1,394

Required

Prepare a table showing cash inflows and cash outflows for the year ended 30 November 20*9.

EXAMPLE OF TRANSACTIONS THAT RESULT IN CASH INFLOWS AND OUTFLOWS

Cash inflows	Cash outflows
Profits	Losses
Interest received	Interest paid
Investment income received	
Dividends received	Dividends paid
Tax refund	Taxation paid
Sale of non-current assets	Purchase of non-current assets
Decrease in inventory	Increase in inventory
Decrease in trade receivables	Increase in trade receivables
Increase in trade payables	Decrease in trade payables
Increase in share capital	Redemption of share capital
Increase in debentures	Redemption of debentures
Increase in long-term loans	Repayment of long-term loans

IAS 7 requires that cash flows should be analysed under the following three headings:

- operating activities
- investing activities
- financing activities.

Some students learn the headings by remembering the capital letters of the first words as 'OIF' or by using a mnemonic such as 'Oprah's in France'.

It is important that you memorise the headings and use them each time you prepare a cash flow statement using IAS 7.

> A **reconciliation of operating profit** to cash flows from operating activities seeks to calculate the actual cash generated through the operating activities of the company.

The operating profit is adjusted for movements in inventory, trade receivables and trade payables as well as for non-cash items included in the income statement. The non-cash items are: annual provision for depreciation charges; annual provision for doubtful debts charges; and any profits or losses on the disposal of non-current assets. They should be clearly identified and shown separately.

> **Net debt** is borrowings less liquid resources.

> The **reconciliation of the movement in cash to the movement in net debt** shows all the cash flows (from the cash flow statement) that affect the net debt position. It includes changes in cash debt and liquid resources. It reconciles the net debt at the beginning of the year with the net debt at the end of the year.

The headings:

OPERATING ACTIVITIES

Cash flows from operating activities are the cash inflows and outflows resulting from operating or trading activities. They are calculated by using figures from the income statement and by comparing consecutive years' balance sheets.

The calculation is done using the profit from operations (that is, profit for the year before deduction of tax and interest).

Add depreciation for the year.

Add loss on sales of non-current assets.

Less profit on sales of non-current assets.

Less income from investments.

Add decrease in inventory.

Less increase in inventory.

Add decrease in trade receivables.

Less increase in trade receivables.

Add increase in trade payables.

Less decrease in trade receivables.

These adjustments from the profit from operations gives the cash (used in)/from operations.

Two further adjustments are required.

Less interest paid during the year.

Less tax paid during the year.

The result is the net cash (used in)/from operating activities.

INVESTING ACTIVITIES

Cash flows resulting from the disposal and acquisition of non-current assets

Cash **inflows** include receipts from the sale of disposal of all types of non-current assets.

Cash **outflows** include payments to acquire all types of non-current assets.

FINANCING ACTIVITIES

Cash flows resulting from receipts or payments from and to external providers of finance.

Cash **inflows** include receipts from a share issue or an issue of debentures; also receipts from other long-term borrowings (but not overdrafts).

Cash **outflows** include dividends paid and payments to redeem shares; and repayment of long-term loans.

There are a number of tricky areas involved in the preparation of the cash flow statement.

CALCULATION OF PROFIT FROM OPERATIONS

Profit from operations is the net profit before tax and interest.

WORKED EXAMPLE

The following information is given for Blodkins plc:

	£000
Profit before tax	713
Debenture interest paid	40

Required

Calculate the profit from operations.

continued ➤

Answer

Profit from operations = £753,000 (713,000 + 40,000).

The following information is given for the year ended 31 July 20*9 for Edcor plc:

	£000
Profit before tax (interest paid 60)	212
Tax	70

Required

Prepare an extract from the income statement showing clearly profit from operations, profit before tax, profit after tax and profit for the year.

Answer

Edcor plc		
Income statement for the year ended 31 July 20*9		
	£000	£000
Operating profit		272
Interest paid		(60)
Profit before tax		212
Tax		(70)
Profit for the year		142

In many questions an income statement extract is not given and it has to be reconstructed from the available information.

The following extracts are taken from the balance sheet of Ocset plc at 31 December:

	20*9 £000	20*8 £000
Current liabilities		
Tax	(120)	(168)
Equity		
Ordinary shares	2,500	2,500
General reserve	400	350
Retained earnings	1,662	1,346

During the year ended 31 December 20*9 debenture interest amounting to £78,000 was paid. Dividends amounting to £150,000 were paid.

Required

Calculate the operating profit for the year ended 31 December 20*9.

Answer

	£000	£000
Increase in profit over year		316
Add Provision for tax 20*9	120	
Debenture interest paid	78	198
Profit from operations		714

An extract from the income statement would have shown:

Income statement extract for the year ended 31 December 20*9

	£000
Profit from operations	714
Less Debenture interest	(78)
Profit before tax	636
Tax	(120)
Profit for the year	516

Statement of changes in equity

	£000
Retained earnings	
Balance at 1 January 20*9	1,346
Profit for the year	516
	1,862
Dividends paid	(150)
Transfer to general reserve	(50)
Balance at 31 March 20*9	1,662
General reserve	
Balance at 1 January 20*9	350
Transfer for the year	50
Balance at 31 December 20*9	400

QUESTION 3

The following information is given for McGarry & Coary plc at 31 March:

	20*9 £000	20*8 £000
Current liabilities		
Tax	112	130
Equity		
Ordinary shares	1,200	1,000
General reserve	120	100
Retained earnings	1,596	1,372

During the year ended 31 March 20*9 interest paid was £27,000. Dividends amounting to £80,000 were paid.

Required

Calculate the profit from operations for the year ended 31 March 20*9.

QUESTION 4

The following information is given for Neal, Harrison & Co Ltd at 30 November:

	20*9 £000	20*8 £000
Current liabilities		
Tax	245	260
Equity		
Ordinary shares	1,700	1,700
8% preferred shares	500	500
General reserve	400	300
Retained earnings	1,849	1,783

During the year ended 30 November 20*9:

- preferred dividends amounting to £40,000 were paid
- ordinary dividends amounting to £110,000 were paid.

Required

Calculate the profit from operations for the year ended 30 November 20*9.

CALCULATION OF THE ANNUAL PROVISION FOR DEPRECIATION OF NON-CURRENT ASSETS

In some cases, the calculation of the provision for depreciation of non-current assets is straightforward. It involves comparing the aggregate depreciation at the start of the year with the aggregate depreciation at the end of the year.

WORKED EXAMPLE

The following extracts have been taken from the balance sheets of Beta and Biga Ltd:

	31 July 20*9		31 July 20*8	
	£000	£000	£000	£000
Non-current assets				
Premises	2,500		2,500	
Less Depreciation	1,850	650	1,800	700
Machinery	1,830		1,830	
Less Depreciation	1,281	549	1,098	732
Office equipment	611		611	
Less Depreciation	369	242	308	303
Vehicles	1,100		1,100	
Less Depreciation	855	245	630	470

Required

Calculate the provision for depreciation for the year ended 31 July 20*9 for each asset.

Answer

	£
Provision for depreciation – Premises	50,000
Machinery	183,000
Office equip.	61,000
Vehicles	225,000

Clearly, examiners may make the calculations a little more difficult (they often do!).

In other cases the calculation of the annual provision for depreciation of fixed assets is less straightforward.

CALCULATION OF CASH FLOWS RESULTING FROM THE DISPOSAL OF NON-CURRENT ASSETS (DERECOGNITION)

WORKED EXAMPLE

The following is an extract from the balance sheets of Neps plc at 30 April 20*9:

	20*9	20*8
	£000	£000
Non-current assets at cost	2,573	2,332
Less Depreciation	1,238	1,021
	1,335	1,311

During the year ended 30 April 20*9, non-current assets which had cost £720,000 had been sold for £274,000. The assets sold had been depreciated by £433,000.

Required

Identify any cash flows resulting from the sale of non-current assets.

Answer

Using 'T' accounts, we can gain a complete picture of the transactions involved in the problem.

Journal entries are given to help you with the timing of the entries:

Non-current assets

May 20*8 Balance b/d	2,332	Disposal	720
Missing figure	_____	Balance c/d	2,573
			3,293
May 20*9 Balance b/d	2,573		

Depreciation of non-current assets

Disposal	433	1 May 20*8 Balance b/d	1,021
1 May 20*9 Balance c/d	1,238	Missing figure	_____
	1,671		
		1 May 20*9 Balance b/d	1,238

Disposal of non-current assets

Non-current asset	720	Depreciation of non-current asset	433
		Bank	274
		Income statement	13
	720		720

	Dr	Cr
Disposal of non-current assets	720,000	
Non-current assets		720,000

Non-current assets are removed from the non-current asset account and are entered in the disposal account.

continued ➤

| Depreciation of non-current assets | 433,000 | |
| Disposal of non-current assets | | 433,000 |

Depreciation 'belonging' to the asset is taken from the depreciation account and entered in the disposal account.

| Bank (not shown) | 274,000 | |
| Disposal of fixed asset | | 274,000 |

The cash inflow is entered in the disposal account.

At this point we need to insert a missing figure £13,000. So:

| Income statement | 13,000 | |
| Disposal | | 13,000 |

The 'loss' made on disposal is entered in the income statement. It is **not** cash but it has been entered in the income statement as an extra expense – it reduces profit but **no** cash has moved!

Enter the closing balances given in the question.

Enter them under the account and take them back diagonally into the account.

Add the non-current asset account and the depreciation account. They will not add unless you put in the two missing figures. The missing figure in the non-current asset account must be either a revaluation or the purchase of further non-current assets. A revaluation has not been mentioned so the missing figure must be non-current assets purchased during the year: a cash outflow of £961,000.

To make the depreciation account balance, this year's charge to the income statement must be inserted, so £650,000 is the amount to be entered in the account and in the income statement.

The profit is reduced by £650,000 but **no** cash has moved.

Both the loss on disposal £13,000 and the depreciation for the year of £650,000 have reduced profit but no cash has moved.

Both have to be added back on to our operating profit to arrive at the cash flow, just like the depreciation on Dougie's van in an earlier example.

QUESTION 5

The following information has been extracted from Kelly plc:

	Balance sheet at 31 August	
	20*9	20*8
	£000	£000
Non-current assets at cost	2,490	2,160
Less Depreciation	910	830
	1,580	1,330

During the year ended 31 August 20*9 non-current assets costing £850,000, which had been depreciated by £610,000, had been sold for £170,000.

Required

Identify all entries that should be made in a cash flow statement for the year ended 31 May 20*9.

QUESTION 6

The following information is available for Kai Hong plc:

Balance sheet extract at	31 December 20*9	31 December 20*8
	£000	£000
Non-current assets	1,346	978
Less Depreciation	488	394
	858	584

During the year ended 31 December 20*9 non-current assets that had cost £400,000 were sold for £82,000. The assets had been depreciated by £320,000.

Required

Identify all entries that should be made in a cash flow statement for the year ended 31 December 20*9.

TREATMENT OF A REVALUATION OF NON-CURRENT ASSETS

A revaluation of non-current assets will clearly have an impact on the balance sheet of the company. However, since such a revaluation is merely a book entry, there will be no movement of cash, so there will be no entry in a cash flow statement.

TREATMENT OF A BONUS ISSUE OF SHARES

Again, such transactions will impact on the balance sheet of the company but will not cause any movement in cash balances. The book entry to record the issue of share will not be shown in a statement of cash flows.

Both revaluations and bonus issues give many candidates problems. Many candidates include them in their answers to cash flow problems.

Don't be one of those candidates!

WORKED EXAMPLE

The directors of Tomkins Smyth & Co plc provide the following balance sheets at 31 May:

	£000	31 May 20*9 £000	£000	31 May 20*8 £000
Non-current assets (Note 1)				
Land and buildings		23,970		18,215
Machinery		1,990		3,370
Vehicles		950		1,050
Investments		6,000		5,050
		32,910		27,685
Current assets				
Inventories	2,000		1,730	
Trade receivables	950		550	
Cash and cash equivalents	183		278	
	3,133		2,558	
Current liabilities				
Trade payables	(1,175)		(1,007)	
Tax	(420)		(380)	
	(1,595)		(1,387)	
Net current assets		1,538		1,171
Total assets less current liabilities		34,448		28,856
Non-current liabilities				
8% debenture stock		(1,200)		(1,200)
		33,248		27,656
Equity				
Called-up ordinary share capital		12,600		12,100
Share premium account		6,150		4,650
Revaluation reserve		3,200		
Retained earnings (Note 2)		11,298		10,906
		33,248		27,656

continued ➤

Notes to the balance sheet

Note 1 Non-current assets

	31 May 20*9 £000	31 May 20*8 £000
Land and buildings		
Cost	31,020	27,815
Revaluation	3,200	
Depreciation to date	(10,250)	(9,600)
	23,970	18,215
Machinery		
Cost	?	6,500
Depreciation to date	?	(3,130)
Net book value	?	3,370
Vehicles		
Cost	1,750	1,650
Depreciation to date	(800)	(600)
Net book value	950	1,050

During the year ended 31 May 20*9 machinery which had originally cost £1,200,000 was sold for £750,000. The depreciation charge on this machinery up to 31 May 20*8 was £480,000. No additions to machinery were made during the year ended 31 May 20*9.

There were no disposals of land, buildings or vehicles during the year ended 31 May 20*9.

Note 2

The summarised income statement for the year ended 31 May 20*9 was as follows (note: a changes in equity statement has not been used):

	£000
Net profit before tax	1,112
Provision for corporation tax	420
Net profit after tax	692
Dividends – paid	300
Profit for year	392

Required

Prepare a statement of cash flows for the year ended 31 May 20*9, using the IAS 7 format.

Answer

Workings

Land and buildings				Depreciation			Cash flow statement	
	27,815				9,600		650	(3,205)
	3,200			10,250	650	MF		
MF	3,205	34,220	MF	10,250	10,250			
	34,220	34,220			10,250			
	34,220							

Revaluation reserve

	3,200

Disposal of machinery

1,200	480
30	750
1,230	1,230

Machinery

6,500	1,200
	5,300
6,500	6,500
5,300	

Depreciation

480	MF	3,130
3,310		660
3,790		3,790
		3,310

Cash flow statement

750	
660	(30)

Net book value at end £5,300 − depreciation = £1,990.

So, balance on depreciation account at year end = £3,310.

Vehicles

MF	1,650	1,750
	100	1,750
	1,750	
	1,750	

Depreciation

800		600
800	MF	200
		800
		800

Cash flow statement

200	(100)

Investments

MF	5,050	6,000
	950	6,000
	6,000	
	6,000	

Cash flow statement

	(950)

Increase in inventories	(270)
Increase in trade receivables	(400)
Increase in trade payables	168
Tax (last year's tax paid this year)	(380)
Dividends paid	(300)
Debenture interest (You might have to deduct debenture interest. The interest paid might be given in the question – or it might not be given, as in this example.) 8% of £1,200,000 = £96,000	(96)
Increase in share capital	500
Increase in share premium	1,500
Revaluation reserve	No movement of cash
Operating profit (profit before tax + interest £1,112,000 + £96,000)	1,208
All these changes should equal the change in the cash at bank and in hand balances	5,636 5,731

Change in cash balances £95,000.

Change in cash flows £5,636 − £5,731 = (£95,000)

Decrease in cash during period	95

We now have all the information needed to prepare our cash flow forecast. Take the figures from your workings and insert them under the correct headings. (Remember Oprah!)

continued ➤

Tomkins Smyth & Co plc
Cash flow statement for the year ended 31 May 20*9

	£000	£000
Operating profit		1,208
Depreciation charges for year		
Land and buildings	650	
Machinery	660	
Vehicles	200	1,510
Profit on disposal of machinery		(30)
Increase in inventories		(270)
Increase in trade receivables		(400)
Increase in trade payables		168
Cash (used in)/from operating activities		2,186
Interest paid		(96)
Income tax paid		(380)
Net cash (used in)/from operating activities		1,710
Cash flows from investing activities		
Purchases of non-current assets	(3,305)	
Proceeds from sale of non-current assets	750	
Purchases of investments	(950)	
Cash (used in)/from financing activities		(3,505)
Cash flows from financing activities		
Proceeds from share issue	2,000	
Dividends paid	(300)	
Cash (used in)/from financing activities		1,700
Net increase/(decrease) in cash and cash equivalents		(95)
Cash and cash equivalents at beginning of year		278
Cash and cash equivalents at end of year		183
Reconciliation of net cash flow to movement in net debt		
Decrease in cash in the period		(95)
Net debt as at 1 June 20*8		(922)
Net debt as at 31 May 20*9		(1,017)

Net debt is borrowings less cash.

So debentures – cash. (1,200 − 278 = 922) and (1,200 − 183 = 1,017)

Chapter summary

- All limited companies (except small companies) must prepare a statement of cash flows.
- IAS 7 requires that cash flow statements must be prepared in the standard format. Remember Oprah's in France!
- All cash movements are shown in the statement.
- Non-cash flows are not shown in the statement (ie issues of bonus shares and revaluations of fixed assets).

SELF-TEST QUESTIONS

- All businesses must prepare a statement of cash flows. True or false?
- Do statements of cash flows calculate the profits of a company?
- Why would a business prepare a statement of cash flows?
- Why is depreciation added back to the profits of a business when calculating cash flows?
- How is a profit on disposal of fixed assets treated in a statement of cash flows?
- How is a loss on disposal of fixed assets treated in a statement of cash flows?

- Land and building have been revalued from £120,000 to £250,000. Under which heading would this be shown?
- Proposed ordinary dividend £31,000; interim ordinary dividend paid £12,000. Under which heading should this be shown in a cash flow statement? How much should be shown?
- How is net debt calculated?
- A company that makes losses does not have to produce a statement of cash flows until it is profitable. True or false?

TEST QUESTIONS

QUESTION 7

The following information is available for Egdal plc:

	31 December 20*9 £	31 December 20*8 £	Cash inflow £	Cash outflow £
Premises at cost	46,000	37,000		
Inventories	6,100	4,200		
Trade receivables	3,700	3,900		
Trade payables	4,750	4,600		

Required

Calculate the cash flows that have taken place during the year.

QUESTION 8

The following information is available for Docht plc:

	31 August 20*9 £	31 August 20*8 £	Cash inflow £	Cash outflow £
Machinery at cost	15,270	17,450		
Inventories	7,930	8,100		
Trade receivables	6,130	5,650		
Trade payables	5,350	4,980		

Required

Calculate the cash flows that have taken place during the year.

QUESTION 9

The following balance sheets are available for Shakoor Ltd:

	At 31 March 20*9 £	At 31 March 20*9 £	At 31 March 20*8 £	At 31 March 20*8 £
Non-current assets at cost		548,000		416,000
Less Depreciation		(156,000)		(118,000)
		392,000		298,000
Current assets				
Inventories	53,700		50,200	
Trade receivables	29,800		31,780	
Cash and cash equivalents	7,600		8,400	
	91,100		90,380	
Current liabilities				
Trade payables	(52,300)	800	(62,910)	(12,530)
Tax	(38,000)		(40,000)	
	(90,300)		(102,910)	
		392,800		285,470
Equity				
Ordinary shares		300,000		200,000
Retained earnings		93,800		85,470
		392,800		285,470

Required

Prepare a detailed analysis of the changes to the cash and cash equivalents during the year.

QUESTION 10

The following balance sheets are available for Tigles plc:

	At 28 February 20*9			At 29 February 20*8		
	£000	£000	£000	£000	£000	£000
Non-current assets at cost			1,462			1,378
Less Depreciation			936			912
			526			466
Current assets						
Inventories		280			312	
Trade receivables		192			182	
Cash and cash equivalents		39				
		511			494	
Current liabilities						
Trade payables		(234)			(213)	
Cash and cash equivalents					(49)	
Tax		(110)			(120)	
		(344)	167		(382)	112
			693			578
Equity						
Ordinary share capital			250			250
Retained earnings			443			328
			693			578

Required

Prepare a detailed analysis of the changes to the cash and cash equivalents during the year.

QUESTION 11

The following information is given for Dixon-Mark & Co Ltd:

	31 May 20*9 £	31 May 20*8 £
Premises – at cost		250,000
at valuation	350,000	
depreciation	(30,000)	(20,000)
Net book value	320,000	230,000

There were no disposals of premises during the year.

Required

Calculate the changes to cash flows that have taken place during the year.

QUESTION 12

The following information is given for Hantar plc:

	31 July 20*9 £	31 July 20*8 £
Machinery at cost	370,000	312,000
Less Depreciation	(91,000)	(72,000)
Net book value	279,000	240,000

There were no disposals of machinery during the year.

Required

Calculate the changes to cash flows that have taken place during the year.

QUESTION 13

The following information is given for Calclot plc:

	31 January 20*9 £	31 January 20*8 £
Plant – at cost	?	240,000
depreciation	?	(100,000)
Net book value	96,200	140,000

During the year ended 31 January 20*9 a piece of plant that had been purchased for £32,000 was sold for £13,200.

The aggregate depreciation charged on the plant to the year ended 31 January 20*8 was £20,000. No plant was purchased during the year.

Required

Identify all entries to a cash flow statement for the year ended 31 January 20*9.

QUESTION 14

The following information is given for Lasopsid Ltd:

	31 October 20*9	31 October 20*8
	£	£
Vehicles – at cost	?	580,000
depreciation	?	195,000
Net book value	250,000	385,000

During the year a vehicle costing £150,000 was sold for £3,000. The aggregate depreciation charged to the vehicle to the year ended 31 October 20*8 was £120,000.

No vehicles were purchased during the year.

Required

Identify all entries to a statement of cash flows for the year ended 31 October 20*9.

QUESTION 15

The following extracts have been taken from the balance sheets of Thomas Tinkle plc:

	31 January 20*9	31 January 20*8
	£000	£000
Equity		
Ordinary shares	3,000	2,000
6% preferred shares	800	600
Share premium account	630	1,630
Retained earnings	1,990	1,920

During the year a bonus issue of one ordinary share for every two held was made, and 200,000 6% preferred shares of £1 were issued at par.

Required

Identify the entries to be made in the cash flow statement for the year ended 31 January 20*9.

QUESTION 16

The following extracts have been taken from the balance sheets of Kerry Harry plc:

	At 31 May 20*9	At 31 May 20*8
	£000	£000
Equity		
Ordinary share capital	4,800	3,600
7½% preferred shares	2,000	1,000
Revaluation reserve		750
Share premium account	150	600
Retained earnings	2,350	1,880

During the year a bonus issue of one ordinary share for every three held was made. A further 1,000,000 7½% preferred shares of £1 were issued at par.

Required

Identify the entries to be made in the cash flow statement for the year ended 31 May 20*9.

QUESTION 17

The following information has been extracted from the books of account of Jasper Turnip Ltd:

	At 28 February 20*9	At 29 February 20*8
	£000	£000
Non-current assets at cost	490,000	362,000

	£000	£000
Depreciation of non-current assets	220,000	140,000
Inventories	52,000	48,000
Trade receivables	18,700	26,700
Trade payables	18,000	23,000
Retained earnings	196,000	136,000
Debenture interest paid	7,000	7,000

During the year ended 28 February 20*9 fixed assets which had cost £70,000 were sold for £17,000. The non-current assets had been depreciated by £60,000 up to 28 February 20*8.

Required

Prepare a statement showing the net cash flow generated from operating activities.

QUESTION 18

The following information has been extracted from the books of account of Raymondec plc:

	At 31 December 20*9	At 31 December 20*8
	£000	£000
Non-current assets at cost	1,782	1,468
Depreciation of fixed assets	668	596
Inventories	298	312
Trade receivables	183	172
Trade payables	106	104
Retained earnings	2,647	2,567
Debenture interest paid	32	32

During the year ended 31 December 20*9 non-current assets that had cost £110,000 were sold for £24,000. The assets had been depreciated by £95,000 up to 31 December 20*8.

Required

Prepare a statement showing the net cash flow generated from operating activities.

QUESTION 19

The following information is given for Currock and Cummersdale plc:

	At 31 August 20*9	At 31 August 20*8
	£000	£000
Machinery at cost	531	488
Depreciation of machinery	262	236
Inventories	92	84
Trade receivables	23	27
Trade payables	37	34
Retained earnings	1,443	1,384
Debenture interest paid	18	18

During the year ended 31 August 20*9 a machine that had cost £102,000 some years earlier was sold for £10,000. The machine had been depreciated by £87,000 up to 31 August 20*8.

Required

Prepare a statement showing the net cash flow generated from operating activities.

QUESTION 20

The following information is given for Denton Homes Ltd:

	At 31 July 20*9	At 31 July 20*8
	£	£
Vehicles at cost	240,000	212,000
Depreciation of vehicles	97,000	88,000
Inventories	53,000	57,500
Trade receivables	51,300	48,600
Trade payables	29,420	34,720
Retained earnings	1,979,000	1,972,400
Debenture interest paid	42,000	42,000

During the year ended 31 July 20*9 a vehicle that had cost £42,000 was sold for £1,000. The depreciation charged on the vehicle to 31 July 20*8 was £25,000.

Required

Prepare a statement showing the net cash flow generated from operating activities.

QUESTION 21

The following information is given for Finnegan and McMeel plc:

	At 30 June 20*9	At 30 June 20*8
	£000	£000
Cash and cash equivalents	152	128
Ordinary shares	2,500	2,000
7% debenture stock	1,500	1,000
Long-term loan	800	750

Required

Prepare a reconciliation of net cash to movement in net debt.

QUESTION 22

The following information relates to Josoap Ltd:

	At 30 September 20*9	At 30 September 20*8
	£000	£000
Cash and cash equivalents	290	248
Ordinary shares	1,200	1,000
6% debenture stock	1,000	600
Long-term loan	280	200

Required

Prepare a reconciliation of net cash to movement in net debt.

QUESTION 23

The directors of Araby & Upperby Ltd provide the following information:

	At 30 April 20*9	At 30 April 20*8
	£000	£000
Cash and cash equivalents	(117)	118
7% debenture stock	1,300	2,000
Long-term loan	750	400

Required

Prepare a reconciliation of net cash to movement in net debt.

QUESTION 24

The information given relates to Stan Wicks plc:

	At 31 October 20*9	At 31 October 20*8
	£000	£000
Cash and cash equivalents	162	(186)
6% debenture stock	500	1,100
Long-term loan	700	350

Required

Prepare a reconciliation of net cash to movement in net debt.

QUESTION 25

The following information is given for McDonnel & Prince plc for the year ended 31 January 20*9:

	£000
Profit from operations	2,167
Debenture interest	(40)
Profit before tax	2,127
Tax	(316)
Profit for the year	1,811

Note

Dividends paid during the year ended 31 January 20*9 amounted to £640,000.

Over the year the following changes have taken place:

	£000
Purchase of non-current assets	1,400
Increase in inventories	12
Decrease in trade receivables	17
Decrease in trade payables	23
Profit on sale of non-current assets	18
Receipts from sale of non-current assets	47
Depreciation of non-current assets	214
Receipts from issue of shares	2,000
Corporation tax paid	298

Additional information

	£000
Cash and cash equivalents at 1 February 20*8	137
Cash and cash equivalents at 31 January 20*9	2,151

Required

Prepare a statement of cash flows using the IAS 7 layout

QUESTION 26

The following information is available for Retrac plc:

Summarised income statement extract for the year ended 31 December 20*9

	£000
Profit from operations	1,783
Debenture interest	(130)
Profit before tax	1,653
Corporation tax	(512)
Profit for the year	1,141

Statement of changes in equity

	£000
Retained earnings	
Balance at 1 January 20*9	986
Profit for the year	1,141
	2,127
Dividends paid	(120)
Balance at 31 December 20*9	2,007

Additional information

During the year the following transactions took place:

	£000
Tax paid in the year ended 31 December 20*9	536
Dividends paid in the year ended 31 December 20*9	120
Purchase of non-current assets	407
Depreciation of non-current assets	215
Receipts from sale of non-current assets	80
Loss on sale of non-current assets	6
Decrease in inventories	9
Increase in trade receivables	28
Increase in trade payables	14
Receipts from share issue	642

Additional information

	£000
Cash and cash equivalents at 1 January 20*9	(461)
Cash and cash equivalents at 31 December 20*9	1,067

Required

Prepare a statement of cash flows using IAS 7 layout.

QUESTION 27

The following extracts from the income statements and balance sheets of Sagoo and Simpson Ltd are given:

Sagoo and Simpson Ltd
Income statement extract for the year ended 31 July 20*9

	£000
Profit before tax (Note 1)	133
Tax	(40)
Profit for the year	93

Statement of changes in equity

	£000
Retained earnings	
Balance at 1 August 20*8	135
Profit for the year	93
	228
Dividends paid	(45)
Balance at 31 July 20*9	183

Note 1
After adding interest received £12,000 and deducting interest paid £8,000.

Balance sheet at 31 July

	20*9 £000	20*9 £000	20*8 £000	20*8 £000
Non-current assets (Note 2)				
Intangible assets		500		95
Tangible assets:				
Land and buildings at cost	612		540	
Depreciation	(300)	312	(280)	260
Total non-current assets		812		355
Current assets				
Inventories	109		99	
Trade receivables	79		67	
Cash and cash equivalents	32		42	
	220		208	
Current liabilities				
Trade payables	(79)		(70)	
Tax	(40)		(38)	
Net current assets	(119)	101	(108)	100
Total assets less current liabilities		913		455
Non-current liabilities				
5% debentures		80		70
		833		385
Equity				
Share capital		650		250
Retained earnings		183		135
		833		385

Note 2
There were no sales of non-current assets during the year.

Required

Prepare a statement of cash flows for the year ended 31 July 20*9.

QUESTION 28

The following information has been extracted from the final accounts of Jaswal and Jarrett plc:

Jaswal and Jarrett plc
Extract from the income statement for the year ended 31 March 20*9

	£000	£000
Profit before tax (Note 1)		4,168
Tax		1,936
Profit for the year		2,232

Statement of changes in equity

Retained earnings
Balance at 1 April 20*8	370
Profit for the year	2,232
	2,602
Dividends paid	(412)
Balance at 31 March 20*9	2,190

Note 1

After adding interest received £291,000 and deducting interest paid £20,000.

Balance sheets at 31 March

	20*9		20*8	
	£000	£000	£000	£000
Non-current assets (Note 2)				
Intangible assets		1,600		1,350
Tangible assets				
Land and buildings –				
at cost	3,514		1,512	
depreciation	(1,494)	2,020	(782)	730
Equipment	1,430		706	
Depreciation	(268)	1,162	(262)	444
Total fixed assets		4,782		2,524
Current assets				
Inventories	436		415	
Trade receivables	39		42	
Cash and cash equivalents	58		6	
	533		463	
Current liabilities				
Trade payables	(39)		(51)	
Tax	(1,936)		(1,216)	
	(1,975)		(1,267)	
		(1,442)		(804)
		3,340		1,720
Non-current liabilities				
6% debentures		(300)		(500)
		3,040		1,220
Equity				
Ordinary share capital		850		850
Retained earnings		2,190		370
		3,040		1,220

Note 2

There were no sales of non-current assets during the year.

Required

Prepare a statement of cash flows for the year ended 31 March 20*9.

QUESTION 29

The following income statement for the year ended 31 August 20*9 is given together with balance sheets at 31 August 20*8 and 31 August 20*9.

Dratas plc
Income statement for the year ended 31 August 20*9

	£000
Profit from operations	1,123
Interest paid	(29)
Profit before tax	1,094
Tax	(447)
Profit for the year	647

Statement of changes in equity

	£000
Retained earnings	
Balance at 1 September 20*8	544
Profit for the year	647
	1,191
Dividends paid	(298)
Balance at 31 August 20*9	893

Balance sheets at:	31 August 20*9		31 August 20*8	
	£000	£000	£000	£000
Non-current intangible assets				
Patents		174		198
Non-current assets				
Premises	895		1,045	
Depreciation	(186)	709	(199)	846
Machinery	995		770	
Depreciation	(447)	548	(348)	422
		1,431		1,466
Current assets				
Inventories	932		634	
Trade receivables	805		656	
Cash and cash equivalents	462		77	
	2,199		1,367	
Current liabilities				
Trade payables	(820)		(606)	
Tax	(447)		(363)	
	(1,267)		(969)	
Net current assets		932		398
		2,363		1,864
Non-current liabilities		(300)		(300)
Equity		2,063		1,564
Ordinary shares of £1 each		1,170		1,020
Retained earnings		893		544
		2,063		1,564

Additional information
1. There were no disposals of machinery during the year.
2. Part of the premises were sold during the year, for £175,000. The profit on the sale was £50,000. There were no additions to premises during the year.
3. Patents originally cost £240,000 and are being amortised over 10 years.

Required
Prepare a statement of cash flows for the year ended 31 August 20*9.

QUESTION 30
The following balance sheets have been prepared for Dixted and Keenan plc together with an income statement for the year ended 31 December 20*9:

Dixted and Keenan plc
Income statement for the year ended 31 December 20*9

	£000
Profit from operations	575
Interest paid	(11)
Profit before tax	564
Tax	(223)
Profit for the year	341

Statement of changes in equity

	£000
Retained earnings	
Balance at 1 January 20*9	196
Profit for the year	341
	537
Dividends paid	(164)
Balance at 31 December 20*9	373

Balance sheets at:	31 December 20*9		31 December 20*8	
	£000	£000	£000	£000
Non-current assets				
Land and buildings	430		480	
Depreciation	(90)	340	(100)	380
Machinery	490		370	
Depreciation	(185)	305	(140)	230
		645		610
Investments at cost		55		
Current assets				
Inventories	370		306	

	£000	£000	£000	£000
Trade receivables	448		410	
Cash and cash equivalents	61		16	
	879		732	
Current liabilities				
Trade payables	(273)		(299)	
Tax	(223)		(192)	
	(496)		(491)	
Net current assets		383		241
		1,083		851
Non-current liabilities				
10% debentures		(100)		(120)
		983		731
Equity				
Ordinary shares of £1		610		535
Retained earnings		373		196
		983		731

Additional information

1. Part of the land and buildings was sold during the year for £110,000. The profit on the sale was £80,000. There were no additions to land and buildings during the year.
2. There were no disposals of machinery during the year.

Required

Prepare a statement of cash flows for the year ended 31 December 20*9.

QUESTION 31

The directors of Gray and Lyons plc provide the following information:

	Gray and Lyons plc			
Balance sheets at:	29 February 20*9		28 February 20*8	
	£000	£000	£000	£000
Non-current assets (Note 1)				
Land and buildings		688		575
Machinery		188		260
Vehicles		60		104
Investments		90		80
		1,026		1,019
Current assets				
Inventories	599		495	
Trade receivables	282		208	
Cash and cash equivalents	23		130	
	904		833	
Current liabilities				
Trade payables	(248)		(201)	
Tax	(172)		(146)	
	(420)	484	(347)	486
		1,510		1,505
Non-current liabilities				
8% debenture 20*9 (Note 2)		(100)		(260)
		1,410		1,245
Equity				
Ordinary shares of £1 (Note 3)		600		390
7% preference shares of £1		400		400
Share premium account				80
Retained earnings		410		375
		1,410		1,245

Statement of changes in equity	
	£000
Retained earnings	
Balance at 1 March 20*8	375
Profit for the year	141
	516
Dividends paid	(101)
Bonus issue of ordinary shares	(5)
Balance at 28 February 20*9	410
Share premium account	
Balance at 1 March 20*8	80
Bonus issue of ordinary shares	(80)
Balance at 28 February 20*9	—

	£000
Revaluation reserve	
Balance at 1 March 20*8	—
Revaluation of land and buildings	125
Bonus issue of ordinary shares	(125)
Balance at 28 February 20*9	—

Notes to the balance sheet

Note 1

	28 February 20*9 £000	29 February 20*8 £000
Non-current assets		
Land and buildings		
Cost		680
Valuation	700	
Depreciation	(12)	(105)
Net book value	688	575

During the year ended 28 February 20*9 the premises were revalued at £700,000.

There were no disposals of premises during the year.

Machinery		
Cost	?	400
Depreciation	?	(140)
Net book value	188	260

During the year ended 28 February 20*9 a machine which had cost £65,000 was sold for £20,000. The accumulated depreciation on the machine to the year ended 28 February 20*9 was £40,000.

No machinery was acquired during the year.

Vehicles		
Cost	550	450
Depreciation	(490)	(346)
Net book value	60	104

There were no disposals of vehicles during the year.

Note 2
£160,000 8% debentures were redeemed on 30 November 20*8 (no transfer to debenture redemption reserve was made).

Note 3
During the year a bonus issue of shares was made. The revaluation reserve and the share premium account had been used for the purpose. Part of the retained earnings was also used.

Income statement for the year ended 28 February 20*9

	£000
Profit from operations	330.6
Interest paid	17.6
Profit before tax	313
Tax	(172)
Profit for the year	141

Required

Prepare a statement of cash flows for the year ended 28 February 20*9.

QUESTION 32

The financial statements and notes to the accounts are given for Appleby and Penrith plc:

Balance sheet at 31 December

	20*9 £000	£000	20*8 £000	£000
Non-current assets (Note 1)		3,670		2,890
Current assets				
Inventories	312		593	
Trade receivables	1,312		937	
Cash and cash equivalents	1,202		1,015	

	£000	£000	£000	£000
		2,826		2,545
Current liabilities				
Trade payables	(718)		(749)	
Tax	(781)		(937)	
	(1,499)		(1,686)	
Net current assets		1,327		859
Total assets less current liabilities		4,997		3,749
Non-current liabilities				
Bank loans (2055–2059)		(800)		(390)
		4,197		3,359
Equity				
Called-up capital (ordinary shares)		2,350		1,950
Retained earnings		1,847		1,409
		4,197		3,359

Statement of changes in equity

	£000
Retained earnings	
Balance at 1 January 20*9	1,409
Profit for the year	784
	2,193
Dividends paid	(346)
Balance at 31 December 20*9	1,847

Note to the balance sheet

Note 1

	£000
Non-current assets	
At 1 January 20*9	5,460
Additions during year	1,340
At 31 December 20*9	6,800
Accumulated depreciation	
At 1 January 20*9	2,570
Charge for year	560
At 31 December 20*9	3,130

Income statement for the year ended 31 December 20*9

	£000
Profit from operations	1,600
Interest paid	35
Profit before tax	1,565
Tax	781
Profit for the year	784

Required

Prepare a statement of cash flows for the year ended 31 December 20*9.

CHAPTER
EIGHT

Performance Evaluation

Financial statements are prepared to convey information to management and the other users of accounts.

The financial statements provide us with much financial information but in order to use this information we must be able to analyse and interpret it. Figures cannot be used in isolation because they can sometimes be misleading. Financial statements use absolute numbers. We need to place the figures in context.

In the days of Charles Dickens a good annual salary was probably £25 per year!

A woman earns $40,000 per year. Is this a good annual income? That depends on whether she lives in Zimbabwe, Singapore, Australia or the USA.

Absolute figures have to be placed in context.

The same is true about accounting information.

A business makes a net profit of £45,000 for the year ended 31 March 20*9. Has the business had a good year?

If the business under review was Freda's Fruit shop in the High Street, what would your answer be? I guess that it would be different if the business was Marks and Spencer plc.

Profits provide only one facet of business activity. Profits are important; they ensure the long-term survival of a business.

The other main facet of business activity is the ability to generate cash. Cash is so important for the day-to-day survival of the business. If a business has insufficient cash then it might be unable to pay staff wages; it might be unable to pay the providers of the utilities; it might be unable to pay its creditors. All of these people are likely to withdraw resources if the business does not pay its debts.

So, two key areas of performance evaluation are: profitability and liquidity.

> **Specification coverage:**
> AQA ACCN3;
> OCR F013
>
> **By the end of this chapter you should be able to:**
> - calculate ratios to assess profitability and liquidity
> - calculate the relevant investors' ratios
> - compare and contrast the results of different organisations
> - analyse and interpret accounting statements using ratios.

PERFORMANCE EVALUATION

How would the users of accounting information decide whether the profitability and/or the liquidity of a business is acceptable?

In the same way that you decide whether the state of your earnings is acceptable or not:

- you compare your earnings this year with your earnings last year
- you compare your earnings with those of your friends
- you compare your earnings with the national average
- you might even compare your earnings with what you planned to earn.

Performance evaluation is about making comparisons.

Ratio analysis is about putting information in context and making comparisons.

The users of accounting information follow similar procedures to the ones that you might use. They ask:

- 'Is the business performing better (or worse) than last year?' They compare previous results with the current year's results.
- 'Is the business performing better (or worse) than similar businesses?' They compare the results of businesses in the same industrial sector.

$$20*9$$
$$= \frac{510}{3,259} \times 100$$

$$20*8$$
$$= \frac{460}{2,395} \times 100$$

$$= 15.65\%$$

$$= 19.21\%$$

This tells us that for every £100 invested in the business in 20*8 the business earned £19.21; a year later the business earned £15.65 for every £100 invested – a worse result.

Could the capital be used elsewhere to earn a greater return? Compare this ratio with the return in similar businesses.

Certainly, there has been a deterioration since 20*9.

GROSS PROFIT PERCENTAGE (ALSO KNOWN AS THE GROSS MARGIN)

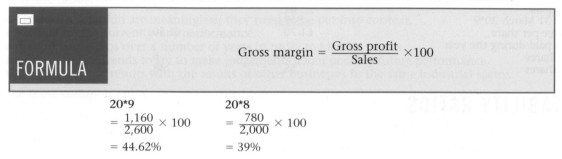

FORMULA

$$\text{Gross margin} = \frac{\text{Gross profit}}{\text{Sales}} \times 100$$

$$20*9$$
$$= \frac{1,160}{2,600} \times 100$$

$$20*8$$
$$= \frac{780}{2,000} \times 100$$

$$= 44.62\%$$

$$= 39\%$$

This shows that for every £100 of sales, the margin was £39 in 20*8. It then improved to £44.62 in 20*9.

The margin will vary from business to business. A business with the need for a rapid turnover in stock will generally have a lower margin than a business with a slower turnover of stock.

The change identified might be caused by a decrease in the cost of goods sold while maintaining selling price or it may be caused by a slight increase in the selling price while the cost of goods sold has reduced.

MARK-UP

This is calculated as follows:

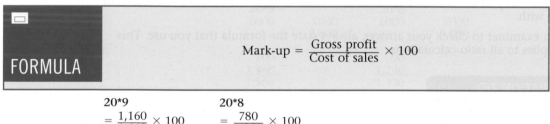

FORMULA

$$\text{Mark-up} = \frac{\text{Gross profit}}{\text{Cost of sales}} \times 100$$

$$20*9$$
$$= \frac{1,160}{1,440} \times 100$$

$$20*8$$
$$= \frac{780}{1,220} \times 100$$

$$= 80.56\%$$

$$= 63.93\%$$

This means that for every £100 of goods purchased the price has been increased to £163.93 in 20*8 and £180.56 in the following year.

Students are advised not to use both ratios in any analysis they undertake.

● EXAMINATION TIP

An increase in the volume of sales will not affect mark-up or margin. These ratios will remain constant. Changes in selling price and/or changes in purchasing price will affect mark-up or margin.

NET PROFIT PERCENTAGE (ALSO KNOWN AS THE NET MARGIN)

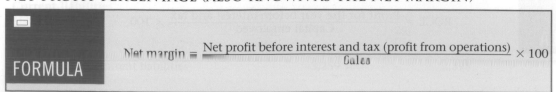

FORMULA

$$\text{Net margin} = \frac{\text{Net profit before interest and tax (profit from operations)}}{\text{Sales}} \times 100$$

$$20*9 \qquad\qquad 20*8$$
$$= \frac{510}{2,600} \times 100 \qquad = \frac{460}{2,000} \times 100$$
$$= 19.62\% \qquad\qquad = 23\%$$

This shows that in 20*8 out of every £100 sales the business earned £23 after all operating costs and cost of sales had been covered. This amount fell to £19.62 the following year.

We can look at this from another angle; it tells us that in 20*8 the business expenses were £16 (£39.00 − £23.00) out of every £100 of goods sold. In 20*9 this amount spent on expenses rose to £25 (£44.62 − £19.62). This begs the question: is the business losing control as far as expenses are concerned?

In absolute terms, expenses have increased by 103% (56% in relative terms) yet sales have only increased by 600/2000, ie 30%. We can perhaps see why this has happened by examining the details of the income statement expenses.

In 20*8 selling and distribution expenses accounted for £7 of each £100 of sales; in 20*9 the figure has risen to £11.92.

In 20*8 administration costs amounted to £9 in every £100 of sales; in 20*9 the figure has risen to £13.08.

Finance charges rose to £1.54 for every £100 of sales in 20*9. It had been 80p for every £100 of sales. This is an increase of 92.5%.

In all this analysis of figures we have simply considered the available information. You must try to develop this technique.

RETURN ON TOTAL ASSETS

This ratio shows how efficiently total assets are being used to generate profits.

FORMULA

$$\text{Return on total assets} = \frac{\text{Profit from operations}}{\text{Non-current assets} + \text{Current assets}}$$

$$20*9 \qquad\qquad 20*8$$
$$= \frac{510}{3,563} \times 100 \qquad = \frac{460}{2,700} \times 100$$
$$= 14.31\% \qquad\qquad = 17.04\%$$

The company was using its assets more effectively in 20*8. For every £1 invested in assets the company earned just over 17p; the following year the return for every £1 invested in assets fell to 14.31p.

QUESTION 1

The following information is given for Trashott & Co Ltd:

Year ended 31 March	20*9 £000	£000	20*8 £000	£000
Sales		1,046		987
Less Cost of sales		(667)		(648)
Gross profit		379		339
Selling and distribution costs	(78)		(67)	
Administration	(58)	(136)	(48)	(115)
Operating profit		243		224
Interest payable		(40)		(38)
Profit before tax		203		186
Taxation		(46)		(42)
Profit for the year		157		144
Capital employed		1,516		1,388

Required

a Calculate for both years:
   i) mark-up
   ii) gross margin
   iii) net profit margin
   iv) overheads (expenses) to turnover
   v) ROCE.
b Comment on your results.

QUESTION 2

The following information is given for Prolill plc:

Year ended 31 December	20*9 £000	£000	20*8 £000	£000
Sales		1,348		1,563
Less Cost of sales		(617)		(599)
Gross profit		731		964
Selling and distribution costs	(112)		(208)	
Administration	(106)	(218)	(132)	(340)
Operating profit		513		624
Interest payable		(30)		(30)
Profit before tax		483		594
Tax		(133)		(152)
Profit for the year		350		442
Capital employed		2,460		2,830

Required

a Calculate for both years:
  i)   mark-up
  ii) gross margin
  iii) net profit margin
  iv) overheads (expenses) to turnover
  v)   ROCE.
b Comment on your results.

FINANCIAL RATIOS

Financial ratios assess the ability of a business to pay its short-term liabilities as they fall due. Liquidity is important since a business has to pay not only its trade creditors but its employees and other providers of resources too. Although creditors are grouped on a balance sheet under headings that indicate payment within 12 months and payments due after 12 months, in reality many creditors require payment in a much shorter time.

> **Solvency** is the ability of a business to settle its debts when they require payment.

Long-term investors are mainly interested in the solvency of the business – they require that the business will survive into the foreseeable future (or at least until their debt can be settled!).

Although solvency means an excess of assets over liabilities, many assets are difficult to dispose of and so many users of accounts are more interested in the liquidity position of the business. They wish to examine and analyse the components of working capital in detail.

CURRENT RATIO (ALSO KNOWN AS THE WORKING CAPITAL RATIO)

There is no ideal current ratio.

The ratio shows how many times the current assets are covering the current liabilities. It is usually expressed as a 'times' ratio, that is the right-hand term should be expressed as unity so the ratio should be expressed as 'something':1. Generally, the ratio should be in excess of unity (i.e. greater than 1:1), although many businesses prosper with a ratio which is less than this.

Once again, we should be looking for trends when we consider the current ratio. If a series of results shows that the current ratio has been declining over a number of years, this may mean that the business might have some difficulties in meeting its short-term obligations in the future.

If the series shows that the current ratio is increasing each year, this could be an indication that the business is tying up an increasing proportion of its resources in inventories, debtors and bank balances, ie non-productive assets, instead of the resources being invested in non-current assets that will earn profit.

Many analysts consider that a reasonable current ratio should fall between 1.5:1 and 2:1 although it is dangerous to be too dogmatic about this. The ratio will depend on the type of business and the direction of any trend.

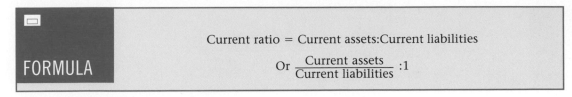

$$\text{Current ratio} = \text{Current assets:Current liabilities}$$

$$\text{Or} \quad \frac{\text{Current assets}}{\text{Current liabilities}}:1$$

FORMULA

20*9	20*8
$\frac{500}{304}:1$	$\frac{900}{305}:1$
1.64:1	2.95:1

The working capital ratio has fallen by around 44% (1.31/2.95). It does appear that in 20*8 rather too many resources were tied up in unproductive resources and it does appear that in 20*9 this was more under control. An examination of the balance sheet reveals that the main change in current assets and current liabilities is that Oyan Magenta & Co Ltd has reduced the cash held in its bank account by £430,000.

Obviously, the greater the number of years' results that are available, the easier it is to identify and confirm a trend.

THE LIQUID RATIO (ALSO KNOWN AS THE ACID TEST RATIO OR THE QUICK RATIO)

Once again, we should be looking for trends when considering this ratio. Liquid assets are current assets and a definition of current assets is that they are assets that are cash or will be cash in the near future. The least liquid of the current assets is stock. The liquid ratio tests the ability of the business to cover its current liabilities with its current assets other than stocks.

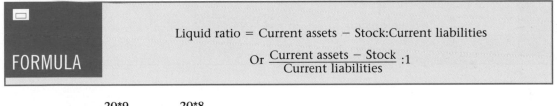

$$\text{Liquid ratio} = \text{Current assets} - \text{Stock:Current liabilities}$$

$$\text{Or} \quad \frac{\text{Current assets} - \text{Stock}}{\text{Current liabilities}}:1$$

FORMULA

20*9	20*8
$\frac{380}{304}:1$	$\frac{790}{305}:1$
1.25:1	2.59:1

Year 20*8 seems rather high so rather too many resources are tied up in a liquid form, not earning profits.

The ratio has improved in 20*9, mainly because of a reduction in the bank balance from £570,000 to £140,000.

The business is still able to cover every £1 owed with £1.25 of liquid assets.

Once again, it is impossible to say what is an acceptable level of ratio – some businesses, for example some supermarkets, perform satisfactorily with a liquid ratio of less than 0.5:1.

DEBTORS' COLLECTION PERIOD (OR DEBTOR DAYS OR AVERAGE COLLECTION PERIOD OR RECEIVABLES COLLECTION PERIOD)

This calculates how long, on average, it takes a business to collect its debts.

Generally, the longer a debt is outstanding, the more likely it is that the debt will prove to be irrecoverable. It is also advisable to have a shorter debt collection period than the creditor payment period.

A question might not identify cash and credit sales; in such cases it is acceptable to use the total sales figure given. It is essential that the same basis is used when making comparisons.

$$\text{Debtors' collection period} = \frac{\text{Trade receivables} \times 365}{\text{(Credit) Sales}}$$

20*9	20*8
$\dfrac{240 \times 365}{2,600}$	$\dfrac{220 \times 365}{2,000}$
= 34 days	= 41 days

Note the rounding of the answer. In 20*8 the actual figure calculated was 40.15 days (that is 40 days, 3 hours and 36 minutes!). We always round to the next full day.

Remember that the calculation will give us an average collection time. It uses all debtors – this may mask the fact that one significant debtor is a very poor payer while the other debtors pay promptly.

30 days' credit is a reasonable yardstick to use. So, using this measure, in 20*8 debts were outstanding for 41 days – perhaps a little too long. There was an improvement in 20*9: debts were collected in 34 days – a week faster.

CREDITORS' PAYMENT PERIOD (OR CREDITOR DAYS OR AVERAGE PAYMENT PERIOD OR PAYABLES PAYMENT PERIOD)

This measures the average time a business takes to pay its creditors.

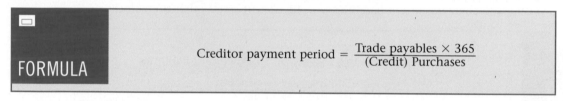

$$\text{Creditor payment period} = \frac{\text{Trade payables} \times 365}{\text{(Credit) Purchases}}$$

20*9	20*8
$\dfrac{159 \times 365}{1,460}$	$\dfrac{176 \times 365}{1,240}$
= 40 days	= 52 days

In 20*8 Oyan Magenta was paying its creditors on average in 52 days; a year later it was paying in 40 days.

The shortening (efficacy) of this 12-day reduction does need investigation.

A comparison of the debtor days and creditor days shows that, in both years, creditors are on average being paid more slowly than cash is being received from debtors. This is a good policy. However, care must be taken to ensure that suppliers are not antagonised by being paid too slowly.

RATE OF INVENTORY TURNOVER (ALSO KNOWN AS STOCK TURN OR RATE OF STOCK TURN)

In every 'bundle' of inventory held by a business there is an element of profit and there is cash tied up. It is essential that this cash is released and that profits are earned as quickly as possible. So the more often inventory can be 'turned over', the better it is for the business.

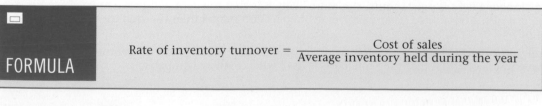

$$\text{Rate of inventory turnover} = \frac{\text{Cost of sales}}{\text{Average inventory held during the year}}$$

20*9	20*8
$\dfrac{1,440}{110}$	$\dfrac{1,220}{100}$
= 13.09 times	= 12.2 times

ADVANCED ACCOUNTING FOR A2

This shows that in 20*8 the company turned its inventory over approximately once a month; it increased this in 20*9.

If you require the time taken to turn inventory over in days, you can either divide 365 by the result of your calculation:

e.g. $\frac{365}{13.09}$ = 28 days and $\frac{365}{12.2}$ = 30 days

or you can use the formula: $\frac{\text{Average inventory} \times 365}{\text{Cost of sales}}$

Clearly, the higher the rate of inventory turnover the better, since this means that inventory is kept in the business for a shorter length of time.

In some industries the need to hold large quantities of inventory at any one time has almost been totally eradicated with the introduction of just in time (JIT) ordering of stock.

WORKING CAPITAL CYCLE

This shows the length of time taken between making payment for goods purchased and the receipt of cash from customers.

The shorter the time between the business laying out cash for the purchase of goods and the collection of cash from sales, the better for the business.

The shorter the cycle, the lower the value of working capital to be financed from other sources.

The cycle can be shortened by:

■ reducing inventory levels held
■ speeding up debtor collection
■ delaying payment to creditors.

FORMULA	Working capital cycle = Rate of inventory turnover (days) + debtor collection period (days) − creditor payment period (days)

28 days + 34 days − 40 days = 22 days	30 days + 41 days − 52 days = 19 days

The main cause of worsening of the working capital cycle is the more rapid payment of creditors.

QUESTION 3

The following information is available for Rywicke plc:

	At 31 August 20*9 £	At 31 August 20*8 £
Sales	730,000	720,000
Purchases	361,000	346,000
Opening inventory	32,000	28,000
Closing inventory	34,000	32,000
Trade receivables	70,000	74,000
Cash and cash equivalents	1,000	14,000
Trade payables	34,000	30,000

Note: All purchases and sales were on credit.

Required

a Calculate the following ratios (show the formulae used) for both years:
   i) current ratio
   ii) liquid ratio
   iii) debtors' collection period
   iv) creditors' payment period
   v) rate of inventory turnover
   vi) working capital cycle.
b Comment on your results for average collection and average payment periods.

QUESTION 4

The following information is given for Bajpan plc:

	At 30 September 20*9 £	At 30 September 20*8 £
Sales (credit)	1,100,000	900,000
Purchases (credit)	524,000	537,000
Opening inventory	50,000	42,000
Closing inventory	52,000	50,000
Trade receivables	102,000	85,000
Cash and cash equivalents	1,000	4,000
Trade payables	44,500	60,000

Required

Calculate the following ratios (show the formulae used). Comment on the current and liquid ratios.

i) current ratio
ii) liquid ratio
iii) debtors' collection period
iv) creditors' payment period
v) rate of inventory turnover
vi) working capital cycle.

INVESTMENT RATIOS

Ordinary shareholders generally have invested in a limited company in order to gain a return on their investment. They are also interested in the market value of their shares.

Before ordinary shareholders are able to receive any return on their investment the providers of long-term loans (debenture holders) and preferred shareholders need to be rewarded.

Debenture holders must receive their interest however profitable or unprofitable the company has been.

The preferred shareholders are entitled to dividends (provided there are sufficient profits) before ordinary shareholders.

The ordinary shareholders return may be at risk if the company's capital is provided mainly by debenture holders and preferred shareholders.

The degree of risk is measured by the gearing ratio or the debt equity ratio.

GEARING

This is the relationship that exists between fixed cost capital and total capital.

So:

> **FORMULA**
>
> $$\text{Gearing} = \frac{\text{Fixed cost capital}}{\text{Total capital}} =$$
>
> $$\frac{\text{Long-term loans} + \text{Preferred shares}}{\text{Long-term loans} + \text{Preferred shares} + \text{issued Ordinary share capital} + \text{all reserves}}$$

$$= \frac{800 + 100}{800 + 100 + 1,500 + 859} \qquad = \frac{200 + 100}{200 + 100 + 1,500 + 595}$$

$$= \frac{900}{3,259} \qquad\qquad = \frac{300}{2,395}$$

$$= 27.6\% \qquad\qquad = 12.5\%$$

The gearing of a company is said to be:

- **high** when the ratio is more than 50%
- **neutral** when the ratio is 50%
- **low** when the ratio is less than 50%.

So: high geared =

- high borrowing

- high debt
- high risk.

   low geared

- low borrowing
- low debt
- low risk.

In the first year 12.5% of total capital employed is provided by people other than ordinary shareholders. In the second year the company has become more highly geared: 27.6% of capital employed is provided by people other than the ordinary shareholders. The company has become more highly geared but on our measure it is still a low-geared company; 72.4% of capital employed is provided by the ordinary shareholders.

Investment in a highly geared company is more of a risk than an investment in a low-geared company because if the company is unable to service its long-term liabilities then it may be forced into liquidation by those long-term investors.

It follows that a highly geared company may find it difficult to borrow further funds because of the inherent risk. Banks may also be reluctant to lend to highly geared companies since they may feel that the ordinary shareholders should be prepared to finance their own company rather than rely on 'outsiders'.

EARNINGS PER SHARE

Earnings are net profit after taxation and after the deduction of preference dividends. That is, earnings that belong totally to the ordinary shareholders.

In year 20*9: Earnings are £325,000 profit after taxation

   Less £6,000 preferred dividend

   £319,000 profits available for ordinary shareholders

In year 20*8: Earnings are £315,000 profit after taxation

   Less £6,000 preferred dividend

   £309,000 profits available for ordinary shareholders

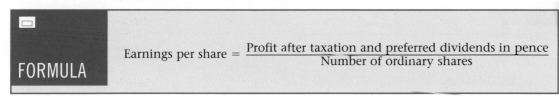

FORMULA

$$\text{Earnings per share} = \frac{\text{Profit after taxation and preferred dividends in pence}}{\text{Number of ordinary shares}}$$

20*9	20*8
$\dfrac{31{,}900{,}000}{1{,}500{,}000}$	$\dfrac{30{,}900{,}000}{1{,}500{,}000}$
= 21.27 pence	= 20.6 pence

The earnings per share has increased in the second year. It has improved by 0.67 pence per share.

● EXAMINATION TIP

The calculation used numbers of ordinary shares issued, not the value. So £2,000,000 ordinary shares of 25 pence each would use 8,000,000 as the denominator in the calculation.

PRICE/EARNINGS RATIO

The P/E ratio relates the market price of the share to the earnings per share. It represents the number of years' earnings that investors are prepared to pay to purchase one of the company's shares.

The higher the P/E ratio, the greater the confidence investors have in the future of the company.

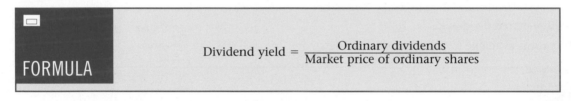

$$\text{Price/earnings ratio} = \frac{\text{Market price per ordinary share}}{\text{Earnings per ordinary share}}$$

FORMULA

20*9	20*8
$= \dfrac{£1.70}{21.27p}$	$= \dfrac{£1.50}{20.6p}$
$= 7.99$	$= 7.28$

Investors are more confident at 31 March 20*9 than they were a year earlier. They are paying almost eight times the earnings to acquire shares in Oyan Magenta.

Since the ratio compares current market price with earnings per share, an increase in market price will increase the ratio. Demand for shares is dependent on investors' perception of the company's future performance. An increase in demand for the shares will generally cause an increase in the shares' price. A high P/E ratio will indicate expected future growth (or an overvalued share). A low P/E ratio indicates expected poor performance in the future (or an undervalued share).

DIVIDEND YIELD

Shareholders invest in a company in order to gain a return (dividends) on their investment. (They also hope that the market price of the share will rise so that if they sell their holding they will make a capital profit – a capital gain.)

The dividend yield expresses the actual dividend as a percentage of the market price of the share. It shows the actual percentage return an investor can expect, based on the current market price of the shares.

FORMULA

$$\text{Dividend yield} = \frac{\text{Ordinary dividends}}{\text{Market price of ordinary shares}}$$

20*9	20*8
$= \dfrac{55,000}{2,550,000} \times 100$	$= \dfrac{48,000}{2,250,000} \times 100$
$= 2.16\%$	$= 2.13\%$

The dividend yield is still low but has increased slightly in 20*9.

Another version of the formula is:

$$\text{Declared rate of dividend} \times \frac{\text{nominal value of ordinary shares}}{\text{market price of ordinary shares}}$$

DIVIDEND COVER

This ratio indicates how likely it is that the company can continue to pay its current rate of ordinary share dividend in the future.

A high figure is good since it suggests that the company should be able to maintain dividends to ordinary shareholders at the current level even if profits fall. It may indicate that the directors operate a conservative dividend policy and that much of the profit is being reinvested in the company.

Low dividend cover may indicate a reckless dividend policy and a small reduction in company profits may have an adverse effect on dividends in future.

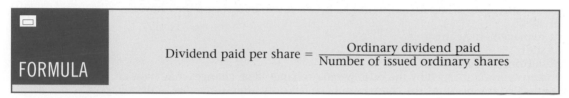

FORMULA

$$\text{Dividend cover} = \frac{\text{Profits available for ordinary dividends}}{\text{Ordinary dividend paid}}$$

20*9	20*8
$= \frac{319}{55}$	$= \frac{309}{48}$
= 5.8 times	= 6.44 times

Both are quite high but there has been deterioration in 20*9. Although profits have increased (3.2%), the dividend paid has increased by a greater percentage (14.6%). Is this a sign of a change in dividend policy?

DIVIDEND PAID PER SHARE

This indicates how much each ordinary share received as a dividend.

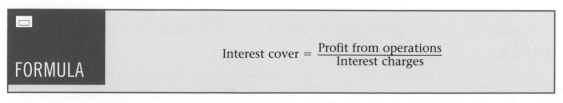

FORMULA

$$\text{Dividend paid per share} = \frac{\text{Ordinary dividend paid}}{\text{Number of issued ordinary shares}}$$

20*9	20*8
$= \frac{55,000}{1,500,000}$	$= \frac{48,000}{1,500,000}$
= 3.67 pence	= 3.2 pence

The amount received by each ordinary shareholder has improved by 14.6% to 3.67 pence per share held.

INTEREST COVER

This shows how many times profits are able to cover current interest payments. It is generally thought that profits before interest and taxation should cover interest payments by at least three times. The ratio shows how secure the interests of the debenture holders are. It also indicates how secure the shareholders' interests are.

FORMULA

$$\text{Interest cover} = \frac{\text{Profit from operations}}{\text{Interest charges}}$$

20*9	20*8
$= \frac{510,000}{40,000}$	$= \frac{460,000}{16,000}$
= 12.75 times	= 28.75 times

Both ratios are high. In the second year the interest cover has reduced by more than half because of the increased debenture interest. Debentures have risen from £200,000 to £800,000 so a full year's interest next year will be £64,000, which could reduce the cover even more.

LIMITATIONS ON USING RATIOS

- The results are based on the use of historic cost because it is objective. However, some results may be misleading if results are compared over a long period. For example, the value of assets shown on a balance sheet from a number of years ago is unlikely to be the same as the market value today. When your great-grandfather first started to work, he may have earned just £2 per week. If he had been given a huge 20% pay rise, this wage would have risen to £2.40. If you or I received a 20% pay rise it would be substantially more than 40p per week.

- Emphasis is placed on past results. Past results are not a totally reliable indicator of future results. If your football team has won its past six matches in the Premiership, there is no guarantee that it will win its seventh game.

- Published accounts give only an overview – perhaps disguising inefficient sections of a business. The return on capital employed may be 27% – however, on closer scrutiny we might find that one section of the business is earning a return on capital of 50% and the other section earns a return of just 4%.

- Final accounts show only the monetary aspects of the business. They do not show the strengths and weaknesses of individual managers or members of staff. They do not show staff welfare. Some businesses are very successful and pay top wages but have workers who hate going to work each day.

- It is extremely difficult to compare like with like between two businesses; they have:
  - different sites
  - different management teams
  - different staff
  - different customers etc.

- The external environment faced by the business may change. The changes may have an immediate effect or the result of the changes may be felt only after a time lag. A devaluation of the currency may cause imported materials to rise in price, but if the business carries large inventory and issues those goods using the FIFO method of issue, increased costs may not be incorporated into product costs for some time.

- Different organisations have different structures; different methods of financing their operation; different expense and revenue patterns. They may use different accounting policies, techniques, methods of measuring and apply different conventions. No matter how similar businesses appear to be from the outside, all businesses are different.

- The final accounts of a business are prepared on a particular date. The balance sheet on that date may well be unrepresentative of the usual position of the business. A fancy goods business may well have low stocks at 31 December, after the Christmas rush. During the rest of the year it may carry large stocks of goods.

- Ratios show only the results of business activity. They do not indicate the causes of good or bad results. Coughs, sneezes and a running nose are the results of having a cold. These symptoms do not indicate how the cold was contracted.

● EXAMINATION TIP

When comparing 'like with like' there may be a need to make adjustments to the figures given. Notional rents and management salaries may need to be included in one set of comparative figures.

EXAMPLE

Business renting premises	Business owning premises –
	Include notional rent of premises
Business employing management team	Business run by owner –
	Include notional manager's salary

QUESTIONS 5 AND 6

The following information is given for two companies for the year ended 31 May 20*9:

	Been & Pole plc £000	Ebyam plc £000
Income statements		
Profit from operations	313	630
Debenture interest	(70)	
Profit before tax	243	630
Tax	(93)	(250)
Profit for the year	150	380
Balance sheet extracts		
Equity		
Ordinary shares £1	250	
Ordinary shares 50p		250
7% preferred shares £1	200	600
Share premium	62	
Revaluation reserve	120	
Retained earnings	95	1,077
	727	1,927
7% debentures	1,000	
	1,727	1,927
Market price per ordinary share	£6.80	£4.10
Dividends paid: preferred shares	14	42
ordinary shares	80	100

QUESTION 5

Calculate the following investment ratios for Been & Pole plc at 31 May 20*9:
i)   interest cover
ii)   EPS
iii)   ordinary dividend cover
iv)   dividend yield
v)   P/E ratio
vi)   dividend paid per share
vii)   gearing ratio.

QUESTION 6

Calculate the following investment ratios for Ebyam plc for the year ended 31 May 20*9:
i)   interest cover
ii)   EPS
iii)   ordinary dividend cover
iv)   dividend yield
v)   P/E ratio
vi)   dividend paid per share
vii)   gearing ratio.

QUESTION 7

The following information is provided for Apacolo plc at 31 March 20*9:

	£000
Ordinary shares of £1 each	3,486
6% preferred shares of £10 each	1,400
7% debenture stock 2025/2026	1,000
Reserves	2,114
Profit from operations	1,250
Provision for corporation tax	380
Dividend cover	6 times
Market price of ordinary shares	£5.50

	Formula	31 March 20*7	31 March 20*8	31 March 20*9
Interest cover		16.4 times	17.1 times	
EPS		17.8 pence	18.74 pence	
Ordinary dividend paid per share		3.1 pence	3.3 pence	
P/E ratio		24.5	25.7	
Dividend yield		0.6%	0.6%	
Gearing		23%	18.62%	

Required

a Calculate the ratios shown at 31 March 20*9.

b Complete the table and comment on the trends shown over the three years.

QUESTION 8

The following information is given for Rowlerby plc at 31 December 20*9:

	£000
Ordinary shares of 50p each	540
7% preferred shares of £1 each	300
6% debenture stock 2018/2019	150
Reserves	410
Profit from operations	303
Provision for corporation tax	49

Dividend cover	7 times
Market price of ordinary shares	£1.30

	Formula	31 December 20*7	31 December 20*8	31 December 20*9
Interest cover		24.6 times	30.8 times	
EPS		16.46 pence	18.59 pence	
Ordinary dividend paid per share		2.04 pence	2.38 pence	
P/E ratio		4.86	5.9	
Dividend yield		2.55%	2.16%	
Gearing		26.4%	29.2%	

Required

a Calculate the ratios shown at 31 December 20*9.

b Complete the table and comment on the trends shown over the three years.

QUESTION 9

The following information is given for two companies for the year ended 31 December 20*9:

	Baliaba plc £000	Firty Leaves plc £000
Profit from operations	260	330
Debenture interest		(63)
Profit before tax	260	267
Tax	(57)	(71)
Profit for year	203	196
Equity		
Ordinary shares of £1 each	195	
Ordinary shares of 25p each		200
8% preferred shares	200	400
Share premium	50	130
Revaluation reserve	100	60
Retained earnings	425	550

	£000	£000
	970	1,340
7% debentures		900
	970	2,240
Market price per share	£4.20	£1.40
Dividends paid during the year: preferred	16	32
ordinary	38	42

Required

a Calculate the following investment ratios for the two companies:
  i)   gearing ratio
  ii)   interest cover
  iii) EPS
  iv)   dividend paid per share
  v)   dividend yield
  vi   P/E ratio.
b Comment on the information gained from each of the ratio calculations.

QUESTION 10

The following information is available for two companies for the year ended 28 February 20*9:

	Becktom plc	Mirtimax plc
	£000	£000
Profit from operations	2,458	1,276
Debenture interest		(300)
Profit before tax	2,458	976
Tax	(983)	(382)
Profit for the year	1,475	594
Equity		
Ordinary shares of 50p each	3,960	
Ordinary shares of £1 each		3,500
6% preferred shares	4,000	1,000
10% debentures		3,000
Share premium	1,320	1,980
Revaluation reserve	500	–
Retained earnings	1,840	638
	11,620	10,118
Market price per share	£1.10	£2.10
Dividends paid: preferred	240	60
ordinary	393	320

Required

a Calculate the following investment ratios for the two companies:
  i)   gearing ratio
  ii)   interest cover
  iii) EPS
  iv)   dividend paid per share
  v)   dividend yield
  vi)   P/E ratio.
b Comment on the information gained from each of the ratios calculated.

● EXAMINATION TIP

Avoid making assumptions where there is no evidence in the question. Do tell the examiner if you do make an assumption. The instruction on the front of the examination paper tells you to do so.

● EXAMINATION TIP

Always state the formulae used. The examiner may have based his or her result on one formula; you may have obtained your results by using an alternative (equally correct) formula. The examiner will not know this if you do not state the formula used.

Chapter summary

- Ratios are used as a method of performance evaluation. 'Ratios' is the generic term used for true ratios, percentages and other measures.
- Ratios are only useful if comparisons are made either with other businesses in the same line of business or with previous years' results – ie trend analysis.
- Ratios can be divided into profitability ratios, liquidity ratios and investment ratios.
- It is necessary to learn the formulae for ratios and produce these before calculating the figures.

SELF-TEST QUESTIONS

- Why are results converted into ratios?
- What do profitability ratios tell us?
- Give an example of a profitability ratio.
- What do liquidity ratios tell us?
- Give an example of a liquidity ratio.
- Give the formula for calculating the net margin.
- Give the formula for calculating the rate of inventory turnover.
- How is average inventory calculated?
- Mary makes a gross margin of 54%. Is this good or bad?
- Mary's debtors pay, on average, in 42 days; she pays her creditors in 19 days. Is this a good or a bad policy? Consider why.
- Give an example of one investor ratio.
- What does the price/earnings ratio tell us?
- Identify two limitations of using ratios as an evaluation of performance.

TEST QUESTIONS

QUESTION 11

The following final accounts for Gerard Guillaume are given:

Income statement for the year ended 31 March 20*9

	£	£	£
Sales			148,120
Cost of sales			88,872
Gross profit			59,248
Expenses			45,811
Net profit			13,437

Balance sheet at 31 March 20*9

Non-current assets			
Vehicle		8,500	
Less depreciation		2,000	6,500
Fixtures		8,000	
Less depreciation		1,600	6,400
			12,900
Current assets			
Inventories		4,650	
Trade receivables		6,348	
		10,998	
Current liabilities			
Cash and cash equivalents	5,078		
Trade payables	4,020	9,098	1,900
			14,800
Capital			14,800

The following ratios are available:

Year ended 31 March	20*8	20*7	20*6	20*5
Gross profit margin	38.2%	37.1%	39.7%	35.2%
Net margin	8.8%	7.7%	10.1%	7.1%
ROCE	89%	87%	89%	82%
Current ratio	1.5:1	1.7:1	2.1:1	2.3:1
Liquid ratio	0.8:1	0.9:1	1.1:1	1.2:1

Required

a Calculate the following ratios for the year ended 31 March 20*9:
   i)   gross profit margin
   ii) net profit margin
   iii) return on capital employed
   iv) current ratio
   v)   liquid (acid test) ratio.
b Comment on your results.

QUESTION 12

The following final accounts for Antoine Ltd at 31 March are provided:

Income statement for the year ended 31 March

	20*9	20*8
	£000	£000
Sales	16,620	12,460
Less Cost of sales	(12,630)	(8,720)
Gross profit	3,990	3,740
Less Expenses	(2,520)	(2,350)
Profit before tax	1,470	1,390
Tax	(800)	(750)
Profit for the year	670	640

Balance sheet at 31 March

	20*9			20*8		
	£000	£000	£000	£000	£000	£000
Non-current assets at NBV			14,200			12,900
Current assets						
Inventories		4,120			2,160	
Trade receivables		4,070			2,100	
Cash and cash equivalents		-			890	
		8,190			5,150	
Current liabilities						
Trade payables	(3,850)			(2,130)		
Tax	(800)			(750)	(2,880)	
Cash and cash equivalents	(2,480)	(7,130)				
Net current assets			1,060			2,270
			15,260			15,170
Non-current liabilities			(3,800)			(3,800)
			11,460			11,370
Equity						
Ordinary shares of £1 each			8,300			8,300
Reserves			3,160			3,070
			11,460			11,370
Dividends paid			640			580

Required

a Calculate for both years:
   i)   gross profit margin
   ii) net profit margin
   iii) return on capital employed
   iv) current ratio
   v)   liquid (acid test) ratio.
b Calculate for 20*9 only:
   i)   rate of inventory turnover

ii)   receivables collection period
iii) payables payment period.
c   (**Note:** transfer price is the price for which shares in a private limited company change hands; this is the equivalent to the market price paid for ordinary shares in a public (plc) limited company.)
Assuming that the transfer price per share was £1.30 at 31 March 20*9, calculate:
i)   earnings per share (EPS)
ii)   price/earnings ratio (P/E)
iii) dividend cover.

QUESTION 13

The following accounts are provided for the year ended 31 January for Vincent and Varsha Ltd:

Income statement for the year ended 31 January

	20*9	20*8
	£000	£000
Turnover	16,550	15,600
Cost of sales	(8,380)	(7,900)
Gross profit	8,170	7,700
Selling and distribution costs	(3,525)	(3,200)
Administration expenses	(1,800)	(1,500)
Profit from operations	2,845	3,000
Interest payable	(88)	(80)
Profit before tax	2,757	2,920
Tax	(850)	(900)
Profit for the year	1,907	2,020

Balance sheet at 31 January

	20*9	20*8
	£000	£000
Non-current assets	18,000	16,500
Current assets		
Inventories	706	680
Trade receivables	4,800	3,800
Cash and cash equivalents	81	1,050
	23,587	22,030
Current liabilities	(6,600)	(6,400)
Total assets less current liabilities	16,987	15,630
Non-current liabilities	(1,100)	(1,000)
	15,887	14,630
Equity		
Ordinary shares of 50p each	8,000	8,000
Reserves	7,887	6,630
	15,887	14,630
Dividends paid	£650	£790
Transfer price of ordinary shares	£1.10	£0.90

Required

a   Calculate for both years, where possible:
i)   gross margin
ii)   net margin
iii)   operating expenses/sales
iv)   return on capital employed
v)   current ratio
vi)   liquid ratio
vii)   interest cover
viii) dividend cover
ix)   earnings per share
x)   price/earnings ratio
xi)   gearing ratio
xii)   dividend yield
xiii) rate of inventory turnover
xiv)   receivables collection period.
b   Comment on ratios (vii)–(xi).

QUESTION 14

The following financial statements are provided to the year ended 31 August for Catas and Trofy Ltd:

Income statement for the year ended 31 August

	20*9 £000	20*9 £000	20*9 £000	20*8 £000	20*8 £000	20*8 £000
Sales (credit)			3,390			2,773
Less **Cost of sales**						
Inventories		184			166	
Purchases (credit)		2,250			1,970	
		2,434			2,136	
Inventories		(198)	(2,236)		(184)	(1,952)
Gross profit			1,154			821
Less:						
Admin, selling and distribution expenses			(584)			(455)
Profit from operations			570			366
Interest payable			(33)			(11)
Profit before tax			537			355
Tax			(190)			(120)
Profit for the year			347			235
Dividends paid: preferred shares		9			9	
ordinary shares		130			70	

Balance sheet at 31 August

	20*9 £000	20*9 £000	20*9 £000	20*8 £000	20*8 £000	20*8 £000
Non-current assets						
Net book value			1,450			870
Current assets						
Inventories		198			184	
Trade receivables		510			380	
Cash and cash equivalents		210			266	
		918			830	
Current liabilities						
Trade payables	(330)			(220)		
Tax	(190)	(520)	398	(120)	(340)	490
			1,848			1,360
Non-current liabilities						
10% debentures			(330)			(110)
			1,518			1,250
Equity						
Ordinary shares of £1 each			700			700
6% preferred shares			150			150
Share premium			70			70
Retained earnings			598			330
			1,518			1,250
Market price per share			£2.10			£1.40

Required

a Calculate for both years (state the formulae used):
   i) gross margin
   ii) net margin
   iii) operating expenses to sales
   iv) return on capital employed
   v) current ratio
   vi) liquid ratio
   vii) interest cover
   viii) dividend cover
   ix) earnings per share
   x) price/earnings ratio
   xi) gearing ratio
   xii) dividend yield.
b Calculate for the year ended 31 August 20*9:
   xiii) rate of inventory turnover
   xiv) receivables collection period
   xv) payables payment period.

QUESTION 15

The following final accounts are provided for the year ended 30 November for two businesses: Del Tipper (a sole trader) and Tanka Continental Traders Ltd:

Income statements for the year ended 30 November 20*9

	Del Tipper		Tanka Continental Traders Ltd	
	£	£	£000	£000
Sales		136,000		1,030
Less Cost of sales:				
Inventories	2,900		140	
Purchases (credit)	60,000		460	
	62,900		600	
Inventories	(1,100)	61,800	(160)	440
Gross profit		74,200		590
Operating expenses		(34,000)		(280)
Profit for the year		40,200		310

Balance sheets at 30 November 20*9

	Del Tipper		Tanka Continental Traders Ltd	
	£	£	£000	£000
Non-current assets		110,000		700
Current assets				
Inventories	1,100		160	
Trade receivables	5,500		120	
Cash and cash equivalents	8,000		85	
	14,600		365	
Current liabilities				
Trade payables	(1,250)	13,350	(250)	115
		123,350		815
Capital		123,350	**Equity**	
			Ordinary shares	500
			Retained earnings	315
				815

Additional information

Both Del and Tanka Continental Traders Ltd are in the same line of business. Both businesses purchase and sell all goods on credit.

Del manages his own business. If he were to work outside the business he would have to employ a manager to run his business. The manager would have to be paid £18,000 per annum.

If Del sold his business he could earn 8% on any capital invested.

Required

a   Calculate for both businesses:
   i)   gross margin
   ii)   net margin
   iii)   expenses/sales ratio
   iv)   return on capital employed
   v)   current ratio
   vi)   liquid ratio
   vii)   receivables collection period
   viii) payables payment period
   ix)   rate of inventory turnover.
b   Comment on your results.
c   Advise Del on the best way of maximising his income in the future.

QUESTION 16

The following balance sheets at 31 August are given for Pawar Ltd:

	20*9		20*8	
	£000	£000	£000	£000
Non-current assets				
Freehold property at valuation		4,000		3,600
Plant and machinery at cost	4,925		2,820	
Less Provision for depreciation	(2,040)	2,885	(1,160)	1,660
Vehicles at cost	2,890		1,450	
Less Provision for depreciation	(850)	2,040	(670)	780
Office equipment at cost	660		220	
Less Provision for depreciation	(140)	520	(110)	110
		9,445		6,150
Current assets				
Inventories	1,160		905	
Trade receivables	520		370	
Cash and cash equivalents	1,250		1,280	
	2,930		2,555	
Current liabilities				
Trade payables	(805)		(590)	
Tax	(412)		(505)	
	(1,217)	1,713	(1,095)	1,460
		11,158		7,610
Non-current liabilities				
7% debenture stock		(1,600)		(700)
		9,558		6,910
Equity				
Ordinary shares of £1 each		2,600		2,600
6% preferred shares of £1 each		3,000		1,000
Share premium		110		110
Revaluation reserve		950		550
Asset replacement reserve		900		900
Retained earnings		1,998		1,750
		9,558		6,910
Market price per share		£3.00		£2.50

Income statement extract for the year ended 31 August 20*9	
	£000
Profit from operations	1,562
Interest payable	(112)
Profit before tax	1,450
Tax	(412)
Profit for the year	1,038
Dividends paid for the year: preferred shares	180
ordinary shares	610

Required

a Calculate for both years:
  i)   current ratio
  ii) liquid ratio
  iii) gearing ratio.
b Calculate for year ended 31 August 20*9 only:
  i)   interest cover
  ii) dividend cover
  iii) earnings per share
  iv) price/earnings ratio
  v)   dividend yield.
c Explain what is meant by:
  i)   earnings per share
  ii) price/earnings ratio
  iii) dividend yield.

CHAPTER
NINE

Business Ownership

Business activity takes place within organisations with varied legal structures. The status of ownership of a business will determine what financial records must be kept and how they must be presented. For example, there is no legal requirement for a sole trader or a partnership to produce a set of final accounts. However, it has long been accepted that it is in the best interests of sole traders and partnerships to produce a full set of accounts in order to be able to provide the information that might be required by Her Majesty's Revenue and Customs (HMRC). This would be a good idea because of the functions of accounting (remember the stewardship and management functions).

Sole traders and partnerships might also want to produce a set of accounts in order to make it easier for them to review their performance in financial terms and perhaps to help them to predict the impact of any suggested changes in their business strategy. In the event of a sole trader or a partnership approaching a bank manager to ask for a loan, they might be asked to present a set of financial statements so that the bank manager can make a judgement about whether or not the business is secure enough for them to agree a loan safely.

Many businesses in the United Kingdom are formed as sole traders and although this type of ownership is usually associated with small businesses, that need not necessarily be the case.

The status of sole trader simply means that one person retains total ownership and control of the business.

Specification coverage:
AQA ACCN3;
OCR F012.

By the end of this chapter you should be able to:
■ distinguish between different types of business ownership
■ identify the advantages and disadvantages of the different types of ownership.

ADVANTAGES OF BEING A SOLE TRADER
1. The owner retains total control of business decisions.
2. Decision-making might be faster because only one person makes all key decisions.
3. The owner will receive all the profits generated by the business.
4. It is easy to set up, as starting a business as a sole trader does not involve many complicated procedures and/or documentation. The individual must notify HMRC that they intend to be self-employed.

DISADVANTAGES OF BEING A SOLE TRADER
1. Although decision-making might be faster, the sole trader might lose out on the benefit of discussion before decisions are made.
2. Just as the owner might receive all the profits, they must also bear all the losses of the business.
3. Sole traders have unlimited liability. This means that in the event of the business having debts that cannot be met from the resources within the business, the owner remains liable for the outstanding debt, even if this means selling personal possessions in order to settle it.
4. Sole traders experience limited access to finance. This is often restricted to what can be raised from personal savings and contacts and from bank loans.
5. However, this disadvantage has been partially offset in recent years as a result of government and European Union grants that have been made available to small businesses.
6. Lack of continuity. If the owner dies or retires, the business ceases to exist.

It is the lack of access to finance that has led many sole traders to take in a partner, or partners, who might not only introduce more ideas to the business but often bring in crucial additional finance. It is extremely rare for any individual to give financial support to a business without requiring something in return. So, what would someone putting money into a business expect? Obviously, they hope for a return on their investment and in order to give some peace of mind regarding the security of their investment, they will usually want a 'say' in the running of the

business, ie some control over business decisions, so meaning that they acquire part-ownership of the business. They become a partner in the business.

The status of the business has now become that of a partnership.

ADVANTAGES OF A PARTNERSHIP

1. Access to additional finance.
2. The introduction of more ideas into the business.
3. The opportunity for discussion to take place before any key decisions are made. This might make decisions more informed.
4. Partnerships can allow for more continuity of business activity, for example when one partner is on holiday or perhaps ill, the remaining partner(s) can ensure that the business continues to function as normal.
5. The introduction of a partner(s) might allow some specialisation to take place, as perhaps each of the partners can specialise in the aspect of the business in which they are most competent.
6. Relatively easy to set up. Setting up a partnership does not require lots of documentation and legal processes to be completed.

DISADVANTAGES OF A PARTNERSHIP

1. Finance is still only mainly available from the partners' personal sources and contacts together with bank loans and any grants that might be available.
2. Agreement might be more difficult to arrive at when decisions need to be made. The more people that are involved in making a decision, the more views there are likely to be and therefore reaching a consensus might slow the decision-making process down.
3. Profits now need to be shared between the partners. This is done in agreed profit-sharing ratios.
4. Partnerships still have unlimited liability, which leaves the personal possessions of all the partners at risk if the business were to be declared insolvent. There is the possibility of forming a limited partnership (see later).
5. Lack of continuity of the business entity. If a partner retires or dies, the partnership (and therefore the business) ceases to exist in its previous form and a new business must be formed if trading is to continue. (See Dissolution of partnerships in Chapter Four.)
6. All partners are liable for the actions of others. They are jointly and severally liable. This means that if the actions of one partner result in debts for the business, all the partners are liable to repay that debt even though they might not have been consulted about the action that had caused the debt.
   For example, you set up a business in partnership with a friend who then, unknown to you, takes out a large bank loan on behalf of the business. However, the money is never used for the business; instead your 'friend' disappears to live in the sun, using the bank loan to buy a house and to finance a rich lifestyle. What happens to the bank loan in a case like this? If your partner cannot be found and the money retrieved, then you, as the remaining partner in the business, will be held liable to repay the whole of the debt to the bank. It is then not surprising that people will tell you that you should not consider going into business with anyone, unless you would trust them with your last penny: that is exactly what they might take, if the situation above occurred – and occasionally it does!

Many partnerships draw up a legally binding document known as a **deed of partnership** that outlines the key terms that have been agreed with regard to such things as how profits are to be shared and perhaps the terms of loans to the business from the partners. It might also include details of the valuation of goodwill and other assets in the case of any structural change.

It should be noted that in cases where a deed of partnership has not been drawn up and a dispute occurs that cannot be resolved by the partners, the dispute will be resolved by recourse to law, ie the Partnership Act 1890. The terms of this Act would then over-rule any verbal agreements that might have been made by the partners. For example, two partners might have verbally agreed a profit-sharing ratio of 3:1 but the Partnership Act 1890 would impose equal sharing of profits unless there was sufficient evidence to prove that the ratio of 3:1 had been the usual practice over a number of years. Therefore, if any partnership wants to agree terms that are not consistent with the Partnership Act then it is advisable that the partners outline all such terms in a deed of partnership that would then be binding on them all.

The situation of partners being '**jointly and severally liable**' might be just the kind of eventuality that partners would want to protect themselves from. This might be easier for partners who are fully involved in the business on a day-to-day basis. What about partners who have put money into a business but who are not involved in the everyday activity of the business? How do they protect themselves? One way is for the partnership to give them **limited**

liability covered under the Limited Partnerships Act of 1907. This Act provides for the personal possessions of partners to be protected in the event of insolvency. However, it also states that at least one partner must have unlimited liability. Limited partnerships are usually formed when someone is willing to inject money into the business, but they do not want, or are not able, to take any part in the running of the business. In the case of a limited partnership, the liability for the debts of the business is limited, to the amount invested, for those partners with limited liability. This offers some security to people who are willing to invest in a partnership but who want to protect themselves from situations similar to the one outlined above. It is often the case that the only partner(s) afforded limited liability are those who put money into the business without actively participating in the business. They are sometimes known as 'sleeping partners'.

Many partnerships can suffer from the same financial starvation as some sole traders because of the limited sources of finance to which they have access. It is for this reason that sometimes people who do not intend to have any involvement in the day-to-day running of the business are approached for financial support – more partners with limited liability.

A change from a partnership into a limited company can meet the needs of those who do not wish to put their personal assets at risk by involvement in a business venture. A change to a limited company gives all the owners limited liability. There are two types of limited companies:

- private limited company
- public limited company.

The process of establishing a limited company, whether private or public, requires the submission of specified documents to the Registrar of Companies. Each company must produce a memorandum of association and articles of association.

A **memorandum of association** is a document that must be filed with the Registrar of Companies before the company can become incorporated. It defines the external relationship of the company to the outside world.

The details filed include:

- the company's name, address and registered office
- details of the share capital
- the company's objectives.

Articles of association state the company's rules which will govern the internal organisation of the company. Details include:

- organisation and control
- shareholders' voting rights
- conduct of directors' meetings
- conduct of shareholders' annual general meeting
- directors' powers
- rights attached to different types of shares.

In the case of a private limited company once these documents have been accepted by the Registrar of Companies, a certificate of incorporation will be issued. Once this formality is completed, a private limited company can begin to trade. However, in the case of a public limited company a prospectus will have to be prepared before shares can be issued for sale to the public.

At this point we need to remind ourselves of the key features and differences between a private limited company and a public limited company by referring to Chapter Six.

Chapter summary

- Businesses differ in their legal structure sometimes according to the number of people involved, eg a sole trader involves only one person whereas a partnership involves between two and 20 people (20 being the maximum for a normal business). This raises issues regarding the ownership and control of a business.
- Businesses can also differ with regard to whether or not they have limited or unlimited liability.

SELF-TEST QUESTIONS

- State two advantages of being a sole trader.
- State two disadvantages of being a sole trader.
- State two advantages of being in partnership.
- State two disadvantages of being in partnership.
- When did the Partnership Act become law?
- When did the Limited Partnership Act become law?
- Sole traders have limited liability. True or false?
- Partners have unlimited liability. True or false?
- What does the term 'jointly and severally liable' mean?
- State how profits are to be shared if there is no partnership deed drawn up by partners.
- The owners of a limited company are known as partners. True or false?
- Identify two items stated in a company's memorandum of association.
- Identify two items stated in a company's articles of association.
- The owners of a limited company have limited liability. True or false?

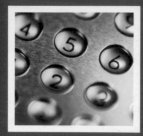

CHAPTER
TEN

Sources of Finance

Finding initial or additional finance is the concern of many businesses at some time or other in their existence.

There are many different sources of finance available but not all of them are accessible to all businesses. Accessibility of finance can depend on the legal status of the business and the amount of security that the business can offer to the potential lender.

PERSONAL FINANCE

Personal savings are often used to provide the first injection of money into a business, however, this is usually a very limited source and there is sometimes a need for finance to be acquired from additional sources. This is often the only source of finance when a person is establishing a business as a sole trader. It is important to recognise that the amount of money made available to a business can often be determined by the degree of risk involved in the investment. The element of risk is reduced for the investor in a company, as business ownership provides for limited liability in the event of the business becoming insolvent. However, in the case of a sole trader, using personal savings to start up or expand a business, their liability in the case of insolvency is unlimited.

FUNDS FROM FRIENDS AND FAMILY

In the early stages of establishing a business, owners frequently seek the help of family and friends to provide some of the required finance. While such contacts might be willing to show their confidence in the business, they might want some security for their investment. This is often the cause of a business that was established as a sole trader transforming its legal status into that of a partnership. By making the providers of finance partners in the business they will now have some control over its day-to-day running and so can, to some extent, protect their investment. However, there is still the possibility that investors might lose all of the money invested and, because partnerships have unlimited liability, their personal possessions might also be under threat in the event of the business becoming insolvent. (See Chapter Six for limited partnerships.)

OVERDRAFT

This is a short-term source of finance obtained from banks. Most businesses will have agreed an overdraft limit prior to any need to use it arising. It is in the interest of businesses to agree an overdraft limit with their bank just in case they find it necessary to use this source of finance. This is because the interest charged on an authorised (agreed) overdraft is usually less than if they had not agreed (unauthorised) an overdraft facility in advance.

It is advisable for businesses to try to negotiate an overdraft limit that is slightly greater than any amount that they feel they might need. This is in order to prevent them going beyond the authorised overdraft limit and so incurring higher charges.

The rate of interest charged on overdrafts tends to be higher than that charged on long-term borrowing, so for this reason a business is only likely to want to use an overdraft in the short term. Although an overdraft could conceivably be maintained in the longer term, it would be an expensive way of raising finance when compared with say, a bank loan. Providers of overdrafts

Specification coverage:
AQA ACCN3;
OCR F013.

By the end of this chapter you should be able to:
■ assess different types of business finance
■ appreciate the relevance of the various sources of finance for different forms of business ownership.

do not require the level of security that they would require when granting a bank loan and therefore the level of risk is much higher for them. The rate of interest charged on overdrafts reflects this higher degree of risk. An overdraft is often used when the amount of additional finance required can only be calculated approximately and the period for which it is required is estimated to be short. If the circumstances of the business are such that the owners feel that they might need additional finance for a longer period of time than would be advisable when using an overdraft, they might then apply to their bank for a loan.

BANK LOANS (SHORT-TERM AND LONG-TERM)

The benefits of arranging a bank loan rather than using an overdraft are that the bank usually charges a lower rate of interest on the amount borrowed. The loan is taken out for an agreed period of time and the repayments are usually for an agreed amount at specified intervals during the loan. The most common arrangement is for equal monthly repayments over the duration of the loan. However, varied arrangements can be made with the lender. For example, some banks might agree to smaller payments being made in the first two or three years of a 15-year loan, with the repayments gradually increasing towards the end of the term. This can allow time for an investment to begin to produce a return before the larger payments need to be paid.

Banks will usually require some collateral (security) for their loan and so loans are often secured by the business's buildings (or owner's/owners' homes in the case of sole traders and partnerships). In the event of the loan not being repaid, the bank would seize the item on which the loan had been secured. It is not uncommon for a bank to require the deeds to property to be handed over to it until the loan is repaid in full. This reduces the risk to the lender because if the business does not repay the loan then they can sell the business property (or the owner's house) if necessary to get their money back. While many loans are for a five- or 10-year period, the length of a business loan is dependent on the amount being borrowed and the length of time for which a lender is willing to lend. Banks usually lend to businesses at approximately 3–4% above their base rate but this again varies with the amount of risk and the length of the loan.

Even though a bank might hold the deeds to the business's property, the loan does not give it any say in the day-to-day running of the business. Therefore, by using a bank loan to raise additional finance, a business is not sacrificing any ownership or control of the business to the outside providers of finance.

ISSUE OF SHARES

When a business raises additional finance through the issue of shares it is actually selling off part of the business. The ownership of the business passes to the shareholders. (If you buy some shares in a business this means that you have bought a 'share' or a 'part' of that business.) For this reason, businesses who choose to raise additional finance through the issue of shares are very careful not to sell too many shares and thus to allow the overall ownership and control of the business to be taken by investors. Theoretically, if the original owners of a business retain 50% plus one share, they would have the deciding vote on key issues because they would always have one more vote than all of the other shareholders put together (assuming that one share equals one vote).

The way in which shares can be sold differs depending on whether the business is a private limited company or a public limited company.

■ Private limited company

In a private limited company shares can be purchased only through private agreements. They cannot be offered for sale to the general public through the Stock Exchange. This can limit the amount of finance that can be made available through the sale of shares.

■ Public limited company

A public limited company can extend the range of people to whom it can offer its shares for sale. Once it has satisfied all the requirements of the Stock Exchange, its shares can be bought and sold by the general public through the stock market.

Note: When shares are issued by a company for the first time, all monies paid for those shares will go to the business in question. However, if the original purchasers decide to sell their shares, the money paid by the next owner of the shares does not go into the company but to the seller of the shares (usually a stock broker). It is similar to Ford selling a car to a Ford garage. When the garage first purchases the car from Ford, the company, Ford, will receive the money. The garage then sells the car to a customer. The garage keeps the money paid for the car, together with any

profit that it has made on the deal – just as if it had bought shares in Ford and later sold them for a profit. Many years later, that same car might have changed ownership four or five times. Each time a sale is made, the seller of the car receives the amount paid for the car – none of the money ever goes to the Ford motor company after that first sale of the car to the garage (the first owner).

This is a common area of misunderstanding for students, particularly when they discuss a fall in share prices; comments are often made by students about the business losing money if the share price falls or that a rise in share prices means more money going into the business. From the example above, I hope that you can see that this is not the case.

DEBENTURES

Debentures are long-term loans made to companies. The loans are made at an agreed rate of interest. The holders of debentures will receive interest payments, usually annually, on the amount loaned. At the end of the agreed period of the loan, the capital sum will be repaid to the lender. This is an efficient way of raising finance for a business as only the interest has to be paid until the time when the repayment is due. For the lender, debentures carry less risk than buying ordinary shares because, in the event of bankruptcy, they will be paid out of the company's assets before any monies are paid to shareholders. However, the downside to this is that if the business begins to gain large profits, that allow it to make bigger dividend payments to shareholders, the debenture holders will continue to receive the same amount of interest that they agreed at the start and they will not gain any additional return as a result of increasing profitability. This is the sacrifice they make for having more security.

VENTURE CAPITAL

This is finance made available by individuals who are looking for return on their money, perhaps from investing in more risky ventures.

GOVERNMENT GRANTS

In a bid to encourage the survival and growth of different sectors of the economy, the Government has, at times, made various grants available to businesses. Such grants have varied with regard to the reason for their being given. Some grants have been given specifically for the purchase of new capital equipment while others have been made available for training the workforce. The type of grant available to a business can depend on what the Government sees as a priority in the economy at that time and also which part of the country the business is in. Some parts of the country are seen to need more help than others when it comes to support for businesses. For example, an area of high unemployment is likely to attract more Government funds than an affluent area that has little or no unemployment.

Grants for various businesses have also been made available through the European Union, again perhaps depending on the factors outlined above.

It is important to realise that the same grants are not always available, as their availability can vary with the economic status of the area in which the business is situated and the needs of other areas either within the United Kingdom or within Europe in the case of a grant from the EU.

TAX ALLOWANCES

HMRC allows businesses to offset certain of their expenses against their tax liability. For example, businesses can claim a percentage allowance against capital equipment being used in the business or an allowance for contributions made to the pension funds of their employees.

These allowances are implemented by HMRC and can vary according to what the Government hopes to achieve in the economy at the time. At times, the Government seeks to encourage the introduction of automated production processes or the increased use of information technology in all aspects of business. At such times HMRC is likely to be allowing a greater percentage of the cost of such investments to be offset (treated as an expense) against any tax that the business is deemed liable to pay. As such allowances are deducted from net profit, this reduces the amount of profit on which the business must pay tax and therefore leaves more money in the business as retained profits.

HIRE PURCHASE

Hire purchase is a means by which a business can acquire assets without paying the full amount at the time of acquisition. Although it is not a source of additional finance for a business, it does allow businesses to conserve any funds that they might have for use elsewhere. When assets are purchased using this method the purchaser would usually pay a deposit followed by regular payments until the full amount has been paid. Until the final purchase is made, the purchaser is legally only 'hiring' the equipment, hence the name 'hire purchase'. When the final payment is made, ownership passes from the vendor to the purchaser. This method of purchasing assets also usually involves the payment of interest on the amount due.

MORTGAGE

A mortgage is usually used to acquire high-value assets whose cost is greater than the current finance available within the business. It is a long-term loan most frequently used for the purchase of the business's buildings. The provider of the mortgage uses the building being purchased as collateral to secure the loan. In the event of a business being unable to finance the regular payments required, the lender would have the right to sell the building in order to recoup their money.

LEASING

This is a means of having the use of assets without ever having to own them. They can be leased (borrowed) from a leasing company. Again, regular payments will need to be made by the business in order to secure the continued use of the asset.

Hire purchase, mortgage and leasing allow businesses to budget because these methods are supported by regular payments being made on the part of the business.

Note: Although assets that are being leased and those that are being purchased on hire purchase technically do not belong to the business, they should nevertheless be included on the business balance sheet since they are being used to generate profits. This is an application of the principle of 'substance over form'. (This is when the person who gains the benefit from the use of an asset is not the legal owner of that asset.)

SALE AND LEASEBACK

Times of cash shortage can sometimes be alleviated by the sale of assets bringing in a lump sum of money realised by their sale. Such assets can then be acquired through a lease company for use in the business. In this way the business gets the money released by the sale of assets and then makes regular (usually monthly) payments for use of the required assets on a lease basis.

One point to remember here is that if a business sells off assets in order, for example, to resolve a cash flow problem, that problem might be solved in the short term but that it can prove to be more expensive to the business in the longer term. This is because previously the business owned the asset but now it must make payments for as long as use of the asset is required. In the short term cash flows in but in the longer term money flows out on a regular basis and for as long as the business wants to use the asset. There is also a danger that when the lease expires the new owner may not renew it, perhaps leaving a business needing to find alternative accommodation and/or equipment.

RETAINED PROFIT

This is probably the most important source of finance for a business because it is this source that ensures that the business is self-financing. If a business constantly has to rely on injections of external finance (from relatives, banks, shares issue, issues of debentures etc) then this source might eventually dry up and if the business is not profitable the result might be its liquidation.

Charles Dickens said many years ago in one of his books that an income of £20 per year(!) with expenditure of £19.99 per year would result in happiness. However, an income of £20 per year with expenditure of £20.01 would result in misery!

If you earn £100 per week from a job and you are spending £120 on a regular basis you will become reliant on external finance to fund your lifestyle. There will come a time when parents

and friends are no longer willing to subsidise your activities. The same principle applies in the case of a business.

Note

When finance is raised from a source that incurs an interest charge, the interest should be charged to the income statement and any capital repayments reduce the amount owed as shown on the balance sheet.

For example, Tom makes a payment of £21,000 to his business mortgage provider. The payment is made up of £1,000 of interest and the remainder is a repayment of part of the capital sum. The financial recording of this transaction would be that £1,000 is charged to the income statement and his long-term liability on the balance sheet would be reduced by £20,000.

● EXAMINATION TIP

When a question asks you to identify sources of finance for a business, take careful note of the legal status of the business in question. The source of finance that you suggest must be one that is available to that particular type of business. Do not suggest that a sole trader raises additional capital by issuing shares, for example, as this source of finance is not available to them unless they change the legal structure of the business and form a limited company.

Chapter summary

- There are many ways in which businesses can raise capital.
- Some are available only to limited companies, eg finance raised from the issue of shares and debentures.
- Other forms of finance are available to all types of business.
- You will have noticed that many of the sources of capital are external to the business but that businesses can also be funded internally by using retained profits.
- Funds can be retained within a business by financing certain activities by using hire purchase, leases etc.

SELF-TEST QUESTIONS

- Name two sources of finance that are available to a sole trader.
- Why might someone worry about putting money into a partnership if they were not going to take any part in the day-to-day running of the business?
- What type of business is allowed to issue shares for sale to the general public?
- To whom can a private limited company sell shares?
- Which form of finance is likely to carry a lower rate of interest: a five-year bank loan or an overdraft?
- Explain why using hire purchase is regarded as a source of finance.
- Outline one benefit of using sale and leaseback.
- Identify one advantage that a government grant has over a long-term bank loan.
- Name one disadvantage of acquiring finance from a relative.
- Explain why a sole trader cannot issue ordinary shares to the general public.
- Why might a Government give a tax allowance to businesses in the northeast of England and not to businesses in the south of England?
- Explain how interest to service a long-term bank loan and capital repayments of the bank loan are treated in a set of financial statements.

CHAPTER ELEVEN

The Valuation of Inventories

In *Introducing Accounting* we considered the valuation of inventories. We said that the over-riding principle that should be used at all times is that inventory should be valued at the lower of cost and net realisable value.

Since this principle causes so many problems to students it is worth a moment's revision.

IAS 2 defines cost as 'the expenditure which has been incurred in the normal course of business in bringing the product or service to its present location and condition'.

The standard defines net realisable value as 'the estimated proceeds from the sale of items of inventory less all further costs to completion and less all costs to be incurred in marketing, selling and distributing ... the items'.

Specification coverage:
AQA ACCN3;
OCR F014.

By the end of this chapter you should be able to:
- understand the main methods of valuing inventory using FIFO and AVCO methods
- calculate the effect of different methods of inventory valuation on profit
- calculate the value of closing inventory when valuing inventory after the financial year-end.

WORKED EXAMPLE

Daphne Baird sells one type of vacuum cleaner. They cost £80 each to purchase. At 31 March 20*9 she has 14 cleaners in stock. The cleaners usually sell for £120 each.

Daphne has one cleaner in stock that is damaged. She intends to have the cleaner repaired at a cost of £35. It can then be sold for £100.

Required

Calculate the value of Daphne's closing inventory at 31 March 20*9.

Answer

Daphne's inventory should be valued at £1,105.

Workings	£	£
13 cleaners at £80 each		1,040
1 damaged cleaner		
Selling price	100	
Less Repair costs	35	65
		1,105

Up to now we have valued most inventories at cost and net realisable value.

Fairly straightforward – or is it?

Consider the following example.

EXAMPLE

Jitesh sells only one product: a 'sedrit'. He provides the following information:

Purchases of sedrits		Sales of sedrits	
January	2 at £10 each	May	4 at £30 each
April	3 at £15 each	December	3 at £35 each
November	4 at £20 each		

You can see that Jitesh has two sedrits remaining in inventory at 31 December.

How should he value the two sedrits remaining in inventory?

He should value them at cost!

Should he choose to value them at £10 each; or £15 each; or £20 each; or one at £10 the other at £15; or . . .?

You can see that there are many combinations that we could choose when valuing Jitesh's closing inventory.

So valuing inventory at cost is not quite so simple as it first seems. The total purchases figure for the year is £145 and the total sales revenue for the year is £225. We could calculate the cost of sales if we could decide on a method by which we could value the closing inventory.

In the example used above it might be fairly straightforward to identify the actual units of sedrits that had been sold and hence identify the two remaining in the business. However, if we had many hundreds of items available for sale this would be well-nigh impossible.

Most businesses will be unable to identify with any precision the actual items that they have remaining as inventories at the end of their financial year, and even if they could it would be a mammoth task to go back through purchases invoices to determine the price paid for each item of inventory.

The valuation of inventory is therefore a matter of expediency rather than strict accuracy.

So in the valuation of closing inventory we do not trace through the actual units that have been sold; rather, we identify certain items of inventory that are deemed to be sold and therefore certain items of inventory are deemed to remain as inventory.

The following methods are most frequently used to identify the goods deemed to have been issued to either a final customer or another department within the same business.

'FIRST IN, FIRST OUT' METHOD OF VALUING INVENTORY (FIFO)

As the name suggests, this method **assumes** that the **first** goods received by the business will be the **first** ones to be delivered to the final customer or the department requisitioning the goods. It assumes that goods have been used in the order in which they were purchased. Therefore any remaining inventory will be valued as if it were the latest goods purchased.

Remember that this is only an assumption.

This is a method of valuing inventories – it is not necessarily the way that goods are actually issued. Goods may be issued in any way that best suits a particular business regardless of when they were received.

A garage mechanic requires a set of spark plugs to fit into the car he is working on. The store keeper in the parts department will issue the first set of plugs he can lay his hands on; he will not waste time seeking out the first set of plugs bought in to give to the mechanic.

WEIGHTED AVERAGE COST METHOD OF ISSUING INVENTORY (AVCO)

The average cost of goods held is recalculated each time a new delivery of goods is received. Issues are then priced out at a weighted average cost.

METHODS OF VALUING CLOSING INVENTORY

Some businesses keep extremely detailed records of the inventories that they hold.

Every transaction affecting the purchase and sale of inventory is recorded in great detail.

The value of inventory is then recalculated after each transaction. (The inventory records look rather like a bank statement.)

The method of recalculating the value of inventory held after each transaction is known as the **perpetual** method.

This method is used by businesses that need to cost their work out to customers very carefully. It is also used in the major supermarkets. Each time a transaction is 'swiped' at the check-outs the bar code is read and records are updated electronically to record the sale. Each time a delivery arrives in the warehouse the goods received will be 'swiped' and the inventory records will be updated with the receipt.

Other less sophisticated businesses may simply value their inventory once, at the financial year-end. The owner of your local newsagents or take-away will probably take inventory at close of business at their year-end. They will list all items remaining unsold on the last day of the financial year; they will then assign a value to each category of goods held as inventory and the total will give the closing inventory figure to be used in the financial statements.

This is known as a **periodic** method of valuing inventory.

Let us examine the results given when we use a perpetual method of valuing inventories.

WORKED EXAMPLE

During the month of February the following receipts and issues of the component SMH/19 took place:

	Receipts of SMH/19	Issues of SMH/19
2 February	8 @ £10	
7 February		6
9 February	9 @ £11	
16 February		10
24 February	7 @ £12	
27 February		6

continued ➢

WORKED EXAMPLE *continued*

Required

Calculate the value of closing inventory of component SMH/19, using the 'first in, first out' method of valuing inventory (FIFO).

Answer

The value of closing inventory using the FIFO method of issue is £24.00.

Date	Receipts	Issues	Balance
2 February	8 @ £10		£80.00 (8 @ £10)
7 February		6	£20.00 (2 @ £10)
9 February	9 @ £11		£119.00 (2 @ £10; 9 @ £11)
16 February		10	£11.00 (1 @ £11)
24 February	7 @ £12		£95.00 (1 @ £11; 7 @ £12)
27 February		6	£24.00 (2 @ £12)

WORKED EXAMPLE

Using the same data for February shown above:

Required

Calculate the value of closing inventory of component SMH/19, using the weighted average cost method of valuing inventory (AVCO).

Answer

The value of closing inventory of component SMH/19 using the weighted average cost (AVCO) method of issuing inventory is £23.70.

Date	Receipts	Issues	Balance
2 February	8 @ £10		£80.00 (8 @ £10)
7 February		6	£20.00 (2 @ £10)
9 February	9 @ £11		£119.00 (Average cost £119.00/11 = £10.82)
16 February		10	£10.82 (1 @ £10.82)
24 February	7 @ £12		£94.82 (Average cost £94.82/8 = £11.85)
27 February		6	£23.70 (2 @ £11.85)

Check the two methods shown above. They are regularly examined at Advanced Level.

Since each method gives a different closing inventory figure, it follows that different gross profits will be revealed by using different methods of valuing inventory.

Imagine that component SMH/19 has been sold for £20 per unit.

What would be the gross profit be for each method of issue?

	FIFO		AVCO	
	£	£	£	£
Sales		440.00		440.00
Less Cost of sales				
Opening inventory	0		0	
Purchases	263.00		263.00	
	263.00		263.00	
Less Closing inventory	24.00	239.00	23.70	239.30
Gross profit		201.00		200.70

The level of profits revealed in a set of final accounts always depends on the way the inventory has been valued.

Now we will calculate the closing inventory using the **periodic** method.

Remember that this method uses only one valuation – at the end of the period being considered.

In the example used above, we consider February as one complete time period (usually the trader will value inventory at the end of a full financial year).

USING FIFO

24 SMH/19 components were purchased during February and 22 were issued, so at the end of the month there were two remaining unsold. Using FIFO, we assume that the first components were the first ones to be issued. The two components that are remaining are deemed to be from the last ones purchased. Closing inventory is therefore deemed to consist of two from the last batch purchased. Closing inventory is valued at £24.00 (2 × £12).

We have arrived at the same figure that we calculated using the perpetual method – coincidence? No: FIFO will give the same result whether you use the perpetual or the periodic method.

USING AVCO

Sorry – there is no shorter version of calculating closing inventory when an average price is taken for issuing goods.

Should you use the periodic method or the perpetual method when answering an examination question? Always use the method you find easiest. Use the method you are most comfortable using. Since the periodic method is, I think, easier, I would use it every time for the FIFO calculation, **unless** the question specifically requires the perpetual method.

QUESTION 1

The following information is available for the purchases and sales of 'pomsels' during October. At 30 September one 'pomsel' costing £100 remained as inventory.

Date	Purchases	Sales
4 October	6 at £100	
7 October		4
12 October	5 at £110	
23 October		6
24 October	7 at £120	
30 October		6

During October the selling price for 'pomsels' was £200.

Required

a Calculate the value of 'pomsels' remaining as inventory, using:
   (i)   the 'first in, first out' (FIFO) method of valuing inventory
   (ii) the weighted average cost (AVCO) method of valuation.
   Use a perpetual method for each calculation.
b Prepare an income statement for each method, using your results from (a).

QUESTION 2

The following information relates to the purchases and issues of 'giottas' during December. At 30 November there were three 'giottas' remaining as inventory; they had each cost £6 when purchased.

Date	Purchases	Issues
2 December	4 at £6	
13 December		6
15 December	5 at £8	
17 December		4
20 December	8 at £10	
30 December		7

During December the selling price of 'giottas' was £25 each.

Required

a Calculate the value of the inventory of 'giottas' at 31 December, using:
   (i)   the 'first in, first out' (FIFO) method of valuation
   (ii) the weighted average cost (AVCO) method of valuation.
   Use the perpetual method of calculation.
b Prepare an income statement for the month ending 31 December for each method, using your calculations from (a).

QUESTION 3

The following information relates to the purchases and issues of 'velspore' during August. At 31 July there were no items of 'velspore' held as inventory.

Date	Purchases	Issues
5 August	2 at £16	
15 August		1
17 August	4 at £17	
21 August		3
27 August	7 at £18	
31 August		6

The selling price of a 'velspore' during August was £40.

Required

a Calculate the value of closing inventory of 'velspores' at 31 August, using the 'first in, first out' (FIFO) method of valuing inventory.
Use a periodic calculation.
b Prepare an income statement for the month ending 31 August, using your results from (a).

QUESTION 4

Gwladys Voisin started trading in January 20*9. She purchases and sells canal long boats. Her transactions during 20*9 are shown:

Month	Purchases	Sales
January	1 at £23,000	
February	1 at £24,000	
March	2 at £25,000	
June		1
August		2
October	2 at £26,000	
November		2
December	1 at £27,000	

The selling price of a canal long boat during 20*9 was a uniform £40,000.

Required

a Calculate the value of long boats held as inventory at 31 December 20*9, using the 'first in, first out' (FIFO) method of valuing inventory.
Use a periodic calculation.
b Prepare an income statement for the year ended 31 December 20*9, using your results from (a).

ADVANTAGES OF USING FIFO

■ Most people feel that this is intuitively the right method to use, since it seems to follow the natural way that goods are generally issued, ie in the order in which they are received.
■ Inventory value is easily calculated.
■ Issue prices are based on prices actually paid for purchases.
■ Closing inventory value is based on prices most recently paid.
■ It is a method that is acceptable to HMRC for tax purposes. It is also acceptable for the purposes of the Companies Act 1985 and IAS 2.

DISADVANTAGES OF USING FIFO

- Because it feels right intuitively, many people feel that this is the way issues are actually made.
- Issues are not at the most recent prices and this may have an adverse effect on pricing policy.
- In times of rising prices FIFO values inventory at higher prices than the other method. This lowers the value of cost of sales and thus increases reported profits. This can be regarded as being contrary to the concept of prudence.

ADVANTAGES OF USING AVCO

- Issues are made at a weighted average price. This recognises that all issues have equal value and equal importance to the business.
- Variations in issue prices are minimised.
- It allows the comparison of reported profits to be made on a more realistic basis, since any marked changes in the price of issues are ironed out.
- Because the average price used for issues is weighted towards the most recent purchases, the value of closing inventory will be fairly close to the latest prices paid for purchases.
- AVCO is acceptable to HMRC, the Companies Act 1985 and under IAS 2.

DISADVANTAGES OF USING AVCO

- It requires a new calculation each time purchases are made. This makes it rather more difficult to calculate than the other method.
- The prices charged for issues will not generally agree with the prices paid for purchases.

ACCOUNTING CONCEPTS AND STOCK VALUATION

Examiners are quite fond of asking which concepts are used when valuing inventories.

Clearly, the **cost concept** is adhered to.

The principle of **consistency** is important since results obtained from financial statements must be able to be used for comparative purposes.

The **concept of prudence** should be adhered to so that profits are not overstated – this means that the lower of cost and net realisable value should be applied when valuing inventories.

The **accruals concept** is used when considering repair costs or delivery charges etc to be deducted from selling price to determine net realisable value.

● EXAMINATION TIP

FIFO and AVCO are methods of valuing inventory. FIFO does not necessarily reflect the way actual issues are made.

IAS 2 states that inventories (and work in progress) should be valued at the total of the lower of cost and net realisable value of the separate items or work in progress. (It allows the grouping of similar items.)

It also states that FIFO and AVCO are acceptable bases for valuing inventories.

INVENTORY RECONCILIATIONS

Goods sent on sale or return remain the property of the 'sender' until the customer indicates that a sale has taken place.

The value of inventories that appears as a current asset on the balance sheet of a business is the result of a physical count and valuation. Although many businesses use a perpetual method of valuing their inventories by the use of bar code technology, the computerised valuation that results from this is invariably incorrect.

How can this be? I hear you shout. Computers never make errors! They are much more efficient than people!

It is true that computers can be much faster than we are. They can be more accurate than some of us. So why use a physical means of checking closing inventories?

The computer relies on accurate inputs by receiving departments of a business – no problem. It also relies on accurate records for issues, and this is where the problem arises.

Consider your local supermarket. Most goods sold in the store do get scanned and inventory records are immediately updated, but what of the goods:

■ stolen by local shop-lifters
■ broken by your unruly young brother
■ eaten by the local mouse population.

None of these 'issues' will be recognised by the computer. This is why a physical inventory count is important to gain an accurate closing inventory figure to complete the financial statements.

One final problem. Sometimes it is not possible to make an inventory count immediately after the close of business on the final day of the financial year. Staff may be absent on the day. It may be too big a job to complete in that one day. No doubt you can think of other reasons why the physical inventory count cannot be made at the right time.

Examination questions based on the inventory count not being completed at the financial year-end are also popular with examiners.

Adjustments need to be made to the figures arrived at if the inventory count and valuation were made after the financial year-end in order to determine the actual inventory figure at the appropriate date.

WORKED EXAMPLE

Albert was unable to physically check his inventory on 31 March 20*9, his financial year-end. However, he was able to complete it on 6 April 20*9. The inventory was valued at £8,430 on that date.

Albert provides the following information of transactions that took place between 1 April and 6 April 20*9.

A gross profit margin of 20% is earned by Albert on all his sales.

(i)   Goods purchased £450.

(ii)   Sales made £600.

(iii) Goods returned by Albert to suppliers £90.

(iv) Faulty goods returned by customers £120.

Required

Calculate the value of Albert's inventory at 31 March 20*9.

Answer

Calculation of inventory 31 March 20*9

	£	
Inventory at 6 April 20*9	8,430	
Less net purchases	(360)	(£450 − £90)
Add Net sales	400	(£600 − £120 = £480 ÷ 1.2)
Inventory at 31 March 20*9	8,470	

Note: The purchases and sales figures are net of returns.

Inventories are always valued at cost (or net realisable value) so the profit margin included in the net sales figure must be eradicated.

Purchases are taken off the inventory at 6 April since they were not with Albert at 31 March. Sales have been added back since Albert did have these goods at the end of March.

QUESTION 5

Krishna was unable to physically check her inventory at her financial year-end on 31 December 20*8. However, she was able to complete it on 5 January 20*9 at which date it was valued at cost as £26,870.

The following information is available:

Krishna has a uniform mark-up of 33⅓% on all the goods she sells.

In the period 1 January to 5 January 20*9 the following transactions took place:

1. Purchases of goods for resale £1,940.
2. Sales of goods on credit amounted to £3,500.
3. Cash sales amounted to £480.
4. Sales returns were £40.
5. Purchase returns were £72.

Required

Calculate Krishna's closing inventory at 31 December 20*9.

QUESTION 6

Vera was unable to physically check her inventory at her year-end on 31 October 20*9.

When she did her valuation on 9 November 20*9 she valued it at £32,840.

The following information is available:

Vera marks up her goods for resale at a uniform 50%.

The following transactions took place in the period 1 November to 9 November 20*9:

1. Cash sales were £2,890.
2. Credit sales amounted to £6,780.
3. Cash purchases amounted to £1,430.
4. Credit purchases were £8,510.
5. Goods returned by customers £290.
6. Goods returned to suppliers £450.

Required

Calculate the value of Vera's closing inventory at 31 October 20*9.

Chapter summary

- FIFO and AVCO are methods of valuing inventory. Both methods are regularly examined at A2 Level.
- They are methods of valuing inventory; they do not necessarily determine the order in which goods are actually issued.
- FIFO may be calculated using either a perpetual method or a periodic method. If a question does not stipulate the method to be used then use the periodic method; it is quicker, easier and you are less likely to make an error.
- There is no right or wrong method of valuing inventories but some methods are more acceptable than others to HMRC.
- The method chosen will determine the level of reported profit.
- If inventory valuation is taken some time after the financial year-end a statement showing the necessary adjustments to the inventory figure must be prepared.

SELF-TEST QUESTIONS

- Which method used to value inventory is acceptable to HMRC?
- Which method is acceptable for the purposes of the Companies Act 1985?
- A greengrocer must always use FIFO as a method of valuing his inventory. True or false?
- Which accounting standard deals with inventories and work in progress?
- Which method values closing inventory at the most recent prices paid to purchase the goods?
- In times of rising prices which method reveals profits later than the other method?

- The closing inventory figure shown on the balance sheet of a business is always determined by a physical count/computer print-out. Delete the incorrect answer.
- Financial year-end 31 May. The physical inventory valuation is conducted on 10 June.
  - How should goods purchased on 7 June be treated?
  - How should sales returns received on 5 June be treated?
- Bill sends Mary some goods on sale or return. Who includes these goods as part of their inventory?
- If closing inventory has been overvalued what effect has this had on reported profits?
- If closing inventory has been undervalued this will .... reported profits. Fill the gap.

TEST QUESTIONS

QUESTION 7

Ray Galpin provides the following information for March. Ray purchases and sells 'ingac'. There were no goods in hand on 1 March. The purchases and sales of 'ingac' are shown:

Date	Purchases	Sales
2 March	5 at £4	
7 March		4
12 March	17 at £5	
21 March		15
24 March	10 at £6	
30 March		7

Required

Calculate the value of closing inventory at 31 March, using:
a the 'first in, first out' method (FIFO)
b the weighted average cost method (AVCO).

Ray uses a perpetual calculation when valuing his inventory.

QUESTION 8

Marion Lycett provides the following information for November. She purchases and sells 'ilins'. She had no inventory on 1 November. The following transactions are given for 'ilins':

Date	Purchases	Sales
3 November	6 at £12	
7 November	9 at £15	
10 November		8
18 November	7 at £18	
23 November		3
25 November		9

Required

Calculate, using a perpetual calculation, the value of inventory at 30 November using:
a the 'first in, first out' method (FIFO)
b the weighted average cost method (AVCO).

QUESTION 9

Jackie Bryan provides the following information for January. Jackie purchases and sells 'glomfos'. Jackie had four 'glomfos' as inventory at 1 January: they cost £200 each. The transactions for January are shown:

Date	Purchases	Sales
6 January		3
8 January	5 at £210	
13 January		4
17 January	12 at £220	
26 January		10
30 January		3

Jackie uses a periodic calculation to determine inventory.

Required

Calculate the value of closing inventory, using:
a the 'first in, first out' method (FIFO)
b the weighted average cost method (AVCO)

QUESTION 10

Tamsin Fretwell provides the following information for September. She purchases and sells 'retyos'. Tamsin had one 'retyo' as inventory at 1 September: it had cost £22. The transactions for September are given:

Date	Purchases	Sales
1 September	40 at £22	
7 September	30 at £23	
12 September		65
18 September	50 at £25	
28 September		51

Tamsin uses a periodic calculation to determine inventory.

Required

Calculate the value of inventory at 30 September, using:
a the 'first in, first out' method (FIFO)
b the weighted average cost method (AVCO).

QUESTION 11

Anil Patel purchases and sells 'derits'. He provides the following information for August. He had 8 'derits' as inventory at 1 August: they cost £12 each. He calculates inventory using a perpetual method. The following transactions are for August:

Date	Purchases	Sales
4 August	10 at £12	
9 August		15
15 August	12 at £8	
21 August	15 at £7	
26 August		28

'Derits' are sold for £15 each.

Required

a Calculate the closing inventory of 'derits' at 31 August, using the 'first in, first out' (FIFO) method of valuation.

b Prepare an income statement for the month of August.

QUESTION 12

Gao Feng purchases and sells 'loits'. He provides the following information for April. He had four 'loits' as inventory at 31 March, valued at cost £30 each. The following information is given:

Date	Purchases	Sales
6 April	4 at £9	
9 April		6
18 April	8 at £6	
23 April		7
29 April	4 at £5	
30 April		5

'Loits' are sold at £20 each.

Required

a Calculate the value of inventory at 30 April, using the 'first in, first out' (FIFO) method of valuation.

b Prepare an income statement for the month ended 30 April.

QUESTION 13

Olivia Oyle purchases and sells 'greftas'. She provides the following information for September.

Date	Purchases	Sales
3 September	8 at £15	
7 September		6
11 September	12 at £16	
14 September		10
23 September	8 at £17	
27 September		6

She had one 'grefta' as inventory on 1 September: it had cost £15. The following information is given:

Greftas are sold for £40 each.

Required

a Calculate the value of closing inventory, using the weighted average cost (AVCO) method of valuation.

b Prepare an income statement for the month of September.

QUESTION 14

Barney Rumble purchases and sells 'ciarfs'. They sell for £110 each. He provides the following information for December:

At 1 December Barney had seven 'ciarfs' as inventory: they cost £40 each.

Date	Purchases	Sales
4 December	4 at £42	
7 December		10
9 December	12 at £45	
14 December		11
20 December	10 at £50	
27 December		9

Required

a Calculate the closing inventory of 'ciarfs' at 31 December, using the weighted average cost method (AVCO).
b Prepare an income statement for the month of December.

QUESTION 15

Gwen Davies was unable to physically value her inventory at her financial year-end on 30 April 20*9. When she did her valuation on 7 May, she valued it at £2,940. The following information is available:

- Gwen marks up all her goods by 25% on cost to achieve her selling price.
- the following transactions took place between 1 April and 7 May 20*9:

1. sales amounted to £1,200
2. purchases amounted to £420.

Required

Calculate Gwen's inventory at 30 April 20*9.

QUESTION 16

John Blunt was unable to physically value his inventory at his financial year-end on 31 October 20*9.

When he did his valuation on 6 November, he valued his stock at £3,670.

He was able to give the following additional information:

- goods are marked up at a uniform rate of 40% on cost to obtain his selling price
- the following transactions took place between 1 November and 6 November 20*9:

1. purchases amounted to £2,560
2. sales amounted to £4,060.

Required

Calculate John's inventory at 30 October 20*9.

QUESTION 17

Siobhan O'Malley was unable to physically value her inventory at her year-end on 31 May 20*9. When she did her valuation on 4 June, she valued it at £14,880.

Using her 4 June valuation for inventory, her draft income statement revealed a net profit of £185,750.

The following information is available:

- she marks up her goods at 20% on cost to achieve selling price
- the following transactions took place between 1 June and 4 June 20*9:

1. sales amounted to £2,400
2. purchases amounted to £850
3. sales returns amounted to £36
4. purchase returns amounted to £84.

Required

a Calculate the value of inventory at 31 May 20*9.
b Calculate Siobhan's corrected net profit for the year ended 31 May 20*9.

QUESTION 18

Jennie McGonagle physically valued her inventory on 8 January 20*9 at £1,720. She had been unable to value her inventory at her financial year-end on 31 December 20*8. She used this figure in her draft final accounts and calculated her net profit to be £56,900.

Jennie marks up all her goods by a uniform 60% to achieve her selling price.

The following transactions took place between 1 January and 8 January 20*9:

1. sales amounted to £1,024
2. purchases amounted to £540
3. purchase returns amounted to £17
4. sales returns amounted to £96.

Required

a Calculate the value of inventory at 31 December 20*8.
b Calculate the corrected net profit for the year ended 31 December 20*8.

QUESTION 19

David Parker was unable to physically value his inventory at his financial year end on 31 July 20*9.

However, he was able to value it on 9 August 20*9 at £2,000.

Using this figure he obtained a draft net profit of £42,870. David marks all goods up by 70% on cost to obtain selling price.

The following transactions took place between 1 August and 9 August 20*9:

1. sales amounted to £1,904
2. purchases amounted to £1,560
3. sales returns amounted to £170
4. purchase returns amounted to £40
5. goods sent on sale or return during July amounted to £510 at selling price. The customer has yet to indicate whether or not he will purchase the goods.

Required

a Calculate the value of inventory at 31 July 20*9.
b Calculate the corrected net profit for the year ended 31 July 20*9.

QUESTION 20

Pat Nicholson was unable to physically value her inventory at her financial year-end on 30 June 20*9. She valued it on 5 July at £3,565. Using this figure, she was able to determine her draft profit as £180,564.

Pat works on a gross margin of 50% on all goods sold.

The following transactions took place between 1 July and 5 July 20*9:

1. sales amounted to £2,360
2. purchases amounted to £980
3. sales returns amounted to £130
4. purchase returns amounted to £58
5. goods dispatched on sale or return during June amounted to £1,420 at selling price. The customer has yet to indicate whether or not she will purchase the goods.

Required

a Calculate the inventory at 30 June 20*9.
b Calculate the corrected net profit for the year ended 30 June 20*9.

CHAPTER
TWELVE

Manufacturing Accounts

So far we have prepared the accounts of traders: businessmen and women who have bought finished goods and sold them on to the final customer. Most of the businesses that you come into contact with in everyday life fall into the category of trading organisations.

QUESTION

Identify three businesses that you use that are trading organisations.

Answer

Your answer may have included Kentucky Fried Chicken, McDonalds, Topshop, Tesco or similar businesses.

The common factor here is that all these businesses buy their products from a manufacturer and sell them on. McDonalds do not make the buns or burgers; Topshop do not make the clothes that they sell to you; Tesco do not make cornflakes, biscuits, CDs, etc.

We have already produced many income statements. Now we need to prepare the final accounts of businesses that make goods that are sold by retailers.

These business organisations prepare manufacturing accounts as part of their financial statements. A manufacturing account shows the costs of running and maintaining the factory in which the final product is made.

A manufacturing business will also trade by selling its finished product to wholesalers or retailers, so it will prepare an income statement as well as a manufacturing account.

> **Direct costs** are defined by the Chartered Institute of Management Accountants (CIMA) as 'expenditure which can be economically identified with a specific saleable cost unit'.

Examples of direct costs include purchases of direct materials and direct labour charges. The purchase of wood and varnish to make a table, and the wages of the person who assembled the parts of the table, are direct costs.

> **Indirect costs** are factory expenses that are not directly identifiable with the final product.

Examples of indirect costs include factory rent and rates and depreciation of factory machinery.

> **Royalties** are payments made to the inventor of a product, process or idea. A royalty is often a percentage of the revenue earned by the user.

A manufacturing account is split into two main sections:

■ the prime cost section
■ overheads.

The prime cost section shows all the direct expenses incurred in production. The expenses can be **directly** and clearly traced to the particular product being produced. For example, in every

Specification coverage:
AQA ACCN4;
OCR FO12

By the end of this chapter you should be able to:
■ prepare the financial statements of manufacturing businesses
■ calculate provision for unrealised profit
■ show relevant entries in income statements and balance sheets.

pair of jeans that you buy you can see the denim used, the studs, the thread and zip. You also know that someone has stitched the pieces together – they have worked **directly** on the jeans. Their wages are a direct cost. The other main direct cost is the payment of royalties.

WORKED EXAMPLE

Hinge & Co are manufacturers of woollen sweaters.

Place a tick beside the expenses that would be used to prepare the prime cost section of the manufacturing account of Hinge & Co.

- Wages of sales staff
- Purchases of wool
- Office heating and lighting expenses
- Wool dyes
- Managers' salaries
- Rent of canteen
- Knitting machine operatives' wages

Answer

You should have ticked purchases of wool, wool dyes and knitting machine operatives' wages. All of these expenses can be traced easily to the final product.

The prime cost section of a manufacturing account contains all the resources used in the manufacturing process:

- Purchases of raw materials
- Direct wages
- Royalties
- Any other direct costs.

The raw materials used in the manufacturing process are not necessarily the raw materials purchased, and so we have to make an adjustment to the raw materials purchase figure in order to find out how many of the raw material purchases were actually used during the year.

WORKED EXAMPLE

Ralph Shoemaker makes footwear. The following information relates to the year ended 31 March 20*9.

Inventory of leather at 1 April 20*8	£4,790
Purchases of leather during the year	£50,790
Inventory of leather at 31 March 20*9	£3,640

Required

Calculate the value of leather used to produce shoes during the year ended 31 March 20*9.

Answer

	£
Inventory 1 April 20*8	4,790
Purchases of leather	50,790
	55,580
Inventory 31 March 20*9	(3,640)
Leather used	51,940

WORKED EXAMPLE

V. Alve manufactures radios from components bought from around the world. The following information relates to the year ended 31 August 20*9.

Inventory of components at 1 September 20*8	£8,790
Inventory of components at 31 August 20*9	£10,460
Purchases of components during the year	£112,900
Wages of assembly workers	£372,610

Required

Calculate the value of components used by V. Alve during the year ended 31 August 20*9.

Answer

	£
Inventory of components 1 September 20*8	8,790
Purchases of leather	112,900
	121,690
Inventory of components 31 August 20*9	(10,460)
Components used	111,230

If you are unsure about this calculation, talk yourself through it.

In the first example, Ralph had £4,790 inventory of leather at the start of the year; he purchased a further £50,790 of leather so he could have used £55,580 worth of leather during the year. However, he didn't use it all: he had £3,640 left so he must have used £51,940.

Talk yourself through the calculation for V. Alve's components in the same way.

The prime cost section can now be prepared.

WORKED EXAMPLE

Trevor Roberts makes cakes for sale to hotels and restaurants. He provides you with the following information for the year ended 30 April 20*3.

Inventory of materials at 1 May 20*8	£376
Inventory of materials at 30 April 20*9	£297
Purchases of materials during the year	£58,748
Direct wages	£27,380
Other wages	£16,492.

Required

Prepare a statement showing the prime costs for the year ended 30 April 20*9.

Answer

Statement showing prime costs for the year ended 30 April 20*9.

WORKED EXAMPLE *continued*

	£
Inventory of raw materials 1 May 20*8	376
Purchases of raw materials	58,748
	59,124
Inventory of raw materials 30 April 20*9	(297)
Cost of raw materials used	58,827
Direct wages	27,380
Prime cost	86,207

Note

Only the direct wages have been included. The prime cost section only lists the resources directly used in the production of the cakes, i.e. the flour, butter, sugar, etc., plus the wages of the people who work directly on producing the cakes – the people who mix the ingredients, bake the cakes and decorate them.

Office workers' wages or cleaners' wages are not included: these people do not work in the factory.

WORKED EXAMPLE

Eliza Doolot produces MP3 players from components purchased from the Far East. Her workers assemble the components using a Japanese design for which she pays royalties.

She provides the following information for the year ended 30 September 20*9.

Manufacturing royalties	£7,500
Purchases of components	£457,300
Inventory of components at 1 October 20*8	£17,450
Inventory of components 30 September 20*9	£26,110
Direct wages	£317,520
Other direct costs	£26,720

Required

Prepare the prime cost section of the manufacturing account for the year ended 30 September 20*9.

Answer

Eliza Doolott.
Prime cost section of manufacturing account for the year ended 30 September 20*9

	£
Inventory of components 1 October 20*8	17,450
Purchases of components	457,300
	474,750
Inventory of components 30 September 20*9	(26,110)
Cost of components used	448,640
Direct wages	317,520
Royalties	7,500
Other direct costs	26,720
Prime cost	800,380

> **Overheads** are described by CIMA as 'expenditure on labour, materials or services which cannot be economically identified with a specific saleable cost'.

Factory overheads are the expenses incurred in running the factory that cannot be easily traced to the product.

QUESTION 1

Moin Syyed owns a manufacturing business. He provides the following information for the year ended 28 February 20*9.

	£
Inventory of raw materials 1 March 20*8	23 658
Inventory of raw materials 28 February 20*9	18 439
Purchases of raw materials	156 364
Direct wages	236 451
Indirect wages	74 590
Royalties	35 000
Office salaries	86 418

Required

Prepare the prime cost section of Moin's manufacturing account.

WORKED EXAMPLE

The following list has been prepared by Brenda Beech, a manufacturer of garden furniture.

Purchases of timber	Depreciation of power saws, planes, etc.
Rent of workshop	Wages of assembly workers
Office manager's wages	Screws and nails
Delivery van expenses	Brenda's drawings
Wood glue	Factory power

Required

Alongside each of these expenses, write PC for prime cost or OH for overhead.

Answer

Purchases of timber, screws, nails and wood glue, and wages of assembly workers, can all be identified as prime costs. Rent of workshop, depreciation of power saws, planes, etc. and factory power are all overheads.

Office manager's wages would appear in the profit and loss accounts; so would delivery van expenses. Brenda's drawings would be deducted from her capital on the balance sheet.

Let us put the two sections together. Initially, you might find it helpful to label the items PC (prime cost) or OH (overhead).

WORKED EXAMPLE

The factory manager of Fawcett Products has supplied the following information for the year ended 30 November 20*9.

	£
Inventory of raw materials at 1 December 20*8	90,000
Inventory of raw materials at 30 November 20*9	80,000
Purchases of raw materials	390,000
Manufacturing wages	212,000
Manufacturing royalties	15,000
Supervisor's wages	27,000
Factory rent	120,000
Factory insurance	30,000
Depreciation of machinery	17,500

Required

Prepare the manufacturing account for the year ended 30 November 20*9.

Answer

Fawcett Products
Manufacturing account for the year ended 30 November 20*9

	£	£
Inventory of raw materials at 1 December 20*8		90,000
Purchases of raw materials		390,000
		480,000
Inventory of raw materials at 30 November 20*9		(80,000)
Cost of raw materials used		400,000
Manufacturing wages		212,000
Royalties		15,000
Prime cost		627,000
Factory overheads		
Supervisor's wages	27,000	
Factory rent	120,000	
Factory insurance	30,000	
Depreciation – machinery	17,500	194,500
Cost of manufacture		821,500

● EXAMINATION TIP

- The most common mistake that examination candidates make when preparing a manufacturing account is to deduct the total overheads from the prime cost. Remember, we are calculating the total cost of manufacturing the product.
- Always label the prime cost and the cost of manufacture – examiners often give a mark for those labels.

Earlier in your studies we saw that carriage inward was included in the income statement.

Carriage inwards always makes purchases more expensive. A manufacturing business is no exception.

Carriage inwards is added to the purchases (of raw materials) in the manufacturing account.

WORKED EXAMPLE

The following balances have been extracted at 31 December 20*9 from the books of Atul Patel, a manufacturer of kitchen furniture.

	£000
Purchases of raw materials	2,470
Manufacturing wages	1,380
Manufacturing royalties	37
Supervisory wages	87
Carriage inward	3
Factory rent	60
Factory power	30
Other factory overheads	27
Depreciation of machinery	42
Depreciation of office equipment	13
Inventory of raw materials 1 January 20*9	89
Inventory of raw materials 31 December 20*9	111

Required

Prepare the manufacturing account for the year ended 31 December 20*9, showing prime cost and cost of manufacture.

Answer

Atul Patel
Manufacturing account for the year ended 31 December 20*9

	£000	£000
Inventory of raw materials 1 January 20*9		89
Purchases of raw materials	2,470	
Carriage inward	3	2,473
		2,562
Inventory of raw materials 31 December 20*9		(111)
Cost of raw materials used		2,451
Manufacturing wages		1,380
Royalties		37
Prime cost		3,868
Factory overheads		
Supervisory wages	87	
Factory rent	60	
Factory power	30	
Other factory overheads	27	
Depreciation – machinery	42	246
Cost of manufacture		4,114

Note:

Office equipment is not used in the factory: it is an office expense and so should be entered in the income statement. Machinery is always used in the factory, hence its inclusion in the manufacturing account.

INVENTORY

In any manufacturing business there are always three kinds of inventory:

- Raw materials: as yet this inventory is in the factory in the condition in which it was bought – the goods have not entered the manufacturing process. The inventory of raw materials from previous examples would include stocks of flour, butter, leather, MP3 player components, wood, etc.

- Work in progress: these are partly finished goods; goods that are still undergoing part of the manufacturing process – e.g. cakes waiting to be decorated, partly finished shoes, MP3 players short of a few components, kitchen furniture without doors and handles, etc.
- Finished goods: goods that have completed the journey through the manufacturing process and are simply waiting to be sold or despatched to a customer.

Inventories are current assets and are shown in the balance sheet. In the case of a manufacturing business, the three types of inventory held have to be identified in the balance sheet.

We have just seen how to treat inventory of raw materials.

You have already worked with inventory of finished goods – in the income statement – because a business usually trades with finished goods.

Work in progress still has to go through the remainder of the manufacturing process before it becomes a finished product, so it should appear in the manufacturing account.

Work in progress appears after the cost of manufacture has been calculated.

The treatment is the same as for all types of inventory. We add the value of work in progress at the start of the period and deduct the value of work in progress at the end of the period.

There are two ways of doing this; both are acceptable and they will be rewarded with the same number of marks in an examination.

Choose one method and always use it. In the following example, we will see both methods, but after that we will use Method 1 (it is usually considered to be easier).

WORKED EXAMPLE

Bert Loggs is a manufacturer. He provides the following information for the year ended 31 July 20*9.

	£
Cost of manufacture	217,432
Work in progress at 1 August 20*8	4,698
Work in progress 31 July 20*9	3,481

Required

Calculate total production costs for the year ended 31 July 20*9.

Answer

Method 1	£	Method 2	£	£
Cost of manufacture	217,432	Cost of manufacture		217,432
Add work in progress 1 August 20*8	4,698	Work in progress 1 August 20*8	4,698	
Subtotal	222,130	Less work in progress 31 July 20*9	(3,481)	1,217
Less work in progress 31 July 20*9	(3,481)			
Total production cost	218,649	Total production cost		218,649

You can see that both methods give exactly the same total production costs.

WORKED EXAMPLE

Laura Shaw is a manufacturer. She provides the following information for the year ended 28 February 20*9.

	£
Inventories	
Raw materials 1 March 20*8	16,500
Work in progress 1 March 20*8	18,200
Finished goods 1 March 20*8	20,600
Purchases of raw materials	237,300
Manufacturing wages	458,900
Office salaries	186,200
Factory supervisor's wages	17,800
Carriage inward	1,500
Rent and rates	
Factory	14,900
Office	7,200
Depreciation	
Machinery	90,000
Office equipment	21,000
Royalties	7,500
Other indirect expenses	
Factory	32,600
Office	28,400
Sales	1,000,000
Inventories	
Raw materials 28 Feb 20*9	16,000
Work in progress 28 Feb 20*9	19,400
Finished goods 28 Feb 20*9	21,350

Required

a) Prepare the manufacturing account for the year ended 28 February 20*9.
b) Prepare a balance sheet extract at 28 February 20*9, showing how inventories would appear.

Answer

Laura Shaw
Manufacturing account for the year ended 28 February 20*9

	£	£
Inventory of raw materials 1 March 20*8		16,500
Purchases of raw materials	237,300	
Carriage inward	1,500	238,800
		255,300
Inventory of raw materials 28 February 20*9		(16,000)
Cost of raw materials used		239,300
Manufacturing wages		458,900
Royalties		7,500
Prime cost		705,700
Factory overheads		
Supervisor's wages	17,800	
Rent and rates	14,900	
Other indirect expenses	32,600	
Depreciation – machinery	90,000	155,300
Manufacturing cost		861,000
Add work in progress 1 March 20*8		18,200
		879,200
Less work in progress 28 February 20*9		(19,400)
Total production cost		859,800

The total production cost is transferred to the income statement in order to calculate the cost of sales figure.

WORKED EXAMPLE

Mike Tong is a manufacturer who has produced the following information for the year ended 31 May 20*9.

	£
Sales	2,913,502
Inventories at 1 June 20*8	
Raw materials	49,780
Work in progress	23,640
Finished goods	40,210
Purchases of raw materials	846,289
Direct wages	750,199
Supervisors' wages	68,720
Indirect wages	187,442
Royalties	19,000
Carriage inward	4,612
Carriage outward	5,218
Rent and rates – factory	48,700
– office	21,300
Insurance – factory	19,170
– office	10,830
Heat and light – factory	4,260
– office	1,830
Factory power	17,282
Other production expenses	5,671
Depreciation – factory equipment	48,000
– office equipment	12,000
Inventories at 31 May 20*9	
Raw materials	48,340
Work in progress	20,119
Finished goods	38,461

Required

a) Prepare the manufacturing account for the year ended 31 May 20*9.
b) Prepare an extract from the income statement for the year ended 31 May 20*9.

WORKED EXAMPLE continued

Answer

(a)

Mike Tong
Manufacturing account for the year ended 31 May 20*9

	£	£
Inventory of raw materials at 1 June 20*8		49,780
Purchases of raw materials	846,289	
Carriage inward	4,612	850,901
		900,681
Inventory of raw materials at 31 May 20*9		(48,340)
		852,341
Direct wages		750,199
Royalties		19,000
Prime cost		1,621,540
Factory overheads:		
Indirect wages	187,442	
Supervisors' wages	68,720	
Rent & rates	48,700	
Insurance	19,170	
Heat and light	4,260	
Power	17,282	
Other indirect expenses	5,671	
Depreciation	48,000	399,245
		2,020,785
Add work in progress 1 June 20*8		23,640
		2,044,425
Less work in progress 31 May 20*9		(20,119)
Total production cost		2,024,306

b)

Income statement extract for the year ended 31 May 20*9

	£
Inventory of raw materials at 1 June 20*8	40,210
Production cost of goods completed	2,024,306
	2,064,516
Inventory of raw materials at 31 May 20*9	(38,461)
	2,026,055
Gross profit on trading	887,447
Sales	2,913,502

QUESTION 2

Fritz Zeller provides the following information.

Inventories	1 January 20*9	31 December 20*9
	£	£
Raw materials	23,500	24,700
Work in progress	17,800	16,300
Finished goods	16,300	17,250

	£
Purchases of raw materials	212,650
Wages – direct labour	143,680
indirect labour	67,340
sales staff	78,290
Factory overheads	56,700
Depreciation – factory machinery	23,000
office equipment	8,000
delivery vehicles	20,000

Required

Prepare

(a) A manufacturing account for the year ended 31 December 20*9.
(b) An extract from the income statement for the year ended 31 December 20*9.

QUESTION 3

Jane Doyle provides the following information.

Inventories	1 August 20*8	31 July 20*9
	£	£
Raw materials	17,650	23,510
Work in progress	8,570	7,340
Finished goods	10,760	10,740

	£
Purchases of raw materials	203,510
Wages – direct labour	123,930
indirect labour	58,900
sales staff	67,500
office staff	37,320
Rent and rates – factory	37,800
office and showrooms	18,450
Factory power	38,900
Lighting and heating expenses – factory	9,450
office and showrooms	6,210
Insurances – factory	14,620
offices and showrooms	5,990
Depreciation – machinery	87,000
office equipment	13,450
delivery vehicles	9,800
Carriage – inwards	1,350
outwards	870

Required

Prepare

(a) A manufacturing account for the year ended 31 July 20*9.
(b) An extract from the income statement for the year ended 31 July 20*9.

Sometimes the managers of a business will wish to gauge how efficiently their factory is operating. They compare the price that the goods cost to produce in the factory with the cost of purchasing the same amount of goods from an 'outside' supplier. If it would be cheaper to purchase the goods externally then it may be in the best interest of the business to cease manufacturing and purchase the goods. (But see marginal costing and social costing later).

MANUFACTURING PROFIT

When the managers of a business transfer the total production cost to the trading account, gross profit is found by deducting the cost of sales (COGS) from sales revenue. This method does have a flaw – there is no indication of how profitable the factory is.

Gross profit is derived in two ways:

- By manufacturing efficiently
- By selling the goods at a price that is higher than the production cost.

We can determine the factory manufacturing profit by finding the difference between the cost of production and the cost of purchasing the goods externally.

Let us look at the manufacturing accounts of Laura Shaw and Mike Tong, produced earlier.

WORKED EXAMPLE

The same number of goods made in Laura's factory could be purchased by Laura's buying department for £900,000.

Required

Prepare

(a) A summarised manufacturing account for the year ended 28 February 20*9 showing the manufacturing profit.
(b) An extract from the income statement for the year ended 28 February 20*9.

Answer

(a)

Summarised manufacturing account for the year ended 28 February 20*9

	£
Prime cost	705,700
Overheads	155,300
Add work in progress 1 March 20*8	18,200
	879,200
Less work in progress 28 February 20*9	(19,400)
Total production cost	859,800
Manufacturing profit	40,200
Transfer price to trading account	900,000

(b)

Income statement extract for the year ended 28 February 20*9

	£
Inventory of finished goods at 1 March 20*8	20,600
Transfer price of manufactured goods	900,000
	920,600
Inventory of finished goods at 28 February 20*3	(21,350)
	899,250
Gross profit on trading	100,750
Sales	1,000,000
Gross profit from manufacturing	40,200
Gross profit on trading	100,750
Total gross profit	140,950

WORKED EXAMPLE

Mike Tong's buying department could purchase the same number of goods made in his factory for £2.5m.

Required

A summarised manufacturing account for the year ended 31 May 20*9 and an extract from the income statement for the year ended 31 May 20*9.

Answer

Manufacturing account for the year ended 31 May 20*9

	£
Prime cost	1,621,540
Overheads	399,245
	2,020,785
Work in progress 1 June 20*8	23,640
	2,044,425
Work in progress 31 May 20*9	(20,119)
Total production cost	2,024,306
Factory profit	475,694
Transfer price to trading account	2,500,000

Income statement extract for the year ended 31 May 20*9

	£
Inventory of finished goods at 1 June 20*8	40,210
Transfer price of manufactured goods	2,500,000
	2,540,210
Inventory of finished goods at 31 May 20*9	(38,461)
Cost of goods sold	2,501,749
Gross profit on trading	411,753
Sales	2,913,502
Gross profit on manufacturing	475,694
Gross profit on trading	411,753
Total gross profit	887,447

● EXAMINATION TIP

It is usual in examination questions to add a percentage to the total production costs in order to arrive at the transfer price.

WORKED EXAMPLE

Olga Stravinska is a manufacturer. The following information relates to her business at 31 October 20*9.

Total production cost	£348,700
Inventory of finished goods at 1 November 20*8	£37,498
Inventory of finished goods at 31 October 20*9	£39,613
Sales	£598,136

Olga transfers goods from her factory to the income statement at cost plus 20%.

Required

An extract from the manufacturing account and income statement for the year ended 31 October 20*9, showing the manufacturing profit and the transfer price of the goods manufactured.

WORKED EXAMPLE *continued*

Answer

Manufacturing account extract for the year ended 31 October 20*9

	£	
Total production costs	348,700	
Factory profit	69,740	(£348,700 × 20%)
Transfer price	418,440	

Income statement extract for the year ended 31 October 20*9

	£
Inventory of finished goods 1 November 20*8	37,498
Transfer price of manufactured goods	418,440
	455,938
Inventory of finished goods 31 October 20*9	(39,613)
Cost of goods sold	416,325
Gross profit on trading	181,811
Sales	598,136
Gross profit from manufacturing	69,740
Gross profit on trading	181,811
Total gross profit	251,551

QUESTION 4

Tabitha Todd supplies the following information for her manufacturing business for the year ended 31 March 20*9.

	£
Total production cost	456,000
Transfer price to income statement	520,900
Sales	873,500
Inventory of finished goods at 1 April 20*8	34,600
Inventory of finished goods at 31 March 20*9	36,200

Required

Prepare:

(a) an extract from the manufacturing account for the year ended 31 March 20*9 showing factory profit and the amount to be transferred to the income statement
(b) an extract from the income statement for the year ended 31 March 20*9 showing the transfer
(c) an extract from the income statement for the year ended 31 March 20*9 showing clearly the total gross profit earned by Tabitha's business.

QUESTION 5

Harry Parker supplies the following information for his manufacturing business for the year ended 31 October 20*9.

	£
Total production cost	1,326,900
Transfer price to income statement	2,100,000
Sales	3,210,600
Inventory of finished goods at 1 November 20*8	186,000
Inventory of finished goods 31 October 20*9	191,450

Required

Prepare

(a) an extract from the manufacturing account for the year ended 31 October 20*9 showing factory profit and the amount to be transferred to the income statement

(b) an extract from the income statement for the year ended 31 October 20*9 showing the transfer
(c) an extract from the income statement for the year ended 31 October 20*9 showing clearly the total gross profit earned by Harry's business.

QUESTION 6

Harpreet Nahal supplies the following information for her manufacturing business for the year ended 31 May 20*9.

	£
Total production cost	842,000
Sales	1,347,500
Inventory of finished goods at 1 June 20*8	62,000
Inventory of finished goods at 31 May 20*9	57,000

Finished goods are transferred from the manufacturing account to the income statement at cost plus 25%.

Required

Prepare:

(a) an extract from the manufacturing account for the year ended 31 May 20*9 showing factory profit and the amount to be transferred to the income statement
(b) an extract from the income statement for the year ended 31 May 20*9 showing the transfer
(c) an extract from the income statement for the year ended 31 May 20*9 showing clearly the total gross profit earned by Harpreet's business.

QUESTION 7

Hilary Nike supplies the following information for her manufacturing business for the year ended 31 March 20*9.

	£
Total production cost	943,750
Sales	1,448,560
Inventory of finished goods at 1 April 20*8	85,820
Inventory of finished goods at 31 March 20*9	87,360

Finished goods are transferred from the manufacturing account to the income statement at cost plus 40%.

Required

Prepare:

(a) an extract from the manufacturing account for the year ended 31 March 20*9 showing factory profit and the amount to be transferred to the income statement
(b) an extract from the income statement for the year ended 31 March 20*8 showing the transfer
(c) an extract from the income statement for the year ended 31 March 20*9 showing clearly the total gross profit earned by Hilary's business.

QUESTION 8

Zack Hill provides the following information for his manufacturing business for the year ended 31 December 20*9.

	£
Total production cost	1,342,700
Sales	3,420,000
Inventory of finished goods at 1 January 20*9	98,400
Inventory of finished goods at 31 December 20*9	102,600

Finished goods are transferred from the manufacturing account to the income statement at cost plus 50%.

Required

Prepare:

(a) an extract from the manufacturing account for the year ended 31 December 20*9 showing factory profit and the amount to be transferred to the income statement

(b) an extract from the income statement for the year ended 31 December 20*9 showing the transfer

(c) an extract from the income statement for the year ended 31 December 20*9 showing clearly the total gross profit earned by Hilary's business.

PROVISION FOR UNREALISED PROFITS

We have seen in an earlier chapter that the overriding principle that governs all valuations of inventories is that all inventories should be valued at the lower of cost or net realisable value (because it is prudent).

This does not pose a problem with raw materials or work in progress. It can cause a problem with finished goods.

Finished goods are stored in a warehouse ready for sale or ready to be despatched to a customer. In all probability, some of these finished goods will be left unsold at the end of the financial year.

How should these inventories be valued?

There is no problem if the finished goods are passed to the warehouse at their cost price. Like raw materials and work in progress, the finished goods would be valued at cost.

A problem does arise when goods are passed from the factory at cost price plus a profit margin.

We have already stated that inventories should be valued at cost (if cost is less than net realisable value) not at cost and some factory profit.

If inventory is valued at cost plus some factory profit, we need to shed the factory profit because it has not yet been earned – we need to find the cost price of the goods.

EXAMPLE

Martin Godin manufactures printed circuits. He passes the goods from his factory at cost plus 25%. At his financial year end, his inventory of finished goods is valued at £250,000.

Required

Calculate the cost price of Martin's closing inventory to be entered in the business balance sheet.

Answer

The cost price of the closing inventory of finished goods is £200,000.

EXAMPLE

Siobhan O'Riley manufactures generators. The finished generators are transferred to the income statement at cost plus 10%. At her financial year end, Siobhan's inventory of finished goods is valued at £385,000.

Required

Calculate the cost price of Siobhan's closing inventory of finished goods as it would be shown in her balance sheet drawn up at the end of the year.

Answer

The closing inventory of finished generators should be valued at £350,000.

QUESTION 9

Value of finished goods	Transfer price to income statement
£	Cost plus
4,080	50.0%
1,080	12.5%
1,450	30.0%
900	20.0%
10,500	75.0%

Required

(a) Calculate the cost price of the inventories of finished goods shown above.
(b) Identify the element of profit added to the cost price of the inventory.

Both methods used to calculate the cost price or the profit element are quite tricky so it is worth practising them.

This is a popular examination topic and many examination candidates find it difficult.

If the value of inventory is increased by the profit element, then the gross profit, and hence the net profit, will also be increased by the same amount.

The closing inventory of finished goods has yet to be sold, so we are anticipating the earning of profit that has not yet been realised.

The concept of prudence tells us that we should not do this. We need to remove the profit element from our financial statements. We do this by creating a provision for unrealised profit.

You saw earlier in your studies how to deal with provisions for depreciation, doubtful debt and discounts. We need to make a provision for the profits as yet unrealised.

All provision accounts look similar.

Dr		Provision for ?!???!!! account		Cr
		Start of year Balance b/d		2,000
End of year Balance c/d	2,150	End of year Income statement		150
	2,150			2,150
		Start of next year Balance b/d		2150

The ?!???!!! could say depreciation, doubtful debts, discounts or unrealised profits.

The balance brought down at the 'end of the year' is shown in the balance sheet (the sheet for balances) as a deduction from the closing inventory of finished goods, while the 'income statement' amount is shown as a deduction from the gross profit on manufacturing in the income statement.

WORKED EXAMPLE

Paquito plc transfers manufactured goods to its income statement at cost plus 30%. The balance brought down in the provision for unrealised profits account at 1 April 20*8 is £1,300. Inventory of finished goods is valued at £6,500 on 31 March 20*9.

Required

Prepare a provision for unrealised profit account showing clearly the amount to be transferred to the income statement.

Answer

Dr		Provision for unrealised profit account		Cr
		1 April Balance b/d		1,300
31 March Balance c/d	1,500	31 March Income statement		200
		(missing figure to be deducted from GP on manufacture in income		
	1,500	statement)		1,500
		1 April Balance b/d		1,500
		(£6,500 × 30 ÷ 130)		

WORKED EXAMPLE

Snodgrass & Co transfers manufactured goods to the income statement at cost plus 25%. The balance on the provision for unrealised profit account at 1 August 20*8 was £3,700. At 31 July 20*9 the inventory of finished goods was £20,000.

Required

Prepare a provision for unrealised profit account at 31 July 20*9 showing clearly the amount to be transferred to the income statement.

Answer

Dr		Provision for unrealised profit account	Cr
		1 August Balance b/d	3,700
31 July Balance c/d	4,000	31 July Income statement	300
		(missing figure to be deducted from GP on manufacture in the income	
	4,000	statement)	4,000
	4,000	1 August Balance b/d	4,000
		(£20,000 × 25% ÷ 125%)	

Frequently in examination questions the whole of the provision account has to be prepared (including the calculation of the opening balance). If you can calculate the closing balance in the questions above, the opening balance should pose no problem.

WORKED EXAMPLE

Seline Smith marks up the goods manufactured in her factory by 35% to transfer them to the trading account. Her inventory of finished goods on 1 March 20*8 was £9,450; one year later, on 28 February 20*9, her inventory of finished goods was £9,720.

Required

Prepare a provision for unrealised profit for the year ended 28 February 20*9.

Answer

Dr		Provision for unrealised profit account	Cr
		1 March Balance b/d	2,450
		£9,450 × 35% ÷ 135%	
28 February Balance c/d	2,520	28 February Income statement	70
		(missing income statement figure)	
	2,520		2,520
		1 March Balance b/d	2,520
		(£9,720 × 35% ÷ 135%)	

WORKED EXAMPLE

Bertram Stink manufactures washing machines. They are transferred to the income statement at cost plus 60%. The inventory of finished washing machines at 1 June 20*8 was £57,600; at 31 May 20*9 it was £60,160.

Required

Prepare a provision for unrealised profit showing the amount to be transferred to the income statement for the year ended 31 May 20*9.

Answer

Dr		Provision for unrealised profit account		Cr
		1 June Balance b/d		21,600
		£57,600 × 60% ÷ 160%		
31 May Balance c/d	22,560	31 May Income statement		960
		(missing figure)		
	22,560			22,560
		1 June Balance b/d		22,560
		(£60,160 × 60% ÷ 160%)		

Like all provision accounts, it is possible that the provision at the end of the financial year could be less than the provision brought down at the start of the financial year. In such cases the amount transferred to the income statement would be added to the gross profit on manufacture shown in the income statement.

WORKED EXAMPLE

Seok Chin manufactures woks. The finished woks are transferred to her trading account at cost price plus 50%. The inventory of finished woks at 1 November 20*8 was £4,500. The inventory of finished woks at 31 October 20*9 was £3,900.

Required

Prepare a provision for unrealised profit showing clearly the amount to be transferred to the income statement for the year ended 31 October 20*9.

Answer

Dr		Provision for unrealised profit account		Cr
Missing figure added to	200	1 Nov Balance b/d		1,500
GP 31 Oct Income statement		(£4,500 × 50% ÷ 150%)		
31 Oct Balance c/d	1,300			
	1,500			1,500
		1 Nov Balance b/d		1,300
		(£3,900 × 50% ÷ 150%)		

QUESTION 10

Denis Walters is a manufacturer. He transfers goods to his income statement at cost plus 30%. He provides the following information.

	£
Inventory of finished goods at 1 February 20*8	6,136
Inventory of finished goods at 31 January 20*9	6,513

Required

Prepare a provision for unrealised profit account for the year ended 31 January 20*9.

QUESTION 11

Doug Down is a manufacturer. He transfers goods to his income statement at cost plus 40%. He provides the following information.

	£
Inventory of finished goods at 1 September 20*8	12,054
Inventory of finished goods at 31 August 20*9	13,356

Required

Prepare a provision for unrealised profit account for the year ended 31 August 20*9.

QUESTION 12

Joyce Black is a manufacturer. She transfers goods to her income statement at cost plus 60%. She provides the following information.

	£
Inventory of finished goods at 1 July 20*8	16,192
Inventory of finished goods at 30 June 20*9	16,416

Required

Prepare a provision for unrealised profit account for the year ended 30 June 20*9.

Finally let us see how the relevant figures are dealt with in the income statement.

WORKED EXAMPLE

Martin Simpson manufactures lawn mowers. He transfers finished goods from the factory to his income statement at cost plus 30%. He provides the following information for the financial year ended 30 September 20*9.

	£
Total production at cost price	76,500
Inventory of finished goods at 1 October 20*8	6,045
Inventory of finished goods at 30 September 20*9	6,864
Sales for the year ended 30 September 20*9	210,000

Required

(a) Calculate the transfer price of goods manufactured for inclusion in the income statement.
(b) Prepare an income statement for the year ended 30 September 20*9 showing the transfer.
(c) Prepare a provision for unrealised profit account for the year.
(d) Prepare an extract from the income statement for the year ended 30 September 20*9 showing total gross profit and the treatment of the provision for unrealised profit.
(e) Prepare a balance sheet extract at 30 September 20*9 to show how inventory of finished goods is treated.

Answer

(a) Transfer price is £99,450: production cost £76,500 plus

$$£22,950 \ (£76,500 \times 30\%)$$

(b)

Income statement extract for the year ended 30 September 20*9

	£	
Inventory of finished goods at 1 October 20*8	6,045	
Production cost of goods completed	99,450	(£76,500 × 130%)
	105,495	
Inventory of finished goods at 30 September 20*9	(6,864)	
Cost of sales	98,631	
Gross profit on trading	111,369	
Sales	210,000	

(c)

Dr	Provision for unrealised profit account		Cr
		1 October Balance b/d	1,395
		£6,045 × 30% ÷ 130%	
30 September Balance c/d	1,584	30 September Inc stat missing figure	189
	1,584		1,584
		1 October Balance b/d	1,584
		£6,864 × 30% ÷ 130%	

(d)

Income statement extract for the year ended 30 September 20*9

	£	£
Gross profit on manufacturing (from part (a))	22,950	
Less provision for unrealised profit	(189)	
Gross profit on trading		22,761
Total gross profit		111,369
		134,130

(e)

Balance sheet extract at 30 September 20*9
Current assets

	£	£
Inventory of finished goods	6,864	
Less provision for unrealised profit	(1,584)	5,280

WORKED EXAMPLE

Ian Rawstron manufactures bedroom furniture. He transfers finished goods from his factory to his income statement at cost plus 70%. He provides the following information for the year ended 31 December 20*9.

	£
Sales for the year ended 31 December 20*9	974,000
Total production at cost price	476,400
Inventory of finished goods at 1 January 20*9	10,540
Inventory of finished goods at 31 December 20*9	15,980

Required

a) Calculate the transfer price of goods manufactured for inclusion in the income statement.
b) Prepare an income statement for the year ended 31 December 20*9 showing the transfer.
c) Prepare a provision for unrealised profit account for the year.
d) Prepare an extract from the income statement for the year ended 31 December 20*9 showing total gross profit and the treatment of the provision for unrealised profit.
e) Prepare a balance sheet extract at 31 December 20*9 to show how finished goods are treated.

Answer

(a) Transfer price £809,880: production cost £476,400 plus

$$£333,480 \ (£476,400 \times 70\%)$$

(b)

Income statement extract for the year ended 31 December 20*9

	£
Inventory of finished goods at 1 January 20*9	10,540
Production cost of goods completed	809,880
	820,420
Inventory of finished goods at 31 December 20*9	(15,980)
Cost of sales	804,440
Gross profit	169,560
Sales	974,000

(c)

Dr		Provision for unrealised profit account	Cr
		1 January Balance b/d £10,540 x 70% ÷ 170%	4,340
31 December Balance c/d	6,580	31 December Inc stat	2,240
	6,580		6,580
		1 January Balance b/d £15,980 x 70% ÷ 170%	6,580

(d)

Income statement extract for the year ended 31 December 20*9

	£	£
Gross profit on manufacturing	333,480	
Less provision for unrealised gross profit	(2,240)	331,240
Gross profit on trading		169,560
Total gross profit		500,800

(e)

	£	£
Balance sheet extract at 31 December 20*9		
Current assets		
Inventory of finished goods	15,980	
Less provision for unrealised profit	(6,580)	9,400

Chapter summary

- Businesses that produce goods prepare a manufacturing account as part of their financial statements.
- A manufacturing account lists all the costs involved in running a factory.
- Goods are often transferred from the manufacturing account to the income statement inclusive of a factory profit.
- A provision account must be opened to eradicate the unrealised profit.

SELF-TEST QUESTIONS

- Name two businesses that prepare a manufacturing account.
- Identify two costs that would be included in the calculation of prime cost.
- Identify two costs that would be included as factory overheads.
- Name the three types of inventory generally held by a manufacturing business.
- Define the term 'direct costs'.
- Give an example of a direct cost for a car manufacturer.
- Define 'indirect costs'.
- Give an example of an indirect cost for a manufacturer of trainers.
- Why might a manufacturing business transfer goods to the income statement at a price exceeding total production cost?
- Why is there a need to provide for unrealised profit?
- Name the two types of gross profit usually earned in a manufacturing business.
- From which type of inventory is the provision for unrealised profit deducted in the balance sheet of a manufacturing business?

TEST QUESTIONS

QUESTION 13

The following information is provided for the year ended 30 November 20*9.

	£
Inventory of raw materials at 1 December 20*8	7,968
Inventory of finished goods at 1 December 20*8	7,670
Inventory of raw materials at 30 November 20*9	8,429
Inventory of finished goods at 30 November 20*9	7,950
Purchases of raw materials	102,177
Sales of finished goods	212,540
Wages – direct labour	82,440
indirect labour	45,670
Manufacturing royalties	1,200

Required

Select the appropriate information and prepare the prime cost section of a manufacturing account for the year ended 30 November 20*9.

QUESTION 14

The following information is provided for the year ended 30 April 20*9.

	£
Inventory of raw materials at 1 May 20*8	16,480
Work in progress 1 May 20*8	13,276
Inventory of raw materials 30 April 20*9	15,981
Work in progress 30 April 20*9	14,538
Purchases of raw materials	232,741
Purchases of delivery vehicles	135,000
Carriage inwards	2,478
Carriage outwards	3,560
Wages – direct labour	168,430
indirect labour	87,549
Manufacturing royalties	15,000

Required

Select the appropriate information and prepare the prime cost section of a manufacturing account for the year ended 30 April 20*9.

QUESTION 15

The following information relates to the Trogle manufacturing company for the year ended 30 June 20*9.

	£
Inventories at 1 July 20*8	
Raw materials	17,480
Work in progress	8,977
Finished goods	12,548
Inventories at 30 June 20*9	
Raw materials	18,597
Work in progress	10,431
Finished goods	13,547
Purchases of raw materials	234,772
Purchases of office equipment	17,400
Wages – direct labour	419,828
indirect labour	21,720
Rent – factory	9,500
offices	12,500
Insurances – factory	8,490
offices	3,510
Factory power	17,460
Depreciation – factory machinery	45,000
office equipment	11,200

Additional information at 30 June 20*9

Factory insurance paid in advance amounted to £360.

An outstanding amount for factory power remained unpaid: £940.

Required

Select the appropriate information and prepare a manufacturing account for the year ended 30 June 20*9.

QUESTION 16

The following information is given for the Duthie manufacturing company for the year ended 31 December 20*9.

	£
Inventories at 1 January 20*9	
Raw materials	23,841
Work in progress	12,402
Finished goods	14,539
Inventories at 31 December 20*9	
Raw materials	19,781
Work in progress	14,701
Finished goods	15,439
Purchases of raw materials	312,741
Wages – direct labour	212,441
indirect wages	126,481
Manufacturing royalties	32,500
Carriage inwards	2,481
Carriage outwards	3,146
Returns inwards	2,548
Returns outwards	1,718
Rent of factory	18,000
Factory insurance	12,461
Factory power	34,772
Factory machinery at cost	500,000

Additional information at 31 December 20*9

Factory rent owing amounted to £2,000.

Insurance paid in advance: £380.

Depreciation on factory machinery is to be provided for at 10% per annum on cost.

Required

Prepare a manufacturing account for the year ended 31 December 20*9.

QUESTION 17

Dreght and Sons own a manufacturing business. Goods are transferred from the manufacturing account to the income statement at cost plus 30%. The following information is available for the year ended 31 March 20*9.

	£
Inventories at 1 April 20*8	
Raw materials	8,162
Work in progress	6,183
Finished goods	7,451
Inventories at 31 March 20*9	
Raw materials	7,466
Work in progress	5,774
Finished goods	8,549
Purchases of raw materials	112,431
Sales	873,442
Carriage inwards	798
Carriage outwards	1,328
Wages – direct labour	189,410
indirect labour	64,822
Factory power	17,231
General factory overheads	21,461
Depreciation of factory machinery	28,000

Additional information at 31 March 20*9

An outstanding amount for factory power, £230, remained unpaid.

General factory overheads, £488, had been paid in advance.

Required

Prepare:

(a) a manufacturing account for the year ended 31 March 20*9
(b) an extract from the income statement for the year ended 31 March 20*9 showing the transfer from the manufacturing account.

QUESTION 18

Jasdeep Gahir owns a manufacturing business. Goods are transferred from the manufacturing account to the trading account at cost plus 20%. She provides the following information for the year ended 30 September 20*9.

	£
Inventories at 1 October 20*8 –	
Raw materials	17,489
Work in progress	11,023
Finished goods	88,149
Inventories at 30 September 20*9 –	
Raw materials	21,603
Work in progress	9,621
Finished goods	99,341
Purchases of raw materials	237,780
Sales	2,177,085
Carriage inwards	1,248
Carriage outwards	2,971
Returns inwards	653
Returns outwards	861
Wages – direct labour	372,005
indirect labour	83,750
Manufacturing royalties	120,000
Factory power	27,473
Factory rent and rates	19,716
Factory insurances	7,483
Factory machinery at cost	316,000

Additional information at 30 September 20*9

Indirect wages accrued and unpaid amounted to £1250.

Factory insurances paid in advance amounted to £272.

Depreciation is to be provided for at 10% per annum on cost.

Required

Prepare:

(a) a manufacturing account for the year ended 30 September 20*9
(b) an extract from the income statement for the year ended 30 September 20*9 showing the transfer from the manufacturing account.

QUESTION 19

Rod Bowler provides the following information for the year ended 28 February 20*9.

	At 1 March 20*8 £	At 28 February 20*9 £
Inventory of finished goods	27,300	32,500

Inventories have been valued at cost plus 30%.

Required

Prepare a provision for unrealised profit account for the year ended 28 February 20*9.

QUESTION 20

Nancy Chou provides the following information for the year ended 31 January 20*9.

	At 1 February 20*8 £	At 31 January 20*9 £
Inventory of finished goods	38,251	42,543

Inventories have been valued at cost plus 45%.

Required

Prepare a provision for unrealised profit account for the year ended 31 January 20*9.

QUESTION 21

Pusmeena Turner provides the following information for the year ended 30 November 20*9.

	At 1 December 20*8 £	At 30 November 20*9 £
Inventory of finished goods	89,250	80,500

Inventories have been valued at cost plus 75%.

Required

Prepare a provision for unrealised profit account for the year ended 30 November 20*9.

QUESTION 22

Jon Fret provides the following information for the year ended 31 May 20*9.

	At 1 June 20*8 £	At 31 May 20*9 £
Inventory of finished goods	42,550	32,200

Inventories have been valued at cost plus 15%.

Required

Prepare a provision for unrealised profit account for the year ended 31 May 20*9.

QUESTION 23

Sandra Gavington provides the following information for her manufacturing business for the year ended 31 December 20*9. She transfers goods from the manufacturing account to the income statement at cost price plus 20%.

	£
Inventories at 1 January 20*9	
Raw materials	7,966
Work in progress	6,200
Finished goods	14,880
Inventories at 31 December 20*9	
Raw materials	8,618
Work in progress	8,000
Finished goods	16,440
Purchases of raw materials	214,283
Sales	900,000
Wages – direct labour	125,750
indirect labour	63,489
Manufacturing royalties	19,500
Factory power	18,240
Factory insurances	7,960
General factory overheads	23,470
Factory machinery at cost	800,000

Additional information at 31 December 20*9

Direct labour wages accrued and unpaid amount to £2500.

Factory insurance was paid in advance: £740.

Depreciation is to be provided on factory machinery at 10% per annum on cost.

Required

Prepare:

(a) a manufacturing account for the year ended 31 December 20*9
(b) an extract from the income statement for the year ended 31 December 20*9 showing the transfer from the manufacturing account
(c) a provision for unrealised profit account for the year ended 31 December 20*9
(d) an extract from the income statement for the year ended 31 December 20*9 showing the total gross profit and the treatment of the provision for unrealised profit
(e) an extract from the balance sheet at 31 December 20*9 showing how all inventories are treated.

QUESTION 24

James Johns provides the following information for his manufacturing business for the year ended 31 August 20*9. He transfers goods from the manufacturing account to the income statement at cost price plus 25%.

	£
Inventories at 1 September 20*8 –	
Raw materials	27,932
Work in progress	13,420
Finished goods	22,500
Inventories at 31 August 20*9 –	
Raw materials	26,880
Work in progress	11,601
Finished goods	25,500
Purchases of raw materials	211,499
Sales	1,780,976
Returns inwards	976
Returns outwards	138
Manufacturing royalties	24,000
Wages – direct labour	477,816
indirect labour	112,420
Factory power	21,961
Factory insurance	9,750
General factory overheads	48,361
Factory machinery at cost	750,000

Additional information at 31 August 20*9

Amount accrued and unpaid for royalties: £1,000

Indirect wages accrued and unpaid: £830.

Factory insurances paid in advance amounted to £370.

Depreciation is to be provided on factory machinery at 10% per annum on cost.

Required

Prepare:

(a) a manufacturing account for the year ended 31 August 20*9
(b) an extract from the income statement for the year ended 31 August 20*9 showing the transfer from the manufacturing account
(c) a provision for unrealised profit for the year ended 31 August 20*9
(d) an extract from the income statement for the year ended 31 August 20*9 showing total gross profit and the treatment of the provision for unrealised profit
(e) an extract from the balance sheet at 31 August 20*9 showing how all inventories are treated.

THIRTEEN

Absorption Costing

It is of vital importance that a manufacturing business is able to calculate what each product (or group of products) has cost to make. This is necessary so that the business can fix a selling price in order to recover the costs incurred in operating the business and provide profits to ensure the survival of the business.

> **Direct costs** are those costs that can clearly be attributable as part of the product being produced.

> **Indirect costs** cannot be identified easily with the product being produced.

CIMA's definition of an indirect cost is 'expenditure . . . which cannot be economically identified with a specific saleable unit'.

QUESTIONS

- Identify a direct cost incurred in the manufacture of the jeans you wear.
- Identify an indirect cost incurred in their manufacture.
- Identify a direct cost incurred in the manufacture of the burger you ate yesterday.
- Identify an indirect cost incurred in its manufacture.
- Your answers for direct costs could have included denim, threads, designer labels, zips etc as the directs costs incurred in the production of your jeans. The indirect costs could have included the rent of the factory, business rates for the factory, factory power etc.
- Beef, buns, relish etc would be direct costs incurred in the production of the burger, while any factory overhead would be included in your answer for indirect costs incurred in production.

You have probably noticed the constituent parts of a manufacturing account already.

A cost centre may be a department, a machine, a person to whom costs can be associated.

> **Cost centre** is defined by CIMA as 'a production or service location, function, activity or item of equipment whose costs may be attributed to cost units'.

Cost centres are usually determined by the type of business being considered. In a college or a large retailer the primary cost centre might be each department. In a garage the cost centres might be the repair department, the sales department or parts department.

> **Cost unit** is a unit of production which absorbs the cost centre's overhead costs.

Cost units in a college might be students while in the garage repairs department the cost unit might be each car being worked on.

Specification coverage:
AQA ACN4;
OCR F014.

By the end of this chapter you should be able to:
- understand the uses and limitations of absorption costing
- allocate and apportion costs
- apportion costs for service departments using the elimination method
- calculate overhead absorption rates
- cost a simple project.

For example, the cost of the paper that this book is printed on is a direct cost. The denim in your jeans is a direct cost.

Direct labour costs can be specifically identified with the finished product (or service).

For example, the wages of the hairdresser styling your hair are a direct cost.

Direct expenses are any other costs that can be specifically identified with the finished product.

For example, royalties payable to the inventor of a process or design of a product; another example might be the costs of hiring equipment needed for a specific job.

Prime cost is the total of all the direct costs.

Prime cost = Direct material costs + Direct labour costs + Direct expenses

Absorption costing determines the total cost of production. (In fact it is sometimes called total costing.)

This means that all costs incurred in the production of the product are absorbed into the cost of production.

WORKED EXAMPLE

The following information is available for the month of January 20*9 for Chaudhry and Son, a manufacturing business. They produce one product: a 'higle'.

Production for January 20*9 was 1,000 units and the costs involved were:

	£
Direct labour costs	78,000
Direct material costs	56,000
Indirect labour costs	34,000
Indirect material costs	17,000
Other indirect costs	26,000
Selling and distribution costs	46,000
Administration expenses	62,000
Royalties	2,000
Depreciation of factory machinery	14,000

Required

a Prepare an absorption costing statement for the month of January 20*9.
b Calculate the cost of producing one unit, using an absorption costing basis.

Answer

a **Absorption costing statement for January 20*9**

	£
Direct materials	56,000
Direct labour	78,000
Royalties	2,000
Prime cost	136,000

	£
Indirect materials	17,000
Indirect labour	34,000
Other indirect costs	26,000
Depreciation	14,000
Total production cost	227,000
Selling and distribution costs	46,000
Administration costs	62,000
Total cost	335,000

b On an absorption costing basis, each 'higle' has cost £335 (£335,000/1,000).

USES OF ABSORPTION COSTING

- Calculation of profit or loss when selling price is fixed.
- Setting selling price in order to achieve a pre-determined level of profit.

CALCULATION OF PROFIT WHEN SELLING PRICE IS FIXED.

If the selling price of higles is fixed at £500 per unit:

The profit on the sale of each higle is £165 (£500 − £335).

CALCULATING THE SELLING PRICE WHEN A PRE-DETERMINED LEVEL OF PROFIT IS REQUIRED.

If Chaudhry and Son wish to achieve a profit of £70 on the sale of each 'higle', the selling price has to be £405 per unit (£335 + £70).

If Chaudhry and Son require a net profit margin of 25%:

Net profit on sales = 25% is the same as 33⅓% on cost of sales.

Cost of sales = £335,000

33⅓% of £335,000 = £111,667

So the net margin is £111,667.

Total cost of producing 'higles'	£335,000
Net profit	£111,667
Selling price	£446,667 or £446.67 per unit (£446,667/1,000)

QUESTION 1

Tucon Ltd manufactures one product, a 'sepyt'. The management provides the following information:

	£000
Material costs – direct	938
indirect	463
Labour costs – direct	461
indirect	726
Manufacturing royalties	20
Selling and distribution costs	612
Administration costs	300
Other indirect costs	84
Depreciation – factory machiney	100
office equipment	48

4 million units of 'sepyt' will be produced in August 20*9.

Required

a Prepare an absorption costing statement for the month of August 20*9.
b Calculate the total cost of producing one unit of sepyt.

QUESTION 2

Llandfferon plc manufactures 'dortees'. The following information is given for January 20*9:

Production for the month is 42,000 units.

	£
Direct labour	210,000
Indirect labour	130,000
Direct materials	67,000
Indirect materials	38,000
Other direct expenses	17,000
Other indirect expenses	42,000
Selling expenses	58,000
Administration expenses	36,000
Depreciation of factory machinery	34,000
Depreciation of office equipment	16,000
Depreciation of delivery vehicles	20,000

Required

a Prepare an absorption costing statement for the month of January 20*9.
b Calculate the total cost of producing one unit of 'dortee'.

QUESTION 3

Cardeter Ltd manufactures one product called a 'dible'. The total cost of producing 20,000 'dibles' is £127,000.

The directors wish to make a profit of £2.18 per 'dible'.

Required

Calculate the selling price of one 'dible'.

QUESTION 4

Transburn Ltd manufactures 'vuiten'. The total cost of producing 40,000 kilograms of 'vuiten' is £312,000. The directors wish to make a profit of £0.50 per kilogram of 'vuiten'.

Required

Calculate the selling price of one kilogram of 'vuiten'.

QUESTION 5

ADTE Ltd manufactures 'treamils'. The total cost of producing 45,000 'treamils' is £159,000. The directors wish to make a net profit margin of 25% on sales of 'treamils'.

Required

Calculate the selling price of one 'treamil'.

QUESTION 6

Froddy Ltd manufactures DT/34, a component for the electronics industry. The total cost of producing 54,000 units of DT/34 is £448,200. The directors wish to make a net profit margin of 33⅓%.

Required

Calculate the selling price of one DT/34.

Well, there does not seem to be much to worry about with regard to absorption costing!

> **Allocation of costs** is the term used to describe the process of charging whole items of expenditure to a cost centre or a cost unit. The costs are easily identified as deriving from the cost centre.

> **Apportionment of overheads** is the process by which some overhead costs are charged to cost centres on some rational basis because they cannot be directly attributed to a particular cost centre.

When all overhead costs have been apportioned to a cost centre the total has to be charged to specific units of production. This process is known as **absorption**.

The examples that we have considered so far have only considered one product. So all overheads have simply been added to the prime cost of the product to arrive at the total cost. The overheads have been absorbed into total cost of the product.

In the 'real world' (and generally in examination questions) things are rarely so simple.

Consider the following scenarios.

Ivor Fillin sets up in business, manufacturing toothbrushes. He employs Harry Sheen to help in the manufacturing process. Ivor rent two units on a local industrial estate.

Ivor can very easily prepare an absorption costing statement since all the costs go towards manufacturing the toothbrushes. He can use the statement to calculate his profits and he can even use it to work out his pricing strategy.

After a couple of successful years, Harry, by now a skilled brush maker, suggests that they should diversify into also producing hairbrushes. Ivor agrees that this would be an excellent idea. In the smaller of the two rented units Ivor continues to produce toothbrushes, while in the larger unit Harry produces hairbrushes.

How would they determine the costs involved in producing the two different types of brushes?

They can very easily allocate the direct costs to each product, since labour costs and material costs are unique to each product.

The problem arises when rent, business rates, electricity charges and other overheads have to be charged to the two products.

These are costs which apply to the business as a whole.

They need to be apportioned on some equitable basis.

BASES OF APPORTIONMENT APPLIED TO INDIRECT EXPENSES

Overhead	Basis of apportionment to cost centres
Rent	Floor area of cost centre
Rates	Floor area of cost centre
Insurance	Value of items being insured
Heating and lighting	Volume of cost centre (if this is not available then floor area may be used)
Depreciation	Cost or book value of the asset in cost centre
Canteen	Numbers of personnel in each cost centre
Personnel	Numbers of personnel in each cost centre

WORKED EXAMPLE

The directors of the Beckmond Engineering Company provide the following budgeted information for the month of February.

The following budgeted overheads cannot be allocated to the two departments run by the company:

	£
Rent	375,000
Rates	90,000
Power	300,000
Supervisory wages	96,000
Depreciation of factory machinery	150,000

Additional information

Total factory area is 240,000 m²	Department A occupies 60,000 m² Department B occupies 180,000 m²
Power used in each department	Department A 60,000 kWh Department B 40,000 kWh
Cost of machinery in each department	Department A £300,000 Department B £600,000
Staff employed in each department	Department A 30 workers Department B 10 workers

Required

Prepare an overhead analysis sheet for February.

Answer

Overhead	Total cost £	Basis of apportionment	Dept A £	Dept B £
Rent	375,000	Floor area	93,750	281,250
Rates	90,000	Floor area	22,500	67,500
Power	300,000	kWh	180,000	120,000
Supervisory wages	96,000	Number of workers	72,000	24,000
Depreciation of machinery	150,000	Cost of machinery	50,000	100,000
	1,011,000		418,250	592,750

QUESTION 7

Bhunit Ltd has the following budgeted costs for October. They cannot be allocated to its three departments.

	£
Rent	36,000
Depreciation of premises	6,000
Depreciation of machinery	210,000
Heating and light	9,000
Supervisors' wages	160,000

The following additional information is also available:

Floor area	Dept 1	2,000 m²
	Dept 2	4,000 m²
	Dept 3	6,000 m²
Number of workers	Dept 1	40
	Dept 2	90
	Dept 3	70
Cost of machinery	Dept 1	£150,000
	Dept 2	£300,000
	Dept 3	£600,000

Required

Prepare a statement showing the apportionment of overheads for October.

QUESTION 8

The directors of Hoolihan Ltd provide the following budgeted overhead costs for March. The overheads cannot be allocated to any of the four departments.

	£
Rent	61,200
Rates	21,240
Canteen costs	3,780
Insurance of machinery	36,000
Power	20,160
Supervisory wages	70,000
Depreciation of machinery	75,000

The following additional information is also available:

Total factory area is 540,000 m² of which:	
Department M occupies	30,000 m²
Department N occupies	180,000 m²
Department O occupies	210,000 m²
Department P occupies	120,000 m²
Staff employed in each department:	
Department M	14 workers
Department N	17 workers
Department O	28 workers
Department P	11 workers
Power used in each department:	
Department M	25,200 kWh
Department N	28,800 kWh
Department O	7,200 kWh
Department P	10,800 kWh
Cost of machinery used in each department:	
Department M	£65,000
Department N	£72,000
Department O	£37,000
Department P	£26,000

Required

Prepare a statement showing the apportionment of overheads for March.

TRANSFER OF SERVICE DEPARTMENT COSTS

Departments that provide services for the production department, and hence other cost centres, clearly are not involved directly in production of finished products. They cannot recoup their costs by incorporating them into the selling price of their product. Yet their costs must be recovered by the business.

The estimated costs of service departments must be apportioned to each production department. This means that each production department will recover its own overheads and some of the overheads incurred by the service department.

Service departments in effect charge the other cost centres in the business for the services that they provide for them.

Sometimes service departments keep detailed records of work completed in each department. In such cases these costs can be allocated to the appropriate department.

This is often the case in a reprographics department of a college or school. Each department will be charged for the photocopying for which they are responsible.

Examples of service departments would include:

- canteen
- stores
- maintenance
- personnel.

WORKED EXAMPLE

Thierity Ltd has three production departments. The company operates a staff canteen for all staff. The following budgeted cost information is given *after* all costs have been allocated or apportioned to the appropriate department.

	£
Department D	412,000
Department E	346,000
Department F	110,000
Canteen	63,000

Required

Prepare a table showing the apportionment of canteen overheads to the production departments.

Overhead	Total	Basis of apportionment	Dept D	Dept E	Dept F	Canteen
Total	931,000		412,000	346,000	110,000	63,000)
Canteen		?	30,000	24,000	9,000	(63,000)
			442,000	370,000	119,000	

Answer

Statement showing apportionment of canteen costs between production departments.
Can you guess how the canteen costs have been apportioned?
What information was missing in the question?
The information that was missing was the numbers of people working in each department. There were ten workers in department D; eight in department E; three in department F. This information was deliberately omitted. Would you have used people working in each department?
Don't worry – the information will be given in examination questions.

QUESTION 9

The Cafcal company has four production departments.

The maintenance department services all four production departments.

The following budgeted cost information is given *after* all costs have been allocated or apportioned to the departments.

Department	Total costs £
Z1	386,100
Y2	227,300
X3	180,400
W4	110,500
Maintenance	69,900

The number of machines in each production department is:

Department	Number of machines
Z1	14
Y2	9
X3	5
W4	2

Required

Prepare a statement showing the apportionment of maintenance costs between production departments.

QUESTION 10

The Teafoo company has three production departments.

The maintenance department services the three departments.

The following budgeted cost information is given *after* all costs have been allocated or apportioned between the departments.

Department	Total costs £
P/15	1,279,800
Q/17	326,400
R/19	807,040
Maintenance	126,000

The number of machines in each production department is:

Department	Number of machines
P/15	35
Q/17	7
R/19	18

Required

Prepare a statement showing the apportionment of maintenance costs between production departments.

Reciprocal services is the term used when a department provides a service for another department and receives a service from the same department.

The picture becomes a little more complicated when reciprocal services are provided.

For example, the canteen provides a service for all the departments including the maintenance engineers; the maintenance engineers keep the canteen equipment in good working order as well as servicing equipment and machinery in all other departments.

The power generating section will provide heating for all departments, as will personnel.

Examination questions will usually have only two service departments as a maximum.

There are three main methods of dealing with inter-departmental transfers of overheads.

Fortunately, for us, examinations at A Level only examine the elimination method.

The elimination method is sometimes referred to as the simplified method, since it does not actually reflect the reciprocity of the service departments to each other.

WORKED EXAMPLE

The cost accountant of Oxian Ltd provides the following information on budgeted total departmental costs after all costs have been allocated or apportioned:

	Production departments			Service departments	
	M	N	P	Q	R
	£	£	£	£	£
Total costs	45,000	60,000	20,000	10,000	12,000

The service departments' costs are to be apportioned as follows:

Department Q	40%	30%	20%		10%
Department R	20%	10%	30%	40%	

Required

Prepare a statement to show how the costs of the service departments are re-apportioned between the production departments.

Answer

	Production departments			Service departments	
	M	N	P	Q	R
	£	£	£	£	£
Total costs	45,000	60,000	20,000	10,000	12,000
Apportionment of Dept R costs	2,400	1,200	3,600	4,800	(12,000)
	47,400	61,200	23,600	14,800	

Note: Department R has now been eliminated.

Always start with the service department with the greater costs.

From above:	47,400	61,200	23,600	14,800	
Apportionment of Dept Q costs	6,578	4,933	3,289	(14,800)	
	53,978	66,133	26,889		

This method ignores the amount to be apportioned to Department R.

Strictly speaking, this method is slightly inaccurate, but the estimated overheads themselves might be inaccurate since they are after all 'estimates'. Also the method of apportioning overheads is only a matter of convention and none of the methods that could have been used can claim to be perfectly accurate. In most cases the figure remaining when the process is completed will be insignificant.

QUESTION 11

The managers of the Philysiac Company provide the following information, based on budgeted total departmental costs *after* all costs have been allocated or apportioned:

	Production departments			Service departments	
	11/R £	12/S £	13/T £	UV £	WX £
Total costs	60,000	120,000	45,000	30,000	20,000

The service departments' costs are to be apportioned as follows:

Department UV	25%	50%	20%	–	5%
Department WX	20%	30%	40%	10%	–

Required

Prepare a statement showing how the costs of the service departments are re-apportioned between the production departments.

QUESTION 12

The managers of Caspen Ltd provide the following information based on budgeted departmental costs *after* all costs have been allocated or apportioned:

	Production departments			Service departments	
	P/3/Q £	R/5/S £	T/7/U £	BZ £	CW £
Total costs	430,000	1,725,000	938,000	125,000	80,000

The service departments' costs are to be apportioned as follows:

Departments BZ	50%	15%	20%	–	15%
Department CW	42%	30%	20%	8%	–

Required

Prepare a statement showing how the costs of the service departments are re-apportioned between production departments.

THE ABSORPTION OF OVERHEADS

After the overheads have been apportioned to the appropriate cost centres we need to calculate the amount of the overhead to be included into the cost of each unit passing through the cost centre.

The amount of each cost centres overheads that needs to be absorbed (added) to each unit of production is termed the **overhead absorption rate** (OAR).

There are a number of different methods of calculating the overhead absorption rate.

DIRECT LABOUR HOUR RATE

When a particular department is labour intensive and there is little machinery used or machine costs are low the overhead absorption rate may be calculated using the man hours required to complete each unit of production.

Direct labour hours per unit is the number of hours (or part of an hour) that a worker would take to produce one unit of output.

WORKED EXAMPLE

Stemods Ltd manufactures two products – 'culas' and 'ginars'.

The budgeted production for each product for October is shown:

	Units	Direct labour hours per unit
Cula	10,000	2
Ginar	8,000	1.5

Budgeted overheads for October are expected to be £75,840.

Required

Calculate:

a the overhead absorption rate for each product, using the direct labour hour method
b the total amount of overheads absorbed by each product if budgets are met.

Answer

Total direct labour hours = 20,000 + 12,000 = 32,000

Labour hour overhead absorption rate = $\dfrac{£75,840}{32,000}$ = £2.37 per hour

a Overhead absorption rate for each unit = cula = £4.74 (2 hours × £2.37)
ginar = £3.56 (1½ hours × £2.37)
b If the budgets are met then the total overheads will be absorbed as follows:

	£	
10,000 units of cula will absorb	47,400	(10,000 × £4.74)
8,000 units of ginar will absorb	28,440	(8,000 × £3.555)
Total overheads absorbed	75,840	

You may find that the two sub-totals calculated above are referred to as the **overhead recovery rates**. So, in the month of October the total overheads £75,840 will be recovered by culas £47,400 and by ginars £28,440.

QUESTION 13

Bonivace Ltd manufactures two products – 'feltos' and 'hevos'.

The budgeted production for each product is shown for July.

	Units	Direct labour hours per unit
Felto	15,000	0.2
Hevo	6,000	1.4

Budgeted overheads for July are expected to be £72,732.

Required

Calculate:

a the overhead absorption rate for each product, using the direct labour hour method
b the total amount of overheads absorbed by each product if budgets are met.

QUESTION 14

Jacobski Ltd manufactures 'supnil' and 'quotanil'.

The budgeted production for each product is shown for October:

	Units	Direct labour hours per unit
Supnil	3,750	1.2
Quotanil	18,000	0.3

Budgeted overheads for October are expected to be £134,739.

Required

Calculate:

a the overhead absorption rate for each product, using the direct labour hour method
b the total amount of overheads absorbed by each product if budgets are met.

> **Machine hours** relates to the number of hours a machine will be used in the production of one unit of output.

MACHINE HOUR RATE

This method is appropriate when production methods are capital intensive or machine costs are relatively high. The overhead absorption rate will take into account the number of machine hours required to produce each unit of output.

WORKED EXAMPLE

Tryndra Ltd manufactures 'dertins' and 'ghilos'.

The budgeted production for each product for February is shown:

	Units	Machine hours per unit
Dertin	4,000	0.5
Ghilo	20,000	0.25

Budgeted overheads for February are expected to be £66,780.

Required

Calculate:

a the overhead absorption rate using the direct machine hour method
b the total amount of overheads absorbed by each product if budgets are met.

Answer

Total machine hours 2,000 + 5,000 = 7,000

Machine hour overhead absorption rate = $\frac{£66,780}{7,000}$ = £9.54 per hour

a Overhead absorption rate = dertin = 0.5 × £9.54 = £4.77
   ghilo = 0.25 × £9.54 = £2.39

b If the budgets are met the total overheads will be absorbed as follows:

	£	
4,000 units of dertins will absorb	19,080	(4,000 × £4.77)
20,000 units of ghilos will absorb	47,700	(20,000 × £2.385)
	66,780	

The total overheads in February will be recovered partly by sales of dertins (£19,080) and partly by sales of ghilos (£47,700).

QUESTION 15

Khuka Ltd manufactures 'klakas' and 'klovas'.

The budgeted production for each product is shown for May:

	Units	Machine hours per unit
Klaka	20,000	2.4
Klova	140,000	0.6

Budgeted overheads for May are expected to be £166,320.

Required

Calculate:

a the overhead absorption rate for each product, using the direct machine hour method
b the total amount of overheads absorbed by each product if budgets are met.

QUESTION 16

Limbachia Ltd manufactures 'peepar' and 'peekar'.

The budgeted production for each product is shown for December:

	Units	Machine hours per unit
Peppar	2,000	4.5
Peekar	5,000	3.2

Budgeted overheads for December are expected to be £240,000.

Required

Calculate:

a the overhead absorption rate for each product, using the direct machine hour method
b the total amount of overheads absorbed by each product if budgets are met.

There are four other possible ways of calculating the overhead recovery rate.

● EXAMINATION TIP

Do check the specification issued by the examination board to determine which methods of overhead absorption it might include in your examination paper.

AQA examines only direct labour hour rate and machine hour rate methods.

DIRECT LABOUR COST RATE

The estimated overheads are expressed as a proportion of the estimated cost of direct wages. The weakness of this method is that overheads will in the main accrue on a time basis whereas wages often accrue in a more complex way depending on the method of rewarding labour. For example, payment may be based on some kind of piecework or a premium bonus method.

WORKED EXAMPLE

Total overheads for April are estimated to be £283,992.

Total direct labour costs are estimated to be £151,060.

Required

Calculate the overhead recovery rate for April, using the direct labour cost method.

WORKED EXAMPLE *continued*

Answer

Overhead recovery rate $= \dfrac{£283,992}{£151,060} = £1.88$ per £1 of direct labour cost.

DIRECT MATERIAL COST RATE

This is a similar method to the direct labour cost method. The total cost of materials is used as the denominator in the calculation. The method's main weakness is that it assumes that time taken to process materials bears some kind of relationship to its cost. So high-value materials will attract more overheads than cheaper materials, regardless of the time taken to process them.

WORKED EXAMPLE

Total overheads for December are estimated to be £1,954,170.

Total material costs are estimated to be £502,350.

Required

Calculate the overhead recovery rate for December, using the direct material cost method.

Answer

Overhead recovery rate $= \dfrac{£1,954,170}{£502,350} = £3.89$ per £1 of direct materials used.

PRIME COST RATE

This method uses prime cost as the denominator. The method has the same weaknesses as the direct labour cost method and the direct material cost method.

WORKED EXAMPLE

Total overheads for July are estimated to be £1,355,500.

Prime cost is estimated to be £412,000.

Required

Calculate the overhead recovery rate for July, using the prime cost method.

Answer

Overhead recovery rate $= \dfrac{£1,355,500}{£412,000} = £3.29$ per £1 of prime cost.

UNIT PRODUCED RATE (COST UNIT RATE)

The total overheads allocated and apportioned to production are divided by the estimated number of units produced. So the overheads are spread over the goods produced. The method can only realistically be used if the business manufactures only one type of product.

WORKED EXAMPLE

Total overheads for May are estimated to be £15,500.

The total number of units produced is estimated to be 14,500.

Required

Calculate the overhead recovery rate for May, using the cost unit method.

Answer

Overhead recovery rate = $\dfrac{£15,500}{14,500}$ = £1.07 per unit

So far, we have considered products that are produced in one department only. Some jobs pass through several departments before completion. As a job passes through a department it attracts a proportion of the overheads of that department. When it passes to the next department, it will attract a proportion of the overheads of the second department and so on until it is complete.

Job ⟶ Prime costs ⟶ Proportion of overheads from Department 1 ⟶ Proportion of overheads from Department 2 ⟶ etc

⟶ Total cost of product + Mark-up = Selling price

WORKED EXAMPLE

Yves Pichot manufactures 'desirs'. A desir passes through two departments on its path to completion.

Information for each department is given:

	Department 1	Department 2
Budgeted total overheads	£40,320	£18,864
Budgeted total labour hours worked	4,800	900
Budgeted total machine hours worked	300	3,600

A desir spends four hours passing through Department 1 and three hours passing through Department 2 before completion.

Required

a Calculate the overhead absorption rate for a desir for each department, using:
   i) labour hours
   ii) machine hours.
b State which method of overhead recovery should be used in the two departments. Give reasons for your answer.
c Calculate the total overheads to be absorbed by one unit of 'desir' if budgets are met.

Answer

a Department 1   OAR using labour hours = £8.40 (£40,320/4,800)
                        OAR using machine hours = £134.40 (£40,320/300)

QUESTION 17

Alex McTavish manufactures 'sporidge'. Sporidge passes through two departments before completion.

Information for each department is given:

	Dept P	Dept N
Budgeted total overheads	£182,466	£262,145
Budgeted total labour hours worked	5,400	30,000
Budgeted total machine hours worked	45,000	2,400

A sporidge spends 9 hours in Department P and 6 hours in Department N before completion.

Required

a Calculate the overhead absorption rate for sporidge for each department, using:
   i)   labour hours
   ii)   machine hours.
b State which method of overhead recovery should be used in the two departments. Give reasons for your answer.
c Calculate the total overheads to be absorbed by one unit of sporidge if budgets are met.

QUESTION 18

Daphne Cherry manufactures 'Frutic'. Frutic is manufactured in two departments before completion.

The information for each department is given:

	Dept I	Dept II
Budgeted total overheads	£668,670	£120,792
Budgeted total labour hours worked	107,850	14,380
Budgeted total machine hours worked	21,570	35,950

A frutic spends 15 hours in Department I and 5 hours in Department II before completion.

Required

a Calculate the overhead absorption rate for frutic for each department, using:
   i)   labour hours
   ii)   machine hours.
b State which method of overhead recovery should be used in the two departments. Give reasons for your answer.
c Calculate the total overheads to be absorbed by one unit of 'Frutic' if budgets are met.

OVERABSORPTION AND UNDERABSORPTION OF OVERHEADS

Overhead recovery rates are based on predictions of future levels of activity and predicted (budgeted) levels of overhead expenditure.

If the actual level of activity is equal to that budgeted and actual expenditure on overheads is equal to budgeted expenditure then the expenditure on overheads will be recovered exactly.

If the actual level of activity is less than the budgeted level and spending on overheads is equal to the predicted level then the actual overheads will not be recovered. There will be an **under-recovery of overheads.**

If the actual level of activity is equal to the level that was budgeted but the actual spending on overheads is greater than the budgeted amount then this too will mean an **under-recovery of overheads.**

If the actual level of activity is higher than the budgeted level and actual spending on overheads is equal to that budgeted then the overheads will be more than recovered. There will be an **over-recovery of overheads.**

If activity levels are the same as those budgeted but actual spending is less than that budgeted then this too will mean less spending on overheads. There will be an **over-recovery of overheads.**

■ Any under-recovery of overheads is debited to the costing income statement.
■ An over-recovery of overheads is credited to the costing income statement.

WORKED EXAMPLE

Bartasil Ltd manufactures kityos. The directors budget for overhead expenditure of £25,000 each month. This figure is based on an output of 5,000 kityos. The overhead absorption rate is £5 per unit.

The following information is given:

	Actual output Units	Actual expenditure on overheads £
January	5,000	24,000
February	4,900	25,000
March	5,100	25,000
April	5,000	25,100
May	5,100	28,050
June	5,100	26,000

Required

Calculate the over- or under-recovery rate for each of the six months.

Answer

	Actual expenditure on overheads £	Overheads recovered £	Over-/under-recovery £
January	24,000	25,000	1,000 over-recovery
February	25,000	24,500	500 under-recovery
March	25,000	25,500	500 over-recovery
April	25,100	25,000	100 under-recovery
May	28,050	25,500	2,550 under-recovery
June	26,000	25,500	500 under-recovery

OTHER OVERHEADS

The other costs incurred by a business must also be recovered if the business is to survive in the long term.

Selling and distribution costs must be recovered.

Administration costs must be recovered and interest charges must be recovered.

These costs are recovered through the mark-up added to the goods before they are sold to the final customer.

These costs are treated as period costs and as such are debited to the income statement as we have done on numerous occasions earlier in the book.

USES OF ABSORPTION COSTING

The total cost of producing goods is necessary when calculating a selling price.

The total cost of producing goods is necessary for long-term planning, since total revenue must cover direct costs as well as overheads.

PROBLEMS ASSOCIATED WITH THE USE OF ABSORPTION COSTING

Overhead absorption rates must be updated on a regular basis. They are derived from budgeted information and are therefore subject to change.

Management decision-making relies heavily on the provision of accurate information; the information provided by absorption costing may be inaccurate since it relies on budgeted information.

ABSORPTION COSTING AND IAS 2

IAS 2 *Inventories* requires that the value of inventories, reported in the final published accounts of limited companies, includes the costs of converting the raw materials used into finished goods.

All 'normal' production costs will be included in the total cost of the product.

Occasionally there may be 'unusual' items of expenditure incurred during production; these might include idle time losses or exceptional wastage because of unforeseen circumstances. These should be excluded in the valuation.

Other overheads may be included if management deems it prudent to do so. Examples might include the accounts department or the personnel department if either has a direct input into the running of the production department.

Managers can use whatever basis they like when producing internal management accounts since IAS 2 does not apply.

ACTIVITY-BASED COSTING (ABC)

Cost pools are groups of costs arising from an indirect activity.

Cost drivers are activities that incur indirect costs.

Total absorption costing has evolved in the manufacturing sector of modern industrial economies. In the manufacturing sector it is relatively easy to identify direct labour hours or machine hours associated with each product.

However, the apportionment of overheads using these methods in the new integrated industrial environment has led to inaccuracies in pricing and an inaccurate distribution of overhead costs.

Activity-based costing (ABC) is based on the premise that business activity results in overhead costs. It attempts to link cost recovery to the activity involved in the production of the finished product.

When the activities that cause costs are identified, these costs can be apportioned to the product(s) with greater accuracy, thus aiding cost recovery. So the cost per unit can be calculated by allocating direct costs and apportioning indirect costs according to their use in the activity and the activity's use in producing the final product.

Activity-based costing analyses the indirect activities of business into groups referred to as cost pools. Factors that affect the costs are identified as cost drivers. A rate based on the frequency and duration of the activity is then calculated. Each unit of output is then charged with an overhead cost based on the rate calculated for the activity undertaken.

Chapter summary

- Allocation of expenditure is used when the cost is incurred for a specific cost centre.
- Expenditure that cannot be allocated is apportioned to the cost centres using some equitable basis.
- Service costs are apportioned to production cost centres.
- In the case of reciprocal service, costs are apportioned by a number of methods: the elimination method is the only one examined at A Level.
- The overheads of cost centres are charged to cost units by using calculated overhead absorption rates.
- At A Level overhead absorption rates are based on direct labour hours if the operation is labour intensive, or on direct machine hours if the operation is capital intensive.
- Higher than budgeted activity and/or lower than budgeted overhead expenditure will result in an over-recovery of overheads.
- Lower than budgeted activity and/or higher than budgeted overhead expenditure will result in an under-recovery of overheads.
- Activity-based costing uses levels of activity, rather than labour or machine hours, to calculate OAR when costing a product.

SELF-TEST QUESTIONS

- Give an alternative name for absorption costing.
- Identify one use of absorption costing.
- Identify one example of a cost centre.
- Identify one example of a cost unit.
- Tick the appropriate box to indicate whether the expense should be allocated or apportioned to the appropriate cost centre:

Overhead	Allocate	Apportion
Direct wages	✓	
Heating and lighting		
Direct materials		
Insurances		
Cost of running the canteen		

- What does the abbreviation 'OAR' stand for?
- Explain what is meant by the term 'reciprocal service departments'.
- Identify two methods of calculating an overhead absorption rate other than by using a direct labour hour method.
- Budgeted overheads are £23,600 and actual overheads are £24,000 and actual activity is equal to budgeted activity. Does this result in an over- or under-absorption of overheads?
- Budgeted overheads are equal to actual overheads and actual activity is 23,000 units of production compared to budgeted activity of 25,000 units. Does this result in an over- or under-absorption of overheads?

TEST QUESTIONS

QUESTION 19

Magreta Ltd is a manufacturing company with four departments. The following information is provided:

Department	B	C	D	E
Floor area (m²)	4,000	3,000	2,000	1,000
Machinery cost (£000)	270	90	60	30
Machinery replacement cost (£000)	300	200	150	150

The following budgeted costs for October have not been apportioned to a department:

	£
Factory rent	90,000
Factory rates	15,000
Factory insurance	21,000
Factory depreciation	7,000
Heating	18,000
Machinery insurance	24,000
Machinery depreciation	27,000

Required

Prepare a statement showing the apportionment of overheads for October.

QUESTION 20

Lethar Ltd is a manufacturing company with four departments.

The following information is provided:

Department	12	14	16	18
Floor area (m²)	2,700	4,800	6,200	1,300
Staff employed	18	46	28	8
Power units (kWh)	1,200	1,000	900	1,400
Cost of machinery (£)	78,000	32,000	40,000	50,000
Replacement cost of machinery (£)	150,000	56,000	100,000	64,000

The following budgeted overheads for February cannot be allocated to any of the four departments:

	£
Canteen costs	68,000
Rent	14,700
Rates	9,600
Supervisory wages	56,000
Insurance – of premises	4,800
of machinery	22,570
Power	36,900
Depreciation of machinery	20,000

Required

Prepare a statement showing the apportionment of overheads for February.

QUESTION 21

The Janu company has three production departments and a canteen that services the three production departments.

The following information is given:

Department	D	E	F	Canteen
Floor area (m²)	4,000	3,500	1,500	1,000
Staff employed	31	35	28	6
Power used (kWh)	800	500	600	100
Cost of machinery (£)	4,250	1,130	1,110	10

The following budgeted costs for November have not been apportioned to a department:

	£
Rent and rates	19,350
Insurance of machinery	35,100
Heat and light	11,460
Supervisory wages	29,000
Power	28,400
Depreciation of machinery	14,950

Required

a Prepare a statement showing the apportionment of overheads for November.
b Prepare a statement showing the apportionment of canteen costs to production departments.

QUESTION 22

The Hedold company has three production departments and a maintenance department that services the three production departments.

The following information is available:

Department	G	H	J	Maintenance
Floor area (m²)	5,000	12,000	11,000	2,000
Staff employed	26	40	16	8
Power used (kWh)	450	600	300	150
Cost of machinery (number of machines in brackets)	£80,000 (8)	£150,000 (12)	£70,000 (5)	100,000

The following budgeted costs for February have not been apportioned to any department:

	£
Supervisory wages	112,500
Power	35,700
Depreciation of machinery	142,400
Rent and rates	38,100
Insurance of – premises	16,530
machinery	9,240

Required

a Prepare a statement showing the apportionment of overheads for February.
b Prepare a statement showing the apportionment of maintenance costs to production departments.

QUESTION 23

The Vilcern Company has three production departments.

The production departments are serviced by a canteen and a maintenance department.

The following information is given:

Department	XY	ZA	BC	Canteen	Maintenance
Floor area (m²)	3,000	1,000	2,000	500	1,500
Cost of machinery (£)	120,000	250,000	150,000	80,000	200,000
Number of machines	14	6	4	2	4
Number of workers	19	6	15	4	6
Power used (kWh)	450	210	180	20	40

The following budgeted costs for April have not been apportioned to any department:

	£
Rent and rates	21,120
Heat and light	17,040
Supervisory wages	220,000
Power	29,610
Depreciation of – machinery	24,000
premises	16,800
Insurance of – machinery	21,720
premises	14,112

Required

a Prepare a statement showing the apportioned overheads for April.
b Prepare a statement showing the apportionment of canteen costs and maintenance costs to the production departments.

QUESTION 24

The Ousrow Company has three production departments that are serviced by a maintenance department and a canteen.

The following information is available:

Department	D/3	E/2	F/1	Maintenance	Canteen
Floor area (m²)	4,500	3,000	3,500	1,000	500
Cost of machinery (£)	400,000	300,000	150,000	100,000	50,000
Number of machines	18	16	10	4	2
Number of workers	120	60	70	7	3
Power used (kWh)	650	200	450	100	10

The following budgeted costs for September have not been apportioned to any department:

	£
Rent and rates	45,000
Heat and light	18,875
Supervisors' wages	494,000
Power	37,224
Depreciation of – machinery	270,000
premises	25,000
Insurance – machinery	15,000
premises	28,750

Required

a Prepare a statement showing the apportionment of overheads for September.
b Prepare a statement showing the apportionment of maintenance costs and canteen costs to the production departments.

QUESTION 25

The Plumet Company has two production departments that are serviced by a maintenance department and a canteen.

The following information is given:

Department	AZ	BY	Maintenance	Canteen
Area (m²)	3,000	5,000	1,000	200
Book value of machinery	£65,000	£25,000	£12,000	£8,000
Number of employees	20	40	10	5

The following budgeted information is given for June:

Department	AZ	BY	Canteen
Direct labour hours	800	12,465	
Direct machine hours	8,310	1,160	
Maintenance hours	800	300	100

The budgeted costs for June not yet apportioned to any department are expected to be:

	£
Rent and rates	47,840
Supervisory wages	172,500
Depreciation of machinery	55,000

Management has been asked to cost job PR/72. The job would require:

- 5 kilos of materials at £9.50 per kilo
- four hours of direct labour at £8.50 per hour.

It would spend two hours in Department AZ and three hours in Department BY.

The job would be marked up by 70% to achieve selling price.

Required

a Prepare a statement showing the apportionment of overheads for June.
b Calculate an overhead absorption rate for each department, using the most appropriate method.
c Calculate the selling price of job PR/72.

QUESTION 26

The Trinkwet Company has two production departments that are serviced by a maintenance department and a canteen.

The following information is given:

	Machining	Assembly	Maintenance	Canteen
Area (m²)	7,000	1,500	200	300
Book value of machinery	£84,000	£10,000	£5,000	£1,000
Number of employees	17	23	6	4

The following information is given for December:

Department	Machining	Assembly	Canteen
Direct labour hours	400	2,400	
Direct machine hours	1,200	300	
Maintenance hours	700	120	80

The budgeted costs for December not yet apportioned to any department are expected to be:

	£
Rent and rates	44,100
Supervisory wages	271,000
Depreciation of machinery	180,000

Job XR 471 would require 9 kilograms of material at £4.30 and three hours of direct labour at £10.40 per hour.

It would spend four hours in the machining department and eight hours in assembly.

The job would be marked up by 20% to achieve selling price.

Required

a Prepare a statement showing the apportionment of overheads for December.
b Calculate an overhead absorption for each department, using the most appropriate method.
c Calculate the selling price for job XR 471.

Marginal Costing

Variable costs vary with levels of activity within the business.

Fixed costs do not vary with levels of business activity.

Semi-variable costs cannot be classified as either fixed costs or variable costs since they contain an element of both.

Specification coverage:
AQA ACCN4;
OCR F014

By the end of this chapter you should be able to:
- use marginal costing for decision-making in respect of 'make or buy' decisions, acceptance or rejection of additional work, price-setting, optimum use of scarce resources
- calculate break-even.

We have seen in the previous chapter that a business must cover all costs in order to be profitable; it must recover all the costs it has incurred by absorbing them into the selling price charged to the final customer.

Absorption costing is the method employed in an attempt to ensure that each product does receive a proportion of the overall costs of running the whole business.

Absorption costing does have weaknesses:

- calculations are based on predicted levels of output, so variations in levels of output are not taken into account and this can lead to overabsorption and underabsorption of overheads
- apportion methods cannot be 100% accurate
- calculations do not take into account differences in cost patterns exhibited by fixed costs, variable costs or semi-variable costs.

MARGINAL COSTING

Marginal costing makes a clear distinction between fixed and variable costs. When using marginal costing no attempt is made to allocate or apportion any fixed costs incurred by cost centres or cost units.

Marginal costs are the costs that are incurred when one extra unit is produced above the planned level.

Marginal revenues are the revenues earned by the sale of one extra unit.

Marginal costs usually comprise extra materials, extra direct wages, extra direct expenditure, other extra variable costs in selling and distributing the product and any extra administration costs that arise when there is an increase in the level of production.

By definition an increase in production (that is an increase in business activity) will not increase fixed costs – they will remain unchanged.

EXAMPLE

Output in units	Fixed costs	Variable costs	Total costs	Marginal costs per unit
	£	£	£	£
1,000	5,000	1,000	6,000	
1,001	5,000	1,001	6,001	1
1,002	5,000	1,002	6,002	1
1,003	5,000	1,003	6,003	1

Note the variable costs change in line with the level of production.

The fixed costs have not changed with the increase in the level of production.

The variable costs are the marginal costs (in this simple example).

Contribution is the difference between selling price and variable costs.

Contribution should more properly be termed 'contribution towards fixed costs and profit' since once fixed costs are all covered contribution becomes profit.

WORKED EXAMPLE

	£
The selling price of a unit of VX/32 is	100
Variable costs per unit – direct materials	27
direct labour	32
royalties	8
Fixed costs per unit	17

Required

Calculate the contribution made by the sale of one unit of VX/32.

Answer

Contribution per unit = Selling price per unit − Variable costs per unit

Contribution per unit = £100 − £67 (£27 + £32 + £8)

Contribution per unit = £33

WORKED EXAMPLE

Emam produces a single product. The following information relates to the production and sales of the product in October:

Costs and revenues per unit	£
Sales revenue	70
Costs – direct materials	15
direct labour	12
royalties	5
fixed costs	20

Production and sales 1,000 units.

Required

Prepare an income statement for October, showing the total contribution and profit.

Answer

Income statement

	£	£
Sales		70,000
Less Direct materials	15,000	
Direct labour	12,000	
Royalties	5,000	32,000
Contribution		38,000
Less Fixed costs		20,000
Profit		18,000

WORKED EXAMPLE

Data the same as the above worked example but 1,001 units produced and sold.

Required

Prepare an income statement for October, showing the total contribution and profit.

Answer

Income statement

	£	£
Sales		70,070
Less Direct materials	15,015	
Direct labour	12,012	
Royalties	5,005	32,032
Contribution		38,038
Less Fixed costs		20,000
Profit		18,038

continued ➤

THE USES OF MARGINAL COSTING

Marginal costing is used in the following circumstances. When a business is:

- costing 'special' or one-off opportunities
- deciding whether to make or buy the product
- choosing between competing alternative actions
- employing a penetration or destroyer pricing strategy
- calculating the break-even level of output.

All of these circumstances tend to be short-term decisions.

SPECIAL OR ONE-OFF BUSINESS OPPORTUNITIES

WORKED EXAMPLE

The Troncell Manufacturing Company manufactures one product: 'troncells'. The following information is available for a production level of 5,000 troncells:

Costs and revenues per unit	£
Selling price	45
Direct materials	12
Direct labour	19
Royalties	1
Fixed costs	8

There is spare capacity in the factory. A Malaysian retailer has indicated that she would be willing to purchase 200 troncells but only if the price to her was £35 each.

Required

Advise the management of the Troncell company whether they should accept the order.

Answer

The order should be accepted. The order will make a positive contribution of £600 (£3 per unit).

Workings   Contribution = Selling price per unit − marginal costs per unit
                      Contribution = £35 − £32
                      Contribution = £3 per troncell

WORKED EXAMPLE *continued*

Note: The special order has no need to cover the fixed costs since they have already been absorbed into the 'normal' selling price.

The Malaysian contract has no need to cover the fixed costs again.

The contract is providing the manufacturer with an extra (marginal) contribution.

We can check to see if the acceptance of the Malaysian contract does make the business more profitable by preparing marginal cost statements.

Non-acceptance of the order	£	£	Accepting the order	£	£
Sales		225,000	Sales		232,000
Direct materials	60,000		Direct materials	62,400	
Direct labour	95,000		Direct labour	98,800	
Royalties	5,000	160,000	Royalties	5,200	166,400
Contribution		65,000	Contribution		65,600
Fixed costs		40,000	Fixed costs		40,000
Profit		25,000	Profit		25,600

Note: The fixed costs have not changed with the increased level of production.

The profit has increased by the amount of the total contribution earned by accepting the order from Malaysia.

CONDITIONS THAT MUST APPLY IF AN ORDER PRICED ON MARGINAL COSTING TECHNIQUES IS TO BE ACCEPTED

Care must be taken when accepting an order based on marginal costing principles.

- There must be spare production capacity in the business.
- The order must not displace other business (if it does then the revenue lost also becomes a marginal cost).
- There must be clear separation of existing customers from customers receiving the order priced at marginal cost (existing customers must be unaware of the cheaper price charged to the customer receiving the goods at the lower price).
- The customer receiving the goods should not be in a position to sell the goods to other customers at a price lower than the regular price.
- The customer receiving the order priced using marginal costing must be aware that the price quoted is for that one order only – the price charged should not set a precedent so that the 'cheaper price' is demanded for future orders.
- Care must be taken to ensure that competitors do not match the price for their regular customers, thus starting a price war where all producers will suffer from lower prices.

A manufacturing business must cover all costs incurred in running the business. A business cannot survive by costing all its production at marginal cost. If it did then none of the fixed costs would be covered (absorbed).

So, generally, any 'special' order which results in a positive contribution should be accepted.

ACCEPTANCE OF AN ORDER THAT WILL RESULT IN A NEGATIVE CONTRIBUTION

A special order that yields a negative contribution may be accepted under the following conditions:

- in order to retain a highly skilled workforce
- in order to maintain machinery in good condition, ie if failure to use the machinery would result in its deterioration
- in order to stimulate further orders at the 'normal price' in the future
- for altruistic reasons, ie because it is a worthwhile thing to do, eg providing a product at less than full cost, for disabled children.

QUESTION 1

The following information is given for T. Cupp, a manufacturer of pottery dinner services:

	£
Direct materials costs	4.50 per unit
Direct labour costs	7.70 per unit
Fixed costs	1.80 per unit

The dinner service sells to retailers at £30. Hallods, a large department store, wishes to purchase 3,000 dinner services at a price of £15 per service to include in its annual January sale.

Required

Advise T. Cupp whether she should accept Hallods' order.

QUESTION 2

The following information is given for Isa Wally, a manufacturer of one type of sports shoe:

	£
Direct material costs	0.80 per unit
Direct labour costs	1.20 per unit
Fixed costs	7.00 per unit

The shoes are sold to retailers at £14.

BBJ sports shops wish to purchase 40,000 pairs at a price of £5 per pair to include in their summer sale as a special purchase.

Required

Advise Isa whether she should accept BBJ's offer.

QUESTION 3

George Thomas manufactures scented candles – they sell for £2 each. The following information is given:

	£
Direct material costs	0.10 per unit
Direct labour costs	0.80 per unit
Fixed costs	0.50 per unit

A retailer in France wishes to purchase 1,000 candles for sale in Marseilles; he will pay £1 per candle.

Required

Advise George whether to accept the order for France.

QUESTION 4

Betty Wong manufactures hand-painted greetings cards. The cards are sold to retailers at £10 each.

The following costs relate to the production of 750 cards:

	£
Direct material costs	0.08 per unit
Direct labour costs	2.42 per unit
Fixed costs	4.00 per unit

A retailer in the USA wishes to purchase 200 cards. She is prepared to pay £2.60 per card.

Required

Advise Betty whether to accept the order from the USA.

QUESTION 5

The Shuttles Bowling Club rents out a room in its clubhouse at £40 per hour.

The costs involved in opening the room are:

Caretaker's wages	£8 per hour
Electricity charge	£1 per hour
Cleaner's wages	£3 per hour

None of these costs will be incurred if the room is not used. The treasurer adds £16 per hour to cover fixed costs incurred by the club.

A local bridge club wishes to use the room for a meeting lasting three hours but are only prepared to pay £50 for the use of the clubhouse.

Required

Advise the club treasurer whether the room should be let to the bridge club.

QUESTION 6

The Towers Hotel owns a sports ground adjacent to the hotel. The hotel accountant provides the following information for the rent of the ground.

Cost that are only incurred when the ground is used.

	£
Groundsman's wage	8 per hour
Petrol etc for the mower	6 per hour
Cleaner's wage for changing rooms	1 per hour
	$\underline{15}$

Additional information:

	£
Mark up to cover fixed costs and profit	20
Charge per hour of use	35

Tiddlers Street Junior School wishes to hire the sports ground for its sports day. It will use the ground for three hours but the school budget can only afford to pay £50 for the three hours let.

Required

Advise the hotel accountant whether the sports ground should be let to the school.

'MAKE OR BUY' DECISIONS

A business may have the opportunity to purchase the product that it currently manufactures itself.

In order to arrive at a decision the managers should consider the marginal costs and revenues.

WORKED EXAMPLE

Alex Droblin manufactures sweatshirts for sports retailers. The estimated costs and revenues for the next financial year are given:

Costs and revenues per unit, based on production and sales of 140,000 sweatshirts

	£	
Selling price	12	
Direct materials	2	
Direct labour	3	
Fixed costs	4	
Total production cost	9	
Profit per sweatshirt	3	Total profit £420,000

A manufacturer in India has indicated that the sweatshirts could be supplied to Alex at a total cost of only £7 each.

Alex has calculated that if existing selling price is maintained then profits will rise to £5 per sweatshirt and total profits will rise to £700,000 next year – an increase in profits of £280,000.

Required

Advise Alex whether, on financial grounds, he should accept the offer from India.

Answer

Alex should not accept the offer. If he did he would be worse off next year than if he continued to manufacture the sweatshirts himself. Profits would fall to only £140,000.
Contribution if he continues to manufacture himself = £7
(Selling price £12 − Marginal (variable costs) £5 (£2 + £3))
Contribution if he purchases from India = £5
(Selling price £12 − Marginal (variable cost) £7).

	Make			**Buy**	
	£	£		£	
Sales		1,680,000	Sales		1,680,000
Direct materials	280,000				
Direct labour	420,000	700,000	Purchase price		980,000
Contribution		980,000	Contribution		700,000
Less Fixed costs		560,000	*Less* Fixed costs		560,000
Profit		420,000	Profit		140,000

Marginal costing statements show the positions clearly:

Note:
It has been assumed that any resources releases by accepting the offer from India could not be used elsewhere by Alex.
It has also been assumed that the fixed costs are in fact fixed and will have to be met whatever decision Alex arrives at.
If the manufacturing space could be sub-let to another manufacturer the income received would be a source of marginal revenue and should be added to the sales revenue as extra income.
If extra costs had to be incurred in transporting the goods to England this would have represented a further marginal cost.
If extra costs were incurred keeping the manufacturing area safe and/or secure, these costs would also represent marginal costs and would have to be included in Alex's calculations.

WORKED EXAMPLE

Alex is faced with the same details given above, however he can sub-let his manufacturing area at a rental of £200,000.

Required

Advise Alex whether, on financial grounds, he should accept the offer from India.

Answer

He should not accept the offer.

With the rental income, the total contribution would rise to £900,000 (original contribution £700,000 + rental income £200,000), which is still less than the £980,000 contribution if he continues to manufacture sweatshirts.

WORKED EXAMPLE

Alex is faced with the same details as given in the original example. But he has to employ a security firm to keep the factory premises secure from vandals. This will cost £120,000 per year and additional maintenance costs of £100,000.

Required

Advise Alex whether, on financial grounds, he should accept the offer from India.

Answer

Alex should not accept the Indian order.

The contribution would only be £480,000 compared with the original contribution of £980,000.

Although in each case the contribution is positive, the new contribution should be compared with the contribution earned if Alex continued to manufacture the sweatshirts.

QUESTION 7

Pierre Dennis manufactures one type of high-quality marble fireplace. The following information is given for each fireplace. The figures are based on production of 80 fireplaces per year.

	£
Direct material costs	40 per unit
Direct labour costs	170 per unit
Distribution costs	30 per unit
Fixed costs	400 per unit
Total costs per unit	640
Profit per unit	360
Selling price per unit	1,000

Pierre has been approached by Angelo, an Italian manufacturer. Angelo can supply a similar fireplace of the same high quality for only £200. This price does not include delivery from Italy. Delivery charges will be £180 per fireplace. The prices are guaranteed for three years. Pierre says 'If I continue to sell fireplaces for £1,000, I will increase my profit to £620 for each fireplace sold'.

Required

Advise Pierre whether he should purchase the fireplaces from Angelo.

QUESTION 8

Fleetfoot manufactures one type of running shoe, the 'Rapide'. The shoe sells to sports shops for £20 per pair.

The manufacturing costs per pair of shoes are:

	£
Leather	2.00
Other materials	1.20
Direct labour	5.10
Selling and distribution costs	0.60
Administration costs	0.10
Fixed costs	4.00
Total costs	13.00
Profit	7.00

Fleetfoot has been approached by a manufacturer based in China who can supply a similar shoe of the same specification and quality for £10.50 per pair. Delivery charges will be £0.40 per pair. Prices are guaranteed for two years.

Required

Advise the managers of Fleetfoot whether to buy their shoes from the Chinese supplier.

MAKING A CHOICE BETWEEN COMPETING COURSES OF ACTION

The managers of a business may have to consider a choice between two or more competing strategies that would incur the same level of fixed costs. If this is the case then only the marginal costs need to be considered. The strategy that provides the greatest contribution should be the one adopted.

WORKED EXAMPLE

Marsha Knit starts a small furniture-manufacturing business. She is only able to produce one type of product. She needs to choose whether to produce tables, chairs or sideboards.

She provides the following predicted information:

Predicted production and sales	Tables 500 £	Chairs 500 £	Sideboards 500 £
Selling price per unit	400	120	380
Direct material costs per unit	80	13	70
Direct labour costs per unit	70	67	110
Total fixed costs	50,000	50,000	50,000

Required

Advise Marsha which product she should manufacture.

Answer

Marsha should produce tables.

Each table produced will give a positive contribution of £250, compared with a contribution of £40 per chair and £200 per sideboard.

Check your answer by preparing marginal cost statements for each type of furniture.

QUESTION 9

The managers of Snuggles have costed the manufacture of two styles of slipper – the 'Comfy' and the 'Warmy'. However, only one type can be manufactured. They provide the following information for the production of one pair of slippers:

	Comfy £	Warmy £
Direct materials	6	5
Direct labour	3	2
Variable costs	4	4
Fixed costs	7	7
Selling price	28	25

Required

Advise the managers of Snuggles which type of slipper should be manufactured.

QUESTION 10

Etomer is an electronics business manufacturing MP3 players and DVD player/recorders. In their first year of this venture they will only be able to manufacture one type of machine. The costs of manufacture are expected to be:

	MP3 players (20,000 units) £	DVD players (15,000 units) £
Direct materials	18	20
Direct labour costs	4	4
Other variable costs	5	9
Fixed costs	15	20
Total costs	42	53
Selling price	49	65

Required

Advise the managers of Etomer which product should be manufactured.

WHEN ONLY A LIMITED AMOUNT OF A FACTOR OF PRODUCTION IS AVAILABLE

A business may be faced by a short-term shortage of one or more factors of production necessary to continue the manufacturing process. There could be a temporary shortage of skilled labour; there could be a temporary shortage of direct materials; or a temporary shortage of storage space. Any shortage of a particular resource will limit the business's ability to maximise profits.

A scarce resource is sometimes referred to as a **key factor**.

It is essential that the managers of a business utilise the scarce resources available in a way that will yield the maximum return to the business.

WORKED EXAMPLE

The Laville Company manufactures four products. The products use the same type of materials and skilled labour.

The following information is given:

Product	P	Q	R	S
Selling price per unit (£)	200	300	100	400
Maximum demand for product (units)	1,000	800	1,200	900
Material usage per unit (kg)	7	12	4	15
Labour hours per unit	3	4	2	6

Materials cost £10.00 per kilogram; labour costs £15.00 per hour.

Required

A statement showing the level of production for each product that would maximise the profits for the Laville Company if:

a   only 25,000 kilograms of materials are available

b   only 10,000 labour hours are available.

Answer

Contribution earned by each product	P £	Q £	R £	S £
Selling price per unit	200	300	100	400
Marginal costs per unit	115	180	70	240
Contribution per unit	85	120	30	160

a

Contribution per kilogram of material used	£12.14	£10.00	£7.50	£10.67
Ranking	1	3	4	2

You can see that the Laville Company should produce as many of product P as possible; if there are still materials available they should produce as many of product S as possible, then product Q and finally product R.

If Laville could produce all products

they would produce	1,000	800	1,200	900
this would use	7,000 kg	9,600 kg	4,800 kg	13,500 kg

since this is not possible

they should produce	1,000	375	nil	900
this would use	7,000 kg	4,500 kg	nil	13,500 kg

This combination will maximise profits while using only 25,000 kilograms of materials.

b

Contribution per hour of labour used	£28.33	£30.00	£15.00	£26.67
Ranking	2	1	4	3

You can see that the Laville Company should produce as many unit of product Q as possible; then produce as many units of product P as possible, then product S and finally product R.

If Laville could produce all products

they would produce	1,000	800	1,200	900
this would use	3,000 hrs	3,200 hrs	2,400 hrs	5,400 hrs

continued ➤

since this is not possible

they should produce	1,000	800	nil	633
this would use	3,000 hrs	3,200 hrs	nil	3,798 hrs

This production pattern would maximise profits while using only 9,998 hours of scarce labour. (They have to produce only 633 of product S since the next unit would be only one-third complete!)

QUESTION 11

Seok Chin plc manufactures tables, chairs and bed headboards in Scunbridge. The same woodworking skills are used by the manufacturing labour.

	Tables	Chairs	Headboards
Annual demand	300	1,000	400
Costs per unit	£	£	£
Direct materials	23	8	10
Direct labour	80	32	16
Other variable costs	7	4	2
Fixed costs	20	6	8
Selling price	230	88	44

Direct labour costs £8 per hour.

In Scunbridge there is a shortage of skilled woodworker labour. There are only 5,000 hours available.

Required

a Calculate the rank order in which the products should be made in order to maximise profits.
b Calculate the number of each product that should be made in order to maximise profits.

QUESTION 12

Jock McTavish manufactures plastic goods. He produces three products; the cost patterns are given below:

	Boxes	Tool boxes	Packing cases
Maximum demand	5,000	2,000	2,000
Costs per unit	£	£	£
Direct materials	4	6	8
Direct labour	3	4	2
Other variable costs	2	1	3
Fixed costs	7	9	6
Total costs	16	20	19
Selling price	29	53	61

Materials cost £2 per kilogram.

There is a world shortage of the plastic needed to produce the products. Jock can obtain only 10,000 kilograms this year.

Required

a Calculate the rank order in which the products must be made in order to maximise profits.
b Calculate the number of each type of product that should be made in order to maximise profits.

QUESTION 13

Ivor Puddle makes wellington boots. Costing for the three types are given below:

	Gents'	Ladies'	Children's
Maximum demand	10,000	8,000	6,000
Costs per unit	£	£	£
Direct materials	6	5.50	4
Direct labour	3	2.50	1
Other variable costs	2	2	2
Fixed costs	7	6	3
Total costs	18	16	10
Selling price	32	24	15

Materials cost 50p per ounce.

There is a shortage of the materials used to make the wellingtons and Ivor is able to acquire only 210,000 ounces for his production this year.

Required

a Calculate the rank order in which the types of wellingtons must be made in order to maximise profits.
b Calculate the numbers of each type of wellington that should be made in order to maximise profits.

QUESTION 14

B. Ristle manufactures three types of brush. The following information is available:

	Toothbrush	Hair brush	Paint brush
Maximum demand	100,000	40,000	30,000
Costs per unit	£	£	£
Direct materials	0.50	1.00	1.50
Direct labour	1.00	1.00	1.50
Other variable costs	0.50	0.50	1.00
Fixed costs	0.50	0.75	1.00
Selling price	4.00	7.50	11.65

The brushes are made with hogs' hair which costs 50p per kilogram.

There is a world shortage of hogs' hair. Ristle is able to purchase only 200,000 kilograms.

Required

a Calculate the rank order of production necessary in order to maximise profits.
b Calculate the number of each type of brush to be manufactured in order to maximise profits.

Required

a Prepare a marginal cost statement for the month of April 20*9.
b Calculate the level of sales revenue that will ensure that Gwenaelle reaches a break-even level of sales revenue.

QUESTION 30

The following information is given for the month of March 20*9:

	Units used	Price per unit £
Direct materials	7,500	2.50
Direct labour	16,000	6.00
Other direct costs	4,000	3.00

Royalties to be paid total £9,000.
Fixed costs for the month will amount to £36,000.
During the month it is estimated that sales revenue will be £208,000.

Required

a Prepare a marginal cost statement for the month of March 20*9.
b Calculate the break-even level of sales revenue.

Standard costing sets levels of costs and revenues that ought to be achievable when reasonable levels of performance are attained, together with efficient working practices to manufacture a product.

Variance is the difference between budgeted (standard) revenue and costs and actual revenue and costs. They arise when actual results do not correspond to predicted results.

Sub-variance is a constituent part of a total variance. Sub-variances added together give the total variance.

Adverse variances reduce predicted profits.

Favourable variances increase predicted profits.

A **budget** is a financial plan prepared in advance of a defined time period. It is based on the objectives of the business.

Specification coverage:
AQA ACCN4;
OCR F014.

By the end of this chapter you should be able to:
- explain the uses of a system of standard costing
- calculate and interpret sales variances, material variances and labour variances
- understand the inter-relationship of variances
- appreciate the usefulness of variance analysis to management.

We all set standards in our everyday lives. Standards are goals – things that we hope to achieve.

- I may try to save £5,000 to add to the trade-in value of my car in order that I may be able to purchase a more up-to-date model.
- You may wish to save a certain sum of money in order that you can purchase a more sophisticated games console.
- You may wish to run 400 metres in a time of 1 minute 10 seconds or less.

All the examples are realistic targets that we believe are achievable.

The same idea is widespread in manufacturing businesses. In order to achieve an efficient production process, a budget will be prepared. The details will set the targets that the business hopes to achieve – standards are set for future performance.

If I fail to save sufficient money to replace my car, then, as a rational person (in my opinion!), I would consider the reason(s) why I was unable to save the £5,000.

If you failed to accumulate sufficient funds to allow the purchase of the games console, I guess you would investigate the reasons why. In both cases it could have been because the target (standard) was unrealistic:

- because income was less than expected or
- other financial priorities took precedence.

If the desired time for completion of the 400 metres was not achieved this could be because of:

- an unrealistic target
- poor training regime
- poor athletic diet etc.

If a business does not achieve the standards set, the managers will also wish to find out why.

MATERIALS VARIANCES

Total direct material variance identifies the difference between the amount that managers thought would be spent on direct materials (the standard set – the budgeted amount) and the amount that was actually spent on the direct materials.

WORKED EXAMPLE

Geoff Whyz has budgeted to use £72,000 direct materials in October. When confirmation is available in November, Geoff discovers that the actual expenditure was £75,000.

Required

Calculate the total direct materials variance for October.

Answer

Total direct materials variance = £3,000 adverse (£75,000 − £72,000).

WORKED EXAMPLE

Ethel Bigome has budgeted to use direct materials costing £36,000 in January. In February Ethel was able to determine that actual direct materials cost £34,800.

Require

Calculate the total direct materials variance.

Answer

Total direct materials variance = £1,200 favourable (£36,000 − £34,800).

Note: The adverse total material variance cost the business more than anticipated and will thus reduce profits (affect profits adversely). The favourable total material variance cost the business less than anticipated and therefore would increase profits (thus having a favourable effect on profits).

It is fine that we can determine whether the price actually paid has cost us more or less than was anticipated but from a management point of view it would be much more useful if we could discover why the variance from budgeted figures had arisen.

The difference in the cost of direct materials used could be because of:

- more materials being used than was expected (adverse variance)
- fewer materials being used than was expected (favourable variance)
- an increase in the prices of materials since the budget was prepared (adverse variance)
- a decrease in the prices of materials since the budget was prepared (favourable variance)
- a combination of a change in the use of materials and a change in prices.

We can identify differences in budgeted and actual expenditure caused by the above factors by calculating **sub-variances**.

Material usage sub-variance will calculate any changes in the total expenditure caused by changes in the quantity of materials used in the process. An adverse variance will indicate that the production process used more materials than was anticipated. Once identified, remedial action can be taken.

A favourable variance will indicate that the production process used fewer materials than was anticipated. If the reasons can be identified, any good efficient practices may be able to be replicated in other cost centres of the business.

WORKED EXAMPLE

R. G. Bahgi provides the following information for raw materials:

	Budgeted	Actual
Materials used	2,000 kgs	2,100 kgs
Materials cost per kg	£8	£8

Required

Calculate the direct material usage variance.

Answer

Materials usage variance £800 adverse caused by using more materials than were budgeted for.

WORKED EXAMPLE

T. Cupp provides the following information for raw materials to be used in production during September:

	Budgeted	Actual
Materials used	830 m^2	810 m^2
Material cost per m^2	£4	£4

Required

Calculate the raw materials usage variance for September.

Answer

£80 favourable variance caused by fewer materials being used than budgeted for.

A **direct material price variance** calculates any differences between budgeted and actual costs caused by sub-variances that arise because of a change in the prices of the raw materials being used.

O EXAMINATION TIP

Always indicate in your answer which variance you have calculated and state whether it is a favourable variance or an adverse variance.

- A **direct material price variance** will arise when the price of the materials changes.
- An **adverse price variance** will arise when the cost of acquiring the direct materials has risen.
- A **favourable price variance** arises when the cost of acquiring the direct materials has fallen.

WORKED EXAMPLE

J. Gwock provides the following information for raw materials to be used in her production process for December:

	Budgeted data
Materials to be used	1,200 litres
Cost per litre	£9.60

In January, the following information became available for December:

	Actual
Materials used	1,200 litres
Cost per litre	£9.80

Required

Calculate the material cost variance for January.

Answer

Material cost variance £240 adverse caused by an increase in the cost of acquiring each litre of the material used.

As you can see, the calculation to determine the variance is relatively straightforward if there is only one variable to consider. But what if there are differences in both the materials used and the price paid to acquire those materials from the amount and price budgeted for?

The simple way to calculate and differentiate between the two types of sub-variances is to use the following grid:

$$Sq \times Sp$$
$$Aq \times Sp$$
$$Aq \times Ap$$

Where: S = the standard (or budgeted) figure
q = the quantity
p = the price
A = the actual figure

So: Sq = the standard quantity
Sp = the standard price
Aq = the actual quantity used
Ap = the actual price of the materials used.

$Sq \times Sp =$ ⎤
⎟
⎟ Any difference (variance) between these two totals must be due to differences in the budgeted usage and the actual usage since the standard price remains the same on both lines.
$Aq \times Sp =$ ⎦ ⎤
⎟
⎟ Any difference (variance) between these two totals must be due to differences in the budgeted price as the actual quantities remain the same.
$Aq = Ap$ ⎦

The two differences combined will amount to the total variance.

WORKED EXAMPLE

The following information is given for the use of materials used to produce 'befures':

	Budgeted	Actual
Direct materials	720 metres	730 metres
Direct material costs per metre	£3.00	£3.50

Required

Calculate:

a the material usage sub-variance
b the material price sub-variance
c the total material variance.

Answer

Sq × Sp

720 × £3   = £2,160

Aq × Sp   £30   To gain full marks, we need
                                                      to identify whether these
730 × £3   = £2,190   variances are adverse or
                                                      favourable.
Aq × Ap   £365

730 × £3.50 = £2,555

The first line tells us that total materials would cost £2,160.

The second line tells us that total materials actually cost £2,190.

Materials in the second line cost £30 more than the budgeted costs on line 1. An increase in costs would have an adverse effect on profits, so £30 is an adverse usage variance.

The second line tells us that materials would cost £2,190.

The third line tells us that materials actually cost £2,555.

Materials on the third line cost £365 more than the cost on the second line. An increase in costs would have an adverse effect on profits so £365 is an adverse price variance.

The material usage sub-variance and the materials price sub-variance together will give the total material variance. So:

Sq × Sp

720 × £3   = £2,160

Aq × Sp   £30 adverse material usage variance

730 × £3   = £2,190

Aq × Ap   £365 adverse material price variance

730 × £3.50 = £2,555

                                     £395 adverse total material variance

We have successfully identified the three variances asked for in the question.

WORKED EXAMPLE

The following information is given for the use of materials in the manufacturing of 'trusmedas':

	Budgeted	Actual
Direct materials	2,400 gallons	2,250 gallons
Direct materials cost per gallon	£8	£10

Required

Calculate:

a   the material usage sub-variance
b   the material price sub-variance
c   the total direct material variance.

Answer

Sq × Sp

2,400 × 8 = £19,200

Aq × Sp   £1,200 favourable material usage variance

2,250 × 8 = £18,000

Aq × Ap   £4,500 adverse material price variance

2,250 × 10 = £22,500

£3,300 adverse total material variance

Materials cost £3,300 more than budgeted for. This was because there was a price increase of £4,500 and a saving of £1,200 because of more efficient use of materials.

QUESTION 1

T. Ravian provides the following information for materials for August:

	Budgeted	Actual
Direct materials	7,000 litres	6,900 litres
Direct material cost per litre	£2.50	£2.40

Required

Calculate:

a   the direct material usage sub-variance
b   the direct material price sub-variance
c   the total direct material variance.

QUESTION 2

Bimson Ltd provides the following information for materials for January:

	Budgeted	Actual
Direct materials	600 kg	530 kg
Direct materials price per kg	£4	£3.75

Required

Calculate:

a the direct material usage sub-variance
b the direct material price sub-variance
c the total direct material variance.

QUESTION 3

Bampa Ltd provides the following information for materials for July:

	Budgeted	Actual
Direct materials	2,900 tonnes	3,100 tonnes
Direct material price per tonne	£200	£220

Required

Calculate:

a the direct material usage sub-variance
b the direct material price sub-variance
c the total direct material variance.

QUESTION 4

Carmichael Ltd provides the following information for direct materials for February:

	Budgeted	Actual
Direct materials	2,130 m²	2,600 m²
Direct material price per m²	£0.50	£0.60

Required

Calculate:

a the direct material usage sub-variance
b the direct material price sub-variance
c the direct material total variance.

QUESTION 5

McThrift Ltd provides the following information for materials for November:

	Budgeted	Actual
Direct materials	9,000 litres	9,100 litres
Direct material price per litre	£1.60	£1.40

Required

Calculate:

a the direct material usage sub-variance
b the direct material price sub-variance
c the direct material total variance.

QUESTION 6

Chang Ltd provides the following information for materials:

	Budgeted	Actual
Direct materials	2,400 metres	2,250 metres
Direct material price per metre	£6.50	£6.70

Required

Calculate:

a the direct material usage sub-variance
b the direct material price sub-variance
c the total direct material variance.

DIRECT LABOUR VARIANCE

Total direct labour variances identify the difference between the amount that managers thought that they would spend on direct labour costs (the standard set – the budgeted amount) and the amount that they actually spent.

WORKED EXAMPLE

Tony has budgeted that direct labour costs for March would be £172,000. The actual amount spent was £178,000.

Require

Calculate the total direct labour variance for March.

Answer

Total direct labour variance = £6,000 adverse (£178,000 − £172,000).

WORKED EXAMPLE

Magdelaine budgeted to use £83,000 of direct labour in May.

In early June she discovered that she had actually spent £82,500.

Required

Calculate the total direct labour variance.

Answer

The total direct labour variance = £500 favourable (£83,000 − £82,500).

Note: In the first example above, labour cost more than was budgeted – this had an adverse effect on profits.

In the second example £500 was saved on the budgeted amount – this would have a favourable effect on profit.

It would be useful for managers of a business to determine whether the total variance was caused by:

■ workers being more efficient (favourable variance)
■ workers being less efficient (adverse variance)
■ workers being paid more (adverse variance)
■ workers being paid less (favourable variance)
■ or some combination of a change in efficiency and a change in wage rates.

We can use the same technique already used to determine direct material sub-variances to calculate sub-variances in the budgeted amount and actual amounts spent on direct labour.

In order to calculate the sub-variances that make up the total direct labour variances we can refer to our grid:

$$Sq \times Sp$$

$$Aq \times Sp$$

$$Aq \times Ap$$

However, we do need to make a couple of changes to our descriptions of the sub-variances:

- labour 'usage' is referred to as 'labour efficiency'
- labour 'price' is referred to as 'wage rate' or 'labour rate'.

Labour is used more or less efficiently than budgeted for.

The price of labour, as you might know from your part-time job, is the 'wage rate' that you are paid.

$$Sq \times Sp$$

$$Aq \times Sp$$

$$Aq \times Ap$$

S = the standard (or budgeted) figure

q = the number of labour hours

p = the rate at which direct labour is paid

A = the actual figure

So:

Sq is the standard number of hours thought to be necessary

Sp is the standard wage rate

Aq is the actual number of hours that were worked

Ap is the actual rate paid to the employees.

$Sq \times Sp$ $Aq \times Sp$	Any difference between these two totals must be because of the hours that managers thought would be worked by direct labour and the hours that were in fact worked.
$Aq \times Ap$	Any difference between these two totals must be because of any difference in the wage rate that had been budgeted and the wage rate actually paid.
	The two differences combined will amount to the total variance.

WORKED EXAMPLE

Katap Ltd provides the following information for direct labour for November:

	Budgeted	Actual
Direct labour	37,000 hours	39,000 hours
Direct labour wage rate per hour	£7	£7.20

Required

Calculate:

a   the direct labour efficiency sub-variance
b   the direct labour wage rate sub-variance
c   the total direct labour variance.

continued ➤

Answer

$$Sq \times Sp$$

$$37,000 \times £7 \quad = £259,000 \; \Big\}$$

$$Aq \times Sp \qquad\qquad\qquad £14,000$$

$$39,000 \times £7 \quad = £273,000 \; \Big\}$$

$$Aq \times Ap \qquad\qquad\qquad £7,800$$

$$39,000 \times £7.20 = £280,800 \; \Big\}$$

To gain full marks we need to identify whether these sub-variances are adverse or favourable.

The first line tells us that the managers of Katap Ltd thought that £259,000 would be spent on direct labour wages.

The second line indicates the change caused by budgeted hours not being achieved. There was an overspend of £14,000; this would affect profits adversely.

When the second line is compared with what actually happened, we can see that another overspend occurred. The profits would be adversely affected by £7,800.

Both sub-variances are adverse.

■ The direct labour efficiency sub-variance is £14,000 adverse
■ The direct labour rate sub-variance is £7,800 adverse
■ The total labour variance is £21,800 adverse

The three variances asked for have been identified.

WORKED EXAMPLE

Bash Ltd provides the following information for direct labour for April:

	Budgeted	Actual
Direct labour	6,200 hours	6,250 hours
Direct labour rate per hour	£9.50	£9.30

Required

Calculate:

a   the direct labour efficiency variance
b   the direct labour wage rate variance
c   the total labour variance.

Answer

$$Sq \times Sp$$

$$6,200 \times £9.50 = £58,900 \; \Big\}$$

$$Aq \times Sp \qquad\qquad\qquad £475$$

$$6,250 \times £9.50 = £59,375 \; \Big\}$$

$$Aq \times Ap \qquad\qquad\qquad £1,250$$

$$6,250 \times £9.30 = £58,125 \; \Big\} \qquad \underline{£775}$$

Adverse direct labour efficiency sub-variance

Favourable direct labour rate sub-variance

Favourable total direct labour variance

QUESTION 7

The managers of Sheddacc provide the following information for direct labour costs for May:

	Standard	Actual
Direct labour	1,400 hours	1,350 hours
Direct labour rate per hour	£9.50	£9.60

Required

Calculate:

a the direct labour efficiency sub-variance
b the direct labour rate sub-variance
c the total direct labour variance.

QUESTION 8

The manager of Typlea plc provides the following information for direct labour costs for September:

	Standard	Actual
Direct labour	24,500 hours	24,750 hours
Direct labour rate per hour	£12.40	£12.25

Required

Calculate:

a the direct labour efficiency sub-variance
b the direct labour rate sub-variance
c the total direct labour variance.

Many examination questions (and indeed real life) give information for both direct materials and direct labour and require the calculation of all seven variances.

WORKED EXAMPLE

The managers of Hasbec Ltd provide the following information for December:

Standard costs:
Direct materials: 430 kg costing £18 per kg
Direct labour: 170 hours at £7.50 per hour.
The **actual costs** incurred in the manufacturing process were:
Direct materials: 425 kg costing £18.10 per kg
Direct labour: 172 hours at £7.40 per hour.

continued ➤

Required

Calculate:

a   the direct material usage sub-variance
b   the direct material price sub-variance
c   the total direct material variance
d   the direct labour efficiency sub-variance
e   the direct labour rate sub-variance
f   the total direct labour variance
g   the total direct expenses variance.

Answer

Direct materials: Sq × Sp

430 × £18   = £7,740.00

Aq × Sp   £90 favourable direct material usage sub-variance (a)

425 × £18   = £7,650.00

Aq × Ap   £42.50 adverse direct material price sub-variance (b)

425 × £18.10 = £7,692.50

£47.50 favourable total direct material variance (c)

Direct labour: Sq × Sp

170 × £7.50   = £1,275.00   £15 adverse direct labour efficiency sub-variance (d)

Aq × Sp

172 × £7.50   = £1,290.00   £17.20 favourable direct labour rate sub-variance (e)

Aq × Ap

172 × £7.40   = £1,272.80   £2.20 favourable total labour variance (f)

Total direct expenses variance = £49.70 favourable (g)

QUESTION 9

The managers of Lesmark Ltd provide the following information for December:

Standard costs:

Direct materials: 1,720 litres costing £1.80 per litre

Direct labour: 810 hours at £8.40 per hour.

The **actual costs** in manufacturing were:

Direct materials: 1,735 litres costing £1.75 per litre

Direct labour: 834 hours at £8.50 per hour.

Required

Calculate:

a   the direct material usage sub-variance
b   the direct material price sub-variance
c   the total direct material variance
d   the direct labour efficiency sub-variance

e   the direct labour rate sub-variance
f   the total direct labour variance
g   the total direct expenses variance.

QUESTION 10

The managers of Slaura Ltd provide the following information for February:

> **Standard costs:**
>
> Direct materials: 1,120 m^2 costing 48 pence per m^2
>
> Direct labour: 310 hours at £16.30 per hour.

The **actual costs** incurred in manufacture were:

> Direct materials: 1,110m^2 costing 50 pence per m^2
>
> Direct labour: 320 hours at £16.20 per hour.

Required

Calculate:

a   the direct material usage sub-variance
b   the direct material price sub-variance
c   the total direct material variance
d   the direct labour efficiency sub-variance
e   the direct labour rate sub-variance
f   the total direct labour variance
g   the total direct expenses variance.

THE FLEXED BUDGET

One of the purposes of using a standard costing system is that problem areas in production are highlighted and so remedial action can be taken. The system will also identify areas of cost saving and therefore good practice which may be emulated in other areas of the business.

The system identifies variances by making comparisons between standard (budgeted) costs and the costs that have actually been incurred.

One of the over-riding principles involved in making comparisons is that we should try, as far as is possible, to compare like with like.

This principle should be applied when comparing standard costs with actual costs. So if actual activity differs from budgeted activity, the budget must be flexed to produce a budget which reflects actual levels of activity.

EXAMPLE

The manager of Bloo Jeans plc has budgeted to produce 100,000 pairs of denim jeans in August. She budgets for the use of 140,000 m^2 of denim in the production process. The actual figures available in September show that only 120,000 m^2 of denim was used and total production was 90,000 pairs of jeans.

Clearly, the production has used less denim than had been anticipated but fewer jeans were manufactured so one would expect less material to be used.

The comparison is 140,000 m^2 with 120,000 m^2.

However, we are not comparing like with like.

- 140,000 m^2 should have made 100,000 pairs of jeans
- 120,000 m^2 actually made 90,000 pairs of jeans.

In order to make a valid comparison to see if the materials have been used efficiently or not, we need to adjust our budget – the adjustment is called **flexing**.

If we had known earlier, when the standard was set, that only 90,000 pairs of jeans would be made, the budgeted figures for materials to be used would have been:

continued ➤

EXAMPLE *continued*

126,000 m^2 (ie 90,000/100,000 or 9/10 of 140,000m^2)

and the figures to be used would be:

Standard costs:

90,000 pairs of jeans would require 126,000 m^2 of denim.

So a comparison can now be made quite easily:

Standard materials usage:

90,000 pairs of jeans will require 126,000 m^2 of denim.

Actual material usage:

90,000 pairs of jeans have required 120,000 m^2 of denim.

We can then see quite clearly that less material has been used than anticipated – thus giving rise to a favourable material usage sub-variance.

WORKED EXAMPLE

The managers of Getang Ltd provide the following information for the production of 'Selvings' during March:

Budgeted output	Actual output
80,000 Selvings	70,000 Selvings
Budgeted use of direct materials	**Actual use of direct materials**
240,000 litres	220,000 litres

Require

Calculate the amount of direct materials saved or wasted during March.

Answer

Flexed budget	Budgeted use of direct materials
70,000 Selvings	210,000 litres (7/8 × 240,000)
Actual usage	**Actual use of direct materials**
70,000 Selvings	220,000 litres

So 10,000 litres of direct materials were used that had not been budgeted for. The reasons for this 'wastage' should be investigated and if possible a remedy sought.

It will also be necessary to flex the standards set for the use of direct labour.

The following information is given for direct labour hours for July for the production of 'Lingts':

	Standard	Actual
Production	250,000 units	225,000 units
Direct labour hours	70,000 hours	65,000 hours

Required

Calculate the direct labour hours to be used in a flexed budget for July.

Answer

225,000 Lingts should use 63,000 hours of direct labour

(225,000/250,000 × 70,000 hours). In fact, 2,000 further hours have been used. An investigation should be undertaken to determine why this has happened and remedial action taken if possible.

● EXAMINATION TIP

Only flex the **standard** quantity of direct materials and/or the **standard** hours of direct labour to be used in your grid. Show your workings.

WORKED EXAMPLE

The following information is given for the production of trapeds:

Standard costs for 1,000 trapeds:	
Direct materials:	220 kg at £5 per kg
Direct labour:	60 hours at £9.50 per hour.
Actual costs for the production of 950 trapeds:	
Direct materials:	204 kg at £5.75 per kg
Direct labour:	58 hours at £9.30 per hour.

Required

Calculate:

a   the direct material usage sub-variance
b   the direct material price sub-variance
c   the total direct material variance
d   the direct labour efficiency sub-variance
e   the direct labour rate sub-variance
f   the total direct material variance.

continued ➤

Answer

$$Sq \times Sp$$
$$7,800 \times £3.85 = £30,030$$
$$Aq \times Sp$$
$$8,000 \times £3.85 = £30,800$$
$$Aq \times Ap$$
$$8,000 \times £3.80 = £30,400$$

£770 favourable (a favourable impact on profit) sales volume sub-variance

£400 adverse (an adverse effect on profits) sales price sub-variance

$\underline{£370}$ favourable total sales variance

● EXAMINATION TIP

The most common type of question relates to calculation of total and sub-variances for direct materials and direct labour. So learn the grid!

QUESTION 13

Budgeted sales for 'graftoos' were 29,300 units at a selling price of £7.96 each. The actual sales were 29,250 units at a selling price of £8.03.

Required

Calculate:

a the sales volume sub-variance
b the sales price sub-variance
c the total sales variance.

QUESTION 14

Budgeted sales for 'chukennies' were 154,000 units at a selling price of 30p each. The actual sales were 150,000 at 28p each.

Required

Calculate:

a the sales volume sub-variance
b the sales price sub-variance
c the total sales variance.

You must learn the grid and how to use it.

You must also be able to tell quickly whether a variance that you have calculated is favourable or adverse.

Calculating variances is only part of the process; with practice, the calculations can be mastered and you should be able to gain accurate results.

However, more important than merely calculating the variances is gaining information from your calculations.

Business managers introduce a system of standard costing because it can highlight variances between the predicted costs and the actual costs.

Variances lead to investigation into the causes of the differences.

Standard costing is the natural extension of budgetary control.

Budgetary control seeks to make sections and departments more efficient and hence improve the performance of the business as a whole.

Standard costing goes into much greater detail than budgeting. It examines in detail the costs of all the constituent parts of the production process for each product.

When variances are identified, action can be implemented to correct adverse variances.

Managers must know the cause of any deviation from standard in order to take remedial action.

You will probably be asked to comment upon or make observations about the variances you have calculated in an examination question.

Variance analysis highlights areas of concern and areas of good practice and you may be asked to explain possible reasons for the variances.

You may also be asked to identify some inter-relationship between different sub-variances.

Many of the comments you may make could be speculative because you will have a limited picture or scenario from the question and thus may lack the detail necessary to arrive at a definitive conclusion. Your answer will require a lot of thought and the application of common sense.

CAUSES OF SUB-VARIANCES

The actual results may differ from the standards because there have been errors in the standards set. These errors could be caused by:

- using incorrect data
- setting unrealistic targets
- managers deliberately setting low standards.

When answering an examination question, show the examiners that you are aware of possible causes of deviations from standard figures, but do not labour the point; rather, make it as a general comment that will apply to all sub-variances.

Direct material usage sub-variances	
Favourable sub-variance:	Adverse sub-variance:
Use of better-quality materials	Use of poorer materials
Use of highly skilled workers	Use of less skilled workers
Use of 'state of the art' capital equipment	Use of poor capital equipment
	Theft of materials
	Deterioration of materials

Note that the first three factors in both columns refer to wastage of materials.

Direct material price sub-variance	
Favourable sub-variance:	Adverse sub-variance:
Deflation – either general or specific to the materials being purchased.	Inflation – either general or specific to the materials being purchased
Supplier reducing price	Supplier increasing price
Use of a cheaper alternative material or less good quality of the same material	Use of more expensive alternative material or better quality of the same materials
Increase in quantity purchased so better trade discount obtained	Decrease in quantity purchased so loss of trade discount
Increase in value of the pound against the value of the euro or the dollar, making imported materials less expensive	Decrease in value of the pound against the value of the euro or the dollar, making imported materials more expensive

Direct labour efficiency sub-variance	
Favourable sub-variance:	Adverse sub-variance:
Use of workers with higher skills	Use of workers with lower skills
Workers using better machinery	Workers using poor machinery
Good working conditions	Poor working conditions
High staff morale – highly motivated	Poor staff morale – poor motivation
Good levels of quality control	Poor levels of quality control

Direct labour rate sub-variance	
Favourable sub-variance:	Adverse sub-variance:
Use of lower-grade workers earning lower rates of pay	Use of higher-grade workers earning higher rates of pay
Wage deflation	Wage inflation – general or specific to workers being used
Reduction in overtime or premium rates being paid	Increase in overtime or premium rates being paid

Sales volume sub-variance	
Favourable sub-variance:	Adverse sub-variance:
More aggressive marketing strategy	Less aggressive marketing strategy
Increased seasonal sales	Decrease in seasonal sales
Less competition in sector: ■ fewer sales by competitors ■ higher market share	More competition in sector: ■ more sales going to competitors ■ lower market share
Change in consumer tastes	Change in consumer tastes
	Defective product

Sales price sub-variance	
Favourable sub-variance:	Adverse sub-variance:
Increase in price to compensate for increased costs	Reduction in selling price for bulk sales
Increase in price after use of 'penetration' (marginal cost) pricing	Reduction in price – to attract new customers; by using marginal cost pricing; to penetrate a new market; to sell off stock quickly etc.

There are inter-connections between sub-variances and generally, in an examination, identification of these inter-relationships will perhaps gain extra development marks.

Here are a few inter-relating sub-variances:

■ Favourable material usage sub-variance and Adverse labour rate sub-variance
  Fewer materials being used   **because**   A higher skilled workforce is being used and has to be paid more

■ Adverse labour efficiency sub-variance and Adverse material usage sub-variance
Workers taking longer to make goods   **this results in**   The machinery spoiling much of
the because of faulty machinery   materials being used.

QUESTION 15

Chan Ltd is a manufacturer. The following is information provided:

■ favourable direct labour rate sub-variance
■ adverse direct labour efficiency sub-variance.

Required

Explain a possible inter-relationship between the two sub-variances.

QUESTION 16

Davmark Ltd is a manufacturer. The following information is available:

■ favourable direct material usage sub-variance
■ adverse direct labour rate sub-variance.

Required

Explain a possible inter-relationship between the two sub-variances.

QUESTION 17

Reayt Ltd is a manufacturer. The following information is available:

■ direct material usage sub-variance is adverse
■ direct labour rate sub-variance is adverse.

Required

Explain any possible inter-relationship between the two sub-variances.

QUESTION 18

Dumy Ltd is a manufacturer. The following information is available:

■ favourable direct labour rate sub-variance
■ adverse sales volume sub-variance.

Required

Explain a possible inter-relationship between the two sub-variances.

Chapter summary

■ Standard costs are pre-determined and reflect possible levels of costs and
  revenues that ought to be achieved under conditions of acceptable levels of
  efficiency.
■ Standard costs are used to prepare budgets and may be used in pricing policies.
■ Variances identify differences between standards set and actual performance.
  They are composed of sub-variances.
■ If actual performance is different from standard performance, the budget may
  have to be flexed.
■ Analysis of sub-variances is necessary in order to eradicate problem areas in
  production or to copy good practice.
■ A sub-variance in one area may cause a sub-variance in another connected area.

SELF-TEST QUESTIONS

■ Total variance = Standard cost less ....
■ Copy out the 'grid' used to calculate sub-variances.
■ Usage is applied to direct materials. What is the word that replaces 'usage' in
  'direct labour.............sub-variance'?

- We say 'material price'. What word do we use for the price of labour?
- Standard quantity direct materials information: 40 units; standard price £10; actual quantity 50 units; actual price £10. Calculate the direct material usage sub-variance.
- X is a manufacturing business. Budgeted production is 1,000 units; budgeted materials used 500 tonnes; actual materials used 550 tonnes. Which figure should be used in the grid for Sq?
- Why is a budget sometimes flexed?
- Explain a possible factor that would result in an adverse material usage sub-variance.
- Explain a possible factor that would result in a favourable labour rate sub-variance.
- Explain how the use of poor machinery might affect a direct material usage sub-variance and a labour efficiency sub-variance.

TEST QUESTIONS

QUESTION 19

The managers of Kambog Ltd provide the following information for direct materials for August:

	Budgeted	Actual
Direct materials	4,200 m²	4,150 m²
Direct materials – price per m²	£3.40	£3.50

Required

Calculate:

a the direct material usage sub-variance
b the direct material price sub-variance
c the total direct material variance.

QUESTION 20

The managers of O'Donnal provide the following information for direct materials for July:

	Budgeted	Actual
Direct materials	7,150 litres	7,300 litres
Direct materials – price per litre	£1.20	£1.15

Required

Calculate:

a the direct material usage sub-variance
b the direct material price sub-variance
c the total direct material variance.

QUESTION 21

The managers of Thomas Ltd provide the following information for direct labour for February:

	Budgeted	Actual
Direct labour	1,200 hours	1,400 hours
Direct labour rate per hour	£8.50	£8.60

Required

Calculate:

a the direct labour efficiency sub-variance
b the direct labour rate sub-variance
c the total direct labour variance.

QUESTION 22

The managers of McStravick Ltd supply the following information for direct labour for October:

	Budgeted	Actual
Direct labour	42,000 hours	41,950 hours
Direct labour rate per hour	£16.40	£16.35

Required

Calculate:

a the direct labour efficiency sub-variance
b the direct labour rate sub-variance
c the total direct labour variance.

QUESTION 23

The managers of Nathwani and Co Ltd provide the following information for May:

Standard costs:

Direct materials: 17,300 kg costing £1.82 per kg

Direct labour: 410 hours at £9.40 per hour.

Actual costs were:

Direct materials: 17,250 kg costing £1.80 per kg

Direct labour: 440 hours at £9.50 per hour.

Required

a Calculate the direct material usage sub-variance.
b Calculate the direct material price sub-variance.
c Calculate the total direct material variance.
d Calculate the direct labour efficiency sub-variance.
e Calculate the direct labour rate sub-variance.
f Calculate the total direct labour variance.
g Calculate the total direct expenses variance.
h Explain one possible reason for the direct material usage sub-variance.
i Explain one possible reason for the direct labour rate sub-variance.

QUESTION 24

The managers of Dactor Ltd provide the following information for January:

Standard costs:

Direct materials: 2,870 litres at £12.00 per litre

Direct labour: 610 hours at £8.45 per hour

Actual costs were:

Direct materials: 2,910 litres at £11.98 per litre

Direct labour: 640 hours at £8.40 per hour

Required

a Calculate the direct material usage sub-variance.
b Calculate the direct material price sub-variance.
c Calculate the total direct material variance.
d Calculate the direct labour efficiency sub-variance.
e Calculate the direct labour rate sub-variance.
f Calculate the total direct labour variance.
g Calculate the total direct expenses variance.
h Explain one possible reason for the direct material usage sub-variance.
i Explain one possible reason for the direct material price sub-variance.
j Explain one possible reason for the direct labour efficiency sub-variance.
k Explain one possible reason for the direct labour rate sub-variance.

QUESTION 25

The managers of Sibi Ltd planned to sell 400,000 units of 'epco' at a price of 87p each in April. When the actual figures were available it was found that 450,000 units had been sold at 85p.

Required

Calculate:

a the sales volume sub-variance
b the sales price sub-variance
c the total sales variance.

QUESTION 26

The managers at Ybsu Ltd planned to sell 56 units of 'Krylo' at £1,940 per unit in November. The actual sales were 58 units at £2,000 per unit.

Required

Calculate:

a the sales volume sub-variance
b the sales price sub-variance
c the total sales variance.

QUESTION 27

The managers of Kopabot have budgeted to produce 30,000 hand-crafted pans in March. They provide the following information:

Standard costs for the production of 30,000 pans:

Direct materials: 16,000 m^2 at £6.10 per m^2

Direct labour: 42,000 hours at £6.80 per hour.

Actual production was 27,000 pans:

Direct materials: 14,500 m^2 at £6.00 per m^2

Direct labour: 37,500 hours at £6.75 per hour.

Required

a Calculate the direct material usage sub-variance.
b Calculate the direct material price sub-variance.
c Calculate the total direct material variance.
d Calculate the direct labour efficiency sub-variance.
e Calculate the direct labour rate sub-variance.
f Calculate the total direct labour variance.
g Explain one possible reason for each of the sub-variances calculated.

QUESTION 28

The managers of Osac have planned to produce 360,000 pencil cases in March. The following information is available:

Standard costs for production of 360,000 pencil cases:

Direct materials: 153,000 m^2 at £1.10 per m^2

Direct labour: 162,000 hours at £5.30 per hour.

Actual production was 320,000 pencil cases:

Direct materials: 134,000 m^2 at £1.10 per m^2

Direct labour: 143,000 hours at £5.40 per hour.

Required

a Calculate the direct material usage sub-variance.
b Calculate the direct material price sub-variance.
c Calculate the total direct material variance.
d Calculate the direct labour efficiency sub-variance.
e Calculate the direct labour rate sub-variance.

f   Calculate the total direct labour variance.
g   Explain one possible reason for each of the sub-variances calculated.

QUESTION 29

The managers of Efax have planned to manufacture 1,400 handbags in October. The following information is available:

Standard costs for production of 1,400 handbags:

Direct materials – leather: 700 m² at £16.40 per m²

Direct labour: 1,050 hours at £8.35 per hour.

Actual production was 1,450 handbags:

Direct materials – leather: 732 m² at £18.30 per m²

Direct labour: 1,090 hours at £8.20 per hour.

Required

a   Calculate the direct material usage sub-variance.
b   Calculate the direct material price sub-variance.
c   Calculate the total direct material variance.
d   Calculate the direct labour efficiency sub-variance.
e   Calculate the direct labour rate sub-variance.
f   Calculate the total direct labour variance.
g   Explain one possible reason for each of the sub-variances calculated.

QUESTION 30

The managers of Adod Ltd have planned to manufacture 240,000 bottles of fruit juice in November. The following information is available:

Standard costs for production of 240,000 bottles of juice:

Direct materials: 245,000 litres at £0.70 per litre

Direct labour: 1,200 hours at £6.17 per hour.

Actual production was 200,000 bottles of juice:

Direct materials: 247,000 litres at £0.75 per litre

Direct labour: 940 hours at £6.25 per hour.

Required

a   Calculate the direct material usage sub-variance.
b   Calculate the direct material price sub-variance.
c   Calculate the total direct material variance.
d   Calculate the direct labour efficiency sub-variance.
e   Calculate the direct labour rate sub-variance.
f   Calculate the total direct labour variance.
g   Explain one possible reason for each of the sub-variances calculated.

CHAPTER
SIXTEEN

Capital Investment Appraisal

We said in *Introducing Accounting* that non-current assets are the wealth generators of a business. They are purchased with the intention that they will generate profits for the business for some years into the future.

The non-current assets used in the business usually consist of:

- land
- buildings
- machinery
- plant
- vehicles
- office equipment etc.

They are used in the business for more than one financial time period.

The managers of a business are always looking for good value when they purchase non-current assets, just as you do when buying clothes, a mobile phone etc.

Like you, the managers of a business do not have unlimited resources; like you, available cash is a scarce resource; and like you, they must plan their capital expenditure very carefully so that they get the best value for their money. They want to ensure that they earn maximum benefits from their purchase, just like you.

Capital projects are appraised (evaluated) according to potential earning power.

Care must be taken when making a capital investment decision because:

- large sums of money are generally involved
- the money may well be 'tied up' for a considerable length of time
- the decisions cannot generally be reversed easily
- the money committed is usually non-returnable.

Consider the family commitment to the purchase of the largest item of capital expenditure – a house:

- a large sum of money is involved
- the money is often tied up for many years
- it might be difficult to resell the house
- once purchased, the house cannot be returned to the previous owners.

It is very important that care must be taken when making a capital investment appraisal. Much detailed information should be obtained from all sources that may be affected by the decision, or that may affect the decision.

Some sources of information that may affect the decision:

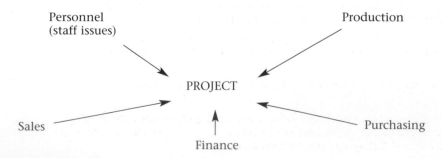

Capital projects are evaluated (appraised) in terms of their potential earning power. If the managers of a business need to replace an obsolete piece of machinery or purchase further pieces of machinery to complete a new project, they must decide **which** new machine to purchase. There would be no choice to be made if there was only one type of machine on the market that would do the job; they would not have to make a choice (other than to buy or not to buy!). In the real world there are usually alternative options from which to choose.

Machines might:

- have different prices
- have different qualities
- produce different quantities of goods
- produce different quality goods
- have different life spans
- have different rates of obsolescence.

These differences apply to most capital purchases in both the business world and other machines in the world outside of business, for example TV sets, DVD machines etc.

There are four main methods of evaluating a capital project. They are:

- the **payback method** – examined by AQA and OCR
- the **accounting rate of return** (ARR) – examined by OCR
- the **net present value method** (NPV) – examined by AQA and OCR
- the **internal rate of return** (IRR) – examined by OCR.

Check with your teacher or specification which methods you could expect to find in your examination paper. All of the methods require predictions about future flows of either cash or profits.

If the predictions are inaccurate, there could be serious problems for the business because of:

- large sums of cash being involved
- long-term commitment of cash and other resources
- the effect on profits.

Note: From this point, reference will be made only to 'projects' but the text does apply to machines also.

So, managers will often use more than one method of appraising a project that could affect the business for many years.

> **Opportunity cost** is the benefit from the alternative use of resources that is foregone when a new project is undertaken.

> **Sunk costs** are unrecoverable expenditures already incurred before a project is undertaken.

Capital expenditure appraisal only considers incremental revenue and incremental expenditure. (The incremental expenditure may include opportunity costs.) That is any **additional** revenue generated by the project and any **additional** expenditure that may be incurred by the project.

Existing revenue and expenditure that has no influence on the new project is disregarded.

THE PAYBACK METHOD

The payback period is the length of time required for the total cash flows to equal the initial capital investment, ie: how long will it take the project to pay for itself?

Risk is an important factor to be taken into account when considering a project lasting a few years. The sooner the capital expenditure is recouped, the better – this is the essence of the payback method.

The method is used widely in practice since most businesses are concerned with short time horizons.

Also, the longer the time horizon involved, the less reliable are the predicted inflows of cash. The earlier the receipts are, the earlier further investments can be made. A long payback period increases the possibility that the initial outlay will not be recouped at all.

The payback period is measured in years.

WORKED EXAMPLE

Olive Branch is considering the purchase of a new machine. Two different machines will suit her purpose.

The cash flows are given:

	Machine A Cost £210,000 Estimated cash flows £	Machine B Cost £180,000 Estimated cash flows £
Year 1	70,000	70,000
Year 2	80,000	70,000
Year 3	90,000	80,000
Year 4	90,000	80,000

Required

Calculate the payback period for each of the two machines.

Answer

Machine A – the initial outlay will be paid back part-way through Year 3 (£70,000 Year 1 + £80,000 Year 2 + £60,000 part-way through Year 3).
More precisely, 60,000/90,000ths through the third year.
Machine A payback is 2 and 60/90th years = **2.67 years**.
Machine B – the initial outlay will also be paid back part-way through Year 3 (£70,000 + £70,000 + £40,000 part-way through Year 3).
More precisely 40,000/80,000ths through Year 3.
Machine B payback is 2 and 40/80th years = **2.5 years**.

If Olive is only concerned with cash flows generated then she should buy machine B.

Note the layout below:
- the date of initial purchase is labelled 'Year 0'
- all cash outflows and inflows are deemed to accrue evenly throughout each year.

QUESTION 1

The managers of Patel Ltd are considering two projects. The information regarding the two projects is given:

	Project 24/JJ Cash inflows/outflows £	Project 25/SM Cash inflows/outflows £
Year 0	(100,000)	(140,000)
Year 1	40,000	60,000
Year 2	50,000	80,000
Year 3	50,000	100,000
Year 4	50,000	110,000

Required

a Calculate the payback periods for both projects.
b State which project should be undertaken and why.

QUESTION 2

The managers of Glenmurray Ltd are considering two projects. The following information is supplied:

	Project RM/416 Cash inflows/outflows £	Project RM/417 Cash inflows/outflows £
Year 0	(400,000)	(500,000)
Year 1	100,000	200,000
Year 2	150,000	300,000
Year 3	200,000	300,000
Year 4	250,000	300,000
Year 5	300,000	300,000

Required

a Calculate the payback period for both projects.
b State which project should be undertaken.

Some questions require that you calculate the projected cash flows to include in your calculations.

There are two types of question:

TYPE 1

When profits are given in the question. Remember that payback uses cash flows, not profits.

WORKED EXAMPLE

The following information is available for two proposed projects:

	Project 2178 £000	Project 2179 £000
Initial costs	(14,000)	(12,000)
Expected profits generated:		
Year 1	3,500	3,500
Year 2	5,000	4,000
Year 3	8,000	5,500
Year 4	10,000	6,500

WORKED EXAMPLE *continued*

Note:

The annual profit for each project has been calculated after providing for depreciation as follows:

£000	£000
1,500	1,200

Required

a Calculate the payback period for both projects.
b State which project should be undertaken.

Answer

Cash flows	Project 2178 £000	Project 2179 £000
Year 0	(14,000)	(12,000)
Year 1	5,000	4,700
Year 2	6,500	5,200
Year 3	9,500	6,700
(a) payback	2 years 2,500/9,500 2.26 years	2 years 2,100/6,700 2.31 years

b Select project 2178 it has a slightly shorter payback period.

QUESTION 3

The managers of Dextok Ltd provide the following projected information for two projects:

	Project Minor £000	Project Nixto £000
Initial costs	(8,800)	(7,400)
Expected profits generated:		
Year 1	3,000	1,500
Year 2	4,000	2,000
Year 3	5,000	2,500
Year 4	5,000	3,000
Year 5	5,000	2,500

The annual profit for each project has been calculated after providing for depreciation as follows:

£600,000   £200,000

Required

a Calculate the payback period for both projects.
b State which project should be undertaken.

QUESTION 4

The managers of Vingard Ltd provide the following information for two projects:

	Project 5432 £000	Project 5433 £000
Initial costs	(18,000)	(8,600)
Expected profit generated:		
Year 1	3,750	2,150
Year 2	5,250	2,850
Year 3	6,000	3,150
Year 4	6,000	4,000
Year 5	6,500	4,500

The annual profit for each project has been calculated after allowing for depreciation as follows:

£750,000   £150,000

Required

a Calculate the payback period for both projects.
b State which project should be undertaken.

TYPE 2

When annual cash inflows and annual cash outflows are given separately.

In this type of question, simply deduct the annual cash outflows (expenses) from the annual cash inflows (receipts) to obtain the net cash flows.

EXAMPLE

■ **Year 1** Cash receipts £100,000; cash expenditure £20,000; net cash flow £80,000.
■ **Year 2** Cash receipts £120,000; cash expenditure £25,000; net cash flow £95,000.
■ **Year 3** Cash receipts £130,000; cash expenditure £25,000; net cash flow £105,000.

QUESTION 5

The managers of Row Engineering Ltd are considering two capital expenditure proposals. The following information is available:

	Proposal 1		Proposal 2	
Initial investment	£100,000		£110,000	
	Annual expenditure £	Annual income £	Annual expenditure £	Annual income £
Year 1	10,000	50,000	12,000	50,000
Year 2	12,000	55,000	13,000	57,000
Year 3	15,000	60,000	15,000	62,000
Year 4	18,000	65,000	17,000	67,000
Year 5	20,000	70,000	21,000	65,000

Required

a Calculate the payback period for both proposals.
b Advise the managers which proposal they should accept.

QUESTION 6

The managers of Townhead Ltd are considering two projects. The following information is available:

	Project PQ/712		Project RS/29	
Initial investment	£220,000		£270,000	
	Annual expenditure £	Annual income £	Annual expenditure £	Annual income £
Year 1	23,000	75,000	45,000	100,000
Year 2	16,000	80,000	50,000	110,000
Year 3	18,000	90,000	50,000	120,000
Year 4	22,000	100,000	48,000	130,000
Year 5	25,000	95,000	50,000	120,000

Required

a Calculate the payback period for both projects.
b Advise the managers which project should be chosen.

In the examples used and in the questions, we have merely considered the financial aspects of deciding on a project. Clearly, the managers of a business would consider all the ways in which a decision might impinge on the business. They would also consider, for example, how a decision might affect:

- the **workforce** – does the decision require more workers?
    – does the decision mean that some workers will lose their jobs?
    – will workers need retraining?
- the **environment** – pollution
- the **locality** – expansion using more space.

ADVANTAGES OF USING THE PAYBACK METHOD

- It is relatively simple to calculate.
- It is fairly easy for non-accountants to understand.
- The use of cash is more objective than using profits that are dependent on the accounting policies decided by managers.
- Since all future predictions carry an element of risk, it shows the project that involves the least risk because it recognises that cash received earlier in the project life cycle is preferable to cash received later.
- It shows the project that benefits a firm's liquidity.

DISADVANTAGES OF USING THE PAYBACK METHOD

- It ignores the time-value of money (but see later).
- It ignores the life expectancy of the project; it does not consider cash flows that take place after the payback period.
- Projects may have different patterns of cash inflows.

For example, consider:

- Project 1 has a payback period of 1 year.
- Project 2 has a payback period of 2.2 years.

	Project 1 £	Project 2 £
Year 0	(10,000)	(10,000)
Year 1	10,000	1
Year 2	1	1
Year 3	1	50,000
Year 4	1	50,000

Payback in this case does not give a realistic appraisal.

If a machine has a scrap or trade-in value, this will be treated as an income in the year the machine is disposed of.

THE ACCOUNTING RATE OF RETURN METHOD (ARR)

This method of appraisal has some similarities to the approach to the calculation of ROCE. It shows the return on the investment expressed as a percentage of the average investment over the period.

Average capital seems rather complicated to calculate – have a look at the way it is calculated and then learn the formula.

WORKED EXAMPLE

A machine is purchased for £100,000. It will be used for two years and will then be traded in for £20,000.

Required

Calculate the average investment on the machine over the two years.

Answer

The machine will incur depreciation using the straight-line method of £40,000 per annum.

(£100,000 − £20,000 = £80,000 ÷ 2 years = £40,000 per annum)

	Start of year	End of year	Average investment over year
Investment Year 1	£100,000	£60,000	£80,000 (160,000 ÷ 2)
Investment Year 2	£60,000	£20,000	£40,000 (80,000 ÷ 2)

So:

- in Year 1 average investment   £80,000
- in Year 2 average investment   £40,000
           £120,000

Average investment over two years = $\dfrac{£120,000}{2}$ = £60,000.

WORKED EXAMPLE

A machine is purchased for £350,000. It will be used for five years after which it will have a scrap value of £50,000.

Required

Calculate the average investment in the machine over the five years.

Answer

Average investment = £200,000

Annual depreciation = £300,000 ÷ 5 = £60,000

continued ➤

WORKED EXAMPLE *continued*

	Start of year £	End of year £	Average investment over year £
Investment Year 1	350,000	290,000	320,000
Year 2	290,000	230,000	260,000
Year 3	230,000	170,000	200,000
Year 4	170,000	110,000	140,000
Year 5	110,000	50,000	80,000
		Total	1,000,000

Average investment over five years = £1,000,000 ÷ 5 years = £200,000 per year.

There is an arithmetic short-cut which gives the correct answer without the long complicated explanation shown in the two worked examples given above.

FORMULA

$$\text{Average investment} = \frac{\text{Initial investment} + \text{Scrap value}}{2}$$

It does seem improbable that the scrap value is added but it does work – trust me, I'm an accountant!

Check the two examples above:

Purchase price £100,000 + Scrap value £20,000 = £120,000

$$\frac{£120,000}{2} = \text{Average investment } £60,000$$

Purchase price £350,000 + Scrap value £50,000 = £400,000

$$\frac{£400,000}{2} = \text{Average investment } £200,000$$

This shorter method works! It always works!

FORMULA

$$\text{Average rate of return} = \frac{\text{Average profits}}{\text{Average investment}} \times 100$$

● EXAMINATION TIP

The calculation of ARR uses profits, not cash flows.

WORKED EXAMPLE

Nancy Betts is considering the purchase of a machine. There are two models that will suit her needs. All profits are assumed to accrue on the last day of the year.

WORKED EXAMPLE *continued*

	Machine Ara Cost £160,000 Estimated profits £	Machine Bibi Cost £210,000 Estimated profits £
Year 1	50,000	70,000
Year 2	60,000	90,000
Year 3	70,000	110,500
Year 4	80,000	88,000
Year 5	60,000	84,000
Year 5 Scrap value	10,000	40,000

Required

a Calculate the accounting rate of return for both machines.
b Advise Nancy which machine she should purchase.

Answer

	Machine Ara	Machine Bibi
Average profit:	$\dfrac{£320,000}{5 \text{ years}} = £64,000$	$\dfrac{£442,500}{5 \text{ years}} = £88,500$
Average investment:	$\dfrac{£160,000 + £10,000}{2}$ $= £85,000$	$\dfrac{£210,000 + £40,000}{2}$ $= £125,000$

a **Machine Ara**: accounting rate of return $= \dfrac{64,000}{85,000} \times 100 = 75.3\%$

Machine Bibi: accounting rate of return $= \dfrac{88,500}{125,000} \times 100 = 70.8\%$

b Nancy should choose Machine Ara because this gives her a higher accounting rate of return than Machine Bibi.

QUESTION 7

Sanvision Ltd presently earns a return on capital of 25%. The directors propose to produce and market a new product. This will require the purchase of a new machine at a cost of £90,000. The machine will last for four years after which it will be traded in for £10,000. The average profits earned by the machine are expected to be £11,400 per annum. Assume that all profits accrue on the last day of the year.

Required

a Calculate the accounting rate of return for the new product.
b Advise the directors whether they should proceed with production of the new product.

QUESTION 8

Nasirah Ltd presently earns a return on capital of 35%. The directors propose to produce and sell 'Judles', a new product. This will require the purchase of a new machine at a cost of £212,000. The machine will last for five years after which it will be scrapped. Scrap value is expected to be £8,000.

The average annual profits are expected to be £46,200.

Assume that all cash flows occur on the last day of the year.

Required

a Calculate the accounting rate of return for the production of Judles.
b Advise the directors whether they should produce and sell Judles.

> **Mutually exclusive.** The pursuit of one course of action will preclude the pursuit of any other action, for example, I can either go to a friend's party or I can go to listen to my favourite band. I cannot do both.

QUESTION 9

A company is considering investing in one of two projects. The projects are mutually exclusive (that is, only one project can be undertaken).

Each project will entail an initial outlay of £300,000.

Assume that all profits accrue on the last day of the year.

Forecast profits are:

	Project 321 £	Project 322 £
Year 1	30,000	16,000
Year 2	30,000	24,000
Year 3	30,000	40,000
Year 4	30,000	60,000

Required

a Calculate the accounting rate of return for each project.
b Advise the finance director which project the directors should invest in.

QUESTION 10

The managers of Absic Ltd are considering investing in one of three projects. The projects are mutually exclusive. Each project will entail an initial outlay of £500,000.

All profits are received on the last year of the relevant year.

Forecast profits are:

	Project 72/GH £	Project 73/GH £	Project 74/GH £
Year 1	70,000	70,000	60,000
Year 2	72,000	75,000	75,000
Year 3	75,000	80,000	85,000
Year 4	80,000	85,000	75,000
Year 5	82,000	90,000	65,000

Required

a Calculate the accounting rate of return for each project.
b Advise the managers which project should be chosen.

ADVANTAGES OF USING THE ACCOUNTING RATE OF RETURN

- ARR is fairly easy to calculate.
- Results can be compared with present profitability.
- It takes into account the aggregate earnings of the project(s).

DISADVANTAGES OF USING THE ACCOUNTING RATE OF RETURN

- ARR does not take into account the time-value of money.
- It does not recognise the timing of cash flows (see same disadvantage for payback).

THE NET PRESENT VALUE METHOD

Which of the following would give you the better value for money?

- Spending £100 today.
- Spending £100 in 10 years' time?

I think that most people would say that £100 spent today would give them the better value. Why?

The future is uncertain – there is an element of risk involved. Also, as time goes on, there is a tendency for money to become less valuable.

When your grandparents bought a house many years ago, they may have spent £20,000. Would that buy the same house today? I don't think so!

The **time-value of money** recognises that £1 received today is worth more than £1 in one year's time or in five years' time.

If £1 were received and invested at 5% per annum, it would be worth £1.05 in one year's time; if it were left to accumulate interest it would be worth just over £1.10 (£1.102) in two years' time and just under £1.16 (£1.158) in three years' time.

Looked at from another perspective:

- If 86.4 pence was invested today at 5% for three years, this would yield £1.
- If 90.7 pence was invested today at 5% for two years, this would yield £1.
- If 95.2 pence was invested at 5% for one year, this would yield £1.

> **Cost of capital** is based on the weighted average cost of capital available to a business.

> The **net present value method of investment appraisal** of a project is calculated by taking the present-day (discounted) value of all future net cash flows based on the business's cost of capital and subtracting the initial cost of the investment.

> A **discounting factor** allows the value of future cash flows to be calculated in terms of their value if they were received today.

Managers of a business invest in capital projects to provide security for the future through profits and cash flows.

As individuals we invest to provide for the future, and we hope that the monetary rewards in the future will be worth waiting for.

In giving up the money today, we expect a reward. The reward is the interest that we will earn on our investment.

In the same way that we may invest in, say, a building society account to get a return on our investment, managers of a business will also invest in projects that will pay a return on their investment.

Managers evaluate a project by comparing the capital investment with the return that the investment will bring in the future.

In order to make a meaningful comparison between the amount originally invested and the income generated in the future by that investment, there is a need to discount the cash flows so that they are the equivalent of cash flows now. Thus, we can compare like with like.

We can compare the initial investment at today's price with future cash inflows discounted to give their values in today's world.

The discounting factor used in net present value (NPV) calculations is generally based on a weighted average cost of capital available to the business.

EXAMPLE

Schiffe Ltd has the following capital structure:

continued ➤

EXAMPLE *continued*

	£
Ordinary shares (currently paying a dividend of 9% per annum)	1,000,000
6% preference shares	500,000
7% debenture stock	200,000
Bank loan (current interest rate payable 8%)	300,000

The weighted average cost of capital for Schiffe Ltd is:

	Nominal value £	Rate paid	Cost of capital per annum £
Ordinary shares	1,000,000	9%	90,000
Preference shares	500,000	6%	30,000
Debenture stock	200,000	7%	14,000
Bank loan	300,000	8%	24,000
Totals	2,000,000		158,000

$$\text{Average cost of capital} = \frac{\text{Cost of capital per annum}}{\text{Nominal value of capital}}$$

$$= \frac{158,000}{2,000,000} = 7.9\%$$

This shows that the average cost of Schiffe Ltd raising further capital would be 7.9%.

Note: The example is correct in principle. However, the interest on debenture stock and the bank loan are revenue expenditure – they reduce profits – they would reduce the amount of tax payable by Schiffe Ltd. So in reality the two figures should be shown in the calculation net of taxation.

More important note: You will be given the discount factor (ie the cost of capital) in a question – 'Thank goodness', I hear you say!

If you are given a number of discounting factors to choose from, select the one identified in the question as the cost of capital.

There is a misconception that a discounting factor is used to take into account the effects of inflation on future cash flows – this is not so. The effects that inflation have on results are self-correcting.

The discounting factor is based on the business's cost of capital, which has been explained earlier.

Generally, what we consider is what would happen if we were fortunate enough to be able to invest, say, £1,000, in a building society account or a business project for, say, four years. We calculate how much our investment would be worth each year if the investment was earning, say, 5% per annum.

At the end of:

Year 1	£1,050
Year 2	£1,102
Year 3	£1,158
Year 4	£1,216

Discounting uses the same principle but in reverse.

If I require £1,000 in four years' time and the interest rate, or rate of return, was 5%, how much would I have to invest today? I would have to invest £823.

The present value gives the value of a future sum of money at today's values.

If you wish to have £100 in four years' time and the interest rates were 7%, you should invest £76.30 today.

Working this in reverse, we can say that £100 received in four years' time is equivalent to receiving £76.30 today.

(£76.30 placed on deposit today and receiving interest of 7% per annum would produce a deposit of £100 in four years' time.)

How did I work these figures out? I used a set of present value tables!

These tables will be given in any examination question requiring the use of net present value.

WORKED EXAMPLE

Calculate the value of:

a £120
b £196
c £42

if the amount were invested for three years at 3% per annum.

The following figures give the value of £1 at a compound interest rate of 3%:

Year 1	1.030
Year 2	1.061
Year 3	1.093
Year 4	1.126

Answer

a £1 invested today would yield £1.09 (£1.093) in three years' time, so £120 invested would yield £131.16 (£120 × 1.093).
b £214.23.
c £45.91.

WORKED EXAMPLE

Calculate the present value of:

a £926
b £62
c £1,380

received in five years' time if the current cost of capital is 9% per annum.

The following figures give the present value of £1 at 9%:

Year 1	0.917
Year 2	0.842
Year 3	0.772
Year 4	0.708
Year 5	0.650

continued ➤

WORKED EXAMPLE *continued*

Answer

a £1 received in five years' time would have a value of 65 pence if received today so £926 received in five years' time has a value of £601.90 today.

b £40.30.

c £897.

The net present value method of capital investment appraisal compares the investment (at today's prices) with future net cash flows (discounted to give the values at today's prices).

Here is a table showing the present value of £1 at a number of different discount rates:

	4%	5%	6%	7%	8%	9%	10%
Period 1	0.961	0.952	0.943	0.935	0.926	0.917	0.909
2	0.925	0.907	0.890	0.873	0.857	0.842	0.826
3	0.889	0.864	0.840	0.816	0.794	0.772	0.751
4	0.855	0.823	0.792	0.763	0.735	0.708	0.683
5	0.822	0.784	0.747	0.713	0.681	0.650	0.621

WORKED EXAMPLE

James Squirrel is considering whether to purchase a new lathe for his workshop. The machine will cost £12,000 and be used for five years after which time it will be scrapped. The following cash flows relate to the lathe.

	Revenue receipts £	Revenue expenditure £
Year 1	8,000	4,000
Year 2	8,500	5,000
Year 3	7,000	4,000
Year 4	5,000	3,000
Year 5	3,000	1,000

The current cost of capital is 10%. All costs are paid and incomes received on the last day of each financial year.

The following extract is taken from the present value tables for £1:

	10%
Year 1	0.909
Year 2	0.826
Year 3	0.751
Year 4	0.683
Year 5	0.621

Required

a Calculate the net present value of purchasing the new lathe.
b Advise James whether he should invest in the new lathe.

Answer

Year	Cash flows £	Discount factor	Net present value £
0 (now)	(12,000)	1	(12,000)
1	4,000	0.909	3,636
2	3,500	0.826	2,891
3	3,000	0.751	2,253
4	2,000	0.683	1,366
5	2,000	0.621	1,242
		Net present value	(612)

James should not invest in the new lathe as it will yield a negative net present value.

Note:

The cash inflows are calculated from the revenue receipts less revenue expenditure. Any project that yields a positive net present value should be considered.

Projects that yield negative net present values should be rejected on financial grounds but may be considered on other grounds, for example to keep a good customer happy; to keep a good, skilled workforce within the business; perhaps to get further orders in the near future.

WORKED EXAMPLE

The managers of Dvorak Ltd wish to purchase a new machine. They will use the machine for four years. There are three machines that are capable of producing the quality of goods that is desired. The current cost of capital for Dvorak Ltd is 9%. The following is an extract from the present value tables for £1.

Year 1	0.917
2	0.842
3	0.772
4	0.708

The following information is available for the three machines. All cash flows arise at the end of the relevant year.

continued ➤

WORKED EXAMPLE *continued*

Machine	78/BA £	92/DC £	36/FE £
Purchase price	88,000	99,000	115,000
Forecast net cash flows:			
Year 1	44,000	47,000	50,000
2	44,000	47,000	49,000
3	40,000	47,000	48,000
4	40,000	45,000	44,000

Required

a Calculate the NPV of each machine.
b Advise the managers of Dvorak Ltd which of the three machines they should purchase.

Answer

a

Machine Present values	78/BA £	92/DC £	36/FE £
Year 0	(88,000)	(99,000)	(115,000)
1	40,348	43,099	45,850
2	37,048	39,574	41,258
3	30,880	36,284	37,056
4	28,320	31,860	31,152
Net present values	48,596	51,817	40,316

b The managers should purchase machine 92/DC because it yields the highest positive net present value.

Note: When a selection has to be made, the machine that yields the highest net present value should be chosen.

If all the machines yielded a negative net present value then no machine should be purchased.

In this example all machines will yield a positive NPV and under different circumstances they would all be worth purchasing.

ADVANTAGES OF USING THE NET PRESENT VALUE METHOD

- The time-value of money is taken into account as adjustments are made to take account of the present value of future cash flows.
- It is relatively easily understood.
- Greater importance is given to earlier cash flows.

DISADVANTAGES OF USING THE NET PRESENT VALUE METHOD

Because the figures are projections, then all of the figures are of a speculative nature:

- inflows are difficult to predict; outflows are equally difficult to predict
- the current cost of capital may change over the life of the project
- the life of the project is difficult to predict.

When the net cash flows to be discounted are the same amounts, time can be saved by totalling the discount factors for the appropriate years and multiplying the amount by this total.

WORKED EXAMPLE

The following net cash inflows are given for a machine:

Year 1	40,000
2	40,000
3	40,000
4	40,000

The present cost of capital is 4%.

All cash flows arise at the end of the relevant year.

Required

Calculate the net present value of the cash flows.

Answer

	Cash flows £	Discount factor	NPV £
Year 1	40,000	0.961	38,440
2	40,000	0.925	37,000
3	40,000	0.889	35,560
4	40,000	0.855	34,200
		NPV	145,200

The same results would be given if 3.63 (0.961 + 0.925 + 0.889 + 0.855) is multiplied by the (constant) £40,000.

Note:

This technique can only be used if the net cash flows are the same amount.

We said earlier that a major drawback in using the payback method was that it did not take into account the time-value of money. We can take the current cost of capital into account by using discounting techniques.

DISCOUNTED PAYBACK METHOD

This method is widely used as a method of selecting a machine or project.

WORKED EXAMPLE

Yvonne Durrant is considering the purchase of a new machine at a cost of £120,000. The estimated net cash flows generated by the machine over the next five years are provided. It is assumed that all cash flows arise at the end of the relevant year.

continued ➤

Required

Calculate the discounted payback period for project 'Helom'.

Two further points to be considered:

- Many discounted cash flow questions are linked with social accounting issues, for example pollution issues, unemployment etc.
  You may have to discuss these issues once you have reached a decision about the project (or machine) that is recommended by the financial aspects of your decision.
- At the end of a project's life there may be some residual or scrap value to be considered. This should simply be treated as further income in the year in which it occurs.

WORKED EXAMPLE

The following cash inflows are generated by a machine:

	£000
Year 1	240
Year 2	320
Year 3	650

At the end of Year 3 the machine will be sold. It is estimated that it will sell for £60,000.

Required

Prepare a schedule of cash inflows generated by the machine.

Answer

Schedule of cash inflows	£000
Year 1	240
Year 2	320
Year 3	710 (£650,000 + £60,000)

Chapter summary

- There are four main methods of capital investment appraisal:
  - payback
  - accounting rate of return
  - net present value
  - internal rate of return.
- Only two are examined by AQA – payback and NPV. If you are studying for the OCR examinations then you also need to cover the accounting rate of return.
- The main disadvantage of payback is overcome by using discounted payback.
- All methods are used to appraise single investment opportunities and they are used to decide between competing strategies.

SELF-TEST QUESTIONS

- Identify two reasons why it is important to appraise capital investment decisions.
- Identify one method of capital investment appraisal that uses cash flows in the calculations.
- Identify one method of capital investment appraisal that uses profits in the calculation.

- A machine is purchased for £600. The net cash inflows are: Year 1 £250; Year 2 £250; Year 3 £250. In which year will the machine pay for itself?
- Identify one advantage of using payback as a method of investment appraisal.
- Identify one disadvantage of using NPV as a method of capital investment appraisal.
- The discounting factor used in NPV is based on the average inflation rate over the period of investment. True or false?
- NPV of Machine A (£4,760); NPV of Machine B (£1,920). Identify the machine that should be purchased.
- £1,000 received in two years' time is worth more/less than £1,000 received today? Delete the incorrect response.
- NPV is an abbreviation for 'new proven value'. True or false?

QUESTION 17

The following information is given for machine X7/5RT:

	£000
Initial cost	35
Net cash inflows – **Year 1**	8
Year 2	9
Year 3	10
Year 4	11
Year 5	12

The current cost of capital is 5% per annum.

Assume that all cash flows arise at the end of the relevant year when calculating NPV and that they arise evenly throughout the year when calculating the payback periods.

An extract from the present value table for £1 at 5% is given:

Year	5%
1	0.952
2	0.907
3	0.864
4	0.823
5	0.784

Required

Calculate for machine X7/5RT:

a the payback period
b the net present value
c the discounted payback period.

QUESTION 18

The following information is given for project 'Rebtom':

	£000
Initial investment	600
Net cash inflows – **Year 1**	180
2	270
3	290
4	300
5	420

At the end of Year 5 the project will be sold for £30,000.

The current cost of capital is 10% per annum.

Assume that all cash flows arise at the end of the relevant year when calculating NPV and that they accrue evenly throughout the year when calculating the payback periods.

An extract from the present value table for £1 at 10% is shown:

Year	10%
1	0.909
2	0.826
3	0.751
4	0.683
5	0.621

Required

Calculate for project 'Rebtom':

a the payback period
b the net present value
c the discounted payback period.

QUESTION 19

The Kapakian government is considering the installation of a new electricity generating facility. The following information is available:

	Type R facility £m		Type S facility £m		Type T facility £m	
Initial cost	2,000		800		3,000	
Estimated cash flows:						
	Inflows £m	Outflows £m	Inflows £m	Outflows £m	Inflows £m	Outflows £m
Year 1	830	620	460	520	1,530	1,240
Year 2	920	415	500	120	1,760	840
Year 3	1,070	540	600	150	2,000	910
Year 4	1,100	600	700	210	2,050	950
Year 5	1,100	580	700	200	2,100	900
Next 15 years	1,100	580	800	250	2,200	900

The current cost of capital is 15%.

Assume that all cash flows arise at the end of the relevant year when calculating NPV and that they accrue evenly throughout the year when calculating the payback periods.

An extract from the present value table for £1 at 15% is shown:

Year	15%
1	0.870
2	0.756
3	0.658
4	0.572
5	0.497

Required

a Calculate for each facility:

i) the payback period
ii) the net present value to the end of Year 5
iii) the discounted payback.

b Advise the Kapakian government which facility it should implement.

QUESTION 20

The managers of Aspar Ltd need to replace an obsolete machine. They are considering two alternative machines as a replacement:

- a 'Yetty', manufactured in Outer Mongolia (a Far Eastern country) and
- a 'Bonbon', manufactured in the EU.

The following information is available for the two machines being considered:

	Yetty £	£	Bonbon £	£
Capital cost	45,000		80,000	
Cash flows:	Revenues	Operating expenses	Revenues	Operating expenses
Year 1	35,000	7,000	44,000	9,000
Year 2	36,500	7,200	46,000	10,000
Year 3	40,500	7,800	50,000	10,500
Year 4	42,000	8,000	52,000	11,000

In addition to the above operating expenses, the Yetty will require a major overhaul costing £2,000 in Years 2 and 4.

The Bonbon will require a major overhaul in Year 4 and this will cost £5,000.

The press has reported that the Yetty pollutes the environment.

Aspar's cost of capital is currently 13% per annum.

Assume that all cash flows arise evenly throughout the year when calculating the payback periods and that they arise at the end of the relevant year when calculating NPV.

An extract from the present value table for £1 at 13% shows:

Year	13%
1	0.885
2	0.783
3	0.693
4	0.613

Required

a Calculate for each machine:
   i) the payback period
   ii) the net present value to the end of Year 4
   iii) the discounted payback period.

b Advise the managers which machine should be purchased.

QUESTION 21

The managers of Agorc Ltd are unsure which one of the following projects should be undertaken. Each will require an initial investment of £68,000. At the end of the project, there would be a scrap value of £8,000.

The following information is available:

Net cash flows:	YP/32 £	WQ/43 £	XR/17 £
Year 1	12,000	25,000	18,000
Year 2	10,000	25,000	18,000
Year 3	15,000	25,000	18,000
Year 4	18,000		19,000
Year 5	20,000		

Depreciation is calculated using the straight-line method.

Assume that cash flows arise at the end of the relevant year when calculating ARR and NPV and that they arise evenly throughout the year when calculating the payback periods.

Current cost of capital is 8%.

Extract from the present value table for £1 at 8%:

Year	8%
1	0.926
2	0.857
3	0.794
4	0.735
5	0.681

Required

a   Calculate for each project:
   i)   payback period
   ii)   accounting rate of return
   iii) net present value
   iv)   discounted payback period.
b   Advise the managers which project should be chosen.

QUESTION 22

The managers of Bancard Ltd are considering selling two new products. The following information is given:

	Product JK £	£	Product MN £	£
Annual sales revenue		220,000		400,000
Cost of sales	110,000		200,000	
Administration costs	80,000		40,000	
Depreciation	8,000	198,000	87,000	327,000
Net profit		22,000		73,000

It is expected that the above results will continue for each year of each product's life.

The capital cost of Product JK is £50,000 and Product MN is £350,000.

Depreciation has been calculated on a straight-line basis and assumes a scrap value of £2,000 for both projects.

The expected demand for each product is expected to last for six years and four years respectively.

Assume that cash flows arise at the end of the relevant year when calculating ARR and NPV and that they arise evenly throughout the year when calculating the payback periods.

Bancard Ltd has a current cost of capital of 7%.

An extract from the present value table for £1 at 7% is given:

Year	7%
1	0.935
2	0.873
3	0.816
4	0.763
5	0.713
6	0.666

Required

a Calculate for each project:
  i)   the payback period
  ii) the accounting rate of return
  iii) the net present value
  iv) the discounted payback period.
b Advise the managers which product should be sold.

SEVENTEEN

Budgeting and Budgetary Control

A **budget** is a short-term financial plan. It is defined by CIMA as 'a plan expressed in money'.

Specification coverage:
AQA ACCN4.

We have already said that accounting fulfils two purposes:

■ the stewardship function
■ the management function.

The management function can be broken down into:

■ planning
■ co-ordinating
■ communicating
■ decision-making
■ controlling.

Budgets help to achieve all five of these functions.

■ The budgets produced by a business are 'plans expressed in money'. The budgets show what the management hope to achieve in a future time period, in terms of both overall plans and departmental plans.
■ The individual budgets are intertwined with each other – they depend on each other and influence each other. There is a need to ensure that the individual budgets are not contradictory or in conflict.
■ Because of the inter-dependency and the co-ordination of the budgets, managers must communicate with each other when preparing budgets. They must also communicate the plans to staff below and management above.
■ The nature of forecasting means that decisions have to be made. If profits are to increase then decisions must be made regarding sales, production levels, etc.
■ Budgets will be compared with actual results. Remedial action can then be taken when actual results are worse than budgeted results. In cases where actual results are better than those budgeted, examples of good practice may be identified and copied elsewhere in the organisation.

Budgeting has the following benefits.

■ The preparation of individual budgets means that planning must take place.
■ These plans need to be prepared in a co-ordinated way and this requires communication throughout all levels of the business.
■ The budgeting process defines areas of responsibility and targets to be achieved by different personnel.
■ Budgets can act as a motivating influence at all levels – this is generally only true when all staff are involved in the preparation of budgets. If budgets are imposed on staff they may have a demotivating effect on morale.
■ Budgets are a major part of the overall strategic plan of the business and so individual departmental and personal goals are more likely to be an integral part of the 'bigger picture'.
■ Budgets generally lead to a more efficient use of resources at the disposal of the business – leading to a better control of costs.

Budgeting has the following limitations.

■ Budgets are only as good as the data being used. If data is inaccurate, the budget will be of little use. Should one departmental budget be too optimistic or pessimistic, this will have a knock-on effect on other associated budgets.

By the end of this chapter you should be able to:
■ understand the need for budgeting
■ explain the limitations of budgetary control
■ prepare budgets for cash; purchases; sales; production; debtors; creditors; labour
■ show how these budgets relate to the master budget.

- Budgets might become an over-riding goal; this could lead to a misuse of resources or to incorrect decisions being made.
- Budgets might act as a demotivator if they are imposed rather than negotiated.
- Budgets might be based on plans that can be easily achieved, so making departments/managers appear to be more efficient than they really are. This could also lead to complacency and/or under-performance.
- Budgets might lead to departmental rivalry.

THE SALES BUDGET

The sales budget is generally the first budget to be prepared, because most businesses are sales led. It shows predicted sales and the revenues that are expected to be generated for the budget period.

Once the sales budget has been drawn up, the other budgets can be prepared using the information from the sales budget. If the sales budget is inaccurate, these inaccuracies will filter through and make the other budgets inaccurate too.

The budget will be based on sales forecasts for the budgeted period.

Sales forecasts are very difficult to prepare because there are so many variables that are out of the control of the managers preparing the budget.

These variables could include:

- actions of customers – customers changing to or from other suppliers
- actions of competitors – competitors increasing or decreasing their price
- the state of the economy –a state of 'boom or bust'
- Government action – e.g. changes in the levels of taxation, changes in government spending, imposition of sanctions.

EXAMPLE

Mentoff Ltd produces one type of machine, the ZT/103. The expected sales for machine ZT/103 for the three months ending 31 October 20*9 are:

	August	September	October
Budgeted sales	10	12	13
Expected selling price per machine	£2,100	£2,100	£2,150

Required
Prepare the sales budget for the three months ending 31 October 20*9.

Answer

	August	September	October
Budgeted sales	£21,000	£25,200	£27,950

THE PRODUCTION BUDGET

A production budget is prepared to determine whether the levels of production necessary to satisfy the anticipated level of sales are attainable. The budget states the quantities of finished goods that must be produced to meet expected sales plus any increase in inventory levels that might be required.

WORKED EXAMPLE

Mentoff Ltd is expected to have an opening inventory of five ZT/103 machines on 1 August 20*8. They require a closing inventory of six machines at 31 October 20*9.

Required

Prepare a production budget based on the budgeted sales used in the previous example. Mentoff Ltd requires an even production flow throughout the year.

Answer

The total production is found by using the following calculation:

Budgeted sales	35 (10 + 12 + 13)
Plus budgeted closing inventory	6
Total production needed to meet budgeted sales and closing inventory	41
Less budgeted opening inventory	5
Budgeted production	36

Note

The calculation has been used to determine the budgeted production for a period of three months. The same calculation could be used to determine the budgeted production for a month, six months, a year, etc.

An even production flow means that Mentoff Ltd will have to produce twelve units per month. The production budget will look like this:

	August	September	October
Budgeted sales	10	12	13
Plus budgeted closing inventory	7	7	6
Total production needed	17	19	19
Less budgeted opening inventory	5	7	7
Budgeted production	12	12	12

THE PURCHASES BUDGET

A purchases budget is required to determine the quantities of purchases required, either for resale or for use in a production process. The calculation to be used is similar to that used in compiling a production budget.

WORKED EXAMPLE

Danst Ltd has the following budgeted sales of 'limts'.

	February	March	April
Budgeted sales	120	140	160

The opening inventory on 1 February is expected to be 26 units of limts and the closing inventory on 30 April is expected to be 41 units of limts.

Required

Calculate the number of limts to be purchased over the three months ending 30 April.

Answer

Budgeted sales	420 (120+140+160)
Plus budgeted closing inventory	41
Total purchases needed to meet budgeted sales and closing inventory	461
Less budgeted opening inventory	26
Budgeted purchases of goods for resale	435

435 units have to be purchased during February, March and April. If an even amount of purchases were required throughout the year, then 145 units (435 divided by 3) would be purchased each month. Therefore, using the figures that we know, the budget will look like this:

	February	March	April
Budgeted sales	120	140	160
Plus budgeted closing inventory			41
Total purchases needed			201
Less budgeted opening inventory	26		
Budgeted purchases of goods for resale	145	145	145

We can now fill in the blanks (we hope) by working backwards.

	February	March	April
Budgeted sales	120	140	160
Plus budgeted closing inventory	*51*	*56*	41
Total needed	*171*	*196*	201
Less budgeted opening inventory	26	*51*	*56*
Budgeted purchases of goods for resale	145	145	145

It is not usually necessary to have an equal flow of purchases each month. However, it might be necessary to have a specified number of units as inventory at the start of each month.

The calculation for this type of budget is the same as that used in the previous example.

WORKED EXAMPLE

Batt & Co supply the following budgeted sales figures:

	July	August	September	October
Budgeted sales	40	72	92	100

It is policy to maintain inventory levels at 25 per cent of the following month's budgeted sales.

continued ➤

WORKED EXAMPLE *continued*

Required

Prepare a purchases budget for the three months ending 30 September.

Answer

We know that the opening inventory each month should be:

July	August	September
10 (25% of 40)	18 (25% of 72)	23 (25% of 92)

We also know that the budgeted closing inventory at the end of September should be 25 (25% of 100).

First, we put in the figures that we know.

	July	August	September
Budgeted sales	40	72	92
Plus budgeted closing inventory	18	23	25
Total purchases needed			
Less budgeted opening inventory	10	18	23
Budgeted purchases of goods for resale			

We can fill in the blanks:

	July	August	September
Budgeted sales	40	72	92
Plus budgeted closing inventory	18	23	25
Total purchases needed	58	95	117
Less budgeted opening inventory	10	18	23
Budgeted purchases of goods for resale	48	77	94

QUESTION 1

Toni is to start a business on 1 May selling food-mixers. She believes that she will sell 300 mixers in May and she expects that her monthly sales will increase by 20% on the previous month's budgeted sales until the end of the year.

Inventory is to be maintained at 10% of the following month's budgeted sales.

Note:

- A 20% increase in sales in July would result in August sales of 518.4 food-mixers. It is impossible to sell 0.4 of a mixer! So sales for August will be predicted at 519 mixers.
- Likewise, inventory held at 31 July could not be 51.84 or 51.9 mixers – we have to keep whole mixers as inventory! Closing inventory at 31 July is therefore 52 mixers.

Required

Prepare a purchases budget for the three months ending 31 July.

QUESTION 2

Lawrence sells calculators. His budgeted sales for January are expected to be 200 calculators. He expects sales to increase by 10% on the previous month's sales until the end of April.

Inventory is to be maintained at 50% of the following month's budgeted sales.

Required

Prepare a purchases budget for the three months ending 31 March.

THE TRADE RECEIVABLES' BUDGET

This budget forecasts the amount that will be owed to a business by credit customers at the end of each month.

The trade receivables' budget is linked to the production budget, the sales budget and the cash budget. It will also take into account the length of credit period that is allowed on outstanding customers' balances.

WORKED EXAMPLE

The managers of Mayne Ltd provide the following budgeted information for the three months ending 31 March.

		£
1 January amounts owed by credit customers		30,000
Budgeted credit sales for	January	40,000
	February	50,000
	March	60,000
Cash sales for	January	12,000
	February	10,000
	March	14,000

All credit customers are expected to settle their debts in the month following the sale of goods. They are allowed and will take 5% cash discount.

Required

Prepare a trade receivables' budget for the three months ending 31 March.

Answer

	January	February	March
Balance brought forward	30,000	40,000	50,000
Credit sales	40,000	50,000	60,000
	70,000	90,000	110,000
Cash received from customers	28,500	38,000	47,500
Discount allowed	1,500	2,000	2,500
Balance carried forward	40,000	50,000	60,000

Note:

Cash sales have not been included. Cash customers do not have an account in the sales ledger. Cash customers are never trade receivables.

	August £	September £	October £
Cash sales	90,963	106,125	116,230
Payments to credit suppliers	29,650	35,050	38,400
Payments for wages	19,100	28,000	21,500
Rent and rates	2,800	2,800	2,800
Other expenses	5,700	5,500	5,300
Payment for purchase of machine		84,000	
Depreciation on machine		700	700

Required

Prepare a cash budget for each of the three months ending 30 October.

QUESTION 8

The following budgeted information relates to Chin Ltd for the three months ending 31 July.

The cash balance at 1 May is expected to be £120.

	May £	June £	July £
Cash sales	6,400	8,000	8,000
Receipts from credit customers	36,800	59,200	56,000
Payments to credit suppliers	25,600	28,800	27,200
Cash purchases	3,680	4,320	3,840
Rent	3,200	3,200	3,200
Wages	12,800	12,800	12,800
Other expenses	2,800	5,696	4,960
Purchase of shop fittings	3,000		
Depreciation of shop fittings	250	250	250

Required

Prepare a cash budget for each of the three months ending 31 July.

THE MASTER BUDGET

Just like all the individual ingredients that are put together to make a successful meal, all the separate budgets that have been prepared are drawn together to create the master budget.

It provides a summary of all the planned operations of the business for the period covered by the budgets. It is a sum of all the individual budgets prepared by the different parts of the business.

It is made up of:

- a budgeted manufacturing account (where appropriate)
- a budgeted income statement
- a budgeted balance sheet.

Examination questions do not usually expect candidates to prepare detailed master budgets, because of the limited time available in the examination.

However, it is possible for an examiner to require candidates to prepare a summarised income statement from a cash budget.

This type of question is designed to test a candidate's ability to:

■ apply the concepts of accruals and realisation
■ differentiate between capital and revenue expenditures and incomes
■ distinguish between cash and non-cash expenses.

WORKED EXAMPLE

The following budgeted information is given for Plum Ltd.

Year 20*9	August £	September £	October £	November £
Credit sales	30,000	40,000	35,000	45,000
Credit purchases	15,000	20,000	15,000	25,000
Wages paid	7,500	7,500	7,500	7,500
Other expenses	8,200	8,400	8,100	9,000
Purchase of machine		10,000		
Depreciation of machine		100	100	100

Credit customers pay one month after goods are sold.

Credit suppliers are paid one month after receipt of the goods.

All expenses are paid in the month in which they occur.

It is expected that cash in hand at 1 September 20*9 will be £1200.

Inventory at 1 September 20*9: £2,000.

Inventory 30 November 20*9: £2,500.

Required

a) Prepare a cash budget for each of the three months ending 30 November 20*9.
b) Prepare a budgeted income statement for the three months ending 30 November 20*9.

Answer

(a) Cash budget for the three months ending 30 November 20*9

	September £	October £	November £
Receipts: cash received from credit customers	30,000	40,000	35,000
Payments:			
Cash paid to credit suppliers	15,000	20,000	15,000
Wages	7,500	7,500	7,500
Other expenses	8,400	8,100	9,000
Purchase of machine	10,000		
	40,900	35,600	31,500
Balance brought forward	1,200	(9,700)	(5,300)
Receipts	30,000	40,000	35,000
	31,200	30,300	29,700
Payments	40,900	35,600	31,500
Balance carried forward	(9,700)	(5,300)	(1,800)

Remember, depreciation does not involve cash leaving the business.

continued ➤

WORKED EXAMPLE *continued*

O EXAMINATION TIP

Always show the months separately when preparing a cash budget.

(b) Cash budget for the three months ending 30 November 20*9

	£	£
Sales		120,000
Less cost of sales		
Inventory at 1 September	2,000	
Purchases	60,000	
	62,000	
Inventory at 30 November	2,500	59,500
Gross profit		60,500
Less expenses		
Wages	22,500	
Other expenses	25,500	
Depreciation of machinery	300	48,300
Profit for the year		12,200

O EXAMINATION TIP

The heading should be precise and include the word 'budgeted', as well as the time period covered.

The sales figure is the total of the budgeted figures for the three months under review – September £40,000, October £35,000 and November £45,000 – **not** the amounts shown in the cash budget. Remember the concept of realisation?

The purchases figure is the total of the budgeted figures for the three months under review – September £20,000, October £15,000 and November £25,000 – **not** the amounts shown in the cash budget. Once again, the concept of realisation is being used.

Depreciation is included in the budgeted income statement because of the concept of accruals – the machine is a resource that has been used to generate the profits, so a charge has to be made.

O EXAMINATION TIP

Do not show separate monthly figures in the budgeted income statement. This is the biggest single error made in examinations in this type of question.

BUDGETARY CONTROL

Budgetary control delegates financial planning to managers. It evaluates their performance by continuously comparing the actual results achieved by their departments against those set in the budget.

Variances arise when there is a difference between actual and budgeted figures.

Responsibility for variances rests with departmental heads. The process requires that variances are analysed and, in the case of adverse variances, any necessary remedial action is taken.

The benefits and limitations of budgeting as outlined at the start of this chapter also apply to budgetary control.

Chapter summary

- Budgets are an important part of the management function.
- Budgets are plans expressed in terms of money.
- Budgets help with the planning and control of a business.
- Individual departmental budgets are summarised in the master budget.
- Labour budgets are prepared in terms of employees, not in cash terms.
- The master budget comprises budgeted income statements and budgeted balance sheets. (A budgeted manufacturing account is also part of the master budget, where appropriate.)
- Cash budgets are the most frequently examined budget.
- Cash budgets are prepared on a cash basis.
- Master budgets are prepared on the basis of accruals.

SELF-TEST QUESTIONS

- Define a budget.
- Identify two functions of budgeting.
- Identify two benefits of budgeting.
- Identify two limitations of budgeting.
- Which budget should usually be prepared first?
- Budgeted sales are 12 units; opening inventory 2 units; closing inventory 3 units. How many units should be produced?
- Name the budget used to forecast the amounts owed by credit customers at the end of each month.
- Identify one reason why a cash budget might be prepared.
- Explain why depreciation is not included in a cash budget.
- What is meant by the term 'master budget'?
- Name one component of a master budget.
- Explain the term 'variance'.

TEST QUESTIONS

QUESTION 9

The following budgeted information is available for Hunter Ltd:

	January £	February £	March £	April £
Credit sales	21,000	28,000	30,000	31,000
Cash purchases	8,000	12,000	9,000	10,000
Cash expenses	21,000	20,000	22,000	18,000
Cash purchase of office machinery		24,000		
Depreciation of office machinery		200	200	200

It is expected that the cash balance at 1 February will be £3,200.

Debtors are expected to settle their debts one month after sales have taken place.

Required Prepare a cash budget for each of the three months ending 30 April.

QUESTION 10

The following budgeted information is available for Slipper Ltd:

	February £	March £	April £	May £
Sales	40,000	38,000	39,000	41,000
Cash purchases	14,000	12,000	13,000	15,000
Cash expenses	16,000	18,000	17,000	19,000
Cash purchase of machinery		60,000		
Depreciation of machinery		500	500	500

It is expected that the cash balance at 1 March will be £2,900.

Cash sales are expected to be 10% of total sales. Debtors are expected to settle their debts one month after the sales have taken place.

Required Prepare a cash budget for each of the three months ending 31 May.

QUESTION 11

The following budgeted information is given for Singh Ltd:

	March £	April £	May £	June £
Cash sales	50,000	40,000	50,000	56,000
Purchases	20,000	30,000	25,000	35,000
Cash expenses	21,000	16,000	24,000	20,000
Depreciation of fixed assets	1,000	1,000	1,000	1,000

It is expected that the cash balance at 1 April will be £1,500 overdrawn.

5% of purchases are expected to be for cash. Creditors will be paid in the month following purchase.

Required Prepare a cash budget for each of the three months ending 30 June.

QUESTION 12

The following budgeted information is given for O'Casey Ltd:

	April £	May £	June £	July £
Cash sales	40,000	60,000	80,000	30,000
Purchases	20,000	20,000	30,000	30,000
Cash expenses	15,000	10,000	14,000	13,000
Depreciation of fixed assets	1,500	1,500	1,500	1,500

It is expected that the cash balance at 1 May will be £800 overdrawn.

10% of purchases are expected to be for cash. Creditors will be paid in the month following purchase.

Required Prepare a cash budget for each of the three months ending 31 July.

QUESTION 13

The following budgeted information relates to the business of Pierre:

	May £	June £	July £	August £	September £
Sales	64,000	62,000	60,000	65,000	64,000
Purchases	30,000	32,000	38,000	42,000	39,000
Wages	12,500	12,500	13,000	12,500	12,500
Other expenses	8,500	8,700	8,300	8,500	8,500
Cash purchase of shop fittings				14,000	
Depreciation of shop fittings	150	150	150	150	150

It is expected that:

- the cash balance at 1 June will be £350 overdrawn
- 5% of sales will be for cash
- 10% of purchases will be cash purchases
- debtors will be collected one month after sale
- creditors will be paid two months after purchase
- wages and other expenses are paid as incurred.

Required Prepare a cash budget for each of the three months ending 30 September.

QUESTION 14

The following information relates to the business of Marcel:

	June £	July £	August £	September £	October £
Sales	34,000	36,000	35,000	34,000	37,000
Purchases	15,000	16,000	15,000	15,000	16,000
Wages	5,600	5,700	5,600	5,800	5,600
Rent	2,000	2,000	2,000	2,000	2,000
Other expenses	4,800	4,900	4,300	4,000	5,000
Cash purchase of delivery van			17,000		
Depreciation of vehicles	300	300	600	600	600

It is expected that:

- the cash balance at 1 August will be £2,570
- 10% of sales will be cash sales
- 10% of purchases will be for cash
- debtors will be collected two months after sale
- creditors will be paid one month after purchase
- wages, rent and other expenses will be paid as incurred.

Required Prepare a cash budget for each of the three months ending 31 October.

QUESTION 15

Tommy Chan supplies the following budgeted information relating to his business:

	August £	September £	October £	November £	December £
Sales	23,000	24,000	29,000	34,000	43,000
Purchases	12,000	13,000	15,000	24,000	35,000
Wages	4,500	4,500	4,500	6,000	6,500
Rent	400		400		450
Other expenses	1,750	1,850	3,400	1,600	980
Depreciation of office equipment	450	450	450	450	450

It is expected that:

- the cash balance at 1 October will be £670
- 10% of all sales will be on credit
- 10% of purchases will be for cash
- debtors will settle their debts in the month following sale
- creditors will be paid two months after purchase
- wages, rent and other expenses will be paid as incurred
- inventory at 1 October is expected to be £7,000; at 31 December it is expected to be £8,000.

Required (a) Prepare a cash budget for each of the three months ending 31 December.
(b) Prepare a budgeted income statement for the three months ending 31 December.

QUESTION 16

Andy Gillespie supplies the following budgeted information relating to his business:

	May £	June £	July £	August £	September £
Sales	34,000	35,000	37,000	40,000	35,000
Sale of old office machine			150		
Profit on sale of machine			50		
Purchases	16,000	16,500	17,000	19,000	15,000
Purchase of new office machine			1,800		
Wages	5,600	5,500	5,600	5,500	5,600
Other expenses	4,570	4,700	3,950	4,780	5,400
Depreciation of office equipment	250	250	265	265	265

It is expected that:

- the cash balance at 1 July will be £580 overdrawn
- 30% of sales will be credit sales
- 20% of purchases will be for cash

- 50% of credit sale customers will pay in the month following sale; the remainder will pay the following month
- creditors will be paid two months after purchase
- wages will be paid in the month after they are incurred
- other expenses will be paid for as incurred
- inventory at 1 July is expected to be £2,000; at 30 September it is expected to be £2,400.

Required   (a) Prepare a cash budget for each of the three months ending 30 September.
                (b) Prepare an income statement for the three months ending 30 September.

CHAPTER
EIGHTEEN

Examination Techniques

Remember what was said at the start of the book about examination technique.

The examination is the final chance that you will have to prove to yourself (and to others) how capable you are. This is what you have been training for over the past couple of years – this is your Cup Final! This is what could gain you entry into the Champions' League! (ie a good job or university)!

The key to success is planning and timing.

Read this section carefully: it may make the difference between gaining an A or a B (or an E and a U). Remember – the difference between one grade and another grade is only one mark – that's right, one single, teeny weeny mark!

Read the front sheet of your examination booklet.

Quickly read through the question paper.

TIMING

In AQA A2 Level examinations one and a third minutes should be allocated to each mark. Make sure that you work out how long you should spend on each question. If you have not finished a 20-mark question in 27 minutes, then move on to the next question (unless you are within two minutes of completing it). Not timing yourself is the surest way of ensuring that you get a lower grade than you deserve.

In OCR A2 Level examinations the paper examining company accounts and interpretation is one and a half hours in length and is worth 80 marks. This means that just over one minute should be allocated to each mark. You should spend a little over 20 minutes (22½ minutes, actually) on a 20-mark question and just over 30 minutes on a 30-mark question.

The OCR management accounting paper is two hours in length and is worth 120 marks, so exactly one minute should be spent on earning 1 mark.

If you run out of time on any question – **move on to the next question**. You might have some time left at the end of the examination to return and complete it. **Keep moving on**!

Many candidates fail to do justice to themselves because they spend too much time on one or two questions early in the examination, so they fail to complete the paper, or later questions, as fully as they could.

To obtain top grades, you **must** attempt all questions and all parts of questions.

MARKS

Look carefully at the number of marks allocated to each written question (you should have done this already in order to allocate your time effectively). The number of marks for a question will give you an idea of how much you should write.

For example, if a written question has been allocated two marks then a two-page answer will not be expected. The answer is likely to be two lines long or perhaps two sentences long.

A recent question asked candidates to identify the method that a trader would use to verify the bank columns in her cash book. It had been allocated one mark. A number of candidates wrote half a side of one page to answer this. Of course, the answer was 'She should prepare a bank reconciliation statement'.

The candidate who wrote a thesis as their answer had not taken heed of:

a the one-mark allocation and
b the word 'identify' in the instruction.

ABBREVIATIONS

As a rule, do not use abbreviations in your answers. 'T & P & L a/c for y/e 31/12/*9' is not acceptable.

If you are short of space then 'Bal b/d' and 'Depn' **may** be acceptable. The acceptance of the use of abbreviations is the remit of the chief examiner. Don't take the chance of dropping a mark. (This mark might be the one mark that makes a difference to your final grade. It might be the one mark needed to get you to the university of your choice.)

Do not use text language in your written sections – this will certainly lose a mark for 'quality of written communication'.

CROSSING OUT

If you have to change a figure, cross it out neatly and show the correct figure clearly. Do not go over the figure you wish to change. The examiner may not be able to tell which figure you want to be considered.

If you cross out a figure that then affects several other figures, do not cross out all subsequent figures, as:

a this will be extremely messy
b you could make many mistakes in any of the sub-totals.

Cross out the major incorrect figure and make a note at the side of how it will affect the final figure.

For example, you prepare an income statement (not inc stat!) and include £2,340 as your opening inventory figure. Just as you finish the whole account, you notice that it should be £3,240. Cross out £2,340 (neatly) and put in £3,240 clearly alongside. Put an asterisk (*) alongside the £3,240, cross out the incorrect net profit and write the corrected net profit alongside together with another asterisk and an indication of why you have made the change.

Do not use correction fluid anywhere on your script.

HEADINGS

Always use a heading for every question and every subsection. Tell the examiner what it is that you are preparing. These are easy marks to gain (every mark is precious. The difference between a grade A and a grade B . . . yes, you've heard it before – but remember this fact – it is vital).

Headings for accounting statements should include the proprietor's name and the statement heading, for example:

R. Lander
Bank reconciliation statement at 31 December 20*9.

WORKINGS

Examiners are not only interested in the actual answer that you produce and submit for marking; they are also interested in the method you used to arrive at your conclusion. This is especially true if you do not arrive at the correct conclusion.

If an examiner sees that you have used an incorrect figure in your answer he or she is interested in your reasoning to reach the incorrect answer. You will have reached your answer by using some logical (to you) thought process; let the examiner see this thought process through workings. In 99% of cases these workings result in part-marks for a partly correct process.

For example:

■ The trial balance shows £79,000 for wages.
■ The notes tell us that £1,000 is still owing at the trial balance date.

- Vanessa does not show workings and answers £80,000, worth 2 marks.
- Ellie shows workings 79,000 (1) + 1,000 (1) and answers £80,000 which is worth 2 marks.

So there is no advantage gained if the answer is correct. **But** and this is a very big **but**, if you make an error in your calculation and don't show workings, you will not gain any marks at all.

- Francesca does not show workings and answers £78,000, worth 0 marks.
- Albert shows workings 79,000 (1) – 1,000 and answers £78,000 and is awarded 1 mark.

You will make unforced errors in your examination answer booklet. Things that you have answered correctly 100 times in class you may answer incorrectly in the examination hall.

What is £6 + £2? Easy! I recently marked a very good script (the candidate probably gained an A grade) in which the answer appeared as £9!

Please, please, please show workings; if you do not, you may be throwing marks away.

(Remember that every mark is precious. The difference between ...)

Identify your workings so that the examiner can trace the workings to the appropriate part of your answer. Use either a heading:

Purchases
26,000
 4,000
30,000

or an instruction W^1
26,000
 4,000
30,000

WRITTEN SECTIONS

Write your answers legibly (remember: do not go over incorrect words – cross them out neatly and insert the correct word). If an examiner cannot read your answer then he or she cannot award marks. Remember that this will be the first time the examiner has seen your writing; they cannot translate it from untidy scribble into English as easily as your class teacher can – they have seen your writing on numerous occasions so they are more used to translating it!

Make marking as easy as possible for the examiner.

Make a plan of what you are going to write – it need only be made using individual words or initial letters; rearrange these into a logical sequence, then, answer the question. This plan, even for very short answers, will help your answer to flow, it will stop you repeating yourself and it will save time.

When answering questions requiring written explanations, pretend that the examiner is a non-accountant and explain things in the most minute detail. Do not assume that the examiner has any prior knowledge of accounting.

Apply the mnemonic **IDA**:

- Identify the key factor(s) of your answer.
- Develop your answer in general terms showing that you understand the concept that you are writing about.
- Apply your answer to the question set by the examiner.

QUESTION

Jock is thinking about changing the rate of depreciation charged on his fixed assets from 10% to 25% per annum. Which accounting concept must he consider and why?

Answer

Consistency (**I**) this means that the same depreciation policy should be applied over the lifetime of the asset (**D**) so he should continue to use 10% as his annual charge for depreciation (**A**).

State the obvious.

QUESTION

How can Glenn improve his profitability?

A student answered along these lines: 'He can conduct a capital investment appraisal to determine which new machine he should purchase. This new machine may produce goods more efficiently at a lower cost so ...'. This may be worth 1 mark.

'He can put up his selling price. If his cost of sales is maintained, or reduced, his profits will increase.' This is also probably worth 1 mark.

When confronted recently with this example, a student replied: 'But everyone knows that!' An examiner does not know what you know unless you tell him or her.

Examiners are trying to find out what you **know**, not what you do **not** know.

Tell the examiner – even the obvious!

Everyone wants you to pass the examinations you take:

- **your relatives** want you to pass
- **your teachers** want you to pass
- **you** want to pass
- **the examiner** wants you to pass.

If an examiner wanted you to fail he or she could guarantee this by asking questions that you would find almost impossible to answer.

Trust your teachers – they will give you all the tools necessary to pass the examination you will take.

Trust yourself during the examination.

In the words of the BBC children's radio programme, 'Go For It!'

IDENTIFY KEY WORDS IN THE QUESTIONS

There will be a clear instruction in the question that tells you how you are required to respond, for example should you give a detailed answer or are you only required to state one or two facts without explanation?

STATE/IDENTIFY

Requires a very short answer – no explanation or development is necessary.

Example:

Q. Identify a source document used to write up the sales day book.
A. Copy sales invoice.

No development is necessary – you will not impress an examiner by extending your answer to cover two sides of A4 paper. It will cost you marks that could have been gained on later questions. You do not have time to do more than is required of you.

LIST

Requires a few short answers (the number will be given). Again, no explanation or development is required.

Example:

Q. List two items that a trader may not have included in the bank columns of his cash book that are shown in his bank statement.
A. Standing orders; bank charges. (No development required or given.)

DISCUSS

Requires arguments for a particular line of action and arguments against such actions. A conclusion should be drawn from your discussion.

Example:

Q. Discuss an issue of ordinary shares as a means of raising capital.
A. Your response would identify benefits to the company then develop these benefits in terms of their implications for the business. Similarly, disadvantages would be identified and developed. Your answer would end with a conclusion as to whether or not this action is likely to be beneficial. Your conclusion should be drawn from (be based on) the arguments that you presented in your answer.

ANALYSE

Looks at reasons why a particular action took place or looks at the likely consequences of taking an action.

Example:

Q. Analyse the effect that a price increase would have on the profitability of a business.

A. The beneficial effects that a price increase would have and the drawbacks of an increase in price should be fully explained.

EVALUATE

This requires a conclusion to be drawn from the arguments presented in your answer (the same as 'Discuss'). Make sure that your judgements are based on the issues raised in your analysis.

Example:

Q. Advise Chetan whether to purchase Machine A or Machine B.

A. You would present the evidence for and against the purchase of each machine. Your final judgement would be to advise which machine should be purchased and why. Your judgement should be supported by the evidence that you have presented.
In answer to this type of question it is important that conflicting advice is not given, ie 'Machine A should be purchased but I think that Machine B is better'.

SOME ADDITIONAL POINTERS!

Do not repeat the question in your answer!

A significant number of candidates start written answers by saying 'I am going to discuss the many advantages and disadvantages of . . . I will list three advantages; I will then list disadvantages. After this I will then go on to . . .' and on and on. This wastes so much time – time that could be gaining valuable marks – and remember that time = marks!

Answer the question set by the examiner – not the question you wish had been asked!

Read the question carefully – if the answer requires action that will affect employees, remember this and don't give your answer from the shareholders' viewpoint or the viewpoint of the managers.

SYNOPTICITY

This means that the examiners must test your ability to incorporate knowledge gained in other units as well as the knowledge specific to the particular unit being examined.

So:

- journal entries
- double-entry transactions
- ledger accounts etc

may also be examined at A2 Level even though they appear as AS units. A2 relies heavily on what you learned earlier. As you go through A2 topics, try to visualise how an A2 examiner might bring topics that you learned last year into the question.

Some areas will be incorporated without much effort, for example:

- double-entry: basic to all accounting, whatever the level
- control accounts: used automatically in incomplete record questions.

FINAL, FINAL WORD!

As I said earlier, one should not wish you 'good luck' – I wish that you 'fulfil your potential'.

My only word of advice to my own daughters before they embarked on their A Level courses was: 'Don't get into the situation in mid-August where you have to say "If only . . .". "If only I had done a bit more revision." "If only I had done all my homework."

This is criminal – you are doing examinations for:

YOU – not parents; not teachers; not friends; not . . . **only for you!**

DO WELL!

CHAPTER ONE

QUESTION 1

Jan

Departmental income statement extract for the year ended 31 December 20*8

	Kitchen goods		DIY goods		Leisure goods	
	£	£	£	£	£	£
Sales		97,876		73,752		102,653
Less Cost of sales						
Stock at 1 Jan 20*8	6,980		4,870		8,820	
Purchases	42,631		30,884		38,005	
	49,611		35,754		46,825	
Stock at 31 Dec 20*8	7,450	42,161	5,090	30,664	7,690	39,135
Gross profit		55,715		43,088		63,518

QUESTION 3

Maurice Duvall

Departmental income statement for the year ended 31 October 20*9

	Cheeses		Meats	
	£	£	£	£
Sales		88,630		125,330
Less Cost of sales				
Stock at 1 Nov 20*8	2,860		1,540	
Purchases	29,960		43,750	
	32,820		45,290	
Stock at 31 Oct 20*9	1,790	31,030	1,680	43,610
Gross profit		57,600		81,720
Wages	12,660		21,110	
Admin salaries	4,280		4,280	
Insurances	2,400		2,400	
Repairs			840	
Electricity	1,600		800	
Rent and rates	4,800		2,400	
Lighting and heating	1,120		560	
General expenses	4,275		4,275	
Motor expenses	2,300	33,435	9,200	45,865
Net profit		24,165		35,855

QUESTION 5

Calculation of total debtors at 31 May 20*9

	£
Original total of debtors	4,775
Less Transposition error	(270)
Add Entry for C. Oyne	718
Less Bad debt written off	(316)
Corrected total of debtors	4,907

Note 2 will affect the control account. Ledger accounts will not be affected.

QUESTION 7

(a) Corrected total creditors as per control account at 31 January 20*9:

	£
Original balance at 31 January 20*9	4,361
Add Clax & Co	301
Balance at 1 January 20*9 not used	2,717
B. Cluck	261
Corrected balance at 31 January 20*9	7,640

(b) Corrected total of debtors at 31 January 20*9:

	£
Correct balance as at 31 January 20*9	7,640
Less – Clax & Co	(301)
J. Fitzwilliam	(991)
B. Cluck	(261)
Incorrect balance at 31 January 20*9	6,087

Note 2. Discounts received are entered in the purchase ledger.
Note 5. Cash sales are not entered in the sales ledger.

QUESTION 9

(a) Journal

		£	£
Suspense account	Dr	100	
Advertising account			100
Purchase ledger control account	Dr	1,440	
Suspense account			1,440
Sales account	Dr	120	
Drawings account	Dr	120	
Purchases account			120
Suspense account			120
Machinery repairs account	Dr	1,600	
Machinery account			1,600

(b) Suspense account

			£
Trial balance difference		Sales account	120
(missing figure)			
Advertising account	100	Ralph Simpson	1,440

Note: The descriptions tell where the other entry can be found. The debit for £1,440 is to the integrated purchase ledger control account – this is the double entry. £1,440 will also be debited in Ralph's account in the purchase ledger although this is not part of the double-entry system; we need to make a note in our own memorandum records that £720 has been paid.

QUESTION 11

(a) Journal

		£	£
Sales account	Dr	5,000	
Capital account			5,000
Commission receivable account	Dr	1,200	
Commission payable account	Dr	2,100	
Suspense account			3,300
Suspense account	Dr	110	
Shirley Knott			73
Andy Knott			37

(b) Suspense account

	£		
Trial balance difference (missing figure)	1,200	Commission receivable account	3,300
Commission payable account	2,100		3,300
	3,300		

No entries are required in the double-entry system for errors 3, 4 and 5.
However, the following adjustments are necessary in the memorandum accounts maintained in the sales ledger:

	Dr		
	£		£
Pippa Bramley	650		650
Pippin Cox			73
Shirley Knott			37
Andy Knott			
D. County account	140		140
S. County account			

These are tricky entries – the changes need to be shown in the personal accounts but as far as the double-entry system is concerned, all the correct entries will be shown in the control account since they are all correctly entered in the subsidiary books, ie the sales day book, the cash book and the purchase returns day book respectively. The subsidiary books 'feed' the control account which is part of the double-entry system. The personal accounts need to be adjusted but these are only memorandum accounts.

CHAPTER TWO

QUESTION 1

	£
Net assets (capital) at 30 November 20*9	50,000
Net assets (capital) at 30 November 20*8	49,590
Retained profits for year	410
Add Drawings for year	13,500
Net profit for year ended 30 November 20*9	13,910

QUESTION 3

	£
Net assets (capital) at 31 December 20*9	70,540
Net assets (capital) at 31 December 20*8	69,300
Retained profits for year	1,240
Add Drawings for year	24,500
	25,740
Less Capital introduced	12,500
Net profit for year ended 31 December 20*9	13,240

QUESTION 5

Debtors

	£		£
Bal b/d	1,792	Bank	121,367
Sales (missing figure)	122,043	Bal c/d	2,468
	123,835		123,835
Bal b/d	2,468		

Creditors

	£		£
Bank	59,846	Bal b/d	815
Bal b/d	1,067	Purchases (missing figure)	60,098
	60,913		60,913
		Bal b/d	1,067

Tamsin Rook
Income statement extract for the year ended 31 August 20*9

	£	£
Sales		122,043
Less Cost of sales		
Stock	8,467	
Purchases	60,098	
	68,565	
Stock	9,566	
		58,999
Gross profit		63,044

QUESTION 7

Motor expenses

	£		£
Cash	8,166	Bal b/d	78
Bal c/d	461	Inc stat (missing figure)	8,549
	8,627		8,627
		Bal b/d	461

Rates

	£		£
Bal b/d	120	Inc stat (missing figure)	1,509
Cash	1,534	Bal a/c	145
	1,654		1,654
Bal b/d	145		

QUESTION 9

	£
Net assets as at 30 April 20*9	37,901
Net assets as at 1 May 20*8	47,682
Retained profit (loss) for year	(9,781)
Add Drawings	18,298
Net profit for year ended 30 April 20*9	8,517

QUESTION 11

	£
Net assets as at 31 August 20*9	103,413
Net assets as at 1 September 20*8	104,629
Retained profit (loss) for year	(1,216)
Add Drawings	20,548
	19,332
Less Capital introduced	(21,000)
Net loss for the year ended 31 August 20*9	(1,668)

QUESTION 13

Trade receivables

	£		£
Bal b/d	840	Cash	73,498
Sales	73,170	Bal c/d	512
	74,010		74,010
Bal b/d	512		

Trade payables

	£		£
Cash	38,910	Bal b/d	3,461
Bal c/d	3,790	Purchases	39,239
	42,700		42,700
		Bal b/d	3,790

Jack Hay
Income statement extract for the year ended 30 June 20*9

	£	£
Sales		73,170
Less Cost of sales		
Inventory	1,791	
Purchases	39,239	
	41,030	
Inventory	2,348	38,682
Gross profit		34,488

QUESTION 15

Trade receivables

	£		
Bal b/d	146	Cash	61,803
Sales	62,254	Discount allowed	310
		Bal c/d	287
	62,400		62,400
Bal b/d	287		

Trade payables

	£		£
Cash	28,718	Bal b/d	28,590
Bal c/d	1,871	Purchases	1,999
	30,589		30,589
		Bal b/d	1,871

Sandra May
Income statement extract for the year ended 31 December 20*9

	£	£
Sales		62,254
Less Cost of sales		
Inventory	982	
Purchases	28,590	
	29,572	
Inventory	1,271	28,301
Gross profit		33,953

QUESTION 17
1. Opening statement of affairs:

	£
Premises	65,000
Equipment	14,000
Inventory	2,519
Credit customers	1,339
Balance at bank	2,347 (Don't forget)
	85,205
Credit suppliers	(2,910)
Accrual	(145)
Capital (assets) as at 1 January 20*9	82,150

2. Already done in question.
3. Adjustments accounts:

Equipment

	£		£
Balance b/d	14,000	Inc stat a/c	3,500
Bank	4,500	Bal c/d	15,000
	18,500		18,500
Bal b/d	15,000		

Trade receivables

	£		£
Bal b/d	1,339	Cash	16,409
Credit sales	16,640	Bal c/d	1,570
	17,979		17,979
Bal b/d	1,570		

4. Final accounts:

Trade payables

	£		£
Cash	23,457	Bal b/d	2,910
Bal c/d	2,341	Purchases	22,888
	25,798		25,798
		Bal b/d	2,341

Dai Johns
Income statement for the year ended 31 December 20*9

	£	£
Sales		81,174
Less Cost of sales		
Inventory	2,519	
Purchases	22,888	
	25,407	
Inventory	2,331	23,076
Gross profit		58,098
Less Expenses	34,692	
Dep'n of equipment	3,500	38,192
Net profit		19,906

Balance sheet at 31 December 20*9

	£	£
Non-current assets		
Premises at cost		65,000
Equipment at valuation		15,000
		80,000
Current assets		
Inventory	2,331	
Trade receivables	1,570	
Bank	2,872	
	6,773	
Current liabilities		
Trade payables	(2,341)	
Accrued expenses	(276)	4,156
		84,156
Capital		82,150
Add Net profit		19,906
		102,056
Less Drawings		17,900
		84,156

QUESTION 19

1. Opening statement of affairs:

	£
Premises	56,000
Fixtures	18,000
Vehicle	8,000
Inventory	1,638
Credit customers	1,649
Rent in advance	600
	85,887
Bank overdraft	(452)
Credit suppliers	(2,225)
General expenses accrued	(127)
Capital (net assets)	83,083

2. Cash book (given in question).

3. Adjustment accounts:

Fixtures

	£		£
Bal b/d	18,000	Inc stat	2,800
Bank	4,800	Bal c/d	20,000
	22,800		22,800
Bal b/d	20,000		

Trade receivables

	£		£
Bal b/d	1,649	Cash	46,880
Sales	45,690	Bal c/d	459
	47,339		47,339
Bal b/d	459		

Trade payables

	£		£
Cash	34,872	Bal b/d	2,225
Bal c/d	2,619	Purchases	35,266
	37,491		37,491
		Bal b/d	2,619

Rent

	£		£
Bal b/d	600	Inc stat	5,000
Cash	6,600	Bal c/d	2,200
	7,200		7,200
Bal b/d	2,200		

General expenses

	£		£
Cash	13,743	Bal b/d	127
Bal c/d	981	Inc stat	14,597
	14,724		14,724
		Bal b/d	981

Commission receivable

	£		£
Inc stat	3,000	Cash	2,000
		Bal c/d	1,000
	3,000		3,000
Bal b/d	1,000		

4. Andre Lefevre
Income statement for the year ended 31 March 20*9

	£	£
Sales		89,424
Less Cost of sales		
Inventory	1,638	
Purchases	41,027	
	42,665	
Inventory	1,744	40,921
Gross profit		48,503
Commission receivable		3,000
		51,503
Less Expenses		
General	14,597	
Wages	24,797	
Rent	5,000	
Depreciation –		
Premises	2,000	
Fixtures	2,800	
Vehicles	4,000	53,194
Loss for the year		1,691

Balance sheet at 31 March 20*9

	£	£
Non-current assets at valuation		
Premises		54,000
Fixtures		20,000
Vehicle		4,000
		78,000
Current assets		
Inventory	1,744	
Trade receivables	459	
Rent in advance	2,200	
Commission receivable owed	1,000	
	5,403	
Current liabilities		
Trade payables	(2,619)	
Bank overdraft	(21,971)	
General expenses accrued	(981)	(20,168)
		57,832
Capital		83,083
Less Loss		(1,691)
		81,392
Less Drawings		(23,560)
		57,832

QUESTION 21
Joe Duff
Income statement extract for year ended 31 December 20*9

	£	£
Sales		240,000
Less Cost of sales		
Inventory	17,993	
Purchases	188,483	
	206,476	
Inventory stolen	7,975	
Inventory	18,501	180,000
Gross profit		60,000

Stolen inventory was £7,975.   (Mark-up 33⅓%)

QUESTION 23

1. Opening statement of affairs:

	£
Equipment	9,700
Vehicle	3,000
Inventory	984
Credit customers	126
Bank balance	1,764
Cash in hand	238
	15,812
Credit suppliers	(1,477)
Capital (Net assets)	14,335

2.

Cash account

	£		£
Bal b/d	238	Wages	4,380
Takings	120,698	Rent	2,400
		Drawings	8,460
		Banked	102,250
		Stolen	3,120
		Bal c/d	326
	120,936		120,936
Bal b/d	326		

3.

Trade receivables

	£		£
Bal b/d	126	Cash	6,479
Sales	6,564	Bal c/d	211
	6,690		6,690
Bal b/d	211		

Trade payables

	£		£
Cash	34,107	Bal b/d	1,477
Bal c/d	1,086	Purchases	33,716
	35,193		35,193
		Bal b/d	1,086

Equipment account

	£		£
Bal b/d	9,700	Inc stat	1,300
Purchases	2,600	Bal c/d	11,000
	12,300		12,300
Bal b/d	11,000		

4. Akit Patel

Income statement for the year ended 30 September 20*9

	£	£
Sales		127,262
Less Cost of sales		
Inventory	984	
Purchases	35,044	
	36,028	
Inventory	1,358	34,670
Gross profit		92,592
Less Expenses		
General expenses	37,328	
Wages	28,141	
Rent	2,400	
Depreciation –		
equipment	1,300	
vehicles	2,000	
Stolen cash		120
Profit for the year		71,289
		21,303

Balance sheet at 30 September 20*9

	£	£
Non-current assets at valuation		
Equipment		11,000
Vehicle		1,000
		12,000
Current assets		
Inventory	1,358	
Trade receivables	211	
Bank balance	899	
Cash in hand	326	
Insurance claim	3,000	
	5,794	
Current liabilities		
Trade payables	(1,086)	4,708
		16,708
Capital		14,335
Add Profit		21,303
		35,638
Less Drawings		18,930
		16,708

CHAPTER THREE

QUESTION 1
Ian and Jenny
Income statement extract for the year ended 31 January 20*9

		£
Profit for the year		26,900
Salary – Ian		(5,000)
		21,900
Share of residual profits – Ian	(14,600)	
Jenny	(7,300)	(21,900)

QUESTION 3
Maria and Nelly
Income statement extract for the year ended 31 March 20*9

	£	£
Profit for the year		74,868
Salary – Maria		(4,800)
		70,068
Interest on capital – Maria	(3,200)	
Nelly	(4,800)	(8,000)
		62,068
Share of residual profits – Maria	(46,551)	
Nelly	(15,517)	(62,068)

QUESTION 5
Queenie and Rusty
Income statement extract for the year ended 28 February 20*9

	£
Profit for the year	63,842
Salary – Rusty	(5,000)
	58,842
Interest on capital – Queenie	(1,800)
Rusty	(1,200)
	55,842
Share of residual profits – Queenie	(27,921)
Rusty	(27,921)
	(55,842)

QUESTION 7
Ursula and Vincent
Income statement extract for the year ended 31 December 20*9

	£
Profit for the year	8,400
Salary – Ursula	(6,000)
	2,400
Interest on capital – Ursula	(500)
Vincent	(3,000)
	(3,500)
	(1,100)
Share of residual loss – Ursula	(660)
Vincent	(440)
	(1,100)

QUESTION 9
Gareth and Darius
Income statement extract for the year ended 31 January 20*9

	£
Profit for the year	27,362
Add Interest on drawings – Gareth	146
Darius	238
	384
	27,746
Share of residual profits – Gareth	(13,873)
Darius	(13,873)
	(27,746)

QUESTION 11
Tramp and Hobo
Income statement extract for the year ended 30 June 20*9

	£
Profit for the year	25,570
Add Interest on drawings – Tramp	267
Hobo	303
	570
	26,140
Salary – Hobo	(2,000)
	24,140
Share of residual profits – Tramp	(14,484)
Hobo	(9,656)
	(24,140)

QUESTION 13
Mark, Noreen and Oswald
Income statement extract for the year ended 31 March 20*9

	£	£
Loss for the year		(818)
Add Interest on drawings – Mark	261	
Noreen	38	
Oswald	279	
		578
		(240)
Share of residual loss – Mark	120	
Noreen	80	
Oswald	40	
		240

QUESTION 15
Rooney and Timms
Income statement extract for the year ended 31 May 20*9

	£	£
Profit for the year		27,967
Add Interest on drawings – Rooney	82	
Timms	179	
		261
		28,228
Salary – Rooney		(3,000)
		25,228
Interest on capital – Rooney	(1,200)	
Timms	(1,000)	
		(2,200)
		23,028
Share of residual profits – Rooney	(11,514)	
Timms	(11,514)	
		(23,028)

QUESTION 17
Gray and Pink
Income statement extract for the year ended 30 November 20*9

	£	£
Profit for the year		37,951
Interest on drawings – Gray	171	
Pink	298	
		469
		38,420
Salary – Gray		(4,000)
		34,420
Interest on capital – Gray	(2,400)	
Pink	(5,600)	
		(8,000)
		26,420
Share of residual profits – Gray	(21,136)	
Pink	(5,284)	
		(26,420)

QUESTION 19
Naylor, Niall and Norbert
Income statement extract for the year ended 31 May 20*9

	£	£
Profit for year		71,560
Interest on drawings – Naylor	460	
Niall	320	
Norbert	411	1,191
		72,751
Salary – Niall		(7,500)
		65,251
Interest on capital – Naylor	(3,000)	
Niall	(2,100)	
Norbert	(2,400)	(7,500)
		57,751
Share of residual profits – Naylor	(24,750)	
Niall	(16,501)	
Norbert	(16,500)	(57,751)

Current accounts

	Naylor	Niall	Norbert		Naylor	Niall	Norbert
Balance				Balance	85		131
Drawings	27,200	17,450	19,350	Salary		7,500	
Interest on				Interest on			
drawings	460	320	411	capital	3,000	2,100	2,400
Bal c/d	175	8,169		Share of			
				profits	24,750	16,501	16,500
				Bal c/d			730
	27,835	26,101	19,761		27,835	26,101	19,761
			730	Bal b/d	175	8,169	

CHAPTER FOUR

QUESTION 1
Pat, Danny and Janice
Balance sheet at 1 January 20*9

	£
Non-current assets	155,000
Current assets	40,000
Current liabilities	(10,000)
	30,000
	185,000
Capital accounts – Pat	90,000
Danny	70,000
Janice	25,000
	185,000

QUESTION 3
Umair, Tim and Eddie
Balance sheet at 1 October 20*9

	£	£
Non-current assets at valuation		
Premises		100,000
Equipment		1,400
Vehicles		12,000
		113,400
Current assets		
Inventory	4,200	
Trade receivables	6,400	
Bank	8,700	
	19,300	
Current liabilities		
Trade payables	(2,700)	
		16,600
		130,000
Capital accounts – Umair		66,000
Tim		54,000
Eddie		10,000
		130,000

QUESTION 5
Mo, Doug and Tracey
Balance sheet at 1 April 20*9

	£
Fixed asset	
Goodwill	12,000
Current asset	
Bank	4,760
	16,760
Capital accounts – Mo	9,010
Doug	4,750
Tracey	3,000
	16,760

QUESTION 7
Victor, Ffiona and Eric
Balance sheet at 1 October 20*9

	£
Bank balance	9,000
Capital accounts – Victor	4,300
Ffiona	(800)
Eric	5,500
	9,000

QUESTION 9
(a) Revaluation account

Capital – Shubratha	32,000	Non-current assets	16,000
Ciaran	8,000	Goodwill	24,000
	40,000		40,000

(b) Goodwill account

Revaluation account	24,000	Capital accounts – Shubrathra	8,000
		Ciaran	8,000
		Jim	8,000
	24,000		24,000

(c) Capital accounts

	Shubratha £	Ciaran £	Jim £		Shubratha £	Ciaran £	Jim £
Goodwill	8,000	8,000	8,000	Balances b/d	20,000	15,000	15,000
				Cash			
Balances c/d	44,000	15,000	7,000	Revaluation	32,000	8,000	
	52,000	23,000	15,000		52,000	23,000	15,000
				Balances c/d	44,000	15,000	7,000

(d) Shubratha, Ciaran and Jim
Balance sheet at 1 January 20*9

	£
Non-current assets at valuation	
Current assets	26,000
Current liabilities	(10,000)
Capital accounts – Shubratha	50,000
Ciaran	16,000
Jim	66,000
	44,000
	15,000
	7,000
	66,000

QUESTION 11
(a)

Revaluation account

	£		£
Equipment	24,000	Land and buildings	75,000
Vehicles	30,000	Goodwill	60,000
Inventory	700		
Trade receivables	200		
Capital – Chuck	53,400		
Todd	26,700		
	135,000		135,000

(b)

Goodwill account

	£		£
Revaluation	60,000	Capital – Chuck	30,000
		Todd	15,000
		Buzz	15,000
	60,000		60,000

(c)

Capital accounts

	Chuck £	Todd £	Buzz £		Chuck £	Todd £	Buzz £
Goodwill	30,000	15,000	15,000	Balances b/d	80,000	50,000	
Balances c/d	103,400	61,700	10,000	Revaluation	53,400	26,700	
				Bank			25,000
	133,400	76,700	25,000		133,400	76,700	25,000
				Balance b/d	103,400	61,700	10,000

(d) Chuck, Todd and Buzz
Balance sheet at 1 April 20*9

Non-current assets at valuation

	£
Land and buildings	140,000
Equipment	10,000
Vehicles	26,000
	176,000

Current assets

	£	£
Inventory	4,100	
Trade receivables	6,000	
Bank balance	22,570	
	32,670	

Current liabilities

	£
Trade payables	(4,570)

Non-current liability

	£
	28,100
	204,100
	(29,000)
	175,100

Capital accounts – Chuck	103,400
Todd	61,700
Buzz	10,000
	175,100

QUESTION 13
(a)

Revaluation account

	£		£
Capital accounts – Gordon	28,000	Non-current assets	50,000
Frances	28,000	Goodwill	20,000
Jacqui	14,000		
	70,000		70,000

(b)

Goodwill account

	£		£
Revaluation	20,000	Capital Gordon	10,000
		Jacqui	10,000
	20,000		20,000

(c)

Capital accounts (£000)

	Gordon £	Frances £	Jacqui £		Gordon £	Frances £	Jacqui £
Goodwill	10		10	Balance b/d	20	10	7
Loan a/c		38		Revaluation	28	28	14
Balance c/d	38		11				
	48	38	21		48	38	21
				Balance b/d	38		11

(d) Gordon and Jacqui
Balance sheet at 31 March 20*9

	£
Non-current assets	84,000
Current assets	12,000
Current liabilities	(9,000)
	87,000
Capital accounts – Gordon	38,000
Jacqui	11,000
	49,000
Loan account – Frances	38,000
	87,000

QUESTION 15
(a)

Revaluation account

	£		£
Equipment	18,000	Premises	65,000
Vehicles	16,000	Goodwill	36,000
Inventory	1,000		

(b)

Goodwill account			
	£	Capital – Ruairi	18,000
Revaluation	36,000	Jock	18,000
			36,000
	36,000		36,000

Capital accounts – Ruairi 33,000
Gareth 22,000
Jock 11,000
101,000   101,000

(c)

Capital accounts (£000)

	Ruairi	Gareth	Jock		Ruairi	Gareth	Jock
	£	£	£		£	£	£
Goodwill	18		18	Balances b/d	60	40	14
Loan a/c	62			Revaluation	33	22	11
Balance c/d	75	62	7				
	93	62	25		93	62	25
				Balance b/d	75		7

(d) Ruairi and Jock
Balance sheet at 31 August 20*9

	£
Non-current assets at valuation	
Premises	110,000
Equipment	5,000
Vehicles	18,000
	133,000
Current assets	
Inventory	10,250
Trade receivables	5,800
Cash and cash equivalents	1,480
	17,530
Current liabilities	
Trade payables	(6,530)
	11,000
	144,000
Capital accounts – Ruairi	75,000
Jock	7,000
	82,000
Loan account – Gareth	62,000
	144,000

QUESTION 17
(a)

Realisation account			
	£		
Premises	70,000	Cash and cash equivalents	133,000
Equipment	30,000	Hazel (vehicles)	10,000
Vehicles	18,000		
Current assets	16,000		
Profit on realisation – Eliza	3,000		
Sze Hang	3,000		
Hazel	3,000		
	143,000		143,000

(b)

Bank account			
	£		£
Balance b/d	3,000	Trade payables	7,000
Realisation: (assets)	133,000	Capital – Eliza	63,000
		Sze Hang	43,000
		Hazel	23,000
	136,000		136,000

Capital accounts (£000)

	Eliza	Sze Hang	Hazel		Eliza	Sze Hang	Hazel
	£	£	£		£	£	£
Realisation (vehicle)			10	Balances b/d	60	40	30
Cash and cash equivalents	63	43	23	Realisation	3	3	3
	63	43	33		63	43	33

QUESTION 19
(a)

Realisation account			
	£		£
Premises	210,000	Discount received	400
Equipment	84,000	Bertram (premises)	300,000
Vehicles	42,000	Chipperfield (vehicle)	5,000
Inventory	12,400	Mills (vehicle)	6,000
Discount allowed	100	Bank (vehicle)	9,000
Costs	6,450	Bank (equipment)	57,000
Capital – Bertram	16,625	Bank (inventory)	10,800
Chipperfield	11,083		
Mills	5,542		
	388,200		388,200

(b)

Bank account			
	£		£
Balance	2,700	Loan – Chipperfield	50,000
Trade receivables	8,100	Trade payables	8,900
Realisation (vehicle)	9,000	Costs	6,450
Realisation (equipment)	57,000	Capital – Chipperfield	106,083
Realisation (inventory)	10,800	Mills	49,542
Capital – Bertram	133,375		
	220,975		220,975

(c)

Capital accounts

	Bertram	Ch'field	Mills		Bertram	Ch'field	Mills
	£	£	£		£	£	£
Realisation (premises)	300,000			Balance b/d	150,000	100,000	50,000
Realisation (vehicles)		5,000	6,000	Realisation	16,625	11,083	5,542
Cash and cash equivalents		106,083	49,542	Cash and cash equivalents	133,375		
	300,000	111,083	55,542		300,000	111,083	55,542

QUESTION 21

Realisation account

	£		£
Net assets	100,000	Agas Ltd	210,000
Capital – Joan	88,000		
Darby	22,000		
	210,000		210,000

Agas Ltd

	£		£
Realisation	210,000	Bank	25,000
		Capital (shares)	185,000
	210,000		210,000

Capital accounts

	Joan £	Darby £		Joan £	Darby £
Ordinary shares in Agas Ltd	148,000	37,000	Balances b/d	60,000	40,000
Bank		25,000	Realisation	88,000	22,000
	148,000	62,000		148,000	62,000

QUESTION 23

(a)

Realisation account

	£		£
Net assets	40,000	Bank	55,000
Capital – Stephen	5,000		
Asman	5,000		
Shably	5,000		
	55,000		55,000

(b)

Bank account

	£		£
Balance b/d	10,000	Capital – Stephen	41,667
Realisation	55,000	Asman	23,333
	65,000		65,000

(c)

Capital accounts

	Stephen £	Asman £	Shably £		Stephen £	Asman £	Shably £
Balance b/d			10,000	Balance b/d	40,000	20,000	5,000
Realisation	3,333	1,667		Realisation	5,000	5,000	3,333
Bank	41,667	23,333		Capital – Stephen			1,667
				Asman			
	45,000	25,000	10,000		45,000	25,000	10,000

QUESTION 25

(a)

Revaluation account

	£		£
Equipment	8,000	Premises	52,000
Vehicles	14,000	Goodwill	60,000
Inventory	400		
Capital – Arbuthnot	44,800		
Barton	44,800		
	112,000		112,000

(b)

Goodwill account

	£		£
Revaluation	60,000	Capital – Arbuthnot	30,000
		Barton	20,000
		Currock	10,000
	60,000		60,000

(c)

Capital accounts

	Arb'not £	B'ton £	Currock £		Arb'not £	B'ton £	Currock £
Goodwill	30,000	20,000	10,000	Balances b/d	65,000	50,000	40,000
				Cash			
Balances c/d	79,800	74,800	30,000	Revaluation	44,800	44,800	
	109,800	94,800	40,000		109,800	94,800	40,000
				Balances b/d	79,800	74,800	30,000

(d) **Arbuthnot, Barton and Currock**
Balance sheet at 1 July 20*9

	£	£
Non-current assets at valuation		
Premises		100,000
Equipment		15,000
Vehicles		20,000
		135,000
Current assets		
Inventory	8,500	
Trade receivables	4,600	
Cash and cash equivalents	42,500	
	55,600	
Trade payables	(6,000)	
		49,600
		184,600
Capital – Arbuthnot		79,800
Barton		74,800
Currock		30,000
		184,600

QUESTION 27

(a)

Revaluation account

	£		£
Equipment	8,000	Premises	40,000
Vehicles	8,000	Goodwill	27,000
Capital – Petteril	25,500		
Eden	20,400		
Calder	5,100		
	67,000		67,000

(b)

Goodwill account

	£		£
Revaluation	27,000	Capital – Eden	18,000
		Calder	9,000
	27,000		27,000

(c)

Capital accounts

	Petteril £	Eden £	Calder £		Petteril £	Eden £	Calder £
Goodwill		18,000	9,000	Balances b/d	50,000	36,000	30,000
Loan a/c	75,500			Revaluation	25,500	20,400	5,100
Balances c/d		38,400	26,100		75,500	56,400	35,100
	75,500	56,400	35,100	Balances b/d		38,400	26,100

(d) Eden and Calder
Balance sheet at 30 September 20*9

		£
Non-current assets at valuation		
Premises		100,000
Equipment		6,000
Vehicles		24,000
		130,000
Current assets		
Inventory	4,200	
Trade receivables	7,600	
Cash and cash equivalents	1,200	
	13,000	
Trade payables	(3,000)	
		10,000
		140,000
Capital accounts – Eden	38,400	
Calder	26,100	
		64,500
Loan account – Petteril		75,500
		140,000

QUESTION 29
Stan and Ollie
Balance sheet at 30 April 20*9

		£
Non-current assets at valuation		
Equipment		40,000
Vehicles		8,000
		48,000
Current assets		
Inventory	10,000	
Trade receivables	9,000	
Cash and cash equivalents	1,500	
	20,500	
Current liabilities		
Trade payables	(8,500)	
		12,000
		60,000
Capital accounts – Stan		36,500
Ollie		23,500
		60,000

QUESTION 31
(a)

Realisation account

	£		£
Land and buildings	40,000	Discount received	300
Equipment	30,000	Bank (stock)	2,000
Vehicles	10,000	Bank (equipment)	17,000
Inventory	3,400	Sukhdeep (vehicles)	6,000
Discount allowed	400	Divya Ltd	60,000
Costs	4,300	Capital – Pritpal	1,400
		Sukhdeep	1,400
	88,100		88,100

(b)

Cash account

	£		£
Balance	2,700	Loan – Pritpal	25,000
Trade receivables	18,000	Trade payables	6,100
Realisation	17,000	Realisation – costs	4,300
Realisation	2,000	Capital – Pritpal	31,900
Divya	30,000	Sukhdeep	2,400
	69,700		69,700

(c)

Capital accounts

	Pritpal £	Sukhdeep £		Pritpal £	Sukhdeep £
Realisation (vehicles)		6,000	Balances b/d		24,800
Realisation	1,400	1,400			
Divya Ltd (Ord shares)	15,000	15,000			
Cash	31,900	2,400			
	48,300	24,800		48,300	24,800

QUESTION 33
(a)

Realisation account

	£		£
Equipment	42,000	Discount received	140
Inventory	17,000	Capital – Jacques	15,000
Discount allowed	300	(inventory)	
Bank (costs)	8,300	Bank (equipment)	25,000
		Capital – Jacques	13,730
		Marcel	9,153
		Guillaume	4,577
	67,600		67,600

(b)

Cash account

	£		£
Balance b/d	800	Loan – Guillaume	30,000
Trade receivables	3,200	Trade payables	6,260
Realisation (equipment)	25,000	Costs	8,300
Capital – Jacques	18,082	Capital – Guillaume	2,522
	47,082		47,082

(c)

Capital accounts

	J'ques £	M'cel £	G'me £		J'ques £	M'cel £	G'me £
Realisation (inventory)	15,000	1,900	10,000	Bal b/d			
Realisation	13,730		4,577	Capital – Jacques		9,153	4,352
Capital – M'l	4,352	9,153	2,901	Guillaume	15,000		2,901
Bank			2,522	Bank	18,082		2,522
	33,082	9,153	10,000		33,082	9,153	10,000

CHAPTER FIVE

QUESTION 1
No. The brand name should not be capitalised. Internally developed intangible assets should be capitalised only where they have an ascertainable market value.

QUESTION 3
The vehicle should be shown in the balance sheet at £30,000 (its carrying amount) since this is lower than its recoverable amount.

QUESTION 5
The property may be revalued. Depreciation should then be charged on the revalued amount over the useful lifetime of the property.

QUESTION 7
The finance director is correct. Purchase cost includes transportation and installation costs. All costs to enable the machinery to function.

CHAPTER SIX

QUESTION 1
(a) **Purlin plc**
Income statement for the year ended 30 November 20*9

	£000	£000
Profit before tax		642
Tax		(120)
Profit after tax		522

(b)

Statement of changes in equity

	£000
Retained earnings	
Balance at 1 December 20*8	997
Profit for the year	522
	1519
Dividends paid	(130)
Transfer to general reserve	(100)
Balance at 30 November 20*9	1,289
General reserve	
Transfer	100
Balance at 30 November 2009	100

QUESTION 3
(a) **Sleerock plc**
Income statement for the year ended 31 July 20*9

	£000	£000
Sales		757
Less Cost of sales		
Inventories	83	
Purchases	312	
	395	
Inventories	(74)	(321)
Gross profit		436
Selling and distribution expenses		(89)
Administration expenses		(112)
Operating profit		235
Finance costs		(36)
Profit before tax		199
Tax		(39)
Profit after tax		160

(b) **Statement of changes in equity**

	£000
Retained earnings	
Balance at 1 August 20*8	844
Profit for the year	160
	1004
Dividends paid	(110)
Balance at 31 July 20*9	894

QUESTION 5
Typleat plc
Balance sheet at 28 February 20*9

	£000
Non-current assets	1,836
Current assets	657
Current liabilities	(349)
	308
	2,144
Equity	
Ordinary shares of £1 each	1,500
Share premium account	50
Retained earnings	594
	2,144

QUESTION 7
(a) **Pitcherdy plc**
Income statement for the year ended 31 December 20*9

	£000
Gross profit	746
Selling and distribution expenses	(88)
Administration expenses	(124)
Operating profit	534
Interest payable	(36)
Profit before tax	498
Tax	(160)
Profit after tax	338

(b) Statement of changes in equity

	£000
Retained earnings	
Balance at 1 January 20*9	1,467
Profit for the year	338
	1,805
Dividends paid	(26)
Transfer to asset replacement reserve	(50)
Balance at 31 December 20*9	1,729
Asset replacement reserve	
Transfer	50
Balance at 31 December 20*9	50

QUESTION 9
Masqik plc
Balance sheet at 30 November 20*9

	£000
Equity	
Ordinary shares of £1 each	1,800
8% preferred shares of £1 each	400
Share premium account	112
Retained earnings	228
	2,540

QUESTION 11
Klobule plc
Summarised balance sheet at 30 September 20*9

	£000
Net assets	3,373
	3,373
Equity	
Ordinary shares of 25p each	1,640
Share premium account	600
Retained earnings	1,133
	3,373

QUESTION 13
Ardbeck plc
Balance sheet at 1 August 20*9

	£000
Net assets	2,500
	2,500
Equity	
Ordinary shares of 10p each	1,800
Share premium account	400
Retained earnings	300
	2,500

QUESTION 15
McTavish-Jones plc
Balance sheet extract at 2 April 20*9

	£000
Equity	
Ordinary shares of £1 each	2,000
6% preferred shares of £1 each	120
Share premium account	1,800
Retained earnings	218
	4,318

QUESTION 17
Omerdoh plc
Balance sheet at 31 December 20*9

Non-current assets	Valuation £	Cost £	Depreciation £	Net £
Premises	250,000			250,000
Equipment		86,000	56,000	30,000
Vehicles		76,000	57,000	19,000
	250,000	162,000	113,000	299,000

Current assets		
Inventories	60,000	
Trade receivables	47,000	
Cash and cash equivalents	58,000	
	165,000	
Current liabilities		
Trade payables	(21,000)	
		144,000
		443,000

Equity	£000
Ordinary shares of £1 each	360,000
Revaluation reserve	76,000
Retained earnings	7,000
	443,000

CHAPTER SEVEN

QUESTION 1

Cash inflows	£000
Decrease in trade receivables	14
Increase in trade payables	9
Tax owed	123
Share issue (including premium)	400
Profits	166
	712

Cash outflows	£000
Purchase of non-current assets	584
Increase in inventories	13
Tax paid	108
	705

Net increase in cash and cash equivalents	7
Cash and cash equivalents at the beginning of the year	39
Cash and cash equivalents at the end of the year	46

QUESTION 3

	£
Profit from operations for the year ended 31 March 20*9	463,000
Less Interest	(27,000)*
Profit before tax	436,000
Tax	(112,000)*
	324,000
Transfer to general reserve	(20,000)*
	304,000
Dividends	(80,000)*
Retained profit for year	224,000*

(Put in all the information supplied * then fill in the missing sub-totals until you arrive at the profit from operations.)

QUESTION 5

Non-current assets account

	£000		£000
Balance b/d	2,160	Disposal	850 (1)
Bank	1,180 (6)	Balance c/d	2,490 (4)
	3,340		3,340
Balance b/d	2,490 (4)		

Depreciation of non-current assets account

	£000		£000
Disposal	610 (2)	Balance b/d	610 (2)
Balance c/d	910 (5)	Inc stat	910 (5)
	1,520		1,520
		Balance b/d	910 (5)

Disposal account

	£000		£000
Non-current asset	850 (1)	Depreciation	610 (2)
		Bank	170 (3)
		Inc stat (loss on disposal)	70 (8)
	850		850

Entries not shown:
(3) Dr Bank 170
(6) Cr Bank 1,180
(7) Dr P & L a/c 690
(8) Dr P & L a/c 70

The cash inflows are £170,000 plus the reduction in profit of £690,000 and profit of £70,000 which will not reduce cash but needs to be added to reported profits to obtain cash inflow. £1,180,000 cash outflow for purchase of non-current assets.

QUESTION 7

	Cash inflow £	Cash outflow £
Premises		9,000
Inventories		1,900
Trade receivables	200	
Trade payables	150	

QUESTION 9
Shakoor Ltd

Cash inflows

	£
Increase in depreciation	38,000
Decrease in receivables	1,980
Provision for tax	38,000
Issue of shares	100,000
Retained profit for year	7,330
Decrease in bank balance during the year	800
	186,110

Cash outflows

	£
Purchase of non-current assets	132,000
Increase in inventories	3,500
Decrease in payables	10,610
Tax paid	40,000
	186,110

QUESTION 11
Depreciation of £10,000 needs to be added to reported profits to obtain the cash inflow for the year.

QUESTION 13

Plant account

	£		£
Balance b/d	240,000	Disposal	32,000
		Balance c/d	208,000
	240,000		240,000
Balance b/d	208,000		

Provision for depreciation account

Disposal	20,000	Balance b/d	100,000
Balance c/d	111,800	Inc stat	31,800
	131,800		131,800
		Balance b/d	111,800

Disposal account

	£		£
Plant	32,000	Depreciation	20,000
Inc stat	1,200	Bank	13,200
	33,200		33,200

The cash inflow is £13,200 plus the reduction in reported profits of £31,800 depreciation debited to the income statement. £1,200 profit on disposal should be deducted from operating profit.

QUESTION 15
Only one cash inflow: £200,000 from the issue of 6% preferred shares.

QUESTION 17
Net cash flow generated from operating activities

	£000	
Operating profit	67	(£196,000 − £136,000 + £7,000)
Depreciation	140	
Profit on disposal	(7)	
Increase in inventories	(4)	
Decrease in receivables	8	
Decrease in payables	(5)	
	199	
Interest paid	(7)	
Net cash flows from operating activities	192	

Non-current assets

	362		70
	198		490
	490		

Disposal

	70		60
	7		17

Provision for depreciation

	60		140
	220		140
			220

QUESTION 19
Net cash flow generated from operating activities

	£000	
Operating profit	77	(£1,443 − £1,384 + £18)
Depreciation	113	
Loss on disposal	5	
Increase in inventories	(8)	
Decrease in trade receivables	4	
Increase in trade payables	3	
	194	
Interest paid	(18)	
Net cash flow from operating activities	176	

Machinery

	488		102
	145		531
	633		633

Provision for depreciation

	87		236
	262		113
			262

Disposal

	102		87
	—		10
			5

QUESTION 3

(a)

	20*9	20*8
Current ratio = $\dfrac{\text{Current assets}}{\text{Current liabilities}}$	3.09:1	4:1
Liquid ratio = $\dfrac{\text{Current assets} - \text{inventories}}{\text{Current liabilities}}$	2.09:1	2.93:1
Debtors' collection period = $\dfrac{\text{Debtors}}{\text{Credit sales}} \times 365$	35 days	38 days
Creditors' payment period = $\dfrac{\text{Creditors}}{\text{Credit purchases}} \times 365$	35 days	32 days
Rate of stock turn = $\dfrac{\text{Cost of sales}}{\text{Average inventory}}$	10.88 times	11.4 times
OR $\dfrac{\text{Average inventory}}{\text{Cost of sales}} \times 365$	34 days	33 days
Working capital cycle	34 days	39 days

(b) There has been an improvement in debtor days; it is getting closer to the 'accepted' 30 days. There has been an improvement in creditor days, although care must be taken not to increase it too much and antagonise suppliers.
In year 20*8, the creditors were being paid rather too quickly – six days on average before debtors settled. There has been an improvement in year 20*9 where the figures match – further improvement should be sought.

QUESTION 5

i) Interest cover = 4.47 times.
ii) Earnings per share = 54.4 pence.
iii) Ordinary dividend cover = 1.7.
iv) Dividend yield = 4.7%.
v) Price/earnings ratio = 12.5
vi) Dividend paid per share = 32 pence.
vii) Gearing = 69.48% (very highly geared).

QUESTION 7

(a) Interest cover = $\dfrac{\text{Operating profit}}{\text{Interest paid}}$ = 17.86 times

Earnings per share = $\dfrac{\text{Profit after tax and preference dividends}}{\text{Number of ordinary shares}}$ = 20.54 pence

Dividend paid per share = $\dfrac{\text{Ordinary dividend}}{\text{Number of ordinary shares}}$ = 3.4 pence

Price/earnings ratio = $\dfrac{\text{Market price per share}}{\text{Earnings per share}}$ = 26.78

Dividend yield = $\dfrac{\text{Dividend per share}}{\text{Market price per share}} \times 100$ = 0.62%

Gearing = $\dfrac{\text{Fixed cost capital}}{\text{Total capital}} \times 100$ = 30%

(b) Interest cover is improving each year. If the debentures have remained the same over the three years, the improvement has been caused by a larger operating profit each year. EPS is improving, again probably because of increased profitability. Dividend per share has improved each year – rather slowly, but shareholders should not be dissatisfied. P/E ratio remains similar to previous years. The dividend yield remains low. Gearing has stayed low but there has been a significant increase in 20*9 – this could affect earnings potential if increased further.

QUESTION 9

(a)

	Baliaba plc	Firty Leaves plc
i) Gearing ratio	20.62%	58.04%
ii) Interest cover		5.24 times
iii) EPS	95.9 pence	20.5 pence
iv) Dividend paid per share	19.49 pence	5.25 pence
v) Dividend yield	4.6%	3.75%
vi) Price/earnings ratio	4.38	6.83

(b) Baliaba is a low-geared company (less than 50% of funding is provided by fixed cost capital), whereas Firty Leaves is highly geared (more than 50% of funding is provided by fixed-cost capital). Firty is able to cover its current interest payments more than five times. Baliaba appears to be more successful than Firty Leaves as its earnings per share are more than four times greater. Around a fifth of earnings per share is paid to shareholders, leaving 76 pence of earnings to be 'ploughed back' into the company. Firty Leaves plc has slightly lower earnings per share and retained profits, however, it is significant to note that the ordinary shares of Firty Leaves plc are 25p compared with the nominal value of £1 per ordinary share in Baliaba. If adjustment were to be made for this then EPS for Firty Leaves would be 80p and dividend paid per share 21p. This is a more valid comparison. Baliaba's dividend yield is slightly better than that of Firty Leaves. Shareholders in Firty Leaves appear to have more confidence in the company than shareholders in Baliaba – indicated by a higher P/E ratio.

QUESTION 11

Gross profit margin = $\dfrac{\text{GP}}{\text{Sales}} \times 100 = \dfrac{59,248}{148,120} \times 100 = 40\%$

Net profit margin = $\dfrac{\text{NP}}{\text{Sales}} \times 100 = \dfrac{13,437}{148,120} \times 100 = 9.1\%$

ROCE = $\dfrac{\text{Net profit}}{\text{Capital employed}} \times 100 = \dfrac{13,437}{14,800} \times 100 = 90.79\%$

Current ratio = $\dfrac{\text{Current assets}}{\text{Current liabilities}} = \dfrac{10,998}{9,098} = 1.2{:}1$

Liquid ratio = $\dfrac{\text{Current assets} - \text{Inventories}}{\text{Current liabilities}} = \dfrac{6,348}{9,098} = 0.70{:}1$

There has been a steady improvement in the gross margin over the five years, with a larger than usual increase in 20*6. However, this larger than usual increase was unsustained in subsequent years. There has been an improvement of £4.8 for every £100 of takings over the five years.
The net margin has also shown a steady improvement (£2 per £100 of takings), reflecting that observed in the gross margin.
There has been a greater than usual increase in expenses in the final year. Having been relatively stable at £29.4 and £29.6 for the past three years, they have now risen to £30.9 per £100 of takings in 20*9 – although this is only £1.30 per £100 of takings this should be investigated to determine the cause of this slight deterioration in control of expenses.
The current ratio has deteriorated steadily over the past five years. Whether this is cause for concern will depend largely on the type of business. The liquid ratio too is falling but again identifying the type of business would be important before commenting. The proportion of stock held is falling each year.

QUESTION 13

	20*9	20*8
i) Gross margin	49.37%	49.36%
ii) Net margin	17.19%	19.23%
iii) Operating expenses/sales	32.17%	30.13%
iv) ROCE	16.75%	19.19%
v) Current ratio	0.85:1	0.86:1
vi) Liquid ratio	0.74:1	0.76:1
vii) Interest cover	32.3 times	37.5 times
viii) Dividend cover	2.93 times	2.56 times
ix) Earnings per share	11.9 pence	12.6 pence
x) Price/earnings ratio	9.24	7.4
xi) Gearing ratio	6.48%	6.4%
xii) Dividend yield	3.69%	5.49%
xiii) Rate of inventory turnover	31 days	–
xiv) Receivables collection period	106 days	89 days

Interest cover has worsened over the two years but it is still very good. Interest could have been paid over 30 times before profits disappeared.

Dividend cover shows how many times the current dividend could be paid out of current profits; the cover has improved over the year.

Earnings per share has deteriorated; profits have gone down; the ratio is an easy to calculate measure of the success of the business.

The price/earnings ratio has improved, perhaps indicating that ordinary shareholders have greater confidence in the future of the company.

Both gearing ratios indicate that a small proportion of the funds invested in the business are provided by long-term creditors.

QUESTION 15

(a)

	Del Tipper	Tanka Continental Traders Ltd	With notional manager's salary
Gross margin	54.56%	57.28%	
Net margin	29.56%	30.1%	16.32%
Expenses/Sales	25%	27.18%	38.24%
ROCE	32.59%	38.04%	18%
Current ratio	11.68:1	1.46:1	
Liquid ratio	10.8:1	0.82:1	
Receivables collection period	15 days	43 days	collection period
Payables collection period	8 days	199 days	payment period
Rate of inventory turnover	12 days	125 days	

(b) The gross margin for the two businesses is very similar. This could be expected since they are in the same line of business. TCT Ltd has a slightly better ratio and this may be caused by economies of scale (purchases of £460,000 compared with only £60,000 in Del's business).

After adjusting for the notional manager's salary, Del's net margin falls from almost 30% to around half of this figure to 16.32% – 16.32% is a fairer representation of his net margin and his ROCE. Using both these ratios, it can be seen that TCT has a better set of figures. Comparison of the amounts devoted to overheads reveals that TCT is managing overheads much more effectively, spending over £11 less per £100 of takings than Del.

It should be remembered that the ROCE calculation depends on the accuracy of the valuation of assets and if these are undervalued (using cost concept, especially in Del's case) then different results could be revealed.

Del's current ratio is much higher than TCT's; in fact, it may be too high. For every £1 owed to trade creditors he has £11.68 of current assets. Perhaps the bank balance could be reduced and the money used in a more productive capacity. The liquid ratio shows that almost £11 in liquid assets cover every £1 of trade creditors – very high. Although TCT's current and liquid ratios are low, they do not pose too much of a problem.

There are great differences between the last three ratios calculated: is Del too strict in getting his debtors to pay? He is certainly paying his creditors too quickly. In fact, he pays his creditors in eight days while receiving money from debtors a week later. TCT, on the other hand, receives money from debtors in 43 days – a little on the long side, especially considering that this is an average collection period – are some debtors taking even longer? The longer debts are outstanding, the greater the chance of them proving to be bad. It is taking TCT almost seven months on average to pay creditors – this is likely to cause problems with suppliers.

Finally, Del's rate of inventory turnover is very much shorter than that of TCT – who are keeping four months inventory in hand. This would seem excessive given that Del keeps inventory for only 12 days before sale. Clearly, more would need to be known about each business in order to comment on the efficiency of these figures.

TCT is overtrading – comparatively large stocks; high proportion of debtors; and high proportion of creditors to liquid assets.

(c) Del currently earns £40,200:

■ If he employed a manager and sought employment elsewhere, he would earn £22,200 plus any income from another employment.
■ If he sold the business and sought employment elsewhere he would receive £123,350 which would currently yield £9,868 per annum. If the business assets were worth in excess of £123,350 and a purchaser purchased goodwill too, the annual income from investing the capital sum might be much greater than £9,868 per annum. In addition there would be the salary earned from the other employment.

CHAPTER ELEVEN

QUESTION 1
(a) (i) FIFO

Receipts	Issues	Balance	Workings
1 @ £100		£100	1 @ £100
6 @ £100		£700	7 @ £100
	4	£300	3 @ £100
5 @ £110		£850	3 @ £100, 5 @ £110
	6	£220	2 @ £110
7 @ £120		£1,060	2 @ £110, 7 @ £120
	6	£360	3 @ £120

(a) (iii) AVCO

Receipts	Issues	Balance	Workings
7 @ £100		£700	7 @ £100
	4	£300	3 @ £100
5 @ £110		£850	3 @ £100, 5 @ £110
	6	£212.50	2 @ £106.25
7 @ £120		£1052.50	2 @ £106.25, 7 @ £120
	6	£350.85	3 @ £116.95

(b) Income statement extract for the month ended 31 October

	FIFO		AVCO	
Sales		3200		3200
Less cost of sales				
Inventory	100		100	
Purchases	1990		1990	
	2090		2090	
Inventory	(360)	(1730)	(350.85)	(1739.15)
Gross profit		1470		1460.85

QUESTION 3

(a) FIFO 3 @ £18 = £54

(b)

Income statement for August

	FIFO	
	£	£
Sales		400
Less Cost of sales		
Purchases	226	
Inventory at 31 August	(54)	(172)
Gross profit		228

QUESTION 5

	£
Inventory as per stock-take of 5 January 20*9	26,870
Less Purchases less returns	(1,868)
Add Sales less returns (3930/1.33)	2,955
Inventory at 31 December 20*8	27,957

QUESTION 7

(a)

FIFO	Receipts	Issues	Balance £	
	5 @ £4		20.00	5 @ £4
		4	4.00	1 @ £4
	17 @ £5		89.00	1 @ £4, 17 @ £5
		15	15.00	3 @ £5
	10 @ £6		75.00	3 @ £5, 10 @ £6
		7	36.00	6 @ £6

(b)

AVCO	Receipts	Issues	Balance	
	5 @ £4		20.00	£20/4 = £4
		4	4.00	1 @ £4
	17 @ £5		89.00	£89/18 = £4.94
		15	14.82	3 @ £4.94
	10 @ £6		74.82	£74.82/13 = £5.76
		7	34.56	6 @ £5.76

QUESTION 9

(a) FIFO 1 @ £220

(b) AVCO 1 @ £218.34

QUESTION 11

(a)

Receipt	Issues	Balance	
8 @ £12		96.00	8 @ £12
10 @ £12		216.00	8 @ £12, 10 @ £12
	15	36.00	3 @ £12
12 @ £8		132.00	3 @ £12, 12 @ £8
15 @ £7		237.00	3 @ £12, 12 @ £8, 15 @ £7
	28	14.00	2 @ £7

(b) Income statement for the month ended 31 August

	£	£
Sales		645
Less Cost of sales		
Inventories at 1 August	96	
Purchases	321	
	417	
Inventories at 31 August	(14)	(403)
Gross profit		242

QUESTION 13

(a)

Receipts	Issues	Balance	
		£	
1 @ £15		15.00	
8 @ £15		135.00	£135/9 = £15
	6	45.00	3 @ £15
12 @ £16		237.00	£237/15 = £15.80
	10	79.00	5 @ £15.80
8 @ £17		215.00	£215/13 = £16.54
	6	115.78	7 @ £16.54

(b) Income statement for the month ended 30 September

	£	£
Sales		880.00
Less Cost of sales		
Inventories at 1 September	15.00	
Purchases	448.00	
	463.00	
Inventories at 30 September	115.78	347.22
Gross profit		532.78

QUESTION 15

	£
Inventory as per stock-take of 7 May 20*9	2,940
Add Sales (£1,200/1.25)	960
Less Purchases	(420)
Inventory at 30 April 20*9	3,480

QUESTION 17

(a)

	£
Inventory as per stock-take of 4 June 20*9	14,880
Add Sales less returns (2364/1.2)	1,970
Less Purchases less returns	(766)
Inventory at 31 May 20*9	16,084

(b) Inventory has increased by £1,204, therefore profit shown on draft accounts will be increased to £186,954.

QUESTION 19

(a)

	£
Inventory as per stock-take of 9 August 20*9	2,000
Add Sales less returns (£1,734/1.7)	1,020
Goods on sale or return (£510/1.7)	300
Less Purchases less returns	(1,520)
Inventory at 31 July 20*9	1,800

(b) Stock has reduced by £200, therefore profit shown on draft accounts will be reduced to £42,670.

CHAPTER TWELVE

1. Moin Syyed

Manufacturing account extract for the year ended 28 February 20*9

	£
Inventory of raw materials	23,658
Purchases of raw materials	156,364
	180,022
Inventory of raw materials	(18,439)
Raw materials consumed	161,583
Direct wages	236,451
Royalties	35,000
Prime cost	433,034

3. Jane Doyle

Manufacturing and trading account for the year ended 31 July 20*9

	£	£
Inventory of raw materials		17,650
Purchases of raw materials	203,510	
Carriage inwards	1,350	
		204,860
		222,510
Inventory of raw materials		(23,510)
Raw materials consumed		199,000
Direct wages		123,930
Prime cost		322,930
Factory overheads		
Indirect wages	58,900	
Rent and rates	37,800	
Power	38,900	
Light and heat	9,450	
Insurance	14,620	
Depreciation of machinery	87,000	
		246,670
		569,600
Work in progress 1 Aug 20*2	8,570	
Work in progress 31 Jul 20*3	(7,340)	
		1,230
Total production cost		570,830
Inventory of finished goods		10,760
Total production cost		581,590
Inventory of finished goods		(10,740)
Cost of goods sold		570,850
Gross profit		342,996
Sales		913,846

5. Harry Parker

Manufacturing account extract for the year ended 31 October 20*9

	£
Total production cost	1,326,900
Gross profit on manufacturing	773,100
Transfer price	2,100,000

Income statement extract for the year ended 31 October 20*9

	£	£
Inventory		186,000
Transfer price of manufactured goods		2,100,000
		2,286,000
Inventory		191,450
Cost of goods sold		2,094,550
Gross profit		1,116,050
Sales		3,210,600

Income statement extract for the year ended 31 October 20*9

	£
Gross profit on manufacturing	773,100
Gross profit on trading	1,116,050
Total gross profit	1,889,150

7. Hilary Nike

Manufacturing account extract for the year ended 31 March 20*9

	£
Total production cost	943,750
Gross profit on manufacturing	377,500
Transfer price	1,321,250

Income statement extract for the year ended 31 March 20*9

	£
Inventory	85,820
Transfer price of manufactured goods	1,321,250
	1,407,070
Inventory	(87,360)
Cost of goods sold	1,319,710
Gross profit	128,850
Sales	1,448,560

Income statement extract for the year ended 31 March 20*9

	£
Gross profit on manufacturing	377,500
Gross profit on trading	128,850
Total gross profit	506,350

9.

	£		
Cost Price	2,720	Profit element	1,360
	960		120
	750		150
	1,115 (rounded)		335
	6,000		4,500

11.

Provision for unrealised profit

	£		£
		Balance b/d	3,444
		Inc stat	372
Balance c/d	3,816	Balance b/d	3,816

13. Manufacturing account extract for the year ended 30 November 20*9

	£
Inventory of raw materials	7,968
Purchases of raw materials	102,177
	110,145
Inventory of raw materials	(8,429)
Raw materials consumed	101,716
Direct labour	82,440
Royalties	1,200
Prime cost	185,356

15. Trogle

Manufacturing account for the year ended 30 June 20*9

	£	£
Inventory of raw materials		17,480
Purchases of raw materials		234,772
		252,252
Inventory of raw materials		(18,597)
Raw materials consumed		233,655
Direct labour		419,828
Royalties		12,500
Prime cost		665,983
Factory overheads		
Rent	9,500	
Insurance	8,030	
Power	18,400	
Indirect wages	21,720	
Depreciation of machinery	45,000	102,650
		768,633
Work in progress		8,977
		777,610
Work in progress		(10,431)
Total production cost		767,179

17. Dreght and Sons

Manufacturing account for the year ended 31 March 20*9

	£	£
Inventory of raw materials		8,162
Purchases of raw materials	112,431	
Carriage inwards	798	113,229
		121,391
Inventory of raw materials		(7,466)
Raw materials consumed		113,925
Direct wages		189,410
Prime cost		303,335
Factory overheads		
Indirect labour	64,822	
Power	17,461	
General overheads	20,973	

(b) Income statement extract for the year ended 31 December 20*9

	£
Inventory	14,880
Transfer price of manufactured goods	662,400
	677,280
	(16,440)
Cost of goods sold	660,840
Gross profit	239,160
Sales	900,000

(c) Provision for unrealised profit

	£		£
		Bal b/d	2,480
Bal c/d	2,740	Inc stat	260
		Bal b/d	2,740

(d) Income statement extract for the year ended 31 Dec 20*9

	£	£
GP on manufacturing	110,400	
Less Prov. fcr unrealised profit	(260)	110,140
Gross profit on trading		239,160
Total gross profit		349,300

(e) Balance sheet extract as at 31 December 20*9

	£	£	£
Inventory: Raw materials			8,618
Work in progress			8,000
Finished goods	16,440		
Less Provision	2,740	13,700	
	2470	13,700	
			30,318
			30,318

CHAPTER THIRTEEN

QUESTION 1

(a) Absorption costing statement for Tucon for August 20*9

	£000
Direct materials	938
Direct labour	461
Manufacturing royalties	20
PRIME COST	1,419
Indirect materials	463
Indirect labour	726
Other indirect costs	84
Depreciation of factory machinery	100
Total production costs	2,792
Selling and distribution costs	612
Administration costs	300
Depreciation of office equipment	48
Total cost	3,752

(b) £3,752,000 = Production cost for one 'sepyt'
4,000,000

= £0.938

= 93.8 pence.

Depreciation of machinery	28,000	131,256
		434,591
Work in progress		6,183
		440,774
Work in progress		(5,774)
		435,000
Gross profit on manufacturing		130,500
Transfer price		565,500

Income statement extract for the year ended 31 March 20*9

	£
Inventory	7,451
Transfer price of manufactured goods	565,500
	572,951
	8,549
Inventory	564,402
Cost of goods sold	309,040
Gross profit	873,442
Sales	

19. Provision for unrealised profit

	£		£
		Balance b/d	6,300
Balance c/d	7,500	Inc stat	1,200
		Balance b/d	7,500

21. Provision for unrealised profit

	£		£
		Balance b/d	34,500
Balance c/d	38,250	Inc stat	3,750
		Balance b/d	38,250

23. (a) Sandra Gavington
Manufacturing account for the year ended 31 December 20*9

	£	£
Inventory of raw materials		7,966
Purchases of raw materials		214,283
		222,249
Inventory of raw materials		(8,618)
Raw materials consumed		213,631
Direct wages		128,250
Royalties		19,500
Prime cost		361,381
Factory overheads		
Indirect wages	63,489	
Power	18,240	
Insurance	7,220	
General overheads	23,470	
Depreciation of machinery	80,000	192,419
		553,800
Work in progress		6,200
		560,000
Work in progress		(8,000)
Total production costs		552,000
Gross profit on manufacturing		110,400
Transfer price		662,400

QUESTION 3

Total cost of producing one 'dible' = $\frac{£127,000}{20,000}$ = £6.35

Selling price = £6.35 + £2.18 = £8.53.

QUESTION 5

Total cost of producing 'treamils' = £159,000
Profit margin = 25% Mark-up = 33⅓%
So selling price = £159,000 × 1.33% = £212,000/45,000 = £4.71 per unit.

QUESTION 7

Overhead	Total cost £	Basis of apportionment	Dept 1 £	Dept 2 £	Dept 3 £
Rent	36,000	Floor area	6,000	12,000	18,000
Depreciation – premises	6,000	Floor area	1,000	2,000	3,000
machinery	210,000	Cost of machinery	30,000	60,000	120,000
Heating and light	9,000	Floor area	1,500	3,000	4,500
Supervisors' wages	160,000	No of workers	32,000	72,000	56,000
	421,000		70,500	149,000	201,500

QUESTION 9

Overhead	Total £	Basis of apportionment	Z1 £	Y2 £	X3 £	W4 £	Maintenance £
					Department		
Total maintenance	974,200		386,100	227,300	180,400	110,500	69,900
Number of machines			32,620	20,970	11,650	4,660	(69,900)
	974,200		418,720	248,270	192,050	115,160	

QUESTION 11

	Production departments			Service departments	
	11/R £	12/S £	13/T £	UV £	WX £
Total costs	60,000	120,000	45,000	30,000	20,000
Apportionment of Dept UV costs	7,500	15,000	6,000	(30,000)	1,500
	67,500	135,000	51,000	–	21,500
Apportionment of Dept WX costs	4,778	7,176	9,555		(21,500)
	72,278	142,167	60,555		–

QUESTION 13

Total direct labour hours 3,000 (felto) + 8,400 (hevo) = 11,400.
Labour hour overhead absorption rate = £72,732 / 11,400 = £6.38 per hour.

(a) Overhead absorption rate for each product:
Felto = 0.2 hours × £6.38 = £1.276
Hevo = 1.4 hours × £6.38 = £8.932

(b) If budgets are met then the total overheads will be absorbed as follows:

	£	
15,000 feltos will absorb	19,140	15,000 × £1.276
6,000 hevos will absorb	53,592	6,000 × £8.932
Total overheads absorbed	72,732	

QUESTION 15

Total direct machine hours 48,000 (klaka) + 84,000 (klova) = 132,000.
Machine hour overhead absorption rate for each product £166,320 / 132,000 = £1.26.

(a) Overhead absorption rate for each product:
Klaka = 2.4 × £1.26 = £3.024
Klova = 0.6 × £1.26 = £0.756

(b) If budgets are met the the total overheads will be absorbed as follows:

	£
20,000 klakas will absorb	60,480
140,000 klovas will absorb	105,840
Total overheads absorbed	166,320

QUESTION 17

(a) Department P:
OAR using labour hours = £33.79 (£182,466/5,400)
OAR using machine hours = £4.05 (£182,466/45,000)
Department N:
OAR using labour hours = £8.74 (£262,145/30,000)
OAR using machine hours = £109.23 (£262,145/2,400)

(b) Department P is more capital intensive so choose machine hours.
Department N is more labour intensive so choose labour hours.

(c)

	£	
Sporidge takes 9 hours in dept P s	36.45	needs to be absorbed
6.5 hours in dept N so	52.44	needs to be absorbed
Total overheads to be absorbed by a sporidge	88.89	if budgets are met.

QUESTION 19

			Department			
Overhead	Total cost £	Basis of apportionment	B £	C £	D £	E £
Rent	90,000	Floor area	36,000	27,000	18,000	9,000
Rates	15,000	Floor area	6,000	4,500	3,000	1,500
Insurance	21,000	Floor area	8,400	6,300	4,200	2,100
Depreciation	7,000	Floor area	2,800	2,100	1,400	700
Heating	18,000	Floor area	7,200	5,400	3,600	1,800
Machinery insurance	24,000	Replacement cost	9,000	6,000	4,500	4,500
Machinery depreciation	27,000	Cost of machinery	16,200	5,400	3,600	1,800
	202,000		85,600	56,700	38,300	21,400

QUESTION 21

(a)

			Departments			
Overhead	Total £	Basis of apportionment	D £	E £	F £	Canteen £
Rent & rates	19,350	Floor area	7,740	6,772.5	2,902.5	1,935
Insurance of machine	35,100	Cost of machinery	22,950	6,102	5,994	54
Heat and light	11,460	Floor area	4,584	4,011	1,719	1,146

Supervisory wages	29,000	Number of workers	8,990	10,150	8,120	1,740
Power	28,400	kWh	11,360	7,100	8,520	1,420
Depreciation – machinery	14,950	Cost of machinery	9,775	2,599	2,553	23
	138,260		65,399	36,734.5	29,808.5	6,318
(b)						
Canteen (figures rounded)		Number of workers	2,084	2,352	1,882	(6,318)
	138,260		67,483	39,086.5	31,690.5	

QUESTION 23

Overhead	Total	Basis of apportionment	Departments XY	ZA	BC	Canteen	Maintenance
	£		£	£	£	£	£
Rent and rates	21,120	Floor area	7,920	2,640	5,280	1,320	3,960
Heat and light	17,040	Floor area	6,390	2,130	4,260	1,065	3,195
Supervisory wages	220,000	Number of workers	83,600	26,400	66,000	17,600	26,400
Power	29,610	kWh	14,805	6,909	5,922	658	1,316
Depreciation – machinery	24,000	Cost of machinery	3,600	7,500	4,500	2,400	6,000
premises	16,800	Floor area	6,300	2,100	4,200	1,050	3,150
Insurance							
– machinery	21,720	Cost of machinery	3,258	6,787.5	4,072.5	2,172	5,430
premises	14,112	Floor area	5,292	1,764	3,528	882	2,646
	364,402		131,165	56,230.5	97,762.5	27,147	52,097
Maintenance		Number of machines	28,052	12,022	8,015	4,008	(52,097)
			159,217	68,252.5	105,777.5	31,155	
Canteen		Number of workers	14,799	4,673	11,683	(31,155)	*
	364,402		174,016	72,925.5	117,460.5		

*Ignores maintenance workers.

QUESTION 25

(a)

Overhead	Total	Basis of apportionment	AZ	BY	Machinery	Canteen
			£	£	£	£
Rent and rates	47,840	Area	15,600	26,000	5,200	1,040
Supervisory wages	172,500	No of workers	46,000	92,000	23,000	11,500
Depreciation of machinery	55,000	Book value of machinery	32,500	12,500	6,000	4,000
	275,340		94,100	130,500	34,200	16,540
Maintenance			22,800	8,550	(34,200)	2,850
			116,900	139,050		19,390
Canteen			6,463	12,927		(19,390)
	275,340		123,363	151,977		

(b) OAR AZ = machine hours = $\frac{123,363}{8,310}$ = £14.85

OAR BY = labour hours = $\frac{151,977}{12,465}$ = £12.19

(c) Job PR/72

	£
Direct materials	47.50
Direct labour	34.00
2 hours in Dept AZ	29.70
3 hours in Dept BY	36.57
Total cost	147.77
Mark-up 70%	103.44
Selling price	251.21

CHAPTER FOURTEEN

QUESTION 1

T. Cupp should accept the order. It will make a positive contribution of £2.80 per service (£15.00 – £12.20) – a total contribution of £8,400.

QUESTION 3

George should accept the order. It will make a positive contribution of 10p per candle (£1.00 – 90p) – a total contribution of £100.

QUESTION 5

Renting the room to the bridge club will make a positive contribution of £14, therefore the bowling club should accept the bridge club's offer.

QUESTION 7

Pierre should not accept the offer from Italy. At present his marginal costs are £240 (£40 + £170 + £30) so contribution is £760. Purchasing from Engelo the marginal costs will be:

	£
Fireplace	200
Delivery	180
Distribution	30
Total marginal costs	410

Contribution will fall to £590. Pierre will be worse off if he accepts Angelo's offer.

QUESTION 9

'Comfy' slippers should be manufactured. They would yield a positive contribution of £15 compared with a contribution of £14 from the 'Warmy' slippers.

QUESTION 11

(a) Tables, then chairs, then headboards.

(b) All 300 tables.
500 chairs.

QUESTION 13

(a) Gents', then Ladies', then Children's.

(b) Gents' 10,000 pairs; Ladies' 8,000 pairs; Children's 250 pairs.

QUESTION 15

(a) Break-even = $\frac{\text{Total fixed costs}}{\text{Contribution per unit}} = \frac{40,000}{9}$ = 4,445 units

(b) £88,900.

(c) 5,555 units